NORTH MA ... 'OU
HIGH A...
OF THE LAKE MICHIGAN ARCHIPELAGO

Histories and trailguides for the hiker and backpacker for these eastern Lake Michigan Islands which are part of The Sleeping Bear National Lakeshore and the Beaver Island Group

By Robert H. Ruchhoft
Associate Professor of History
The University College, University of Cincinnati

FIRST EDITION
SIXTH PRINTING

All contemporary photographs by the author except where otherwise noted

P.O. BOX 19161
CINCINNATI, OHIO 45219

ACKNOWLEGMENTS

If this book does not enrich the reader seeking information about these islands for use use either as a a meaningful help in exploring them or for their historical interest I must accept the blame. But if this mountain of words is at least in part successful, the literary climb was far from being a solo ascent. In turning my original tape recorded trail descriptions and excerpting and abstracting many gathered sources into the brief histories to the final printed page, I know the manuscript's organization, information, and readability has been improved by the special knowledge and talents provided by the following individuals: My two editors, Cynthia Dews and Edith McCabe who read all of the original manuscript, gave me their experienced judgement on content and style, improving the readability and grammatical correctness of the work immeasurably; to my hiking companions, Bob Coats, Rob Milton, Herb Rodenberg, Ed and Cynthia Dews, who not only shared with me many of the island trails but also gave me a viewpoint other than my own of their feelings about the islands; Rob Milton was also helpful in early problems with my word processor; Stan Meyerson and Mike Sears critically read short sections; many of the personnel of the Sleeping Bear Dunes were especially helpful, Charles Parkinson, now retired made me acquainted with many unpublished manuscripts and photographs, Rangers Cathy Bietau and Bill Herd, read much of my manuscript on the Manitous and offered valuable suggestions, Cathy was also great help in answering my many questions when I was hiking the Manitous, as was her fellow ranger Chuck Kruch; Former Manitou islanders Glenn Furst, Ethel Furst Stormer, Fred Burdick, George Hutzler, Doris Shirk and Paul Maleski Jr. shared with me many of their own personal Island experiences; Ethel Stormer and Paul Maleski also graciously allowed me to use many of their photographs as did George Grosvenor; Susan Wasserman, whose family has ties with North Manitou for generations, corrected many historical errors and added much new information as well as critically reading my history of that island; Dick Moran, former head biologist for Michigan's Department of Natural Resources offered general information on High and Garden Island, and arranged for my use of the D.N.R. cabins on both islands; my knowledge of Garden Island was further enhanced by information given to me by William Wachtner Jr., his son Don, and Keewaydinoquay; Don Cole arranged my first passages to High Island and also also permitted me to use photographs of High Island as did his fellow Beaver Islander Archie La Freniere; credit goes to Ed Wojan for introducing me to both these gentlemen as well as sharing island information and giving me maps; Abbey and P. J. White helped in my introduction to High Island and allowed me to share the D.N.R. cabin with them; both Larry Wakefield and Steve Harold of Traverse City furnished me with important photographs; my computer and typesetting woes were often graciously solved by Mike Breen, who often stepped in and changed a day of frustration and near despair to one of productivity

TABLE OF CONTENTS

Part I Prologue

Part II South Manitou Island

Part III North Manitou Island

Part V Garden Island

Part V High Island

Maps and Illustrations

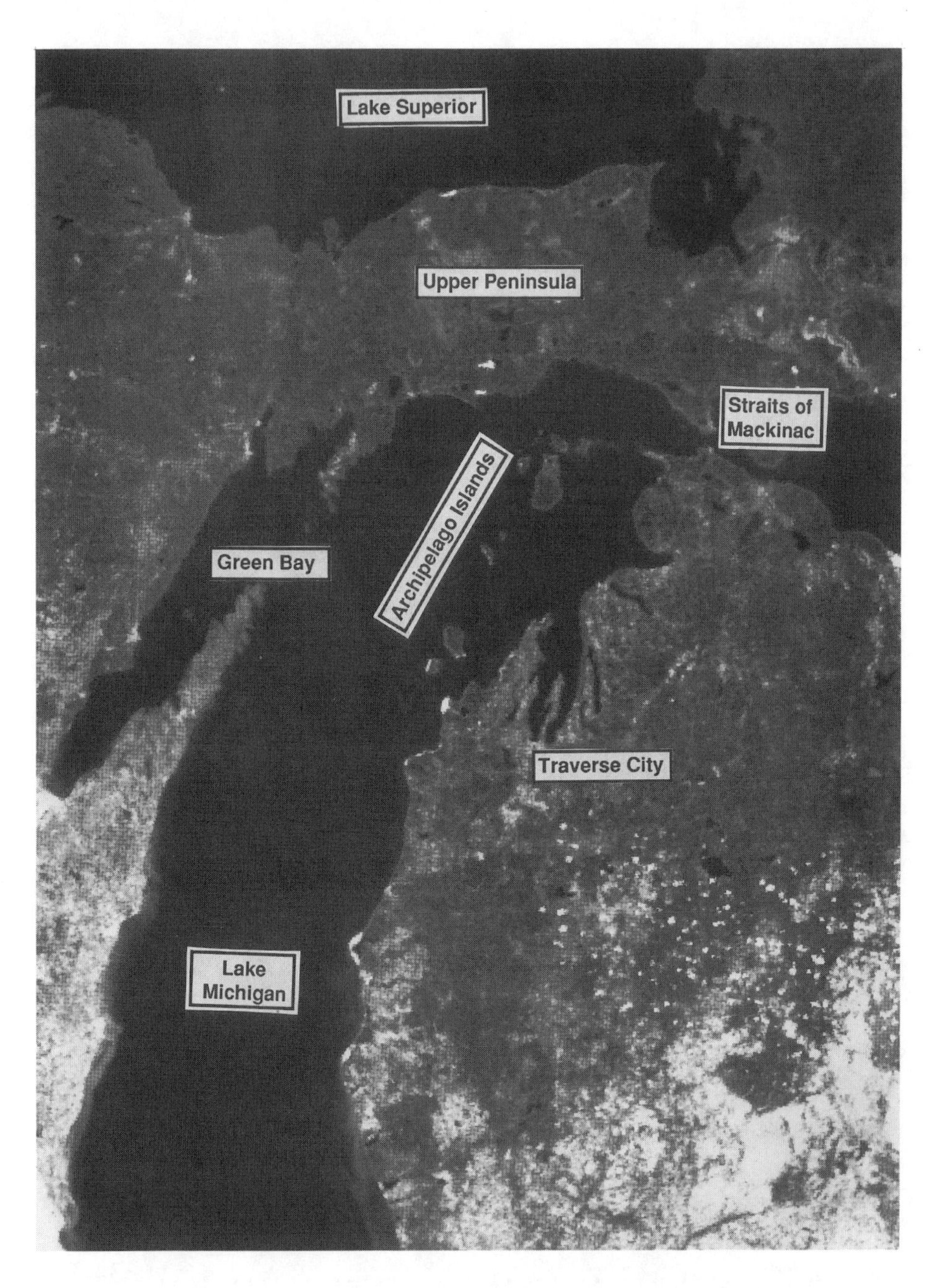

Satellite view of Upper Lake Michigan

Courtesy of the Environmental Research Institute

PART I Prologue

Chapter I

How to Use this Book and other Introductory Matters

If you begin this book reading at leisure, soaking up a bit of the romance of these islands, continue with the paragraph below and read on. When you are not pressed for time you will gain a good overall view of what such an island adventure has to offer and what to expect on your first visit to one of them. If time is of the essence and you are making definite plans that must soon be expedited start with the chapter entitled Makin**g Plans for Island Hiking, Which Island to Choose**, then follow that by reading the chapters devoted to the island you have chosen. If your first reading happens on the ferryboat while heading to one of the islands and the lake is giving you a gentle introduction with small to moderate swells, start reading the introductory chapter devoted to the island of your destination. The hurried visitor could skip the chapters entitled The Natural Setting and A **Brief Early History of the Lake Michigan Archipelago for a later time. Although for** full appreciation of island visits these chapters should be read, they could be put on "hold" for later consumption. Since they usually will increase the enjoyment of an island visit and give the reader a better appreciation and understanding of the islands, they could be saved for evening reading in camp. Sometime during or before a visit to a specific island, reading the individual history of that island will also help the visitor feel the flavor of its individuality and enrich the experience of being there.

What is included in the Archipelago

Starting about 17 miles south of Michigan's Upper Peninsula a chain of islands that begins with diminutive Squaw island in the north runs in a general southwesterly direction for about 60 miles to South Manitou Island. They are not the broken end of a long point of land like the Washington Island group which extends from the Door Peninsula on the Wisconsin side. This group of Michigan islands stand independently well out in the lake.

When looking at a map that shows these northeastern Lake Michigan offshore islands, reasonable questions arise. Do they have a unified group name? Are they subdivided into sub-groups? How many of them are there? What distinguishes them from other island chains and what areas do they cover? Not all sources agree on a group name nor what should be included in the name. Although this entire grouping is usually called the Lake Michigan Archipelago it is often divided into three sub-groups. The first and largest one contains those islands that cluster around Beaver Island and are known as the Beaver Group. A middle group has the two Fox Islands which lie about 11 miles southwest of Beaver. In some publications the Foxes are included with the Beaver Group and are referred to as the aforementioned Lake Michigan Archipelago, leaving out the two Manitous. There are two reasons for this classification, which omits the two southern islands. First, the 19 mile distance between them

High dunes, western side of South Manitou

and South Fox Island does isolate them from the larger grouping to the northeast. The second reason is the main port for the Beaver group is found at the City of Charleviox, while the usual debarkation point for the Manitous is Leland. Although by a straight line the two towns are only about 40 miles apart, the entrance to Grand Traverse Bay lies between them. This isolates the groups into two different spheres and places them many road-miles apart. But the classification of including the Manitous in the archipelago seems to make better sense when one realizes that no island of any size exists south of the Manitous all the way to Chicago, and the first land mass encountered north of Squaw Island is the Upper Peninsula.

The number of islands in the Archipelago depends largely on the criteria for what constitutes a real island. If one counts every minute particle of land rising above the lake surface that some cartographer has honored with a name the number reaches 15. But specks of land like Hat, Shoe and Grape Islands are no more than shoals that in severe weather are sometimes completely awash. Having no trees and supporting almost no amount of heavy vegetation, they are mainly of interest to nesting birds and navigators who are studiously trying to avoid them. Those large enough to support tree life and having enough area to appear with names on some state road maps number 12, with Squaw Island having the double distinction of being the northernmost and smallest of this group. Beaver is the largest and the only island of the group which now has a human population for the entire year.

In the late nineteenth and earlier parts of this century, five of the other islands were also inhabited by year-round occupants. Four of those islands that once sustained mortal life for the 12 calendar months are the subjects of this book. The other is South Fox.

Why Four Islands Were Chosen

Since all the islands are not included in this book, the reader may reasonably ask why, of the 15-odd islands of this archipelago, were only four chosen and what factors influenced the decisions in choosing those particular four? Only these four islands fit into categories in what I considered my major aims in writing this guide. It is a hiking guidebook, intended for use by serious hikers and backpackers who are looking for places to hike in approximate wilderness settings. The islands to be included then should be those that were primarily being allowed to turn back to wilderness and would probably stay that way over an extended of time. This meant that to make sure the islands would remain that way, they should be publicly owned, with policies in force to protect the natural and historical setting, and be immune from further encroachment by real estate developers or logging operations. Since all four of the chosen islands are almost entirely owned by federal and state governments where such plans to protect their natural and historical heritage are now in force, they became candidates for inclusion.

There are other islands which also fit this requirement but have other drawbacks that keep them from being good prospects for inclusion. Size was a factor, since some of them are so small, or so much of their surface area is in swamp, any possibility of extended hiking on them is impossible. Accessibility is another factor. The Manitous are easily reached by ferry. High and Garden Islands are close enough to Beaver Island that only a short charter boat ride is called for. All of the included island except North Manitou have natural harbors, making access to them easier.

The other islands of the Archipelago require longer journeys over water. Their lack of natural harbors also makes approaches to them hazardous in any but the mildest of weather. The four chosen islands have existing trails. Some are maintained but many are not. Many of the non-maintained ones are still easy to follow. They offer the hiker easy access to many parts of the island without extensive boondocking. But if that is your favorite mode of travel and you wish to lose yourself among forests and dunes, there are plenty of available areas to go cross-country. The other islands, although smaller, are so seldom visited that they require almost constant boondocking. Most of them are privately owned as well. So the islands chosen are not only big enough that campers can comfortably sequester themselves away from motor vehicles and commercial establishments but they have various hiking possibilities lasting several miles without trespassing on someone else's land. They can exist close to the microcosm of the natural world without the effort of hiking many extended miles into wilderness areas, or the dangers that may be experienced when civilized outposts lie many days away.

The basic format for this work is not unlike my two previous books, and its writing was influenced by them in many ways. They were also written for hikers who were looking for something more than an easy Sunday afternoon stroll. Many ideas used here were adopted from my experiences in writing those two books. I was also helped by the reactions to them by the many people who have used them and shared their thoughts with me through the years. If you are curious how this history prof, whose special area of professional interest lies eastward across the Atlantic Ocean, whose previous major recreational hours were taken up by hi fi systems, record collecting and general lethargy, came to write books on hiking and backpacking, read on. If not, skip the next few paragraphs and go to the heading entitled **Historical Significance**.

During a Christmas season of the early 1970s one of my presents was Colin Fletcher's book, The Complete Walker. After enthusiastically devouring its pages, I felt strong pangs to do something to reverse my tendency to become more and more of an addicted couch potato. The fascination of being able to carry my own portable house into wilderness settings apparently stimulated some back channel of my mind. This possibly was linked with a wish to return, partly at least, to my distant pre-historic ancestral past. I had taken up jogging

Eastern shore of High Island

sometime before I read Fletcher's book, mostly to help fight a growing depression. Today, I think the depression was a symptom of a typical mid-life crisis. The jogging did help to alleviate the depression, but as a bonus, it also helped in the physical preparation for the up and down miles of trailwalking. Fletcher's book really turned on the creative juices, and I began taking easy overnight backpack hikes sponsored by the local chapter of the Sierra Club. When time from my university job and family responsibilities allowed, I became an avid day hiker and backpacker. Unknowingly, this new activity was also preparing me for a new time-consuming undertaking.

One of the areas a few hours from my Cincinnati home where I could indulge myself in this new activity was in Kentucky's Daniel Boone National forest. Known as the Red River Gorge, the area is famous for the highest concentration of natural arches in the United States, including Kentucky's well-known Natural Bridge. Large recess caves known as rock shelters, high sandstone cliffs and over a thousand varieties of flowering plants also add to the area's magnetic charm. I was surprised to learn there was no published general history or trail guide to the area so I took the plunge and wrote one. Originally, published in 1976, Kentucky's Land of the Arches has undergone several printings and now, in its revised edition, is the standard guide to this beautiful area.

Seasoning my skill as a backpacker with longer hikes in the Smokies, Isle Royal and Wyoming's Wind River range, I began to wonder if there were regions in Southern Ohio where I might enjoy backpacking closer to home. Finding several, I decided to let other Ohioans and anyone else who was interested know about them, and started my second book. Many years of research and writing finally culminated in 1984 when I published Backpack Loops and Long Day Trail Hikes in Southern Ohio. In both books, the major areas described are almost entirely on public land, preserved for recreation. Most of the trails are maintained and the areas are being allowed to return to wilderness. The favorable response to this approach has led me to follow pretty much the same format for this present work.

The Romance of the Islands
A personal View

Islands for many of us hold an attractiveness that is sometimes hard to classify. What does make a place take on an aura of mystery just because it is surrounded by water? Not everyone who willingly romanticizes about islands will have the same criteria of what is necessary to make an isolated piece of land suddenly take on an atmosphere of dreamy wonderment. What is the atmosphere that will raise our individual excitement or stimulate our romantic imaginations?

Those islands that have held the greatest fascination for me are, first, ones not attached to the mainland by bridges. Other stimulating factors are size: not big enough to have a continuing feeling that it might be just another chunk of mainland; few roads and vehicles or better yet no roads or vehicles at all; people, the fewer the better, and abundant wildlife nestled in a rich natural terrain with few or no buildings. Other types of islands are truly fascinating but more for their components of current and sometimes vulgarized human activity, like Manhattan. Others are primarily interesting because of their exclusive hunk of legend, ethnic background, literary references and history such as England and Ireland. Their watery isolation undoubtedly affected the course of their human history and our appreciation and enjoyment of them, but the reality that they are islands almost seems secondary.

Another part of my early life also led me to have more than a passive interest in these species of off-shore real estate. The love of the smaller idealized type of island more removed from great centers of long-term human activity are undoubtedly influenced by my childhood reading of Treasure Island, Robinson Crusoe and The Swiss Family Robinson, but my love for them was also highly influenced by actual events and associations that came quite early. My parents inherited a large rambling wooden summer home built by my grandfather before World War One on an island in Lake Minnetonka near Minneapolis. My parents were married on the front lawn in front of that large wooden frame building which overlooked the lake. Then, Minnetonka seemed far removed from the great northern metropolises of the Twin Cities. No bridge tied the island to the mainland and one had to row a boat 3/4 mile to the designated landing for the island. If my youthful memory serves, the island was about 3/4 mile long and a half-mile wide. It contained 13 summer homes, an ice house and a tennis court. The main water supply was a hand pump found near the center of the island close to the ice house. The single dilapidated tennis court was always in dire need of having its clay surfaces smoothed and its sagging net and fences patched. The island contained no roads or motor vehicles; not a single cottage had the luxury of indoor toilets; its total summer population probably never reached 50, and as late as 1955 the island was without electricity. There, each summer, I became a sort of Tom Sawyer who ignored shoes from the day I arrived till the day I left. The weeks were full of fishing, boating and swimming on a carefree time schedule which came in welcome contrast to my citified life the rest of the year in Chicago. On several occasions, in good Tom Sawyer fashion, it included whitewashing large sections of our next door neighbor's board fence. There were enough other young boys also summering there to join forces and indulge in all sorts of mild nefarious island activities. Also in residence were a sufficient number of girls to tease and mildly torment. Nights were often filled with singing; telling ghost stories and popping popcorn near open fires either along beaches or in front of large fieldstone fireplaces. Reading and games were carried out by mantled gas lamps whose mild hiss is still a part of my audible memory.

On this island I began to learn of the world of Poe, Dickens and Hawthorne but I much preferred the then popular publications consisting mostly of cartoons, known as "Big Little Books." It was a carefree isolated summer world of a young boy, historically suspended between two cataclysmic periods of war, in the latter of which he would take part. Like the title of Thomas Wolfe's book, You Can't Go Home Again, I knew I could never relive or duplicate those childhood days, but the seed of island fascination had been planted by my youthful island stays and remained with me into adulthood. So it was not surprising that when events of my life brought me to northern Michigan for repeated summers, the close presence of those islands, seen when scanning Michigan road maps, worked their magic upon me and built up a curiosity about them that I had to satisfy.

Although no one lived year round on that small Minnetonka island known as Crane, it did help me to identify with other youths, now far older than I, who had once lived the full year cycle on these Michigan Islands. The stories of their early island lives I was later to partly know. Since they were year round residents I could only comprehend, vicariously and in part, the feelings of what it was like to spend ones formative years in such an island existence. By reading and later by personal contact, I began at least to know in part Williard Smith, John Maleski Jr, Charles Anderson, Glenn Furst, Ethel Stormer, George Hutzler, Fred Burdick and John Wachtner Jr. Their early lives in these isolated water-bound hamlets deeply affected their destinies long after they left the islands. And the waters of Minnetonka, famous as they are, can never command the fierce majesty inspired by the enormity of the fresh-water sea known as Lake Michigan. Those youths are now old and one of them has recently died, but even as children they were well aware of how close their families' destinies were identified with that lake. Theirs was an all-encompassing world during their youth while mine was no more than a summer idyll. Nor was my small isle close to a major watery highway of commerce as were these Lake Michigan islands, replete with histories of struggling immigrants, lighthouses, shipwrecks, sea rescues and small villages now ghost towns. But, my own boyhood summers and a general romantic inclination gave me more than enough stimulation to be interested in these island communities.

Historical Significance

Although my career as a teacher of history mainly focused on the European area, my training in that discipline made me aware of the unique historic role these Lake Michigan

Abandoned farm on South Manitou

training in that discipline made me aware of the unique historic role these Lake Michigan islands played as stopover points on this important northern major water route. This link between Buffalo and Chicago had furnished transportation for much of the commerce and immigration that helped develop the northern Midwest. A few of the islands also provided new hardworking immigrants acreage for homesteading where, within a generation, their families changed from non-English speaking foreigners, to becoming totally American. Another point of historical interest happened when a few Ottawa and Ojibwa Indians retreated to the more remote islands and used them as the last havens against the white man's world. For a brief time at least, a few of the islands acted as last holdouts for a handful of Indians who only partly accepted the civilized world, but were eventually swallowed up by it. All these factors make for a fascinating historical microcosm of developing Midwest America from the eighteenth through the twentieth century. The four islands today are returning to wilderness. The people who once settled them are dead and their descendents have long since moved elsewhere. There are only remnants left of these ghost island communities but knowing about these past human events adds to the spice of exploring them. These unusual stories were more than enough to prime the pumps of my historical enthusiasm.

Disclaimer to the Historical and the Natural Setting Chapters

The reader should understand that the human histories, the geology and the naturalist sections are not to be interpreted as critical studies. These sections are not for specialists, but are general introductions and brief surveys to enhance a visit to the islands by

Channel between North and South Manitou as viewed from the top of North Manitou's largest blowout called Old Baldy

interested laymen. In discovering the unique history of the islands, combined with my intense interest in hiking and experience in writing two similar books, a guidebook devoted to brief histories and the recreational possibilities these islands afforded seemed a natural. The historical text here is far longer than I originally intended, and is more extended than corresponding sections found in my previous books. The human story of the islands is so much a part of the complete experience, that I feel a hiker may enjoy the pages devoted to this past. Those looking for a definitive history of the four islands in this book will be disappointed. Historical sections on the Two Manitous have been taken largely from readily available sources, and contains very little original research. High and Garden Islands are another matter. An in-depth historical survey of those lesser-known islands has yet to be written. A few good articles on specific areas do exist and were of great help. In piecing together the short narratives on High and Garden Islands found in these pages much is original and has never before been published. These brief chronicles are still often fragmentary. Parts are far sketchier than I would like and I occasionally have assumed some things that later evidence may not fully support.

Knowing that some sections of these island histories are incomplete and possibly even inaccurate, I am in hopes that persons who have evidence which will substantiate a more complete and accurate story will share such information with me. It is also hoped that someone at a future date will do definitive histories. Since I am trained in that field, readers may ask why I did not undertake the task of doing the necessary research and writing my own critical historical survey of the two smaller islands. My first and primary purpose for writing

South Manitou's South Island Dunes Trail

this book was to supply a work that would be useful to hikers. Reading it would increase their enjoyment of an island visit and make the best use of their time while there. The history sections were written to supplement and enrich that hiking experience, playing a secondary role to it, not the other way around. Second, such an intensive study would take many added months of investigation. Interesting as it would probably be I have already spent almost six years in researching and writing this book. I feel the time necessary for a first-rate historical survey of High and Garden Islands would delay publication of the book far too long. Possibly this narrative will encourage someone to take on such a project.

I am neither a geologist nor a naturalist. Everything found in those sections was taken from existing sources written by knowledgeable people in those fields. As is often the case I found that authorities did not always agree. These sections were gleaned from such works to serve as a general survey for the layman, composed by this author, who claims no expertise in either area. Despite elementary college courses in Geology and having some of the natural environment rub off on me after all those years of rambling about in the woods I am a neophyte in both areas. If experts of these areas take umbrage at some of my statements and would like to inform me of my inaccuracies and colossal ignorance, I would be glad to hear from them. I could possibly incorporate their knowledge into later editions.

About the Maps

The major island trail maps were made from the appropriate U.S.G.S. 7.5 minute series topographic maps. Although I was often aided by existing area maps issued by the state and federal governments the trail markings in this book were made by me. I feel they are adequate for giving the hiker, regardless of his/her map reading skill a good general idea of where the trails go. I found many small errors in the existing trail maps, and made appropriate corrections. Some minor mistakes and misinterpretations may turn up in mine and with time; new trail routes made by man and nature will call for occasional revisions.

Although I make no claim to be any professional type of cartographer, I think I am reasonably safe in stating that, at this writing, my trail maps, if not as artistically done, are at least as accurate and in some cases more accurate for hiking purposes than any existing trail

Old farm road, South Manitou

maps of these areas. Since many trails discussed in this book are not shown on the U.S.G.S. Maps, and since some trails shown on them no longer exist, hikers will find the maps included here more useful for their purposes, and a lot easier to carry around. The hiking areas in this book are found on five different 7.5 minute quadrangles. Those who wish to do extensive boondocking on the islands will find the 7.5 quads useful, for their colored surfaces distinguish features that cannot be equaled in black and white reproduction.

Rating the Trails. Distance and Time

Those of you who are familiar with my other two books know that at the beginning of each trail I have included three useful pieces of information: the length of the trail, the difficulty of the trail and an approximate time necessary to complete it. I have followed the same pattern in this volume with one exception. I have eliminated rating the difficulty of individual trails in this work. Since both my other books are about areas found in the foothills of Appalachia there are many strenuous up and down sections. Except for an occasional dune climb all the trails on these islands are fairly level, making their mileage the essential factor in determining their difficulty. The necessary walking time to cover a trail has to be somewhat arbitrary for the speed of various hikers ranges from those whose pace approximates giant sloths to those whose speed would embarrass a gazelle. My walking times tend to favor the slower-paced hiker, the ones who are in no hurry, whose pace is governed by the hours it takes to enjoy the scenery. Any well-conditioned serious hiker, who is used to backpack trips covering many miles over hilly terrain in a single day, will find my stated

Southern shore of North Manitou looking toward Dimmick's Point

times are at a snail's pace level. Those who are out of shape and burdened with a load of flab may find them more than a bit testy.

When It's Time to Hit the Trail

If you have prepared yourself well both Physically and mentally, and carry with you sensible hiking equipment, your visits to these islands may number among the most rewarding walks you will ever take. Each island is different enough to give you a uniqune hiking experience that won't be quite like any other walking venture of your life. As your boots stir up the faint dust of the trails you may hear the silent singing of forests, no longer threatened by the kettledrum thunder of the woodsman's axe. But remember, you are the visitor and not the possessor of these lands. The natural creatures that live there own them, and except for an occasional fish taken from the lakeshores or the necessary deer hunt at North Manitou, they should be left to live and to perish as nature intends. As you hike thsrough the islands keep in mind sthe following old Algonquin saying:

It is every man's responsibility to so walk the Sun's trail that he honor those who walked before him, honors those who walk with him and is remembered with honor by those who walk after him

Chapter II

Making Plans For Island Hiking

Which Island to choose

GENERAL REMARKS. Because of the usual embarkation points for these islands, they nicely divide themselves into two groups. Those wishing to go to the Manitous, will most probably take the ferry from the port of Leland. Others, who are primarily interested in High and Garden Islands will usually begin the first leg of their lake journey by taking the ferry or flying from the more northern city of Charlevoix to Beaver Island. The question then arises, "Which island should I visit?" The best answer for many would be, "All of them." But, time considerations and other factors will often make that answer impractical. One might assume that since the islands are so close together, they are pretty much the same so it doesn't make much difference which one you choose. In some ways that is true, but overall the dissimilarity between the four is significant and each has enough unique features to make the hiking experience on one vastly different from the others.

To best decide destinations for your planned visit and to choose which island you would first like to explore read the section immediately below entitled General Island Information. This introductory section includes those things applicable for all four islands under different headings and contains many vital facts about trips to any of them. Then, if the Manitous seem to be your choice, read the section entitled Introduction to Hiking the Manitous beginning on page 20. If High or Garden Islands are your first choice read Introduction to Hiking High and Garden Islands beginning on page 26. Then, to further fine-tune your trip, read the introductory chapter devoted to each island. There are also five history sections. The first covers the combined history of the islands up until they were occupied by the first white settlers during the second quarter of the nineteenth century. From there, the history of each individual island is treated separately. By reading these brief histories, the reader will not only have a better understanding of the general environment of the islands, but also a better idea of how to choose one for a first or only visit.

General Island Information

For your hiking palate, all four islands offer at least a triple treat, a taste of the sea, a taste of nineteenth century nautical and agricultural history and a taste of semi-wilderness. You can hike miles and miles of deserted sandy beaches, or higher up along the edge of huge sand cliffs which plunge hundreds of feet to the edge of the deep blue water. These walks give the viewer marvelous ocean-like vistas across what seems like an endless expanse of fresh water. You can also traverse the easily followed and mostly level trails that once were the island roads through recently deserted farms and lumber towns into the recovering forests that once supplied millions of board feet of lumber for the furnaces of the woodburning lake steamers and the commercial market.

What to Bring

Since there are no commercial facilities for either food or accommodations on any of the four islands you must carry everything you need. Backpackers will already have a good idea of what this should include. If you are staying overnight or longer the following items should make your trip a pleasanter one. Food for as many days as you plan to stay plus a day or two extra. Occasionally high seas make it impossible for the ferries to dock at the Manitous or chartered boats from Beaver to pick you up from the shores of High or Garden. It is quite possible that you might find yourself marooned for an extra day or two, and you should be prepared for it. Unless you are planning to eat only cold food, you will need a stove of some kind. Remember, fires are forbidden anywhere on the islands except at the few fire rings shared by campers in the official campgrounds on the Manitous. Even then, available supplies of dead wood may be scarce or thoroughly soaked from a few days of torrential rain. A good backpack stove is best, but if you are staying at a campground close to the Manitou docks or set up a base camp near the water on High or Garden and day-hike from there, the old two burner Coleman will suffice.

Along South Manitou' s Old Dock Road

Since rainy days are frequent, a substantial tent is more than a luxury. If you like sleeping out under the skies peeking from time to time of brief wakefulness at the fabulous show of a billion stars unfiltered by our filthy city air, please do. But, make sure you have a portable house to retreat to if less pleasant weather puts out the lights or a horde of mosquitoes zeroes in on your face. If you buy one of those discount house super-cheepie tents, beware. I once asked a camping companion who had one how he liked it. He replied. "They're really wonderful until it rains." Its best to test any tent you have in a hard rain at home before you come. Make sure the tent has adequate screening and zip-up enclosures to keep out mosquitoes and other unwelcome night visitors. It is also nice to have a lightweight rain fly for cooking outside during rainy periods.

A good quality insect repellent which has from 80 to 95% DEET is helpful, but not

Lifeboats at Sleeping Bear Point Maritime Museum

always effective. Ground cloths, flashlights with fresh batteries and reading material are not absolutely essential but still nice to have. A small first aid kit and sun lotion should be carried. If you are hiking on North Manitou, High or Garden Islands you must have some way to purify water. Boiling is tedious and uses lots of fuel. Iodine and chlorine can be used if you know the proper solutions. There are also commercial preparations, but sometimes they are hard to find. I have found that using one of the popular backpack water filters has worked very well.

Clothing should include not only adequate dress for sensible summer walking, but also enough warm garments for cold, blustery, wind and rain-driven days. Although summer days are usually warm it cools down considerably in the evening and temperatures in the low forties and high thirties are not unknown. It has even snowed in late August. Generally, sunny days are slightly cooler on the islands than the mainland, for the lake effectively lowers island temperatures. Still, temperatures in the 90s are sometimes recorded. Long-sleeved shirts and long pants are a must, especially if you want to do any shore walking in July and August. If you don't wear them the sand fly, which seems to be immune to any type of bug repellent, will eat you alive. I have been told that Avon "SkinSoSoft" sometimes is effective in warding off these viciously persistent pests. Good hiking shoes, broken in before you arrive, should be worn with a liner sock next to your feet encased in a heavy woolen outer sock.

A good quality rain parka, poncho or cagoule should also be carried. Rain pants are nice to have. You may be blessed with a string of warm, sunshine-filled days but don't count on it. Things can turn more than a little bit soggy if one encounters what is known thereabouts as a three-day blow. You may find your tent has developed serious leaks from the wind and

Chief Boswain demonstrating use of Lyle Gun at South Manitou Station Similiar eqipment is on display at Sleeping Bear Point Museum

Courtesy of S.B.D. National Lakeshore

pelting rain, and your down bag is rapidly collapsing after making contact with a mysterious puddle that suddenly appeared on what was supposed to be your waterproof floor. You are faced with the realization that the envisioned idyllic island experience is rapidly degenerating into a fight for survival. You wisely decide to return to the mainland on the next boat, only to discover that the ferry trip has been scrubbed because of high seas or your charter boat captain has no way of knowing that you would like to leave the island days before your appointed rendezvous. Well, if you are not the adventurous type, there are several mainland resorts anxious to coddle your wish for total creature comfort at exurbanite prices.

Preliminary Mainland Excursions

If you can arrange the time, an ideal way to familiarize yourself with the geography, history and geology of the islands would be to visit three different nearby locations maintained by the National Park Service. These locations are especially handy for those going to the Manitous. They are a bit out of the way for the northern two islands but if you have the time, a visit to these mainland locations is still rewarding. All three are less than 25 miles from Leland and conveniently close to one another. The first is the Philip A. Hart Visitor's Center at the Sleeping Bear Dunes headquarters at Empire, Michigan on Route M-

72 near its junction with Route M 22. This visitor's center has excellent displays and slide presentations which help explain the geologic and historical development of the area as well as how dunes are formed and why they are constantly changing. There, free maps and brochures are obtainable and rangers on duty will to answer any questions you might have. They also have a nice collection of books displayed for sale. These include histories and books of local interest, with many publications on flora and fauna.

Since both the Manitous and Beaver Island once had active life saving stations whose buildings still survive, a visit to the Sleeping Bear Point Coast Guard Station near Glen Haven on Route M 209 off Route M 22 will acquaint the visitor with how these stations were once utilized. The Glen Haven Station is now a museum run by the National Park Service dedicated to showing the individual function of each building, complete with the equipment and furnishings that were used during their active days. Much Great Lakes nautical and Coast Guard history is also included, with many photographs of old ships and shipwrecks. On moderately clear days North Manitou is easily seen from the beach in front of the station.

The last of these three points of interest is the 7.6 mile Pierce Stocking Scenic Drive loop. This is a one way auto loop found on Route M 109 off Route M 22. Although there are several points of interest on the drive, the one most meaningful to prospective Manitou Island visitors is Point #10. This takes you to the top of the awesome sand bluffs some 440 feet above Lake Michigan. From here on clear days you can look across the open water and see the south end of South Manitou some seven miles away. By following the path northward past the first wooden overlook to a second overlook both North and south Manitou are visible on clear days. If you later camp at South Manitou's Weather Station Campground, you will be able to look back and see the whole expanse of this mighty mainland dune escarpment which runs for almost three miles.

Manitou Passage Underwater Preserve

If you look out across the water from these Sleeping Bear cliffs not only are the islands you see a part of this historic natural area but the waters that surround the entire shoreline of the Manitous and the mainland coast are also part of a historic preserve. To manage and protect "submerged cultural resources" that lie on the bottom in the vicinity of the Manitou Passage, the Michigan Legislature established this famous nautical graveyard as an underwater preserve. Enclosed within the boundaries of this 282 square mile preserve established in 1988 are the wrecks of over 50 ships. Because the waters of Lake Michigan are clear enough to allow underwater visibility up to 25 feet and most of the wrecks lie in less than 40 feet of water, this creates an exciting recreational opportunity for skin divers and those equipped and trained for Scuba diving. Although the cold waters of the lake will discourage many divers used to the inviting temperatures of the Caribbean, these chilly temperatures have helped slow down the deterioration of the wrecks, and some of them are well preserved. The water of the straits do tend to be somewhat warmer than the open lake. Because of the excellent visibility, a few of the wrecks can be viewed from the surface by snorkelers. By law, the sunken hulls are protected and anyone caught removing any artifacts or damaging the remains of these ships is subject to heavy fines. Some underwater hulls are marked by buoys, making their location easy to find for perspective divers. Further information may be obtained about this preserve from the previously mentioned Visitor's Center at the park headquarters, or the Glen Haven Coast Guard Life Saving Museum. Another excellent source of information about the preserve and the location of known wrecks is the:

Northwest Michigan Maritime Museum
324 Main Street
Frankfort, Michigan 49635

Those interested in buying or renting diving equipment or charting a dive boat may contact:

Scuba North
113380 W. Bay Shore Drive
Traverse City, Michigan 49684
(616) 947 2520

How to get to the Islands

Regularly scheduled commercial ferry service is available in season to both the Manitous and Beaver Island. The latter island is the usual intermediate stop to High and Garden Islands. Most visitors will take advantage of one or the other commercial boat service in getting to the islands. Since these services are completely different for the two sets of islands, both in boat companies and embarkation points, available ferry services to the two areas are discussed under their individual sub-headings in this chapter.

Getting to the Islands on Your Own

If you have a boat seaworthy enough to handle the big water of Lake Michigan and the seamanship to operate it, the closest deepwater port with a protected harbor for the Manitous is found at Leland, Michigan. Many private boats also sail from Frankfort. The usual embarkation point for the Beaver group is Charlevoix. Crescent Bay at South Manitou and a similar bay at High Island do offer boaters some harbor protection, which is quite adequate unless there are strong breezes from the east. Boaters dropping the hook in these harbors should set their anchors with wind shifts in mind and remember that passing squalls, especially from an easterly direction can create serious wave conditions. Garden Island is the only one of the four that has a snug harbor with good protection from wind and heavy waves from almost any direction. Much of it is shallow, however, and it takes some careful maneuvering when entering or leaving. There is no safe anchorage at North Manitou so if you drop the hook offshore someone must be with your craft at all times in readiness to return to Leland if the weather turns nasty. There are no long-term docking facilities or fuel on any of the four islands.

Those with smaller boats who are capable of handling all but the roughest Lake Michigan weather, and would like to use them for visits to High and Garden, can avoid the 27-mile open-water journey to Beaver by having the Beaver Island Ferry take their boat across to St. James. Reservations for doing so must be made well in advance with the Beaver

Island Boat Company.

Sea Kayaks.

If you are a skilled sea kayaker (not a whitewater river kayaker which calls for different skills and equipment), completely equipped with wet suit and are comfortable in five to six-foot swells, these islands offer many possibilities for combination hiking and kayaking trips. The Beaver Island Ferry can easily take your boat to St. James which puts you in comfortable range for both High and Garden Islands. Advanced reservations for transporting your kayak should be made. The Manitou ferries are much smaller and not really equipped to regularly carry anything as large as a sea kayak, so you will have to negotiate a trip across open water. The closest mainland take-off for North Manitou is at Pyramid Point, some five miles from the southern end of the island, but getting to the water at that location is so difficult it negates its two-mile advantage over departing at Leland. Those sea kayakers wishing to go to South Manitou will have an easier time getting to Glen Haven near Sleeping Bear Point, where a trip of almost eight miles of open water is needed to cross the straits to the island. This is still a lot shorter than the 14-mile distance between South Manitou and Leland.

The Use of Small Boats for Transportation to the Islands

If you are stupid enough to try these crossings in a canoe or other small craft designed for smaller lakes and rivers, make sure your life insurance is paid up and inform any dependents you might have to get ready to enter the job market.

When to Come

During the winter months the accumulation of Lake Michigan shore ice, violent storms, discontinued ferry service and official closings, pretty much restricts sensible visits to the islands to a period from late Spring though early Fall.

For the wildflower lover May and early June are best with thousands of blooms almost anywhere one looks. The number of campers at that time of year is also quite small. Temperatures are cooler and are the best for pleasant walking. Conversely, these early months are generally still too cool for comfortable sunbathing and the waters of Lake Michigan seem absolutely frigid.

May through July is the active nesting season for the gulls, and terns. Watching the nesting antics of these birds with binoculars at a respectable distance will be enjoyed by many. These early months also seem to be the worst for mosquitoes and other annoying insects. By the middle of June temperatures have warmed considerably and with them comes an ever increasing number of sun-seeking visitors, especially on South Manitou.

By late July, the insect population has decreased greatly, but beach walkers will soon realize they have been inundated by another plague, the sand fly. In this writer's estimation, they are worse than all the other insects put together. Fortunately however, they are generally found only along the shoreline areas. By the middle of August, the summer

Coast Guard boat in ice near North Manitou shore
Courtesy of S.B.D. National Lakeshore

crowds visiting the Manitous have fallen off slightly, and stay generally smaller except for the Labor Day weekend. It is rare that you will find more than a handful of people on either High or Garden Island at any time throughout the season.

After Labor Day, the visitors to the Manitous diminish almost to nothing. The cooler temperatures and the feelings of Fall with its turning colors, can make it one of the loveliest times for those seeking solitude in an isolated natural setting. By the second week of October, South Manitou is officially closed and ferry service is stopped. At this writing, North Manitou is open until the end of the deer hunt in early November. Ferry service is available through that period, albeit at a higher price and following no regular schedule. The Beaver Island private charter boats, which most people use to get to High and Garden Islands are usually pulled from water by late fall. I have often thought how lovely it would be when these islands are blanketed with snow to cross-country ski across them unhampered by the sounds of autos or skimobiles. But, even if the islands were not officially closed once the shore ice begins to build, the hazards and expense of getting to them would be so great that it would negate any sensible plan for such an excursion.

An occasional exception sometimes happens in January and February when the lake surface between Beaver and Garden Islands is like icy steel. If conditions are right the two-mile distance between them can easily be traversed by cross country skiers. Check with authorities on Beaver Island on the condition of the ice before you leave on any such adventure, because this crossing is not possible every year and the times such a passage can be made vary a great deal.

These preceding pages should give you a good idea of which group of islands you would prefer. The two sections that follow, **Introduction to Hiking the Manitous** and **Introduction to High and Garden Islands** furnish you with more specific information on each group.

Introduction to Hiking The Manitous.

GENERAL REMARKS. Prospective visitors might consider some of the following comparisons in deciding where their introductory visit to the Manitous should begin. Of the four hiking islands emphasized in this book, most hikers will find that these two southernmost islands of the Lake Michigan Archipelago are the most often visited. Administered by the National Park Service as part of the Sleeping Bear Dunes National Lakeshore, the Manitous are the only islands in this chain controlled by that branch of the federal government. They are larger than High and Garden Islands, and are a lot easier to get to, since both have regular passenger ferry service from late spring through early fall. Not only are there park rangers residing on the Manitous to aid visitors during the summer months, there are also many miles of maintained trails for the hiker to follow.

The nineteenth and early twentieth century chronicle of the Manitous gives these islands a unique history, which in itself is an enhancing bit of romance that many visitors will enjoy. Since this area of northern Michigan was originally penetrated by ship, the Manitous, which were strategically placed along the mainstream of that commerce, played an important role in that development. During the nineteenth century, the impact of the white man on the Manitous was considerable, because these sister islands form the western side of the critically important Manitou Passage. Thousands of ships funnelled through that narrow seaway on their way north or south each year. Both the Manitou islands had year-round white settlers many years before the adjacent mainland, and the relatively safe harbor of South Manitou made it a natural haven for sailing and steam powered ships that often sought protection from storms or a convenient place to resupply and refuel. But the once active sawmills, farms and small lakeside villages that thrived during the heavy sea traffic days, as well as the small summer communities, are now things of the past. Most of the buildings that accompanied those activities have disappeared, lie in ruin or will be allowed to deteriorate. The orchards and farm fields are being reclaimed by nature and only a few of the historically important structures continue to be maintained.

North Manitou is almost three times as large as South Manitou and nearly twice as long. If you want to backpack, North Manitou will be your obvious choice, for once you are out of the village area camping is at-large. The official trail system has about 20 miles of maintained paths and there are another 20 miles of non-maintained trails that are fairly easy to follow. Except for the village area human intrusion is far less visible here than on its sister island to the south. It also has more of that get-away-from-it-all feeling, for fewer people visit North Manitou and hikers have more room in which to disperse. Reasons for this smaller number of visitors include the following: even during the height of the season, the ferry service to the island does not run on a daily schedule as is the case with South Manitou; the number of days the ferry makes the trip fluctuate with demand, which is usually three times a week; the ferry does not lay over at North Manitou, so there are no day-trip visitors; landing the ferry at the island has become difficult for the ferry because the lake level has dropped

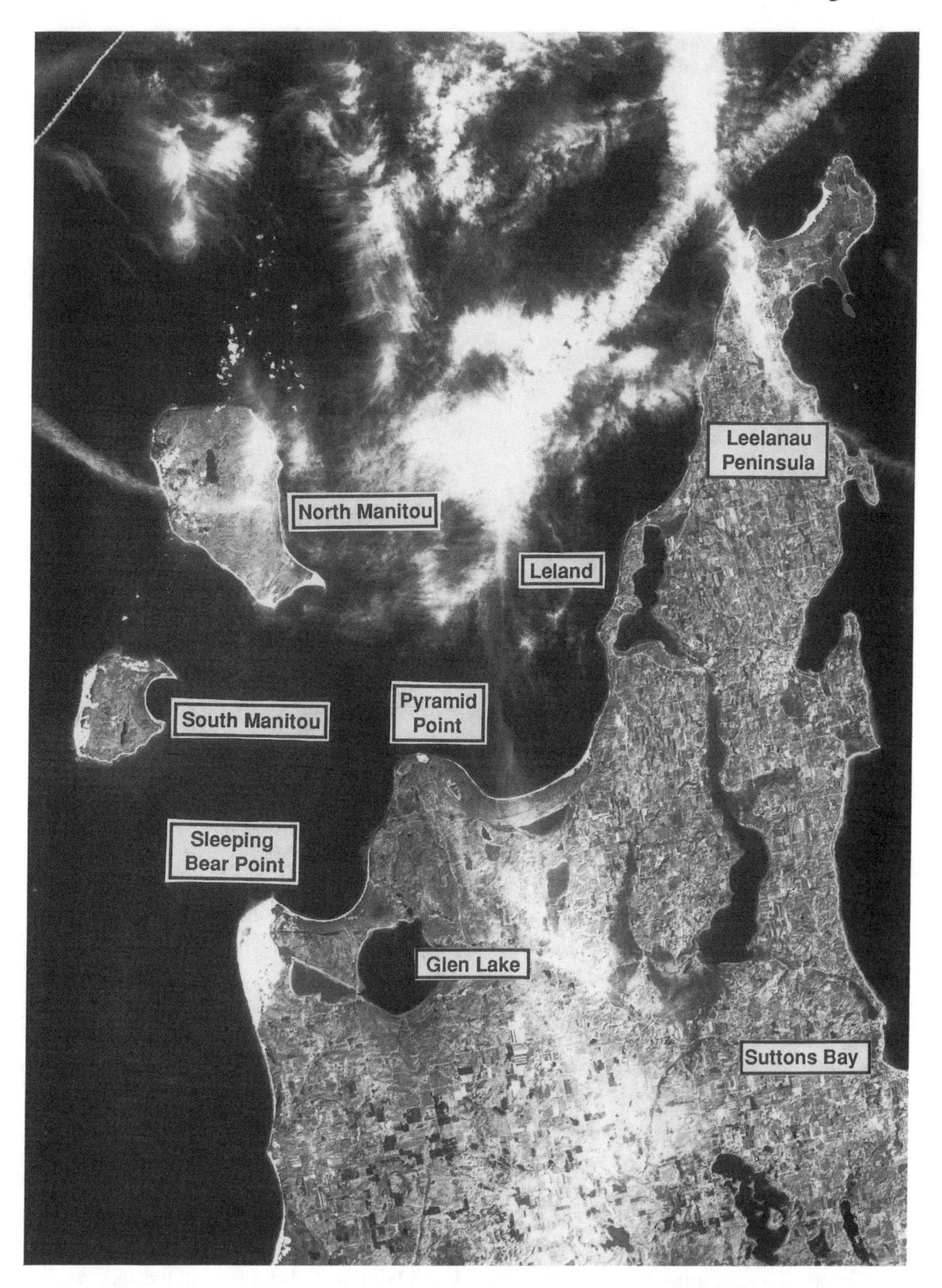

Satellite photo of the Leelanau Peninsula and the Manitou Islands

Courtesy of the Environmental Research Institute

making the water around the N.P.S. Dock too shallow. Winds from the east sometimes cause

Campsite on the bluff at South Manitou's Weather Station Campground

wave action that makes the ferry change its landing site.

Because North Manitou does not have a natural harbor there is no safe anchorage for private boats so they may not be left unattended for long periods of time. Even at its busiest periods North Manitou never seems overburdened with humanity. If you are looking for a hike in isolated and wilderness-oriented atmosphere, North Manitou would be the obvious choice between the two islands. The possible exception would be during the October and early November deer hunt held annually on the northern island. Recreational hiking is still permitted, but not recommended during this period.

If you are not enthusiastic about backpacking South Manitou may be your preferred choice, for there is no at-large camping permitted and overnighters must stay in one of the three designated campgrounds. With the advantage of the daily ferry service between Memorial Day and Labor Day, it is easier to schedule a trip around your own personal free time. It can be used as a weekender island by arriving on a Friday or Saturday morning and leaving Sunday afternoon. The walk to two of the campgrounds is not long, so once camp is set up hikers have the opportunity of day-hiking without the burden of a pack.

The island is small enough that any major point of interest on the island is within the roundtrip range of any conditioned walker in a single day. There are more apparent things of a historical and cultural interest on the island, and both the lighthouse and the spectacular view from the top of the island's western sand bluff just aren't matched on North Manitou. For those who are looking for R and R, all three campgrounds are close to excellent beaches. As long as a strong wind doesn't blow out of the east, the protected harbor allows those with boats suitable for Great Lakes navigation a sheltered place to drop the hook. But with this come the people. Lots of 'em, especially day trippers, particularly in late June, July and early August.

If you are an addicted beach walker both islands have marvelous miles of sand-covered shoreline to explore. Many feel that the best hiking on these islands are the extended beach walks. Both islands have rangers living on them in season who are available for questions or emergencies. Both islands also have direct communication with the mainland in case of emergencies. Neither island has a store nor any type of commercial lodging, so you must bring everything you need for your stay. Except for emergency first aid, there are no doctors, nurses or medical facilities on any of these islands, so don't come if you are ill or have a medical problem that you cannot handle on your own.

South Manitou is the only one of the four islands that has a public telephone (attached to the south wall of the building containing the flush toilets near the boathouse). Outgoing calls may be made either by using a telephone credit card or reversing the charges. The phone will not take coins, nor is it equipped to receive incoming calls. There are no public telephones on North Manitou. Drinkable water is available at or near the three South Manitou campgrounds. The only place where treated water can be obtained on North Manitou is at the ranger station.

Rules and Regulations for the Manitous

Except for the small historic corridor on South Manitou where the island's motorized tour is allowed, these islands are designated as wilderness areas. If you are staying overnight on the Manitous, you must register for a backcountry permit on your arrival, and you can extend your stay for as long as 14 days. Leave Fido and your motor scooter at home, for no pets or any type of wheeled vehicle are allowed. When staying in the campgrounds, you choose one of the assigned sites for which you must register. No more than six people may occupy a single site. There are also several large group campsites available on South Manitou which can accommodate up to 25 people. Advanced reservations for the group campsites are necessary before you arrive at the island and may be made by calling the Park headquarters at Empire. Telephone (616) 326-5134. Individual campsites cannot be reserved in advance. Since the campsites are primitive, low-impact camping is practiced. There should be no ditching of tents and all trash must be carried out. Trash cans are located at the N.PS. docks on both Islands.

Following the wilderness ethic, portable radios, if played at all, should have the volume at a very low level. Loud raucous parties do not fit into the peaceful scheme of the islands. If you have conjured up images of long evening beach strolls gathering up driftwood along the way to build a blazing fire on a distant beach for roasting hot dogs, marshmallows and other goodies, forget it, for the only places open fires are allowed on either island are in a few metal-encased fire rings provided by the park service. With one exception the rings, which are shared by several campsites, are found only at the official campgrounds. This exception is a single fire ring found on South Manitou's Crescent Beach next to the Bay Campground. You may use only downed deadwood in these rings. The camps do have toilet facilities.

Ferry Service to the Manitous.

The Manitou Island Transit Company has two substantial boats used in the ferry service to both Manitous from their home port of Leland, Michigan. This family owned business has been operating ferry and mail boats to the two Manitous for over 50 years. Mike Grosvenor, the present manager and owner of the ferry service, is the fourth generation of his family to be involved with the Manitous. His grandfather, Tracy, who began the ferry service and his father, George both grew up on North Manitou. George continued to run the service his father began and is still active as one of the pilots. He has, however, turned the

The Manitou Island ferries

management of the company over to his son and daughter-in-law, Beth.

Ferry service to South Manitou usually begins running on weekends about the middle of May. Wednesday and Monday sailings are sometimes added if there is enough passenger demand to warrant it. Starting Memorial Day weekend, a seven day a week trip schedule is begun and continues through Labor Day. After the Labor Day weekend a shortened schedule to South Manitou is again followed through the first part of October. Ferry service stops when the park service officially closes the island. This usually happens during the first or second week of October. The boat departs from its Fishtown dock in Leland harbor promptly at 10:00 a.m. for the 14 mile trip to South Manitou, and arrives at the island about 11:30 a.m. The boat lays over at the island until 3:30 p.m. when it departs for the mainland arriving at the Leland dock about 5:00 p.m.

Regular ferry service to North Manitou usually begins Memorial Day weekend and

Ferry Captains George and Mike Grosvenor

runs to the beginning of the controlled deer hunt held on the island in October and November. Sailings are scheduled three days a week on Wednesdays, Fridays and Sundays leaving the same dock at Fishtown at 10:00 a.m. and arriving at the island about 11:10 a.m. The boat returns to Leland as soon as returning passengers are aboard, for there is no layover at North Manitou. This makes one-day round trips with on-shore visiting to North Manitou impossible. You can still go to North Manitou to hike during the time of the annual October deer hunt, but there are reasons that make it not an Ideal time to go. The ferry service is far more costly during the hunt and does not follow a regular schedule. Possible severe weather conditions and the chance that an inexperienced and excitable hunter might mistake you for a deer also add to the hazards.

Those holding reservations for a trip to either island should arrive at the company's office called "The Port Hole," located at the Fishtown Dock on the Leland waterfront, by 9:30 a.m. to confirm their reservations. Reservations may be made be calling **(616) 256-9061** between 9:00 a.m. and 9:00 p.m. between June 1 and Labor Day. If no one answers the phone during the week in September and May, or if you wish information during the off-season, call (616) 271-4217. At this writing, reservations need no advance deposit. You may also write:

Manitou Island Transit
P.O. Box 591
Leland, Mich. 49654

If you arrive at Leland without reservations, go to "The Port Hole" dock office at 9:00 a.m. and put your name on the waiting list. Often, people with reservations don't show, and you may be able to get on. Reservations are held until 9:45 a.m. At this writing, the roundtrip cost to either island for campers is $16.00 for adults and $12.00 for children 12 years old or younger. Day trips to South Manitou are $2.00 cheaper. Vehicle parking on a nearby lot is available for $1.00 a day. A weekly rate is also available. If you are leaving your car, get to the dock office as close to 9:00 a.m. as you can to deposit your gear at the office, then get your car parked and be chauffeured back to the dock in plenty of time for departure. During the busy months there is often a huge morning traffic jam in the vicinity of the office. Remember if you have reservations, you must claim them before 9:45 a.m.

Scheduled departures sometimes have to be cancelled because of Inclement weather. This rarely happens on the South Manitou run because the deep water harbor allows debarking and boarding in all but the roughest of weather. North Manitou is a different matter. At this writing, lower lake levels have placed the new N.P.S. dock in water that is too shallow to allow the ferries to approach it. When weather permits, passengers disembark on

Leland Harbor with North and South Manitou in the distance. The "Port Hole" ferryboat office is the building on the left

beaches at the southern end of the island. If you are going to North Manitou it is always wise to carry enough food for a couple of extra days.

If the wind is blowing from the west, the ferries can usually make the run to either island, even if the swells are large. But remember that Lake Michigan is not Walden Pond and strong winds producing good-sized waves can seem to reduce the Leland ferry to cork-size proportions on a stormy sea. This often causes some passengers' summer tans to take on a bilious green hue as they rush across the pitching deck to feed their digesting breakfast to the fishes. As far as your personal security is concerned, the Leland ferries have an outstanding reputation for safety with not a single serious injury in many years of service. But this is of little comfort to the person who has been adversely affected by the pitching deck, and for the moment, wishes to die anyway. Remember, this is big water. Usually the ride, made through gently rolling swells and bathed in blue sky sunlight, will be one of the most pleasant parts of your visit. If it turns out otherwise, you only have a little over an hour to suffer before your feet will again be on terra firma.

Although both islands had aircraft landing strips at one time, they have not been maintained. Landing on them today would not only be unduly hazardous but because of their wilderness classification, is also against the law.

Introduction to High and Garden Islands

GENERAL REMARKS. Hikers trying to escape all vestiges of the hand of the white man will find High and Garden Island more removed from the civilized flows of the last two centuries than the Manitous. High and Garden Islands, not being directly on the important sea lane that bordered the Manitous, were less affected by nineteenth century nautical commerce. This resulted in a historical development which was shorter-lived, involving

The Beaver Island group of the lake Michigan Archipelago

Courtesy of the Environmental Research Instsitute

decidedly fewer people, but fascinating in its own way. Their closeness to Beaver Island, which is the largest of the entire archipelago, also heavily influenced their historical destinies. Although both islands once had small year-round communities, today the islands are deserted except for researchers involved in bird and botanical studies. Unlike the Manitous, there are no summer rangers in residence. The islands have no telephone connections and their trails, once the roads for the island's inhabitants and lumbering operations, receive little or no maintenance. They are part of the Beaver Island State Wildlife Research Area, which also includes Hog Island and much of the southern end of Beaver Island. Administered by Michigan's Department of Natural Resources, High, Garden and Hog Islands are being allowed to return to nature.

For those looking for solitude and isolation, with little or no human contact, High Island is the ideal choice, with Garden Island a close second. You are pretty much on your own on these islands, so they are a poor choice for beginning campers, those people new to backpacking or those not in excellent health. Although primarily maintained as places for environmental research studies, the islands are open to hikers, campers, fishermen and hunters. All those engaged in the latter two of these activities must hold valid Michigan licenses and follow the state's hunting and fishing regulations. Despite their nearness and inclusion in the same natural ecosystem, the two islands are distinctively different. These differences are discussed in the introduction to each island and to avoid redundancy, are not repeated here.

First, Stopover Beaver Island

GENERAL REMARKS. Since both High and Garden Islands lie close to this largest island of the Lake Michigan Archipelago many will use it as a stopover on their way to the smaller islands. Beaver Island itself can be a wonderful adventure for the beachcombing hiker. Its unique history and removal from the intense beehive of the mainland's concentrated humanity brings about a welcome slower-paced inhabited world. Although it has about a hundred miles of road the island, at this writing, still has not one traffic light. With a year-round population of about 200, the island may have as many as 1,000 summer visitors at one time. They are, however, spread out through the 14-mile length and 6-mile width of the island. Except for Homecoming Weekend the island never seems congested.

I had originally planned to include the trails and beachwalks of Beaver Island in this volume, but it became impractical for several reasons. First, I found that as the writing of the book's major four hiking islands progressed it was becoming far longer than I had originally forecast. Adding the hiking areas of Beaver would have increased its size to encyclopedic proportions. Secondly, although about a third of the island is state-forested land, and the long beachwalks are of the best, there is still a lot of civilization nearby. It doesn't have that all-out exclusiveness devoted almost entirely to hikers. This experience is enhanced on High and Garden Islands by the total absence of motor-operated land vehicles. It doesn't mean that you can't escape the madding crowd on Beaver Island. There are backpackers who get off the ferry at St. James harbor and disappear into the island's forests and secluded beaches sometimes for weeks at a time.

After having spent considerable time on the island I became aware that those visiting Beaver would better be served by a comprehensive book designed to acquaint the visitor with the island's own unique high points. Although there are many fine published books and articles in print about the island's history and natural features there is no comprehensive guidebook to the island. There is one small guide available containing limited information called The Beaver Island Guide. I highly recommend it, not so much for its scant descriptions, but for the excellent large colored map of the island done by two longtime islanders, William

Arriving at the Port of St. James, Beaver Island

Cashman and Ed Wojan. Printed on durable rain-resistant paper and on sale at reasonable cost, this map shows and names all the island's roads, trails, lakes and bays, including public and private land.

In this author's opinion a book, combining a short comprehensive island history and a more extensive island guide would be welcomed by visitors and widely read. The island traveler, moving by foot or auto, would have a sourcebook of what he was seeing that would weave the historical content of the locations into their geographical descriptions and locations. With all the things of tremendous interest that this island holds such a book, properly done, would reach sizable proportions. Undoubtedly some author, possibly this one, will take up the task sometime in the future.

At this time the Cashman, Wojan cartographic effort remains the best source for getting about the island and it is unlikely that anyone will ever make a better island map. Meanwhile, those who seek existing printed matter about the island should visit or contact the Beaver Island Historical Society, housed in the Old Mormon Print Shop in the island town of St. James. Displayed in their combination bookshop and museum are an excellent selection of available books about the island which are for sale. The society has published three volumes of collected articles about the island entitled The Journal of Beaver Island History which are also sold there and are well worth reading by anyone interested in the island.

Getting to High and Garden Islands via Beaver Island

Unless one has a large seaworthy vessel and can proceed directly to High or Garden

The Beaver Island ferry returning to Charlevoix

Island, the usual way to get to these destinations is to proceed first to Beaver Island. From there one can hire one of the local carriers or proceed in his own vessel if it is seaworthy enough to handle offshore waters. You can get to Beaver either by boat or by air.

THE BEAVER ISLAND FERRY. This company has two ferries, both capable of carrying passengers and vehicles. Ferry service is available from Charlevoix to Beaver Island's town of St. James from the middle of April to December 24. Because of the great seaworthiness of their vessels they seldom miss a run because of bad weather. The port-to-port distance is about 27 miles and usually takes two hours and 15 minutes. During the middle of June the Beaver Island Boat Company begins daily round trips to the island. From the end of that month through the first week of September, there are two roundtrips a day during the week, and three on Fridays and Saturdays. Fares are reasonable and walk-on passengers usually do not need advance reservations. About the only time the boats reach full passenger-carrying capacity is during Homecoming which is held the second weekend of August. Inexpensive long-term mainland vehicle parking is also available. If you are leaving your car on the mainland, make sure you arrive at least an hour before sailing, for the parking area is not at the dock. Reservations for motor vehicles and boats are absolutely necessary, and should be made well in advance. An advance deposit is required, and you must have your vehicle and or boat at the dock at least an hour before sailing time. Each year the Beaver Island Boat Company publishes a ferry schedule card which includes sailing dates, times of sailings, fares and other pertinent information. To obtain one, make reservations, or for other enquiries write or call the:

Beaver Island Boat Company
102 Bridge Street
Charlevoix, Michigan 49720
Phone (616) 547-2311

ARRIVING BY AIR. If you are bothered by mal de mer, are in a hurry, or would like to see the islands from above and have access to an airplane, the island has two airports. The privately-owned Welke Airport located 1 1/2 miles south of the town of St. James has two runways measuring 2,700 and 3,500 feet with tie-downs available. The Welkes operate the Island Airways, offering regular flights between Charlevoix and the island, as well as charter service to other points. Although it is a non-scheduled airline, there are almost hourly flights in twin engine aircraft from Charlevoix during the summer season. For further information call or write:

Island Airways
St. James, Michigan 49782
Phone (616) 448-2326
or Charlevoix Airport on U.S. 31 (616) 547-2141

If you are flying in by private plane, you may use the Welke or the Township Airports with tie-down services at either landing area. The township airport has three landing strips, the largest of which is paved and long enough to handle jet aircraft. Taxi service is available from either airport. If you fly in on a private aircraft, make sure you have plenty of fuel for it is available only for emergencies at the Welke airport. You may not land on either High or Garden Island, for they do not have landing strips. Although there are open areas where a helicopter could put down on those two islands, it is against the law to do so because of their wilderness classification.

Getting to High and Garden Islands from Beaver

Unless you have taken a personal boat to Beaver Island by ferry that can handle offshore water, the next step is to take a charter boat to either High or Garden Island. You should make reservations with the charter captain before your visit. Two that I have had personal experience with are Danny Higdon and Jack Urber. Both their boats are licensed by the Coast Guard for carrying commercial passengers. Danny's boat is open, while Jacks has an enclosed cabin. Jack's boat is also seaworthy enough that he can make the run from Charlevoix directly to either High or Garden Island, but the cost for doing so is higher than taking the Beaver Island Ferry across to that larger island first. At this writing, Danny lives on the island year-round while Jack winters elsewhere. Danny's telephone number is (616) 448-2309. During the season call the local operator for Jack's current island number. The

Beaver Haven Marina also offers this service and may be reached by phone (616) 4482-300. There may be others offering this service with whom I am not acquainted. You may be able to find other charter services by writing or calling:

The Beaver Island Civic Association
P.O. Box 5, Beaver Island
ST. James Michigan 49782
(616) 448-2505

Plans should be made with local carriers days before your expected arrival.

Beaver Island Plans. If you are using one of the local charter boat operators, they usually have their boats in St. James harbor so it is an easy walk from the ferry dock to their moorings. By taking the morning Beaver Island Ferry from Charlevoix you would arrive at the harbor well before noon. If the weather is cooperating and your carrier knows when you are arriving this would leave you with plenty of time to take the smaller boat to either High or Garden Island the same day. If weather conditions become particularly nasty, or you want to spend some time on Beaver before you migrate to the other islands, there are two campgrounds and two handy motels for overnight or longer stays. The Township Campground, found 1.3 miles from St. James, is the closest of the two. It sits on a high bluff which overlooks Garden Island, some two miles away. The more attractive state campground, which has a beautiful sandy beach, has the disadvantage of being 7.5 miles from St. James, making it a bit much for an overnight stay if your car is back on the mainland.

Taxi service is available, but costly, not because the local operators are trying to gouge the tourists, but because of the high cost of gasoline on the island. Both camps have outhouses and water but no other facilities, and a camping fee is charged. The two motels are right in town less than a half block from the ferry dock. Both are moderately priced, but reservations during the season are absolutely necessary, for they are often fully booked weeks ahead of time. They are the Erin Motel, phone (616) 448-2240 and the Harbor View II, phone (616) 448-2201. There are also cabins to rent, and bed and breakfast places. For a complete list of facilities contact the Beaver Island Civic Association.

If you are looking for something beside fast food, there are two excellent island restaurants a short distance out of town. They are the Beaver Island Lodge (phone (616) 448-2396) and the circle M Supper Club (phone (616) 448-2318). Reservations, especially on weekends, are also usually necessary and may be made by phone. The in-town Shamrock (phone (616) 448-2278) also has a kitchen and menu. All three serve alcoholic beverages. If you wish to write to any of the above for an address simply use the name of the company followed by Beaver Island, St. James, Michigan 49782

One plan I have used on my backpack trips to High and Garden is to try to get to the island I have chosen the same day I arrive on Beaver, but make a motel and dinner reservation for the date I intend to return to Beaver. It's nice to have a hot shower, a leisurely dinner and a comfortable bed after a few days of backpacking. Then, the following morning, refreshed and clean, I immensely enjoy the easy paced ferry ride back to Charlevoix.

If you are staying on Beaver only for a short stay the expense of transporting your car to the island is hardly worth the cost. The Beaver Island Boat Company usually conducts

Cabin ruin in "House of David" ghost town, High Island

If you are staying on Beaver only for a short stay the expense of transporting your car to the island is hardly worth the cost. The Beaver Island Boat Company usually conducts an Island tour during the busy months. For a moderate fee, this tour is an excellent introduction to the island. If you intend to spend a few days on Beaver, a car is a mighty handy thing to have when exploring the sights, beaches and trails of the island. Fill your tank with gas before you cross the waters, because fuel costs are almost double what you will pay on the mainland. Do not load up extra gas cans for this is against Coast Guard regulations. For grocery items, Gilespie's Dockside I.G.A. Grocery store is immediately adjacent to the ferry, and McDonough's well-equipped supermarket is about a quarter mile northeast on Main Street paralleling the harbor.

Ferryboat Manitou Isle leaving Leland Dock for North Manitou while Mishe-Mokwa passengers await departure for South Manitou

Ferryboat Beaver Islander passing the M 31 Bridge at Charlevoix on way to Port of St. James, Beaver Island

Chapter III

The Natural Setting

The Glacier, the Dunes and the Plant communities

The Glacier and A Short Geologic History

The most influential factor in shaping the basic outlines of the Great Lakes was an extended period of geologic time which saw huge glaciers covering much of the northern part of the North American continent. Before this time, the geologic history is quite complicated and of little interest except to the specialist. This early period can briefly be summed up as follows. An extended lowland region known as the Michigan Basin was surrounded by mountainous areas called "Shield" uplands. This broad basin, nearly circular in shape extended south into Illinois, Indiana and Ohio. Its lowest point is found around the middle of Michigan's Lower Peninsula. For a period of about 600 million years, this basin underwent different cycles of uplifting and sinking often rearranging the major drainage patterns from northeast to south.

During these up-and-down movements, various sediments were deposited in shallow seas, swamps and by stream action. They were then partly eroded and turned into various stone layers by the pressure of later deposits above them. Sometimes they were turned into sedimentary strata or metamorphosed by greater pressure into more weather resistant layers. One geologic explanation describes this as a collection of huge mixing bowls, the lower bowls being larger and older then the ones immediately above. These mixing bowl layers were deposited during a long geologic age geologists call the Paleozoic, which is divided into six sub-periods. From the oldest to the youngest, they are named the Cambrian, Ordivician, Silurian, Devonian, Mississippian and the Pennsylvanian. The deposits made during these six major Paleozoic periods represent a time expanse of about 250 million years. The eastern fringe of one of these bowls deposited during the Devonian period forms the basic pre glacier bedrock of the Lake Michigan Archipelago islands (See Diagram A).

A period immediately following the Paleozoic, which began over a million years ago, is the one most influential in determining the present surface features of the Lake Michigan Archipelago. Known as the Pleistsocene epoch, it contains several periods of intense glaciation. For reasons not entirely understood, temperature averages across the globe underwent a universal decline, which brought on these ice ages. These lowered temperatures of the Pleistocene epoch made the building of vast continental ice sheets, covering much of North America. They were not continuous, and there were long warming periods in-between, causing the ice sheets to retreat or to disappear entirely. When another cooling cycle would begin, the new advance of ice would obliterate existing land surface features left by the previous one.

If the cause of these extended ice age temperature drops is still open to debate, the growth

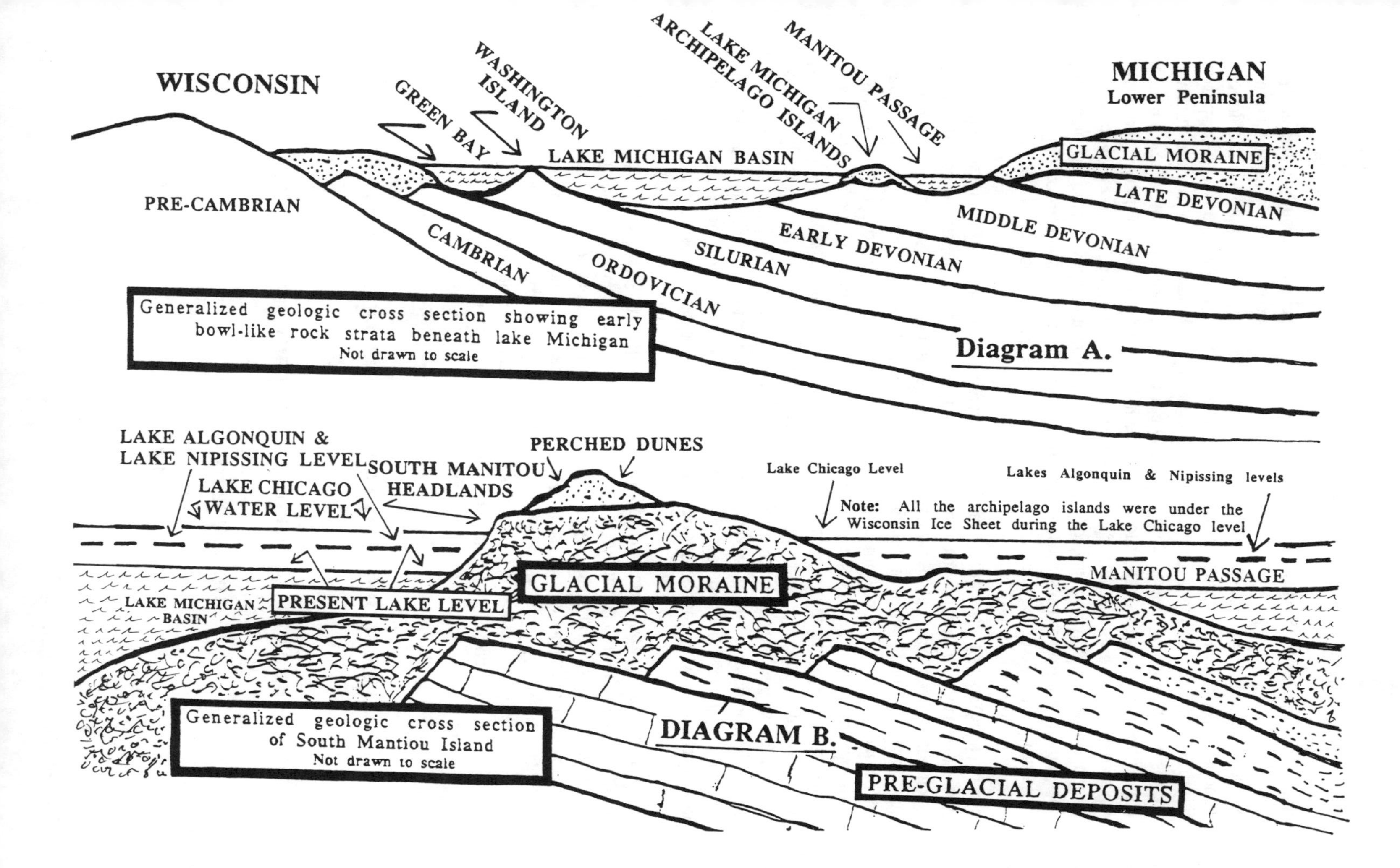
WISCONSIN
GREEN BAY
WASHINGTON ISLAND
LAKE MICHIGAN ARCHIPELAGO ISLANDS
MANITOU PASSAGE
MICHIGAN
Lower Peninsula
LAKE MICHIGAN BASIN
GLACIAL MORAINE
PRE-CAMBRIAN
LATE DEVONIAN
MIDDLE DEVONIAN
EARLY DEVONIAN
SILURIAN
CAMBRIAN
ORDOVICIAN
Generalized geologic cross section showing early bowl-like rock strata beneath lake Michigan
Not drawn to scale
Diagram A.
LAKE ALGONQUIN & LAKE NIPISSING LEVEL
LAKE CHICAGO WATER LEVEL
SOUTH MANITOU HEADLANDS
PERCHED DUNES
Lake Chicago Level
Lakes Algonquin & Nipissing levels
Note: All the archipelago islands were under the Wisconsin Ice Sheet during the Lake Chicago level
MANITOU PASSAGE
GLACIAL MORAINE
LAKE MICHIGAN BASIN
PRESENT LAKE LEVEL
Generalized geologic cross section of South Mantiou Island
Not drawn to scale
DIAGRAM B.
PRE-GLACIAL DEPOSITS

of glaciers is readily understood. When you have many years in a row where more snow falls than summer temperatures can melt, you have an accumulating ground cover of snow. By partially melting during periods of warmer weather, followed by refreezing and pressure from new fallen snóws, these lower layers turn into ice creating icefields. These icefields have their beginning in existing valleys since they are more protected from the warming rays of the sun. New layers are piled on top of old ones and as they thicken the ice begins to flow. This turns an icefield into a glacier. The first movement of the glacier is down the valleys but as the size of the glacier increases it eventually expands covering the area between the valleys as well. It gradually becomes an ice sheet hundreds of miles wide and thousands of feet thick. As the glacier expands across the land surfaces rocks and other debris get frozen to its bottom. When the glacier moves outward the debris, trapped in the glacier's bottom, acts like a giant bulldozer and planes off existing topography. The glacier moves across the land surfaces in this scouring action following the path of least resistance down old river valleys. This indicates that the major basins of the Great Lakes were once large river valleys. Glaciers, acting like gargantuan conveyor belts, also carry a tremendous amount of rocky debris within, and on, them. When glaciers melt, this debris, known as moraine, is left behind, deposited on top of the older geologic deposits.

There were four major great ice sheets that were separated by periods of warmer non-glaciated times, but only the last and largest of them is pertinent to this short history. Known as the Wisconsin Ice Sheet its frozen center began forming in the region of Hudson Bay about 50,000 years ago. At its largest stage, reached sometime between 25,000 and 35,000 years ago, its southern border reached almost to the Ohio River and was largely responsible for bringing that stream into existence. Its greatest thickness was somewhere between 5,000 and 10,000 feet high. If you visit one of the islands, sometime during your stay look upward, and imagine a wall of ice rising almost two miles above your head.

When the Wisconsin Glacier began to retreat, it did so in a series of stages. Warming trends would cause a noticeable retreat of the ice. These retreats were halted at least seven times by the return of long stretches of colder weather. These colder periods often maintained the glacier at this new, slightly smaller size for an extended time. Sometimes these cooling periods were long enough that the glacier again began to spread southward, but they never lasted long enough to bring the glacier back to anything near its largest size. The long-range temperature patterns favored long warming trends, which brought a steady if not contiguous retreat of the glacier northward.

The deeper river valleys which had been the first early routes of the glacier's southward movement were the last areas to melt. With these valleys as their centers, the melting ice left behind huge lobes known as the Erie lobe, the Saganaw lobe and the Michigan lobe. These lobes are the rough ancestral outlines which form the basins of Lakes Erie, Huron and Michigan. When the lobes began to retreat, they exposed gaping holes that had been deepened and gouged out by the glacier. These large holes, found along the melting edge of the lobes, began to fill with the melt waters. Satellite lobes also appeared as the thickness of the glacier decreased. These were located in the smaller tributary valleys of the main stream, which were at a higher elevation. As these lobes melted, their areas filled with melt water and became extended bays of the fossil lakes. When lake levels dropped, some of these old gouged-out valleys became separate, smaller lakes. Others, closer to the main lobe, remained as bays of the larger lake, such as Grand Traverse Bay. Some of these bays were isolated from the larger lake at a later period by sand spits that built up between them and the lake. This

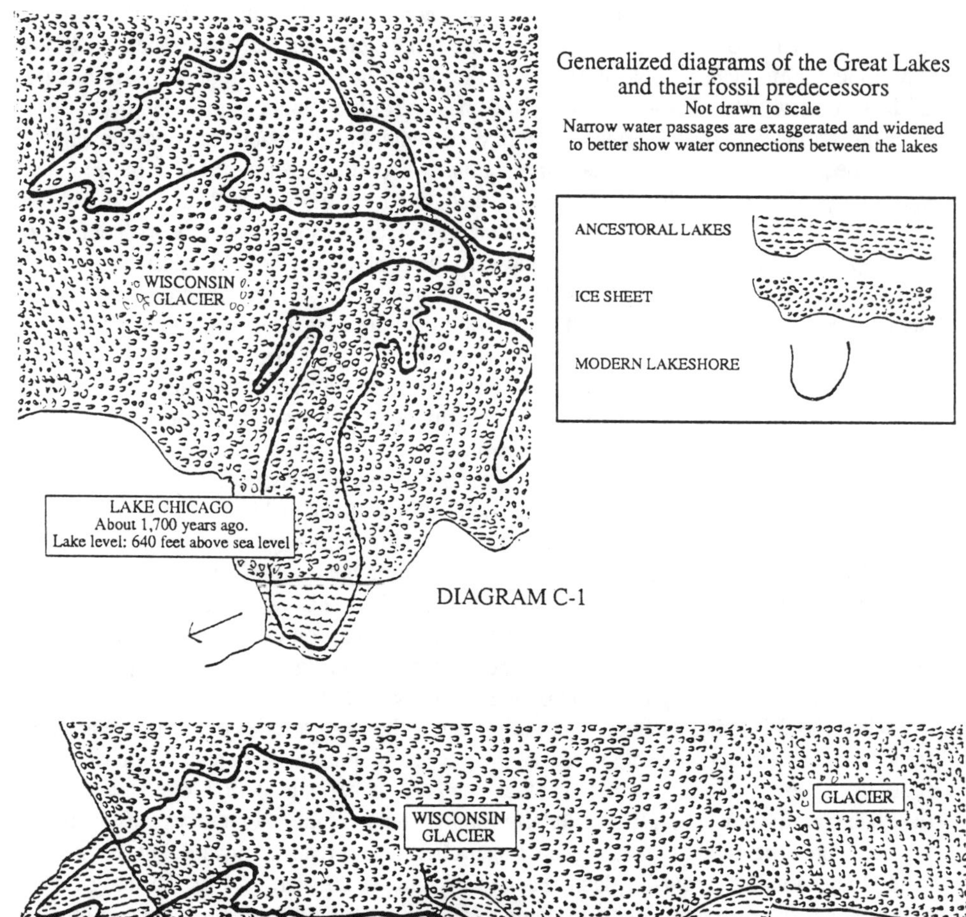
Generalized diagrams of the Great Lakes
and their fossil predecessors
Not drawn to scale
Narrow water passages are exaggerated and widened
to better show water connections between the lakes
ANCESTORAL LAKES
ICE SHEET
MODERN LAKESHORE
WISCONSIN
GLACIER
LAKE CHICAGO
About 1,700 years ago.
Lake level: 640 feet above sea level
DIAGRAM C-1
WISCONSIN
GLACIER
GLACIER
LAKE ALGONQUIN
About 11,500 years ago.
Lake level: 605 feet above sea level
DIAGRAM C-2

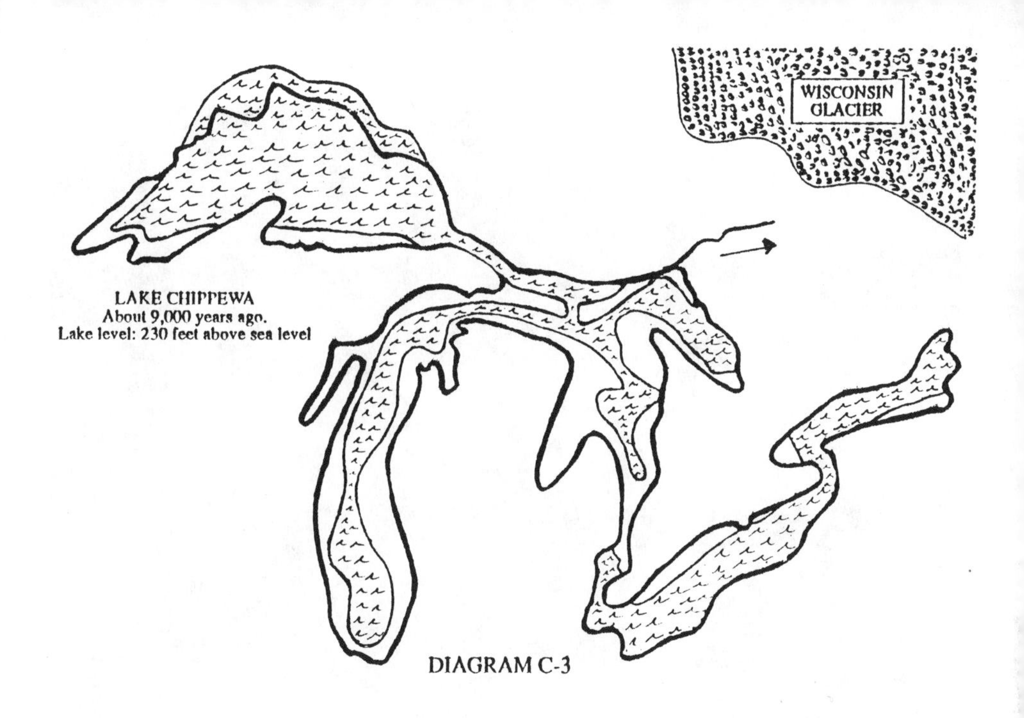

DIAGRAM C-3

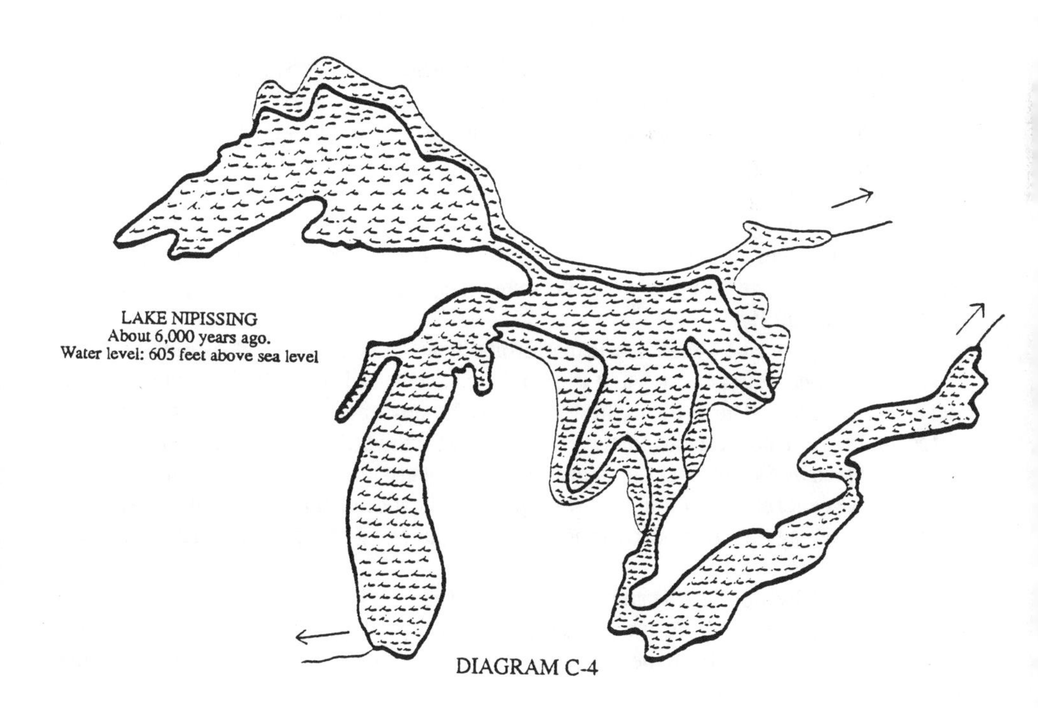

DIAGRAM C-4

High Island's Lake Maria-one of the typical island lakes with no established drainage stream

created other new lakes close to the shoreline of Lake Michigan. A good example of this bay-to-lake transformation is found at Glen Lake adjacent to Sleeping Bear Dune.

With the retreat of the glacial ice, modern Lake Michigan did not immediately appear, but underwent several stages of fossil lakes. These ancestral lakes had both higher and lower levels than today's average of about 578 feet. These various levels were made by changes in the drainage pattern. Sometimes a resurgence of the remaining glacier in the north would cut off earlier established outlets forcing higher lake levels. As the glacier again retreated, new drainage openings would be found, bringing corresponding changes in the lake level (See Diagram B).

The earliest of these lakes formed near the southern end of modern Lake Michigan. Known as Lake Chicago it is thought to have had a high water level of about 640 feet above sea level. This is the highest water level of any of the ancestral lakes and is over 60 feet higher than the present water level. It drained southward down the same valley which is now occupied by the present DesPlaines River in northern Illinois (See Diagram C-1). This early lake was entirely wiped out by a resurgence of the glacier southward only to reappear when the glacier again retreated to the north. This final retreat of the ice began about 16,500 years ago.

One of the most important of these ancestral lakes, which existed about 11,500 years ago, is called Lake Algonquin. It was the first of the ancestral lakes to exist where glacial ice was almost entirely gone from the vicinity of the Lake Michigan basin. The remnants of the Wisconsin Glacier immediately to the north were still significant enough to block any drainage in that direction. With lake drainage only possible from the south, it created a high lake level of 605 feet, approximately 28 feet higher than the modern lake. Before the Lake Algonquin stage, the ancestral Lake Chicago existed as a separate body of water. It was during the Algonquin stage that the Lake Michigan basin became linked with the Lake Huron basin (See Diagram C-2). The costal lowlands of modern Lake Michigan were underwater at the Lake Algonquin stage.

Following the Algonquin period further retreats of the glacier to the north allowed newer and lower drainage systems to open in that direction. This effectively lowered the water levels of the ancestral lake in a series of stages. The lowest of these stages happened about 9,000 years ago and is known as Lake Chippewa. During this stage the water level dropped over 370 feet to the lowest point it ever reached. At this new low water level of 230 feet, the islands of the Lake Michigan Archipelago were not islands at all but were linked to the mainland. All southern outlets were now high above the lake level so drainage was entirely to the north (See Diagram C-3).

It is thought that the earliest human inhabitants may have roamed through the coastal regions at this time, but since these fossil shorelines were considerably lower than the present lake level their temporary encampments would be at least 300 feet below the present surface of the water.

Another significant geological event began during this low water Lake Chippewa period. With the great weight of the glacier removed the compressed earth, previously buried beneath the ice sheet began to "rebound." This uplifting action caused the basin of the lake to refill with higher elevations of water, until the southern drainage was again reactivated. This rise of land surrounding the lake continued raising the level of the existing drainage systems until the water level was again at 605 feet. This created another body of water known as Lake Nipissing, which is somewhat larger than today's lake. The high water level of Lake Nipissing was reached about 6,000 years ago and drainage outlets were again functioning both in the north and the south (See Diagram C-4). Erosion made by the continuous stream action of the exiting rivers began to lower the lake level. This level has continued its slow fall until it reached the present day average of about 578 feet.

Today, the archipelago islands are made up of glacial moraine left behind by the various retreating glaciers. These deposits are thick enough to have buried the pre-glacial Devonian bedrock far beneath them (See Diagram B). The formation of the many smaller lakes found on the archipelago islands is significantly different than their mainland counterparts. These island lakes were not found in former pre-glacial river valleys, as were most of the nearby mainland lakes. The mainland lakes generally have well established runoff streams down their ancestral valleys, which follow pretty much the same direction as their pre-glacial ancestors. The island lakes have no well-developed runoff streams, and several have no outlets. This peculiarity stems from the fact that the island impoundments had never been part of a river valley system, and so normal runoff streams had never existed and were not part of satellite lobes of ice. Glacial ice, however, had much to do with their formation.

Occasionally hollowed out lower areas developed on the islands that were slightly below the surrounding surfaces in the moraine. These lower areas are called kettels. Huge ice boulders that centered in the kettels remained as ice long after other glacial ice had retreated northward and isolated them. The weight of these huge ice blobs kept enough pressure on the underlying surfaces that they did not immediately rebound like the surrounding land. Gradually the isolated hunks of glacial ice melted, but in doing so not much of their melt water drained off the island. Instead, these melting ice boulders filled the holes that they had helped to create, leaving behind a lake without an established drainage system. Natural drainage patterns were not allowed to develop as they might elsewhere because the forces of These are often in the form of dunes that inhibit the growth of runoff streams.

The Dunes

A sand dune is a large mass of sand that was placed in its present location by the wind. The small size of sand grains, 1/16 to two millimeters, are easily carried in suspension through the air. Many grains are pink or white particles of feldspar, red garnet, black magnetite and other minerals, but the most common sand grain is quartz. Because quartz is

Hiker standing on perched dune, South Manitou Island

very hard it becomes an effective tool of erosion when the wind blows the grains against surfaces of softer material. These basic mineral particles were originally part of the glacial moraines.

The long expanse of open water across Lake Michigan, combined with the prevailing southwesterly winds, makes the windward sides of the Lake Michigan Archipelago islands ideal places for dunes to develop. But active dune development in this area is restricted to no more than a mile inland from the shoreline, for at that distance active plant growth restricts the erosive force of the windblown sand and stabilizes sand movement. Over a period of years, intensive plant growth initiates other soil-building activities, resulting in a humus groundcover.

Classification of Dunes. There are four major classifications of dunes found on these islands and on the adjacent mainland. The first and most common of these is known as a beach dune. These dunes form close to the lake level on coastal lowlands. Wave action kicks up sand from the shallow bottom and deposits them on the shore. After they dry out onshore winds pick up these beach deposits and carry them inland to low level areas next to the beach. Some of these dunes reach a significant elevation above the shoreline. Examples of this type of dune are common along the western ridges of the Manitous and High Island.

The perched dune is similar to the beach dune, with one distinct difference. It too

Old Baldy blowout, North Manitou Island

is created by windblown sand along the western edge of the lakeshore, but instead of being deposited on adjacent lowlands, this type of dune develops when there is an existing high plateau made up of old glacial deposits just behind the beach. Here the wind blows the sand up the sloping face of this headland, and deposits it on top of the plateau, forming a dune. This dune is "perched" on top of the existing plateau several hundred feet above the lake level.

Two beautiful examples of perched dunes are found on the western shoreline of South Manitou and the mainland's Sleeping Bear Cliffs. The base plateau of South Manitou is over 300 feet high while the one at Sleeping Bear Cliffs exceeds the height of South Manitou's by over 100 feet. The accumulation of windblown sand on its top is the perched dune. A combination of gravity and wind action builds a sloping cliff on the western edge of these lakeside plateaus, which is close to an angle of 34 degrees. This is known as the angle of repose, for it is the maximum angle at which sand will stay on the cliffside without falling

Ghost forest on South Manitou

back to the beach below. Generally, these cliff faces are slightly more gradual than this angle, and as strong prevailing winds climb their sides, their angled surfaces are gradually eroded. When heavier particles such as large pebbles and rocks are loosened from the escarpment by this wind action, they tumble down to the beach area. Sand and grains of clay are carried uphill over the top of the dune. As the wind curves over the dune top, it loses some of its velocity and drops the sand a short distance beyond the top to become part of the dune. The clay particles, being lighter, often become completely airborne and travel distances far beyond the dune before settling to the earth.

Sometimes whole forests that once grew on top of these plateaus get buried by the accumulating sand and disappear completely. Later, wind erosion exposes them, leaving behind a ghost forest of these once living trees. The perched dune at South Manitou has some small isolated patches of such a ghost forest.

In some areas, substantial vegetation can establish itself on top of the dunes. Small trees and heavy shrubbery establish a crown on both the beach and perched dune tops and often will move down the western slope of the dune for some distance. Occasionally, however, the wind will again cut a narrow path windward uphill through this vegetation, obliterating it and exposing the sand clear to the ridge-top. At the base of these exposed channels, known as blowouts, is usually a bowl-shaped area of open sand. Both the Manitous and High Island have excellent examples of this erosive feature, the most famous and possibly the largest on these islands is Old Baldy on the southern coast of North Manitou.

Falling dunes develop on the leeward side of perched dunes. When sand migrates downhill into a lowland existing behind the plateau of the perched dune, it creates a falling

Western shore of North Manitou showing beach, dunes and shrub zones

dune. With time the falling dune moves away from the perched dune. In effect the dune has become de-perched which gives this type of dune its name.

The Plant Community Zones.

Proceeding inland from the shoreline, the changing environment allows different types of vegetation to exist. Various types of plants, able to survive in that environment, establish themselves there. They form a plant community that is distinctly different from others close by where environmental conditions are somewhat different. The plants that most commonly establish themselves in that environment and tend to dominate it bring about distinctive plant communities which can be divided nicely into five distinct growing zones. If you walk from the shoreline inland, you will often find it is easy to identify the change in zones, but interruptions, both natural and man-induced, usually interfere in one way or another, preventing a beautiful textbook sequence of all five zones in a row. The existing borders of the zones themselves are often indistinct, with much overlapping of plant growth from one zone to another.

The Beach Zone. With a combination of almost constant wave action, the full force of offshore winds and the baking rays of the sun, the shoreline beach is a zone of hostile environment for plant growth. Only an occasional plant, partly sheltered by beach boulders, trunks or stumps of dead trees washed up on the shore, can establish a fragile existence in this severe environment.

The Dune Zone. Moving inland from the beach this zone has an environment that is almost as hostile as the beach zone. Although it usually escapes the wave action of the beach zone the winds are almost as strong and there is no relief from the burning rays of the sun. Although growing conditions are only slightly modified hearty dune grasses will often establish themselves in this zone. They help slow down the force of the wind and offer limited shade which can eventually lead to limited humus soil buildup.

The Shrub Zone. With the increasing distance from the lakeshore wind velocities have usually slackened somewhat. This zone is often a region of older dunes where limited amounts of top soil have developed. This allows a variety of dense, hardy low lying shrubs to establish themselves and gradually cover much of the surface area of the old dune. This, in turn, greatly decreases the eroding force of the wind and allows further soil buildup.

The Pine Oak Forest Zone. A distinct and dramatic borderline is often discernible between the shrub zone and the Pine Oak Forest Zone. That border is established by a growth of trees, made up mostly of varieties of pine and oak, that presents a solid wall of forest growth along its perimeter. They have established themselves on areas that formerly were ancient beaches and dunes. This forest could establish itself on this older dune because it was allowed to develop through the aforementioned zones. Unlike the beach, dune and shrub zones, this one is quite stable. Unless it is subjected to serious forest fires, logging operations or other interferences, it will survive for long periods of time without serious change. During such long stretches, its soil floor becomes much richer and more moist, possibly preparing it for transformation into the following zone.

The Beech-Maple Forest Zone. This is the last of the zones and can only develop after the area has passed through some or all of the earlier zones. During those extended periods of time, a rich covering of thick moist soil must accumulate, making it possible for its namesake trees to exist there. Although beech and maple are the most dominant species, black cherry, hemlock, yellow birch, basswood, white ash and others are often found in this zone. If left undisturbed, this forest does not change into another type of zone, but will remain stable for hundreds of years. It is, therefore, known as a climax forest. In the spring, before the ground is darkened by a canopy of leaves, the damp, rich forest floor is often covered with an abundance of wildflowers.

Chapter IV

A Brief Early History of The Lake Michigan Archipelago

Indian Ancestors

The progenitors of modern American Indians first entered the North American continent from Asia by crossing the Bering Straits about 40,000 years ago. Subsequent migrations of these paleolithic nomads occurred with the most significant in number probably happening about 12,000 B.C. The great glacial age would have kept these stone-age people from penetrating present day Michigan until the retreat of the last great glacier began over 11,000 years ago. Scanty evidence suggests that aboriginal people, classified by archaeologists as the Paleo Indians, may have occupied areas of the southern part of the state as soon as human habitation was possible. It was impossible for such people to occupy the Lake Michigan islands then, for this area was still buried under the glacier and the islands did not exist.

Although the last of the great ice sheets, known as the Wisconsin, did help create the island chain as it retreated northward, the forming of modern Lake Michigan underwent several stages, which saw the lake level both far higher and a good deal lower than its modern level of about 580 feet. Spear points and other flint fragments identified as Paleo Indian, dating from about 6000 B.C., have been found in the Upper Peninsula. These people were mainly nomadic hunters who covered a large range and may have migrated from as far away as the state of Wyoming. Flints found over many parts of the western Great Lakes region suggest that these roving bands did pass through the general vicinity of the islands. They apparently hunted close to the edge of the huge retreating ice sheet, but never stayed long enough in one area to establish any type of long term settlement.

The first irrefutable evidence that the immediate vicinity of the islands was inhabited by a more advanced aboriginal culture occurred during the period which is called the Archaic. Dating from 8,000 to 600 B.C., the earlier parts of the period saw vegetation and wildlife recovering from the denuding of the area by the glacier. As the land became reforested, with game animals and fish becoming plentiful, it was possible for the Archaic Indians to inhabit the region for longer stretches of time, and they probably did so. During the middle stages of the Archaic period, it is believed that people concentrated along the lakeshore, but archaeological evidence of this is lacking for a very good geologic reason. At that time, the ancestral body of water that existed here has been named by geologists as Lake Chippawa. The level of this fossil lake was four hundred feet below the surface of the modern lake. Whatever aboriginal lakeshore encampments that existed then are now buried under several hundred feet of water.

The earliest evidence that Indians occupied the actual islands happend during the Late Archaic period when there was a developing ancestral lake known as Nipissing. During this period lake elevations had risen above the present level. One of the first meaningful island discoveries made during this lake stage was found on North Manitou Island. It was a copper awl of large size, which has been dated to about 3000 B.C. Other early traces of Indian occupation of the islands have been found along the Ageline Bluffs on the western side of Beaver Island. These sites were apparently temporary summer fishing encampments, established between 2,500 and 2,000 B.C. The artifacts include spear points, flint chips and heat-cracked rocks used for boiling food. They were found along a fossil lakeshore which was much higher than today's level.

The last period of Indian culture before contact with the white man is classified as the Woodland. Lasting from 600 B.C. until 1620 A.D. the major cultural difference between these people and their earlier ancestors was the making of pottery and the use of the bow and arrow. There are several Woodland sites that have been discovered in the last few years on both the Manitous and Beaver Island. Discoveries of flint chips, stone tools and pottery show

Count Castlenau's Drawing of Indian village along Lake Michigan shoreline, 1838 Library of Congress

the activities and the periodic occupation of these island locations for better than a thousand years. Pieces of pottery, flint chips and more rarely, arrow heads are occasionally found today in various vacant lots and clearings in Beaver Island's town of St. James. These sites were not major settlements, which would suggest anything as large as a village. They were short-term summer encampments, where the Woodland Indians fished, hunted and gathered wild crops of berries and rice.

Outside of the partial story pieced together by archaeologists and before the written records of historic times, about the only other source of information of the Indian past comes from Algonquin Indian legends. These old Algonquin stories and language are the ancient heritage of both the Ottawa and Ojibway tribes that inherited this area of Michigan during the historic period.

From one of the most famous of these legends,, both the national lake shore and the two Manitou islands received their names. Although there are many slight variations in the tale, the one most often repeated tells of a mother bear and her two cubs attempting to escape the scorching heat of a raging forest fire along the Wisconsin shore. They plunged into the protective covering of Lake Michigan's cool waters and headed for the safety of the eastern shore. Once on land the mother bear anxiously looked across the water to see how close her tired cubs were to the safety of the land. In the murky evening darkness she could not see that the exhausted cubs had slipped beneath the surface of the water and perished, just a few miles from shore. Refusing to continue without her cubs the bear lay down to sleep, waiting there for her cubs until death took her too. To honor the patience of this courageous and loyal mother bear the great Indian spirit known as the Manitou raised a huge mound of sand along the shore where the mother had slept. The Manitou then created two islands in the lake marking the locations where her offspring had drowned.

These two southern islands of the archipelago are not the only ones named after this Indian deity for these Algonquin stories of this great spirit were known throughout the Great Lakes region. In three of the five Great lakes one may find islands called Manitou.

Although there were no Indians living on either of the Manitous when first visited by white explorers, they probably were living on Beaver. It is generally thought that the Indians found the lands of the mainland so bountiful in supplying their needs that there was little necessity for them to isolate themselves on these small islands, especially through much of the long winter. Modern Indians also were well acquainted with legends about the Manitous which may have contributed in part to their largely ignoring the islands.

There is one such story about South Manitou, which told of a strong war party from the Upper Peninsula invading the mainland near the islands and killing all except seven of the local warriors. After this blood bath, the war party crossed over to South Manitou to bivouac for the night. Under cover of darkness the remaining seven braves also crossed the Manitou straits, and shielded by the dark night, hacked most of the invaders to death. Since the survivors did not see the avenging assassins, they blamed the death of their comrades on evil spirits that inhabited the island. The legend suggests that this land of evil spirits was no place for an Indian to live, so the superstitious red men avoided the islands, believing they were the residences of bad spirits and omens. One early nineteenth century writer also pointed out that the Indian's name of Manitou implied that the islands were probably looked upon as sacred ground, dwelling places for the spirits of their departed ancestors. A far more practical reason was simply that there were no deer on any of these islands so there was no compelling reason to occupy them.

The coming of the White men and the beginning of the Historic Period

No one is sure who were the first white men to see the islands, but they were probably French explorers, Jesuit missionaries and traders. Their multiple purposes included seeking a way to China, an extension of the valuable fur trade and the spread of Christian theology among the Indian tribes. When the Indians developed major trade routes on the waters of the Great Lakes, their major north-south passage on Lake Michigan did not follow the eastern shore of the lake. They skirted along the south shore of the Upper Peninsula then down the Wisconsin side of the lake. During the seventeenth century the five nations of the Iroquois tribe attempted to control the lucrative fur trade. That powerful group moved war parties into the Lower Peninsula to drive out rival tribes. As a result much, of Michigan's Lower Peninsula then became a no man's land between the warring Indian factions. This made the eastern shore quite hazardous, so the Indian traders opted for the safer Wisconsin side. This western passage also protected them from the strong prevailing winds from the West. These winds crossing 60 miles of open lake without interruption often bring heavy seas along the eastern shore which are largely avoided on the western side. It is not surprising that the French would also make their first explorations following this same westerly route.

The name Michigan was originally a combination of two words taken from the Algonquin language meaning big or great lake. French explorers called the Indians that lived

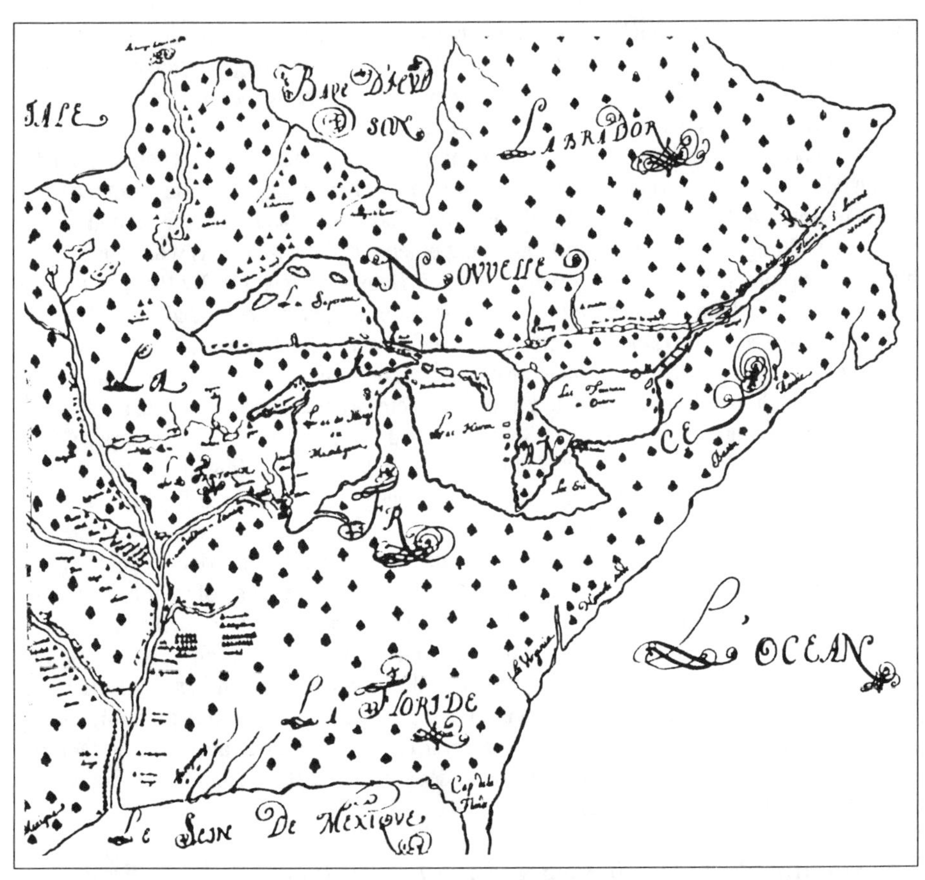

Section of Joliet's 1673 map. First map to show the Lake Michigan Archipelago Islands. Although geographic features are out of proportion and scale, the accuracy for its day is amazing

Library of Congress

along its shores as the Michigamies. The initial discovery of the lake by Europeans was made in 1634 when a Frenchman named Jean Nicholet stumbled onto it while seeking a water route to the Orient. After landing on the present site of Green Bay, Wisconsin, he was so sure that he was stepping ashore in China that he donned the robes of a Chinese mandarin. Another 41 years would pass before the eastern shore of the lake would be traversed by the French.

The first known trip by white men along the Michigan side of the lake was brought about by the illness and death of a well-known French explorer-missionary, Father Marquette. This famous Jesuit had earlier established a mission on the Upper Peninsula at Sault Ste. Marie, the first permanent white settlement in Michigan.

In 1673, Father Marquette joined a fur trader and cartographer named Louis Joliet who had been commissioned by the French governor to explore the lands west of Lake Michigan. They followed the usual Indian route hugging the northern shoreline of Lake Michigan into Green Bay. There they followed the Fox River upstream then portaged to the

French fur traders in their voyageur canoes

Library of Congress

Wisconsin River and followed it until they ran into and discovered the Mississippi River. They proceeded south on the great river to the confluence of the Arkansas River, but fearing possible interception from the Spanish they proceeded no further.

Marquette was anxious to visit the northern area of the present state of Illinois, for Indian tribes had invited him to found a Christian mission there. By following the Illinois River northward the two explorers eventually arrived at the southern end of Lake Michigan. Their arrival made them the first known white men to visit the area that would become the great metropolis of Chicago. A year later, though he was in ill health, the 43 year old missionary-priest, returned to the southern end of the lake to establish a mission to convert the Illinois tribes. When he arrived, his condition worsened and he realized he was probably dying.

To reach his missions in the Upper Peninsula before his death, he decided not to go up the lake on the usual western side, but to save time he would try the here-to-fore unexplored eastern side of the lake. He died on the way, either at the present sites of Ludington or Frankfort, Michigan, but two of his followers continued northward along the lake's eastern coast, passing the islands on the way. The two men, Jacques Largilier and Pierre Porteret made it safely back to the northern mission. Although earlier French fur trappers might have preceded them, these two became the first men of European origin to have their names recorded as having definitely passed through the Manitou Passage in sight of many islands of this eastern archipelago.

The first written record that definitely establishes the existence of the archipelago was made by Joliet. On his return journey to Montreal, Joliet's journal and personal effects were lost when his canoe upset in a rapids. Nonetheless, he sat down and drew from memory a map of much of the eastern part of North America. On this map, which is extraordinary for its time, he called this lake the *Lac des Illinois ou Michigami.* This seventeenth century map is the first to show any of the Michigan Archipelago islands. It is believed that three of the five islands shown are probably Beaver and the two Manitous.

French fur traders then shore-hugged the eastern side of the lake as well as the western. Their large voyageur canoes used crews of up to 14 men, and were capable of carrying three and a half tons of cargo. Heading southward, they would pass close by the Manitous because these islands lie closer to the mainland than the others in the group. These two southern islands were easily accessible and offered relative safety from Indian attack for the Frenchmen's north and south journeys. Although there are no written records to substantiate their doing so, it is a reasonable assumption that some of these French fur traders beached their canoes on the welcome sands of the eastern shores of the Manitous and bivouacked briefly there. Possibly they paid brief visits to the more outlying Beaver group as well. The protective lee of the Manitous was also an excellent place to lay over during periods of stormy weather for they were shielded from the prevailing southwesterly winds.

Another Frenchman, Robert Cavalier Sieur de la Salle, was the first to envision using the lakes for moving bulk goods in large quantities. Hoping to reduce some personal debts by amassing a large quantity of furs on the western side of Lake Michigan then shipping them straight through to the eastern end of Lake Ontario, he started to build the first large vessel on the Lakes. Launched in 1679, the 60 foot long ship was named the Griffin after that famous mythological bird that was prominently displayed on the crest of the French Governor of Canada.

The Griffin was the first sailing ship built in the European tradition on the upper Great Lakes. At 45 gross tons she also became the first cargo ship of any size which could carry many times the amount of goods that could be accommodated in a voyageur canoe. In September of that year. LaSalle successfully sailed the Griffin from the headwaters of the Niagara River to Green Bay, where he collected enough furs to load her hold. Wishing to explore further south, but also wanting to get his cargo back to Montreal to ease his indebtedness, he sent the ship back without him. The ship was never seen again. No one knows where she went down, but one theory has her possibly sinking in the offshore waters of the Lake Michigan Archipelago.

LaSalle also wrote the first surviving written account that specifically mentions the Manitous. On his famous trip, during which he would become the first white man to follow the Mississippi all the way to the Gulf of Mexico, he sent one of his subordinates down the eastern shore of Lake Michigan through the Manitou passage. From him, LaSalle learned about the Manitou Straits, and he noted in his diary that the sand bars lying off the islands were a considerable danger to ships. It is the first written warning of the treacherous waters that seamen could expect to find navigating the Manitou Straits. This geographical fact would play an important role in the later history of the Manitous.

For the next hundred years, the crude map and the single log entry stood as the only written references about the islands. Part of this was caused by the major economic activity of the area, in which both Indians and French were mutually involved. Fur trading was so lucrative that the royal French government discouraged any type of colonization in these regions for fear it would disrupt that profitable enterprise. The fur trade would remain the dominant economic activity of the area well into the first third of the nineteenth century.

How much contact the French had with the islands of the more northerly Beaver

First large sailing ship on the great Lakes. LaSalle's "Griffin" of 1673

Group is open to much speculation. It is possible that the modern name for the largest island in the group came from the French "Isle du Castor" (Beaver Island). But, concrete proof that the French ever occupied the island is lacking. James Strang, the Mormon leader who made himself "King" of the island in 1850, wrote extensively about an active French colony he claimed existed there in the seventeenth century. His research for this claim seems to be more from a curious flight of his imagination than any historical or archaeological evidence. It also contradicts the expressed French policy of keeping settlers out of the area to cause no serious disruption to the fur trade.

The Ojibway, who had contact with the French, were definitely on the island during the seventeenth century, for several fragments of local flint shaped in an odd rectangular pattern have been found along the shore of the island's main harbor. They had been carved by the Indians to be used as gun flints on a type of flintlock muzzle loader that was in wide use before 1670. They are identical to ones manufactured in Europe, but made of local material. The Ojibway obviously got The guns by trading furs for weapons. Although the

Indians might have been engaged in trapping the island's extensive beaver population in order to trade their pelts with the French for guns, firewater and other accouterments of civilization, their name for the island did not come from that large aquatic rodent. They knew the island as "Kitchi Miniss," meaning "large island" in their native language. They also were not year-round occupants but used the island as a sort of summer residence for hunting, fishing and trading activities. After the seventeenth century, Indian occupation of Beaver Island seemed to drop off.

In 1832, a priest named Father Barga became the first white man to land on Beaver Island and write about it. In his report to his order, the Leopoldine Foundation of Austria, he wrote that he found a few pagan Indians whom he wished to convert living in eight flimsy hovels. Though High and Garden Islands are in close proximity to Beaver, there is no evidence that white men occupied them until the middle of the nineteenth century.

At the conclusion of the French and Indian War in 1760, the entire area came under British control. The former French policy of protecting the fur trade by discouraging white homesteading in northern Michigan was continued by the governments of George II and George III. British disinterest in the area for other types of commercial exploitation or colonial activities is shown in the fact that not a single English writer has a word to say about Lake Michigan until the American Revolution. The only document written during the time when the area was indisputably under the flag of the Union Jack was written In 1773. The author was a French trader named St. Pierre, who was sent by English representatives into the Lake Michigan area aboard the British sloop Felicity, to establish relationships with the Indians. On his return trip he mentions in his journal sailing by the two Manitous and anchoring briefly in the lee of North Manitou until threatening weather from the west had passed. Six years later during the third year of the American Revolution, the British commander at Mackinac sent that same 100 ton sloop into Lake Michigan to collect or destroy any products that might prove useful to the rebellious colonials. On his return, the skipper of the Felicity mentioned that he also used the lee of the Manitous to shelter his sloop during a period of nasty weather.

America's Acquisition of the Michigan Territory

After the end of the American Revolution, the Peace of Paris signed in 1783, stipulated that Great Britain would recognize the southern side of all the Great Lakes except Lake Michigan and the western tip of Lake Superior as the boundary between the remaining English territories and her former colonies. This made Lake Michigan the only one of the Great Lakes to lie entirely within the boundaries of the United States. Much of this northern area was claimed by Virginia with a counter claim for the lower part of the territory by Massachusetts. As early as 1780, Congress had suggested that all western territories should be ceded to the nation. At the urging of Thomas Jefferson, the states did relinquish their claims and left it up to the Congress to decide how these frontier lands would be partitioned and governed.

In 1787, Congress passed the Northwest Ordinance which stipulated that the territory bounded by the Ohio River, the Great Lakes and the Mississippi River would be initially overseen by a governor and three judges, until there was sufficient population to set up legislative governments. This Northwest Territory was to be divided in the future into smaller territories, which eventually would become not less than three nor more than five new states.

In 1803, the Territory of Indiana was established from part of the Northwest Territory. It included all the present State of Michigan. Two years later, the Michigan Territory, which contained all the Lower Peninsula and the eastern half of the Upper Peninsula, was extracted from the Indiana Territory.

Twenty five years after the first Northwest Ordinance, much of the Michigan Territory was almost lost back to the British. A general feeling of hostility and suspicion between the newly formed United States and the British lands to the north continued to exist, particularly in the Great Lakes region. The Indians too, felt more uncertainty toward the Americans than their British counterparts. In the western areas of the Great Lakes, the Canadians seemed content to carry on the old fur trade economy, while the Americans were actively seeking new farmland for settlement. This antagonism festered on and vented its full fury during the War of 1812. The American attempt to annex Canadian lands during that war were totally frustrated by a series of military disasters on land. General Hull's surrender of Detroit to the British, and the Indian massacre of the Fort Dearborn garrison at the bottom of Lake Michigan, effectively placed Lake Erie and all Michigan territories under British control. This debacle of the fortunes of the infant United States were miraculously reversed by a 28 year old naval Captain whose name was Oliver Hazzard Perry. He decisively defeated the British Lake Erie Naval squadron near Put-in-Bay, which restored American control over Lakes Erie and Michigan, and the Michigan territories.

Though the treaty ending the conflict did not specify the exact boundaries between the two belligerents, Perry's victory on Lake Erie permanently decided that these northern territories including Lake Michigan would stay under American control. With the American boundary reestablished during the first quarter of the nineteenth century, the winds of change were bringing on a whole new era. During this period, both the Upper and lower Michigan Peninsulas were in a state of transition between Indian and U.S. domination. The fur trade was still the major enterprise, and up to this point there is no existing evidence that any American Caucasian had set foot on any of the archipelago islands.

Land-hungry immigrants and eastern Americans looking for new opportunities wanted to penetrate into the largely undeveloped prairie lands of the Midwest. The opening in 1825 of the Erie Canal between Albany and Buffalo furnished a watery highway that extended from New York City via the Hudson River, the canal and the Great Lakes all the way to the fledgling community of Chicago. Railroads were in their infancy, for in 1830 there were only 23 miles of track in the entire United States. The first rail connection from the East Coast to the upper Great Lakes did not reach Buffalo until 1852 and Chicago in 1856.

The important all-water route between Buffalo and Chicago passed close to and was in sight of many of the Archipelago islands especially the two Manitous. This water route meant easy access to much of the territory of Michigan's Lower Peninsula that were coveted by land and timber hungry whites. But this meant penetration and annexation of traditional Indian lands.

Louis Cass, who had risen to high military rank during the War of 1812, was appointed governor of the Michigan Territory in 1813. He was well aware that this large wilderness area was mostly under Indian control, and they would have to be dealt with before the area could be opened for settlement and timber exploitation. He was genuinely liked by the Indians, who affectionately gave him the nickname "Big Belly," and his negotiations with them were honorable and genuinely honest. He was, however, a man of his times and openly

The Canadian ship "Frontenac." First steamship on the Great Lakes, 1816
Courtesy Canada Steamship Lines, Canadiana collection

expressed the opinion that the Indians were naked aboriginal savages who would keep these lands in useless wilderness restraining industrious whites who would bring the land under useful cultivation and further America's Manifest Destiny.

In 1820, in order to embark on an exploratory trip by voyageur canoe along the south shore of Lake Superior, he crossed Lake Erie on the first steamboat to ply the waters of the upper Great Lakes. He took along with him a young topographer named Henry Rowe Schoolcraft. Apparently the two men got along well together, and in 1822 Cass appointed Schoolcraft the federal Indian Agent for the north Michigan Territory, with his headquarters at Sault Ste. Marie. These two men became the most important individuals in determining the fate of these northern Indian lands. Both negotiated several treaties with the Indians, in often stormy but peaceable negotiations, which always eventually ceded more Indian lands to the White Americans. During one stage of touchy negotiations for the southern side of Sault Ste. Marie, the dissatisfied Indians raised the British flag over land Cass considered strictly American. The angry Cass personally tore down the flag and informed the Indians that he would order his troops to fire on them if they raised the Union Jack again.

As the governor's official Indian agent, Schoolcraft negotiated no less than 22 treaties with the tribes, and was instrumental in working out a new and final agreement with the Indians. The Treaty of Washington, signed in 1836, effectively turned over the lands of the northwestern section of the Lower Peninsula, including the offshore islands, to the United States Government. This cleared the way for Michigan's statehood, which occurred the following year. Then Schoolcraft was looked upon as being a great friend of the Indians and a real protector of their interests. The terms of the treaty would suggest otherwise. Believing that the treaty set aside important insular lands of the territory in perpetuity for exclusive tribal use the Indians signed the treaty. After the treaty was signed the Indians discovered that its terms gave the tribes sole rights to those lands only for the short period of five years.

With the general sympathetic view prevalent today toward the ruthless takeover of Indian lands, it is easy to condemn the policies of these two nineteenth century Americans. On the other hand, in the prevailing attitudes of the early nineteenth century, the absorption of the Michigan territory by white Americans was inevitable. For their time, both Cass and Schoolcraft were reasonable men, and they negotiated treaties which, however unfair they were to the Indian side, did prevent serious Indian wars where the predominant war making power of White Americans would have led to bloody Indian annihilation.

Congress foolishly wanted to move the remaining Indians to the territory of Kansas, but to transplant these woodland people to the plains would have been an ethnic disaster. The Ottawas fought this decision, and were able to gain much public support. By staying in Michigan, they were forced to adjust to the ways of the white man, and take part in his economy, which many of them successfully did. A few moved to Beaver, Garden and High islands where the influence of the white world was felt in lesser degrees. Some of them managed to survive on these islands and maintain part of their traditional heritage for over a hundred years.

During the long period that Schoolcraft served as the Indian agent for this northern territory, he lived among and studied the ways of the resident native Americans. In 1823 he took as his wife the granddaughter of an Ojibway chief. From his research, he published one of the most enormous works on Indian life that has ever been written. Although written in a largely disorganized fashion Its 4,995 pages, discussed at length Indian legend, religion and customs. This inspired Henry Wadsworth Longfellow to write his epic poem, The Song of Hiawatha. On a lake journey in 1820, Schoolcraft passed through the Manitou Straits. He became the first American to write a description of the passage and make a survey of its shoreline. He also wrote a vivid description of the mighty sand cliffs there. In this published work, he was the first to use the Indian name Sleeping Bear. Aware of the Indian legend he referred to the two offshore islands not as the Manitous but as the Sleeping Bear Islands.

New Developments in Lake Transportation

The period between the War of 1812 and the Civil War was a time of rapid development, which saw commercial shipping expand rapidly on Lake Michigan. Many technical advances in the art of ship building, between these two war periods, furnished the lake with ships of greater speed and larger freight-holding capacities. Most important of these new innovations was the introduction of steam powered ships to the Great Lakes.

Construction of the first successful ship on the Great Lakes to be powered by steam was begun by Canadians, almost immediately following the end of the War of 1812. Christened the Frotenac, this ship of 740 gross tons was launched in 1816 on the waters of Lake Ontario. With a bow like a clipper ship, and rigged as a three-masted schooner, this 171 foot ship could make 9 knots an hour without the aid of sails. Her paddle wheels were driven by a noisy high-pressure steam engine that used wood for fuel.

Two years later, Americans built the first steamboat on the upper Great Lakes. They

First steamship on the upper Great Lakes named "Walk-in-the Water" passing Detroit in 1820
Courtesy of Dossin Great Lakes Museum

named it Walk-in-the-Water after an Indian chief who lived along the Detroit River. Smaller than the Frontenac, this ship weighed in at 338 gross tons, measured 135 feet and was rigged as a two-masted schooner. She was slower than her Canadian counterpart, for the best her engines could make in calm weather was about six knots. Nonetheless, this ship made many successful runs between Buffalo and Detroit, carrying both Cass and Schoolcraft as passengers on the first leg on their fateful westward trip of 1820. Like the sailing ships which they resembled, these early steamboats were steered from the stern. The Walk-in-the-Water even had a raised quarter deck aft, a common feature of large sailing ships of the day. Similar side wheelers were soon built, and by 1825 seven of these early steamboats were making regular runs between Buffalo and Detroit.

The next important development in Great Lakes shipping was largely the work of a New England soldier named Oliver Newberry. He had served in the Buffalo area during the War of 1812, and remained there after the conflict ended. He opened a grocery store where he also did fur trading with the Indians. But in 1820 he felt the urge to move westward, and reestablished his business in Detroit. Although he was a bit of an eccentric, he was also a far seeing businessman, and he became involved as an investor in shipping companies. Seeing the great potential for shipping on the lakes he began building and operating his own ships. The most famous and revolutionary of his fleet, which was also his first steamboat, was launched in 1833. Christened the Michigan, this side wheeler was a 472 ton ship, 172 feet in length. The innovative hull of this new ship drastically departed from the sailboat type hull of the earlier paddle wheelers like the Walk-On-Water. Known as the longitudinal sponson hull, its main deck was elevated in such a way that it ran continuously from bow to stern. It was also revolutionary in having a passenger cabin built on the main deck. This new type hull would become the standard for side wheelers, until they disappeared from the lakes. The

Buffalo waterfront in 1835. Note early lighthouse on right
Courtesy New York Public Library

Michigan was much faster then the earlier paddle wheelers for she could reach 15 miles an hour in smooth water. The ship would stay in service on the lakes for 34 years.

With the opening of the Erie Canal in 1825, the flood of immigrants increased dramatically. Newberry soon realized that the major western terminus for this activity was the infant town of Chicago, and he felt that he should have an agent to represent him in this rapidly growing city. He was fortunate to find an ambitious and competent young man named George W. Dole to look after his interests in Chicago. Dole did so well that Newberry, who was now known as "Admiral of the Lakes," made him a partner. in 1832, during an Indian uprising in southern Illinois known as The Blackhawk War in which the young Abraham Lincoln served as a captain, Chicago began running out of food. Realizing this, Dole built and put into operation a slaughterhouse to fill the immediate need, and was soon producing a surplus. Three years later, the great numbers of immigrants into the city caused a great shortage of flour. Again, Dole organized flour mills that also soon began to produce a surplus.

At that time, the immigrant passengers moving westward were the major source of revenue for the steamboats. But once the passengers embarked at Chicago, there were few making the return trip. Newberry and Dole soon realized that agricultural developments were creating new cargoes that could fill the holds of their ships on the return voyages. New farmlands, particularly suited for the growing of grain and corn, were being opened to cultivation in Illinois, Iowa and Wisconsin. They were soon producing valuable food surpluses that were often moved to Chicago to be loaded on ships bound for eastern Great Lakes ports. These shipping enterprises paid off handsomely for the partners, and Newberry became Detroit's first millionaire.

This two-way traffic on the lakes continued to increase during the 1830s and 1840s. The Buffalo-Chicago run of about 900 miles was the longest and among the busiest on the lakes. New steamboats were being built to serve this rise in lake traffic, often incorporating the innovations first tried on the Michigan. This flourishing trade encouraged other new ideas in shipbuilding, both in invention and in size. In 1838 the largest side wheeler on the lakes,

First shipment of grain from Chicago.
Note-Newberry & Dole buildings
Courtesy of the Chicago Historical Society

the Great Western, was launched at Huron, Ohio. Although she was only 11 feet longer than the Michigan, her 781 tons was over two-thirds greater that of the earlier ship. The high tonnage for this length was in part due to another new and unusual feature. The upper cabin deck ran from the stern almost to the bow. Despite these innovations, parts of the Great Western's structure still clung to the past. She had a clippers ship type bow, and she was rigged as a schooner. A smaller and equally successful ship launched in the same era was the Illinois. She was one of the first to eschew sailboat rigging and the clipper bow. From end to end, she was a complete steamboat. These two ships were the most popular on the Buffalo-Chicago run, and their arrival in port became a real social event among the urban populations. Though these vessels and others like them continued to operate successfully for years, further innovative ideas were being tried that would soon make them obsolete.

In 1841, a new ship was launched upon the waters of the Great Lakes that to the casual observer appeared to be a throwback to the old sailing days. This new ship, named the Van Dalia, had a clipper ship bow and was rigged as a sloop, with no evidence of paddle wheels at her sides. She had an unpretentious length of 91 feet and weight of 138 tons, and only a smokestack near her stern suggested something revolutionary. She was the first ship on the Great Lakes driven by the creation of a Swedish inventor named John Ericsson, the screw propeller. The Van Dalia became the first commercial ship driven by screw propellor in the world. For years, Great Lakes sailors would distinguish between the paddle wheeled craft and those driven by screw propellers by calling the former steamers and the latter

The Great Western, 1838
Courtesy of the Mariners Museum, Newport News Virginia

The S.S. Illinois. Note lack of sails
Library of Congress

propellors.

Another first for American ships on the Great Lakes was not long in coming, and was the result of a border squabble between Canada and the United States. In the late 1830s the British, feeling it was necessary to protect their Lake borders, built two steam driven gunboats and placed them on Lake Erie. Daniel Webster, who was then serving as Secretary of State, sent a letter of protest to the British ambassador which produced from London a curt and stinging reply. Rhetoric in Congress grew hot and sabre rattling began, which resulted in a new armed naval vessel being constructed on Lake Erie. Launched in 1843 at Erie, Pennsylvania, the U.S.S. Michigan was a pace setter, for her hull was made of iron. She became the first iron-clad ship on the Great Lakes and the first iron-hulled ship in the U.S.

The propeller Van Dalia, from a sketch made in 1841
Courtesy of the Chicago Historical Society

Navy. She would sail the waters of the Great Lakes as a commissioned ship of the navy for the next 80 years, and was not scrapped until 1949.

By 1851, Chicago had the largest corn market in the United States. It had become a great center for the transshipment of corn, grain, livestock and timber, which created a demand for more cargo-carrying ships. By the beginning of the Civil War, the commercial propellors on the Great Lakes numbered 197, far more than the remaining 137 less efficient side wheelers. But the greatest number of cargo carriers were still propelled by sail, for the schooners, ketches, sloops and barkentines actively sailing the lakes then numbered over 1,100. A high percentage of these ships were used in trade from Chicago ports which would eventually pass through the Manitou Passage.

It was not until the Civil War that a ship made its initial appearance on the lakes, which first linked together these previous steamship innovations. Unusual for its time, this new 190 foot ship, launched near Buffalo in 1862, was the first iron-hulled ship on the lakes to be driven by a propellor. Designed to be a combined passenger and cargo ship, and Christened the Merchant, she was put into service on the Buffalo-Chicago run. She was the prototype of the modern Great Lakes steamer, but with the coming of better rail transportation the ships developed more as freight carriers, with less emphases on passenger service.

These innovations had much to do with the nineteenth century development of the Lake Michigan Archipelago, especially the Manitous, for geographic factors pushed these islands into the limelight. By sailing east of the Archipelago, through the Manitou Straits rather than on the open westward side of the islands, mariners saved over 60 miles on their north-south journey. During the fourth decade of the nineteenth century these strategic locations made the Manitous the most important pieces of nautical real estate on the whole eastern shore of Lake Michigan. Because no other refueling stops existed in the 200 mile

The U.S.S. Michigan. First ironclad in the U. S. Navy, 1843
Courtesy of the Mariner's Museum, Newport News, Virginia

distance between the Manitous and Chicago, they were among the earliest refueling stops on Lake Michigan on that northern run from Chicago. Both the Great Western, the Illinois and many other side wheelers and propellors refueled at the Manitous.

In the 1840s and 50s South Manitou had almost a virtual monopoly in succoring of ships between Chicago and the Straits of Mackinac, for during those decades she had the only harbor deep enough to accommodate large ships on that 300 mile run. The accessibility of the harbor and its nearby forests made it not only an easy refueling stop for the woodburning steamships, but also made it a logical place for both s, soon appeared on both islands.

At that time, Lake Michigan's eastern shore was wilderness, and except for the area around the Straits of Mackinac, these two islands were the only areas of the upper part of Michigan's Lower Peninsula to have white settlements of any size. This made the two Manitous the first important outposts of civilization in the eastern part of northern Michigan south of the Mackinac Straits.

With the heavy lake traffic, improved navigational aids were desired, and the first lighthouse on Lake Michigan was built at Chicago in 1834. Six years later, the first light on the Manitou Passage was in operation on South Manitou. Great Lakes traffic continued to expand after the Civil War. By 1869 over 12,000 ships came to or departed from the Port of Chicago in a single three months period and a high percentage of them passed through the Manitou Passage.

The Merchant, 1862. This forerunner of modern Great Lakes steamships was the first ironclad on the lakes to be driven by a propellor
Drawing by M. Soller

Although the Manitous had become the sole domain of the white man, High and Garden islands were becoming outposts of another kind. Indians began to immigrate to them from their traditional mainland homes. For them, these islands had become a haven where they might escape the corrupting influences of the Caucasian world. On these isolated islands, the Indians tried to keep alive the cultural identity of their woodland heritage.

Although in a few aspects the continuing history of these four islands is similar, there is enough diversity in their stories to make each one unique and from this point the history of each island is handled separately. These history chapters are included in the individual sections devoted to each island.

PART II
SOUTH MANITOU ISLAND

Chapter V
Introduction and General Remarks

The reader should be aware that much important information about a visit to the islands is in the chapter called Making Plans for Island Hiking, Which Island to Choose. Practical matters such as Rules and Regulations and What to Bring are included in that chapter. To avoid redundancy, much other specific information which directly concerns a visit to the Manitous is given there and not repeated here. It is suggested that you read both sections to gain knowledge that will greatly aid you in planning a trip.

Lying 6 miles from the closest mainland shore, at Sleeping Bear Point, and 17 miles from the port of Leland, this 5,260, acre, four-mile-long island is at the southern end of the Lake Michigan Archipelago. This second largest of the four hiking islands in this book serves as the anchor of that island chain, and is the last island found on the eastern side of the lake all the way to Chicago.

A Personal Introduction

My first conscious awareness of the island came almost as an accident, several years before the national lakeshore had become a reality. My wife and I were enjoying a visit with our musician daughter at the National Music Camp at nearby Interlochen. On a non-performance day at the camp, we decided to do some local sightseeing and the nearby high cliffs of the Sleeping Bear seemed a logical place to go. At that time, one of the "in" things tourists did was to take a commercial dune ride that skirted the top of those great sand cliffs, in special open touring cars built by the Ford Motor Company. From this high escarpment, I saw South Manitou for the first time. The day was overcast, and as I stood looking across that vast horizon of this westward sea over 400 feet above the water, the island seemed to hover mysteriously on an indistinct horizon line, partly swallowed in a veil of blue gray haze. It stimulated my romantic frame of mind into thinking that here was a lost Valhalla, tugging at me like a magnet quietly saying "You must come, you must come."

This first view from the mainland's high escarpment kindled my wish to see this island. Ideas for the future national lakeshore were just beginning to incubate, and it was becoming the subject of hot controversy among local residents. South Manitou itself was still mostly in private hands, and the circumstances of my life excluded any visit then or in the immediate future. But I made a mental note to answer that call, and began collecting information on the island. Though many years would pass before a visit to the island was possible, It definitely stood high on my list of places to explore when time and circumstances would allow. When it came about it did so in an odd way.

My introductory visit began as a trial run, filled with both hope and fear precipitated by the only serious accident I have ever had in thousands of miles of hiking. While winter backpacking in 1980 doing field work for a hiking book on southern Ohio, I fell and broke

The Mishe-Mokwa at Park Service Dock in South Manitou Harbor

my ankle. Since my fiftieth birthday was already a few years past, I wondered if my backpacking days were permanently and sadly over. Fortunately, the break was not serious, but worry over my future hiking ability increased, for my recovery was much slower than I was told it reasonably should be.

I realized that a visit to South Manitou, which, meanwhile, had become a part of the national lakeshore, could be an ideal opportunity to answer some burning questions about my hiking future. I knew that the walks to any of the island' three campgrounds were not excessive. It seemed like a great place to test the endurance of my newly-mended ankle while carrying a backpack. If I survived that short weight-bearing trip, and physical limits allowed, I could then shed my portable house, and find out if I could function as a day-trip trail walker as I went sightseeing around the island.

This experiment with a series of island day-hikes, plus at least two short load-carrying trips between campground and boat dock, would pretty much tell me if I could still manage a forty-pound pack and go on progressively longer pack-free day-hikes. The trip was a great success, for I found that although my ankle was not yet 100%, I could still hike with a pack, and the island's scenic rewards exceeded my highest expectations. It was then that I began formulating ideas for this present book. I could see that the recreational opportunities the island offered were unique and varied, and would appeal to many types of would-be visitors.

What's Special About the Island

For the history buff, South Manitou is the most fascinating of the four islands in this book. During most of the nineteenth century, the eastern side of Lake Michigan was the major north-south highway of the region, for both commerce and population. The island's location on the west side of the narrowest section of the Manitou Passage meant that both passenger ships and freighters, squeezed between the mainland and the island, would come close to the inviting anchorage of the island's deep and protective harbor. Because its eastern shore borders this important shipping lane and its harbor is the best natural one within 300 miles, the history of the island is steeped in the nautical romance of Great Lakes exploration and settlement.

Of this book's four major hiking islands, South Manitou's 5,000 acres make it the second largest. It is the only one that has daily ferry service during the months of June, July and August, making it by far the handiest to get to. It is also the easiest one to find your way around, for most of its trails are on well-defined and easily followed roads, well marked by strategically placed signs. Short of doing some off-trail boondocking through its forests, your chances of getting lost on this island are almost nil. Furthermore, the National Park Service has enough rangers and volunteers stationed on the island that seeking answers to your questions is rarely difficult. The Park Service has also erected signs at important historical points of interest, with detailed facts about these locations. Under these circumstances, you may wonder why a guidebook is necessary at all. For many it really won't be. On the other hand, the organization of material presented on these pages may help you in planning your trip, and using your time efficiently while on the island, allowing you to establish a priority of areas to visit and things you most want to do. You may also find it a handy reminder of how to get from place to place, and the historical significance of these locations.

Several of South Manitou's special features are decidedly different from the other three islands, and place it in a sightseeing class all by itself. The walk across the island's west side perched sand dunes, and the westward views from the top of the escarpment, approximately 350 feet above the water's edge is, in this writer's opinion, the single most spectacular view found on any of the four islands. This panorama, unhampered by forest, gives the hiker a spectacular lake vista from the edge of this high sand escarpment. Being close to three miles in length this escarpment covers almost the entire west side of the island. Its only rival as a spectacular cliff-side walk in the Great Lakes area is found at the Sleeping Bear cliffs on the nearby mainland. True, the mainland cliffs rise about a hundred feet higher than those of South Manitou and continue for several more miles making the mainland overlook even more breathtaking. But the advantage of the Manitou walk over its mainland counterpart is that hikers can enjoy this island perspective in splendid isolation, avoiding the hordes of people encountered at the overlooks along the mainland's Pierce Stocking Drive. At the top of the escarpment of the Sleeping Bear Cliffs, a serious mainland viewer, standing among many hurried uninterested tourists, often experiences a loss of much of the essence of this natural phenomenon. The presence of others seems to destroy or decrease a deeper human identification and unity with the natural world. To me, the insular separation and isolation of the Manitou cliffs often gives the solitary walker a feeling of being absorbed into, and becoming part of this magnificent panorama.

If the escarpment and dunes of this island are its most outstanding natural enticement, it also has a manmade masterpiece in its lighthouse, with its 99 foot tower. Although there are three non-functioning lighthouses on other islands in the Lake Michigan Archipelago, none of them is found on the four publicly-owned hiking islands in this narrative, nor do any of the existing ones match either the height or magnificence of the Manitou Light complex. In the long tradition of American lighthouses, this high structure, almost at the water's edge, strategically overlooking the narrow Manitou passage and the Sleeping Bear Cliffs some seven miles away, makes it one of the most aesthetically pleasing anywhere.

Park Service dock and former Coast Guard buildings-South Manitou Harbor. Boathouse on right is ranger contact station

The lighthouse and the island's high sand escarpment are not the only things of interest that one may enjoy on an island visit. There is the grove of giant virgin white cedars, containing the largest known tree of that species in the world. You may view a shipwreck, lying in the shallow water about a half mile from the island's south shore. Although rapidly alling prey to the lake's winter ice, there is still enough of its hull and some of its superstructure left above the water line to attract those interested in things nautical. You can take yourself back in time by walking the delightful narrow dirt one-lane roads that lead you through this rural setting. You may pass the now deserted late nineteenth and early twentieth century farm buildings and machinery that comprised this once successful agricultural community.

When I became familiar with the island's history, its remaining buildings and physical surroundings, I found, as I walked the narrow roads past the island's now-deserted farms that I was more aware of a disappearing form of agricultural America. The other islands have a bit of this also, but it is more evident on South Manitou. One feels in touch with that recent past when, with a small financial investment and hard work, it was possible for an immigrant farmer to till less than a hundred acres and still make a living adequate to support a large family. Industriousness was aided by their location on a strategic stopover on the major mass transit system of the Great Lakes during the last two thirds of the nineteenth century. Before the coming of the automobile, and the slow growth of railroads into the northern part of Michigan's lower peninsula, these were the halcyon days of the sailing ships and woodburning steamboats that used the island as a regular stopover for supplies and fuel. The farmers had a good market for anything they raised, and supplies came in regularly in all except the winter months.

Times became more difficult for the island farmers during the first third of the twentieth century. With the improved reliability of automotive machinery, traveling on all weather roads, and larger coalburning steamships which no longer stopped at the island the direct market connection and supply route with Chicago that the island once enjoyed was hampered severely.

Yet the record of a large farming community of small farms passing through several island generations is a success story that lasted here for almost a hundred years. Much evidence of this agrarian existence can still be sensed, as one hikes the delightful one lane sand and gravel roads, through the remnants of a once thriving community of farming homesteaders. For those who love beach walking the various possibilities are many. But, South Manitou is not exclusive here. At least two of the other islands have excellent long beach-shore walks.

The easternmost protrusion of the island known as Gull Point was once one of the largest rookeries in the Great Lakes for both the Ring-Billed and Herring Gulls. Although the number of nesting birds has declined significantly in recent years, they are still high enough to make the rookery an area of interest for many visitors. Trespassing into the Point's nesting area is not allowed, but there is an overview which gets you close enough to watch the antics of the gulls whose breeding season lasts from late May through July.

An Introduction to the World of Overnight Hiking

For those hikers not used to long treks, or not caring to transport a portable bedroom and kitchen over long distances, yet conditioned enough to take level walks of a few miles, all points of the island are within easy roundtrip day-hikes from the established campgrounds. General backpacking is not allowed on the island, and campers must stay in one of the three camps, but the walk to two of the three campgrounds is short and once your camp is set up, there is no toting of camp gear until departure day. It really is a wonderful area for a beginning backpacker because one must carry gear over distances long enough to get the feel of wearing a loaded pack without causing undue stress if the load is heavy or the hiker is out of shape. It also gives you a shakedown experience, getting used to dealing with tents, sleeping bags and pads, tiny stoves, camping utensils and general organization of ultra light equipment.

Because the Leland ferry lays over for about four hours at the island on its daily round trip, a high percentage of visitors stay only for those few hours, which gives time for only a slapdash look at the island. Some will take advantage of the convenience of the ferry to take a restful weekend of doing little except enjoying the sun and the sand, away from the mainland hordes of people and traffic.

For the hurried island visitor there is a motor vehicle sightseeing trip that carries passengers to inland points of interest, such as the cemetery, some of the old farm sites and schoolhouse. Aside from this open touring vehicle the only other motorized conveyances one is likely to hear are miniature flatbed four-wheel scooters the park personnel use to move small supplies or maintenance tools to nearby points along the historic corridor. Much of the island has a wilderness classification, where all types of motorized or wheeled vehicles are prohibited.

If getting away from people is part of the island experience you wish, you may be better served by visiting one of the other islands especially from late June through early August. But even then there are periods between Monday and Thursday on South Manitou when the island seems lonely. Once, during a long weekend visit I made in early September, I found that a threat of rainy weather caused all the campers to take Sunday's late afternoon ferry back to the mainland. I was expecting a return to Leland the following day but because

Farm road alongside former Hutzler-Riker Farm

of high winds the Monday boat could not make the crossing. Since the ferry did not make a Tuesday run then the resident ranger and I were the sole occupants of the island. For two and a half-memorable days I was the solitary occupant of the island's country lanes and the only tourist viewer of its many vistas.

If you wish to identify with the island's past and the presence of other people will disrupt your identification with it, plan a trip in September, when you too can enjoy hiking these nostalgic farm lanes in relative seclusion. The only other human presence you are likely to encounter are the spirits of the people who for many generations lived and died on these island homesteads. Or if you love solitary walks through dazzling fields of trillium, lady slipper and other wildflowers, come in late May. If you can put up with near-freezing temperatures at night and love the zesty tang and colors of early fall try late September or early October. Ferry schedules are not as regular then and bad weather delays are more frequent, but you can roam the island almost as though it was your own personal feudal domain.

For someone who has a real interest in the island's many sightseeing and walking adventures, a single day visit becomes a frustrating exercise in futility, for it leaves one knowing little more about the island than the mainland visitor who views it from afar. The day return trip can however, serve as a quick introduction to whet one's appetite for a bigger bite of vacation time at a later date. In this writer's estimation it takes a minimum of two full 24-hour periods on the island uninterrupted by arriving, leaving or setting up camp to enjoy the island's major features and soak up the feeling of its history and beauty. This can be done nicely on an extended weekend. Of course, longer periods on the island gives one more time for meditative beachcombing, soaking up the oceanic-like water-side atmosphere, and the peaceful and nostalgic moods of the inland farms.

Campsite near South Manitou Harbor

If your mind has a romantic bent capable of imagining the voices of the island's ghosts, when walking near the lighthouse you may hear the haunting and forlorn cries of two children of the last century as they seek in vain for their drowned lighthouse-keeper father and his wife. As you pass the cemetery, the voice of an old woman might be heard grieving over a small child's grave near her own. You might also feel the presence of the unknown skeleton lying in that same cemetery, hopelessly searching for his named identity. Or if you camp near the Bay Cemetery you may hear audible night-time proof of a nineteenth century legend. Sailors, dying of dreaded and highly contagious Cholera, were hurried into their wooden tombs before they had totally expired. The legend maintains that the victims protest their live burial by moaning throughout eternity.

If poltergeist utterances are not part of your audio imagination, it is only a minor part of the island's worthwhile features. There are abundant diverse reasons many people may spend a worthwhile week of rest and relaxation on the island anytime from late May through early October, especially when the weather cooperates.

Chapter VI

A Brief History of South Manitou Island From the 1830s to the present

The historical development that precedes the American occupation of South Manitou is given in the chapter entitled, A Brief Early History of the Lake Michigan Archipelago. Indian legends about the Manitous and the first white contacts with the islands are given in that chapter. To avoid as much redundancy as possible, detailed historic information of specific island locations is often given in the South Manitou trails chapter at those locations, and not repeated or only casually mentioned in this history.

Reasons for Change From Wilderness island to Early Settlement

From the first appearance of the Paleo Indians in Michigan up through the early nineteenth century, South Manitou had been touched only for brief periods by the hand of man. The great fur trade had dominated commercial activity of the region for the better part of two hundred years was dwindling into insignificance. Important factors attracted Americans to look at other commercial possibilities afforded by South Manitou's unique geographical location. During the first third of the nineteenth century rapidly changing economic and political conditions brought on radical changes, which would bring the first permanent white settlers to the island. Robert Fulton's steamboat was rapidly changing the way man traveled over water. In 1819, the first steamship on the upper Great Lakes made her maiden voyage into Lake Michigan, and introduced the only Great Lake entirely inside the United States to the age of steam. The opening of the Erie Canal in 1825 stimulated the movement of new settlers and trade routes into the northern Midwest. By 1834, there were 34 steamers plying Great Lakes waters. These new steamships, and hundreds of sailing vessels, used the Great Lakes as major watery highways to penetrate the Midwest heartlands.

South Manitou was strategically placed on the major north-south shipping lane between Chicago and the Straits of Mackinac. This major shipping route funnelled most of the sea traffic into the narrow Manitou Straits, adjacent to South Manitou. Having the only easily accessible, deep natural harbor between Mackinac and Chicago The island was a logical place for the passing mariners to stop for fuel and food. The first island settlers came to exploit the commercial possibilities of by this unique geographical position.

No one knows when the first white men visited and explored the island nor who they were. The first written records mentioning ships stopping on south Manitou, date from the 1830s. One of the earliest was written by a passing English tourist whose name was Harriet Martineau. In 1836, while making an extensive sight-seeing trip through America, she wrote of passing through the Manitou Straits. She explained that there was great anticipation among the ship's passengers as they approached the islands, for they knew about the Indian legends, which described the Manitous as Indian spirit islands. These romantic illusions were further

Manitou passage in a storm with Sleeping Bear Bluffs in background. Drawing by Count de Castlenau

Library of Congress

enhanced by the islands being surrounded by early morning midst. She noted that the Manitous were apparently deserted, and the land had not yet suffered from the invasion of land speculators. The year following the Martineau visit, an American passenger named Thomas Nye passed through the straits en route to Chicago, and noted in his journal that his ship stopped at South Manitou, "to wood."

The dangerous waters of the Manitou Straits during violent weather were becoming better-known, and of great concern to mariners. After suffering through severe squalls in the Manitou Passage, a European nobleman, named Castelnau, described these turbulent waters as being severer than those he had encountered on either the Atlantic or the English Channel. Describing a passage through the straits he wrote:

> "We were a plaything of the giant waves. . . . I have seen the squalls off the banks of Newfoundland . . . And the hurricanes of the Gulf of Mexico. Nowhere have I witnessed the fury of the elements comparable to that found on this fresh water sea."

Such writings and comments by sea captains attracted the attention of the federal government. In 1837, Naval Lieutenant G. J. Pendergast was sent by U.S. authorities to locate possible sites where navigational beacons could be strategically placed to aid the ever-increasing number of passing ships.

In his report, the Lieutenant strongly suggested that a prime location for a rotating beacon was on the southern end of South Manitou. A year later, Lieutenant James Housman visited the island and picked a site for a lighthouse where the present structure stands today. It is near the island's southern end, as Lieutenant Pendergast had previously suggested. In his submitted report to the Secretary of the Treasury, he also mentioned that all large commercial vessels stopped at the island either to fuel or for protection from unfavorable weather or both. He stressed the fact that the island had the only deep-water harbor able to accommodate large ships in the 300 mile distance from the Straits of Michimilimackinac to Chicago. In 1838, Congress authorized $5,000 for the building of the island's first lighthouse. In today's climate of governmental cost overruns it is interesting to note the actual building cost of the first lighthouse was $4,567. Construction began in 1839 and the first lamp was lit at the building's completion in the spring of the following year. A light from its and other replacement towers at this location would burn for the next 118 years. The Manitou Light was built just in time to welcome the first screw driven steam vessels to the lakes in 1841.

The Island's First Entrepreneur

With the convenience and safety afforded by its harbor, South Manitou's untouched forests furnished another asset that became vastly important. There was a gradual increase in steam powered vessels on the Great Lakes that used wood for fuel. With the double advantage of a ready supply of timber and the only accessible harbor for over 300 miles that did not need dredging, the island had all the prerequisites of a natural refueling point for these tall-stackers on the runs to and from Chicago.

Probably the earliest white occupants of the island were timber men, exploring the possibilities of supplying the island's wood to feed the furnaces of these hungry woodburning boats. The first recorded permanent island resident was a timber merchant named William W. Burton. He was known to have been active on the island before 1840, and was probably on the island the year that Miss Martineau sailed by. The actual date of his first stay on the island is not known, but it might have been as early as 1835. Although he then owned no land on the island, he had probably begun cutting and selling timber to passing boats sometime around that date. His first legal ownership of island land does not occur until 1849, when his name appears on a title for 50 acres of island territory. It is said that at one time he made claim to the entire island, but there are no known records of his trying to make this a legal reality.

In 1840, after being recommended by other islanders, he was appointed to become the first keeper of the lighthouse at a salary of $350 a year. He did such a poor job of attending his duties at that crucial job the government removed him from the position three years later. His failure was probably not from laziness but from having stretched himself too thin. His involvement in more than one major enterprise used up all his time. He, with the aid of his son, had established South Manitou as a major refueling station for the woodburning steamboats. An 1847 island survey mentions a dock, a general store, a blacksmith shop and a three-mile wooden railway used to haul felled logs to the dock. This was the nucleus of the island's first small village which was located along the shores of Crescent Bay. Much of it was probably owned and supervised by Burton. The pier became known as, "Burton's Wharf," and in later years "The Old Dock." South Manitou's first sawmill was also established by him. Burton and his son remained the island's major entrepreneurs until sometime after 1880, when their island holdings were sold and the family moved to California.

Stepping Stones of Civilization

When the nineteenth century began, the northwestern shore of Michigan's Lower peninsula was still wilderness. South Manitou became the first island pioneer settlement to be established along the peninsula's western coastline, bordering Lake Michigan. Indians paddled to the island by canoe from an Ottawa village on the nearby mainland to trade in Burton's store, for no such establishment could then be found on the Leelanau Peninsula. This hamlet of about 300 Indians was situated on a hill, near a small stream that entered Lake Michigan close to the Manitous. Their name for the future location of Leland, Michigan was "Mishi-mi-go-bing," meaning "a place where the Indians run their canoes up the river because there is no harbor." One writer called South Manitou the "jumping off place," because it was from this island base that settlers would first move across the Manitou Straits carrying civilization to the Leelanau Peninsula. Migrants from The Manitous eventually founded several communities along its coast including the town of Leland. That future town did not receive its first white settler until 1848. He was an Indian trader named Lerue, who moved his business from South Manitou to be closer to his trading customers. These small mainland communities offered no real competition to South Manitou in supplying fuel and food to the passing ships, for at least two more decades.

Beginning of Farming and the First German Immigrants

Although Burton did not plan for or take part in it, he did encourage another important island enterprise that flourished and prospered well into the twentieth century. Starting about mid-century there was a steady growth of independent farms, which greatly enhanced family living. Most of the early island farms were envisioned and created by European immigrants, who primarily came from Germany. These immigrant families played an important part in the settling and development of the island for the next hundred years. Since South Manitou was an uninhabited wilderness at the beginning of the nineteenth century, unknown in Germany or anywhere else, the discovery of this island was made more by happenstance than direct knowledge by the German immigrants.

The first arrival to establish a farm who would have long-standing ties to the island was not German by birth, but was originally a New Yorker. Putnam Burdick became the first of four generations of Burdicks to make the island their home. Besides farming he apparently was involved in fishing and other island activities. His great-grandson, Fred Burdick, was the last member of the old pioneer families to live on the island for any extended period of time. Fred spent several years years promoting the island as a summer resort, a hundred years after the coming of his great-grandfather.

The first German immigrant to establish a permanent home on the island was George Johann Hutzler. The story of the Hutzler family is beautifully told in a book written by his great-grandson, Myron H. Vent entitled South Manitou Island, From Pioneer Community to National Park. After extensive research, Vent was able to chronicle the story of his family from its German origins through their extended stay on the island. It is the best of three published books on island history, and from it this writer gleaned much of the information used in this far shorter narrative.

Born in a small Bavarian village in 1814, George Johann was the son of humble parents who most likely knew nothing of the struggle between the young United States and England. They probably would have been astonished if they knew that this struggling country would be the adopted homeland of their newborn son. In 1842, this son of a basket weaver and hops grower married Margaretha Ziegler, who lived in a nearby Franconian village. Part of their attraction for each other might have been the fact that both George and Margaretha were Lutherans in an area of Germany that is predominantly Catholic.

The series of revolutions that shook Europe and especially a disunited Germany during 1848-49 brought on particularly hard economic times. By 1853, with five children to feed and no real economic opportunity to look forward to, Hutzler decided to try his luck in the new world. It was no small undertaking for a man almost 40 years old with little formal education, who spoke not a word of English. In October of that year, the family embarked on a stormy winter Atlantic crossing. That journey, on a crowded sailing ship named Sir Issac Newton, took the painfully long time of three months and three days to reach American shores at the port of New York. Proceeding on to Buffalo, both husband and wife found tragedy awaiting them during the summer heat. Falling victims to a dreaded Cholera epidemic they barely survived. The disease claimed the life of their eldest son, ten-year-old George Junior, who didn't live long enough to meet the Indians he so much wanted to see. A year later, another son was born. He was also named George in honor of his departed brother.

Buffalo's geographic location at the east end of Lake Erie played a decisive roll in determining the future and happier life of the Hutzlers in America. In the spring of 1855, George Johann was able to secure a job on a new large side wheeler steamboat of 1000 gross tons, named the Iowa. She regularly sailed from Buffalo to Chicago, which gave the senior Hutzler an opportunity to become acquainted with the Great Lakes. Actively seeking a new place to relocate his family, he quickly rejected Chicago. Although it was the favorite place to settle for westbound immigrants, dirt streets that turned into mucky swamps in rainy weather and other unhealthy overcrowded conditions made George Hutzler aware that in its present primitive stage, Chicago was a breeding ground for further epidemics. With the recent loss of his son foremost on his mind, he looked elsewhere for a safer place to settle his family.

When the Iowa stopped At South Manitou for refueling, George Hutzler liked what he saw. A beautiful island, isolated from the hazards of city life, but still on an important line of commerce that offered various possibilities for making a secure and comfortable living and a healthy location for raising a family. Fortunately George Burton's wharf was a beehive of activity, and he was in sore need of woodcutters. George Hutzler hired on, and with his strong German work ethic, he favorably impressed Burton and they became friends. Hutzler soon decided that he wanted to bring his family to the island, but lacked the money to pay for their passage. It took him several months to accumulate enough cut wood to pay for passage money but an untimely fire wiped out that investment. Burton then lent him the money, and after a year's separation, sometime near the end of 1856 George was reunited with Margaretha and their five children.

Once the Hutzlers were established on the island, they encouraged a German immigrant family named Haas, then residing in Buffalo, to settle on the island. George Johann Hutzler, also encouraged his half-brother in Germany, whose first name was also George, to immigrate to the island. This was the beginning of a second branch of the Hutzler family on the island. They can be told apart by the use of the middle names. George Johann's younger half brother is George Conrad. These three German families were later joined by the Beck family, who arrived before 1870. With the qualities of thrift, determination and hard work, these four German immigrant families became the backbone of the island's farming community, and remained so well into the twentieth century. They frequently intermarried,

Historic German immigrant farm, South Manitou

entwining the families together, and most of the farm buildings still standing on the island are identified with one or the other of these original German immigrants.

The Homestead Act of 1863 gave George Johann an opportunity a German immigrant would highly covet; owning the land he worked. On the mainland he walked the entire 30 mile distance to Traverse City to register his claim and walked back. This made him the legal owner of his 80-acre farm. it was something that would have been impossible for a man of his station to achieve back in his native Bavaria. By 1865, he was raising both cows and horses, as well as the usual grain crops, for which he needed a large barn. That year, such a barn was raised, using giant timbers and wooden pegs, but nary a nail. It remained in excellent condition until the 1930s when it was struck by lightning and burned to the ground.

When he arrived in 1855 at the age of 42, George Hutzler owned little more than the clothes on his back. By 1870, he was the most successful farmer on the island, and was considered one of its foremost citizens. He became an outstanding example of the American dream: the poor European immigrant who transplanted his family to this country and within a generation established himself as a successful, worthwhile and productive citizen. Before the turn of the century, various members of the Hutzler clan would own 1/5 of the entire island.

George Johann requested that at his death he be laid to rest in the middle of an orchard he had planted. When he died at the age of 74, the request was carried out. With the demise of the orchard in this century, the grave was lost in new forest growth. Myron Vent, who remembered visiting it as a young boy, rediscovered it and today there is an easily followed trail to the site. George Hutzler's equally hard-working wife survived him by more than 20 years, living until 1909. Together, as island pioneers, adapting to a culture and language that was foreign to them, they built a home and successfully raised their surviving children. But in a pattern that would be followed by the other immigrant families, most of their children would abandon the island in adulthood, seeking the wider career opportunities of the mainland. Only one of George Johann's sons would stay to operate the family farm.

His death in 1944 ended the island saga of this branch of the Hutzler family which had begun 89 years before.

The Island's Most Prosperous Decade

The 1870 census listing of the island's resident families showed that six of them were of German origin, four were American, two from England and one from Ireland. All of these families were again listed in the census of 1880. Since most of them were farmers, it suggested a decade of stability and family life on the island. It was around this time that the island reached its largest number of year-round residents, with a population of 98. It was also during the years between 1870 and 1880 that the island reached its happiest bucolic state. Families living on the island during this period had children of varying ages, in enough numbers so that active social life flourished. Although they were isolated from the nearby, but still largely undeveloped mainland, these self-sufficient farmers with a mixture of American, German and English heritages were also able to furnish their own entertainment. Barn dances, spelling bees, anniversary and marriage celebrations flourished. With an abundance of horses and snow-covered periods lasting for months, recreational sleighrides were common. Although there was no resident minister or church on the island, revival meetings were major social events and were well attended.

1858 combination lighthouse and keeper's residence Courtesy of S.B.D. National Lakeshore

The economic base of this insular existence depended largely on the continuing flow of the Chicago-run lake traffic, with boats regularly stopping at the island. Fortunately for the islanders, from the 1850s through the 1880s the need by north and south-bound ships for the island's services and protection continued to increase. This resulted in a period of general prosperity for the islanders in servicing the ships and using their holds to send their agricultural products to Chicago markets.

Because of ever increasing lake traffic during these decades, the first lighthouse built in 1840 was considered inadequate. Its light was so weak that an unknown scoundrel on the mainland occasionally placed a light along the slope of the Sleeping Bear cliffs. To find the northern entrance of the Manitou Straits and Crescent Harbor, mariners moving north would seek out the Manitou light. If they mistaking identified the illegal mainland light as the legitimate one they would be lured into steering a course too far east, and run aground. The land pirate then would plunder the ships when the crews and passengers abandoned ship.

In 1858, a similar but larger structure replaced the original house with a higher wooden light tower extending from its roof. A fog signal building, separate from the lighthouse, was built near it. In it, the first steam driven foghorn on the Great Lakes was placed in 1875. Before that time, ships were warned of the nearby fog bound shores by the sounding of a large bell, weighing a half ton. At the beginning of the Civil War, there were

Photograph showing enclosed corridor connecting the 1858 keeper's house to the 1871 lighthouse

197 screw-driven steamers on the lakes. Known as propellors, they were more efficient and faster than the remaining 137 side-wheelers sailing these inland seas. But sailing ships still dominated the waters, for there were 1,122 sail-propelled vessels on the Great Lakes at that time.

A government report written in 1869 again stressed the importance of the South Manitou light. It pointed out that more ships passed this island point than any other place on Lake Michigan. It also stated that the island's nearby harbor was used more often as a refuge shelter from severe weather than any other harbor on the lake. The existing light was low enough both in height and power, that passing ships often mistook it for lights aboard anchored vessels in Crescent harbor. The report suggested that South Manitou needed a higher and more powerful light, so navigators could use its beam as a reference for skirting the island as well as a beacon to guide them into the harbor. Funds were then appropriated to build a new higher tower that would contain a more powerful beacon, in front of and

Wreck in South Manitou harbor
Courtesy of Ethel Furst Stormer

separate from the existing house. The new tower was finished and operational late in 1871. At 99 feet in height, it was one of the tallest and most important lights on the Great Lakes, and is today one of the most beautiful lighthouses anywhere. What is not seen is its foundation, which extends better that 70 feet below the surface (See "The Lighthouse" in Trail section). The nautical traffic relying upon the new tower had increased significantly since the Civil War, for in season more than 100 ships passed through the Manitou Straits on almost any single day. With this increase in numbers It was felt that one lighthouse keeper could not operate the new facility in an expedient manner by himself, so an assistant was duly hired in 1872. But even with the new light and protective bay, the Manitou Straits often proved treacherous.

It was in this decade that the sea traffic passing South Manitou was at its busiest. This eastern ship passage was the nineteenth century's nautical equivalent of Michigan's modern interstate highway I-75. Steamships often made as many as 35 trips a year between lake freeze-ups. Since they would burn between 100 and 300 cords of wood on a single trip, the convenient location of Crescent Harbor and an adequate supply of island timber made the harbor a busy place. This gave the farmers of South Manitou easy access to the markets of Chicago for their crops and cattle. They also made sales directly to the ship's commissaries for consumption on the ship's voyages. Still, the bulk of the ships moved under sail with general cargos of grain and lumber. It was reported that during the busiest seasons there were often as many as 100 ships at anchor in Crescent Harbor. A great number of them were schooners, often three or four masters. The combined masts gave the appearance of a thick but leafless forest of straight trees. Other types of sailing vessels including fore'n'afters, barques and barquentines were also frequently seen.

Development of the Rescue Service

Even with the added safety of the new lighthouse and the easily approached harbor, the Manitou Straits continued to be an especially hazardous place, and a true graveyard for ships during extreme weather conditions. Nearly 70 vessels have been recorded lost in the area of the Manitou Straits since records were kept, and the exact number is probably double that. The first wreck was recorded in 1835, the last in 1960. Although there was certainly no shortage of wrecked steam vessels, the toll among sailing ships was far higher, for of the reported 42 disasters, sailboats accounted for 31 of them. Relying solely on wind for power a sailing ship close to shore ran a far greater danger of finding its power source driving the vessel towards shore and destruction. Blinding snowstorms often blotted out the welcome Manitou light as well. In the deadly November storms, crews whose ships ran aground on offshore reefs or sand bars often found the damaged hulls only partly sunk, as they bottomed in the shallow depths. Under less stormy conditions, they would be within easy swimming or wading distance of land. With their way to safety on the shore blocked by huge waves the crew would climb the rigging to escape the churning, freezing seas, and await rescue from the shore. There, with the stinging spray of gale force winds soaking the helpless sailors, they would freeze to death. The masts of those doomed ships had become trees of death with strange fruit dangling frozen in the ice-covered rigging.

Many of these catastrophes were caused by trying to squeeze in as many sailings in as possible before winter ice made the lakes impassable. The month of the most frequent and violent storms is November, and the list of lake victims of November weather is far longer than that of any other month. Because most grain crops are harvested in the later months of the growing season, there was always a rush to get the crops to markets before the season closed. Delaying shipment after November called for the added expense of storing the grain until the following spring.

Extreme storms in the later part of the nineteenth century, both on the Great lakes and the Eastern Seaboard, received much newspaper attention, and made the public more aware of these disasters. One such severe storm that wrecked and sank many vessels and received much publicity in newsprint, happened along the New York coast during the summer of 1848. People not familiar with the sea became more aware that dangerous weather could happen anytime. Almost as bad as the wrecks themselves, were the subsequent looting of the derelict ships by coast inhabitants before their cargos could be salvaged by their legitimate owners. These storms and the consequent vandalism that often followed were directly responsible for and eventually lead to the construction of the most important building complex that is still in use on South Manitou. Congress began appropriating small sums of money to furnish volunteer lifesaving crews along the eastern coast with surf boats and other equipment to aid shore-to-sea rescue. The volunteer concept did not function well, so a few haphazardly organized professional crews were tried in some locations.

After a series of nautical disasters, a congressional committee of 1871 concluded that an organized, professionally trained rescue service was necessary for both seacoasts and the Great Lakes. The U.S. Life Saving Service was then established under the jurisdiction of the Treasury Department, and stations began to be built. Had such a station been placed at the southern end of the Straits shortly after the establishment of the Service it would have proven most useful and productive in saving lives and cargos during the decade of the 1880s. Since the period between 1865 and the late 1880s were the peak years for sailing vessels on the Great Lakes, severe weather conditions brought on the destruction of the greatest number of ships. In studies and reports on desirable locations for the service there was general agreement that the Manitou Straits were prime locations for one of the new lifesaving stations. A hotly debated item was where this station would be located.

The first station to be authorized on the Straits was built on North Manitou, and put into operation in 1877. It was soon realized that the new station was a little too far north of the narrowest and the most treacherous parts of the Manitou Passage to be fully effective in many rescue operations. It was felt that another station, located further south, would be a great help in aiding vessels in distress in the passage's narrowest and southernmost sections. Some suggested that the station should be at Sleeping Bear Point on the mainland, while

Residence for the keeper and crew's quarters for the South Manitou Life Saving Station, circa 1910. Note-lack of front porch
Courtesy of S.B.D. National Lakeshore

1990 view of South Manitou's former Life Saving Station

others argued that South Manitou some six miles away on the western side of the passage, was the better site. Despite pleading letters from concerned individuals, the government procrastinated for over 20 years, postponing a decision for either location. In the two decades between 1878 and 1898, severe storms wrecked close to six thousand ships on the Great

Surfmen from South Manitou Life Saving Station transfering a cargo of lumber from a schooner wrecked off South Manitou to another ship-first decade of the twentieth century

Both photos courtesy of Ethel Furst Stormer

Lakes, with tremendous loss of life, when a station in either location could have been most effective. It was finally agreed that the Straits were of such importance there should be a station on both the mainland and the island, but bureaucratic bumbling delayed authorization until the beginning of the new century. The actual building of the South Manitou facility was not finished until 1902, long after the peak years of shipping and passengers service on the Great Lakes were over. On the twentieth of August the station was made operational with a captain and three surfmen. The normal compliment of a skipper (also sometimes called the keeper) and six permanent surfmen was soon realized.

Many island residents served as both permanent and temporary surfmen during the station's 56 year active existence, but only two native islanders were among the seventeen men who served as captain of the station. In 1915, the Life Saving Service was combined with another existing offshore government agency called the Revenue-Cutter Service, which became the U.S. Coast Guard. Although the station was decommissioned in 1958, the buildings were so solidly built that they survived nicely between the time of the abandonment and the takeover of the island by the National Park Service. Two of the largest buildings of this substantial complex were adapted to fill new rolls in the island's changed purpose. The residence of the keeper and his crew is used as the Island's ranger station, and the boathouse now serves as the visitor's contact station. Its sister station on the nearby mainland at Sleeping Bear Point near Glen Haven has also become part of the National Lakeshore, and now serves as a maritime museum. The buildings of the old Coast Guard complex on the mainland have been restored to show how these stations were used and equipped. If time permits, a tour of this museum before proceeding to the island will greatly enhance enjoyment and understanding of island history for anyone visiting South Manitou.

Although a lifesaving station did not become a reality on the island during the 1870s, the addition of the new lighthouse and other factors showed that this was South Manitou's most prosperous decade. The island was incorporated as a township in 1873, and opened its first official post office in 1879.

The Coming of Formal Education

Although the island residents had been paying school taxes for many years, this predominantly German settlement apparently felt self-sufficient and secure in educating its own. There was no school or teacher on the island in the 1870s, nor did the islanders ask for one. In 1882, two events changed the island's educational environment. The first was Michigan's first compulsory education act, passed by the legislature that year. It specified that all children under the age of 14 must attend school for at least six months a year. The other was the arrival of a new lighthouse keeper named Martin Knudsen. He insisted that the new act be implemented as soon as possible, and was instrumental in bringing the island's first elementary teacher from Traverse City. With his first six months contract and the aids of slate boards and the famous McGuffy Readers, a teacher from the mainland, whose name was Bert Green, began instructing the island's children in the three R's. Even with a professional teacher, the island's German speaking residents showed little enthusiasm for formal education, for the existing schoolhouse was not built until 1899.

Growth of Mainland Competition

Despite the growth of similar commercial activity on the nearby mainland the 1880s was a decade when economic factors continued to smile on the island residents. The bulk of north and south trade still traveled on lake boats instead of by railroad, and the business of supplying wood to the steamers was at its height. But there were definite signs that the commercial winds were changing and the island was beginning a period of gradual economic decline.

Before the 1850s, the adjacent mainland had remained as wilderness, and had offered no direct competition to the island. Commercial development of the nearby mainland, furnishing direct economic challenge to the Manitous and eventually surpassing them, began as early as 1848. During that year, a timber merchant, named Manseau, who normally operated out of North Manitou, began cruising the nearly mainland shore looking for a suitable site on which to build a sawmill. Needing water power to operate the mill he found a desirable location alongside a stream later known as the Carp River. Water from this short stream, which passed through the area that is now the town of Leland, came from a chain of three small lakes. In 1853, to ensure a steady water supply for his newly constructed mill, Manseau, and a partner named John I. Miller, built a dam on this stream. This raised the water level of the inland lakes several feet and combined the three small lakes into one, forming today's Lake Leelanau. The saw mill built at the dam site was to be used for supplying fuel to the wood burning steamer trade.

To function as a wooding station, a company dock was necessary. It was subsequently built on the north side of the stream, and was in operation by 1859. Business was so good a competing dock was built on the south side of the stream in 1861. Further competition to the island's once-exclusive wood business came from nearby Glen Haven, a scant six miles from South Manitou. In 1857 a sawmill was built there by C.C. McCarthy, near where the mainland lifesaving station would be located over 40 years later. In 1865, he added his own dock at Glen Haven, which soon became another important wooding station. Known as the Center Dock, it passed into the hands of the well-known lumber king, D. H. Day, in 1885. This Glen Haven dock, being much closer to the islands than the ones at Leland, also functioned as the principal mainland landing site for islanders up through the first half of the twentieth century.

Although there were now three nearby mainland locations competing with the island as wooding stations, the easy accessibility of South Manitou's harbor and the tremendous demand for wood fuel meant there was plenty of business in the wood trade for everyone, and demand would not seriously deteriorate as an income source until well after 1880. When that decade had been reached, the population of Leland had grown to almost 400 souls, while South Manitou's was less than 100. The most important civilizing center of the area had left the island and had permanently moved east to the mainland.

Another factor which would not only bring on rapid expansion of the northwestern sections of Michigan's Lower Peninsula, but would also begin to seriously challenge the area's almost sole reliance on Lake Michigan as its major highway, was the introduction of railroads. In 1856, Congress passed a land grant act which gave midwestern states title to thousands of acres of land to be turned over to fledgling railroads, to encourage expansion into areas previously void of track. In the following year, the Grand Rápids & Indiana Railway Company was given 823,204 acres of north Michigan land, agreeing to build a rail line from Grand Rapids to a point somewhere on Grand Traverse Bay. A general financial panic in that same year, followed by the Civil War, delayed the beginning of construction of the new line until 1869. This allowed a few more years of an exclusive monopoly of lake traffic transportation in the area, but the handwriting of its demise was on the wall.

By 1871, this land grant railroad had extended its track as far north as Cadillac, and by November of the following year it reached Traverse City. In 1873, a passenger could board a regularly-scheduled train in Traverse City any day of the week and arrive in Grand Rapids nine hours later. The editor of a Traverse City newspaper wrote that when he traveled overland through that same area only 12 years before, he had to ride a wagon over sandy roads. Those so-called roads, he said, were not much more than footpaths through the wilderness. He prophetically remarked that the new rail line would bring a new wave of civilization to the Traverse City region. In 1874, the main line of the Grand Rapids and Indiana Railway was extended all the way to the Straits of Mackinac: another blow to the once exclusive lake traffic.

S. S. Fred M. Green extracting sand and gravel from the bottom of Crescent Bay close to South Manitou's harbor shoreline

Courtesy of S.B.D. National Lakeshore

The 1880s also saw a major change and improvement in lake transport vessels. New lake steamboats were not only much larger but were using coal for fuel. Considering the amount of cargo they could carry, the new ships were far cheaper to operate than the smaller woodburning craft or schooners. They could also easily carry enough fuel and food for an entire voyage, which meant that they usually bypassed the island. With the rapid decline in the number of wood burning steamers and sailing vessels that still plied Lake Michigan, the business of selling wood and supplies to passing ships was all but over. By this time, a high percentage of the island had been denuded of trees and much of its surface consisted of a forest of stumps. The disappearance of the demand for wooden fuel gave the island a reprieve from further timbering saving the few remaining groves of standing timber. This breather in lumbering activities on the island also permitted a slow return of its wooded lands.

Sand Becomes an Export Commodity

In 1871, a catastrophic event that happened 220 miles south of the island soon brought about a great buying up of South Manitou shore property. In October 8 of that year, a great conflagration burnt two thirds of Chicago to the ground. 18,000 buildings, mostly of wood, were consumed by the flames. Rebuilding the city of less flammable materials created a tremendous demand for sand and gravel. The Garden City Sand Company of Chicago began buying up as much island shore line as was available, so they could operate dredges paralleling the beaches to scoop sand and gravel from the shallow offshore lake bottom. The company eventually owned about a fourth of the island's water frontage, including almost all of Crescent Harbor. For several years, a whole series of lake boats and barges loaded their holds with thousands of tons of nearby lake bottom, and hauled them off to help rebuild the metropolis to the south.

In those days no one worried about the ecological destruction that is caused by the removal of protective offshore sand and gravel bars. This author once visited the ruins of a shoreline town in England that was totally destroyed by a ferocious storm after a protective reef had been removed for use in World War I. Sometimes ships removed sand and gravel less than 70 feet from south Manitou's shoreline. The company continued to extract sand from the shallow near coastal waters of the island well into the 1920s. Since no records have been kept concerning the island's shoreline erosion, how much serious damage has been done to the less protected beaches of South Manitou can only be a matter of speculation.

First Attempts at Recreational Development

About the turn of the century, when the immediate need for sand and gravel had subsided executives of the Garden City Sand company decided to exploit their island holdings in another way. Since the company owned a great amount of waterfront property, and access to the island from Chicago was easy, a lakeside resort was envisioned and promoted. With the entrepreneurial zeal of visionary real estate developers, they proposed an elaborate development plan. The scheme included building a whole block of streets in the area of Crescent Harbor, and extending several inland roads. They also gave island roads already in existence new names. Streets running in a north-south direction were given the names of states, while those running in an east-west direction were named after cities. They also planned to build a grand boulevard following the sweeping shoreline curve of Crescent Bay. Prospective summer home owners did not materialize in any number and the whole development fizzled out. If the scheme had caught on, and there had been a proliferation of hundreds of summer cottages built on the island, it not only would have drastically changed the whole atmosphere and general character of the island, but the combined power of many landowners might have been enough to circumvent the island's future as part of the national lakeshore. There are at least two historical remnants left on the island from that developer's scheme. The present narrow road that runs due west from the site of Burton's old dock is known both as Old Dock Road and Chicago Road. The major north-south road of the island that passes both the schoolhouse and the cemetery still bears the state name given to it by the company over 80 years ago. It is named after my home state of Ohio.

Revival of Timbering

If the resort plans for the island at the beginning of this new century were short-lived, the last gasp of the once-active timbering industry happened during its first two decades. A good part of the island's extensive forest had disappeared during the heyday of the woodburning boats, but over 20 years had passed, allowing partial rejuvenation of the island's forests. Because excessive lumbering on the mainland had used up most of those great forests, timbermen became interested in lesser groves and smaller operations that they would have previously ignored. There now was enough island timber for profitable smaller scale commercial cutting, and two island sawmills were built and operated during this period. One mill that specialized in processing hardwood for the lumber trade, was found a half mile inland at the southwest corner of the junction of Ohio and Chicago Roads. A horsedrawn wooden tram railway was used to move the processed lumber from near the schoolhouse to

Wreck of Schooner Margaret Dahl in South Manitou Harbor. Old Dock and cedar sawmill in background, circa 1910

Courtesy of S.B.D. National Lakeshore

the bay. The millhands received a wage of one dollar and board and room for a 10 hour workday. A few scattered remnants of the mill's foundation are still visible today.

The other mill was located at the site of the original Burton mill near the old dock on Crescent Bay. This was a much larger operation than its inland counterpart, hiring up to 50 workmen in season. The two mills were not in direct competition, for the waterfront mill specialized in cutting shingles from cedar logs. By 1913, this mill had closed, for the island's supply of cedar trees was exhausted. For some reason, the woodsmen missed a section in the southwest corner of the island which is the only original climax forest left on South Manitou. No one is sure why this area of the island was never logged, but it is indeed fortunate that it was overlooked, for it contains the largest known white cedar in the world. There are several others in this same grove almost as large. Two factors which might have helped save this and other large virgin cedars in the grove are their remoteness and distance from the sawmills, and sand, which penetrated deeply into the tree's gnarled bark and played havoc with the woodcutter's saw blades. Still very much alive, the tree is thought to be at least 500 years old.

Economic and Population Changes

Although the hardwood mill would continue operating into the 1920s, its days were limited because the hardwood forests of the island were about depleted. Even at its height, this small operation offered little to the island's economy. Passenger steamship timetables of this early period of the twentieth century showed that no regular service was available for the island. Most of the north-south lake freighters now sailed by, without stopping at the island, their holds carrying only one type of cargo, usually grain or iron ore. Farmers were losing the ships both as customers and as haulers for easy access to the Chicago markets which started a decline in the farming population. But if the ships no longer stopped, they still needed protection passing through the Straits and rescue if they ran aground. The Lighthouse Keeper needed two assistants, not only for operating the light, but for keeping the steam operated fog signal sounding when needed in those pre-radar days.

The opening of the island's Life Saving Service in 1902 brought a component of six to seven more men living on the island. Usually the skipper of the station, the Lighthouse Keeper and his assistant were married, which added three families to the island community. Some surfmen also had wives living on the island. Added to these government employees and families, there were at least six farm families and one commercial fisherman still maintaining year-round homes on the island. This population formed a small but still stable and vibrant community during the first quarter of the twentieth century.

Because most lake boats now bypassed the island, the islanders became more dependent on the nearby mainland instead of Chicago for the accoutrements of civilization. The development of small power boats made it easier for island residents to get back and forth to the mainland. Except during storms, trips to Glen Haven and Leland were almost daily occurrences during the warm seasons of the year. Winter months were a different matter. Shore and channel ice closed the passage between the island and the mainland for long periods that sometimes extended up to six weeks. Occasionally the lake would freeze solid enough to permit walking or riding across the ice to Sleeping Bear Point. With no protection from wind or other elements, that one-way walk of six miles under conditions of bone chilling cold could often be an unpleasant experience. It could be dangerous, too. A few islanders lost their lives by attempting to cross the ice during unstable conditions.

At the beginning of this century, the island's only general store was located near the center of Crescent Bay. Set back about a hundred yards from the shore along the Old Dock Road, near the site of Burton's Dock, its sign proclaimed "Burdick's General Merchandise." It was run by the third generation of the Burdick family living on the island. These descents of Putnam Burdick would continue to be active in island affairs up to the time when it was taken over by the Department of the Interior. During the decade following the first World War, most of the islanders would meet in front of Burdick's store to celebrate the Fourth of July with various foot and bag races, as well as a baseball game. The store was run by the

Burdick Store on Chicago Road near Old Dock, circa 1910 Courtesy S.B.D.National Lakeshore

wife of the lighthouse keeper, James Burdick, who was a grandson of Putnam Burdick. Hired by the Light Keeping Service in 1901, he was promoted to Keeper in 1908. He held that position until he was transferred in 1928, longer than any other Keeper of the Manitou Light during its 118 year existence. The dilapidated remains of this original Burdick store along the Old Dock Road are still existent.

With the closing of the island's logging operations and the falling-off of the number of docking steamships, the old Burton Dock fell into disrepair, and the Life Saving Station became the main embarking and debarking point for the island. The center of community activity also gradually shifted south from the old dock to the area around the Life Saving Station. In 1923, this shift was further emphasized when the Burdicks moved the general store from its "Old Dock" location about the middle of the bay shore to another building further south, just a short distance southwest of the Coast Guard Station. The store's new location was within easy walking distance of the lighthouse, and functions today as the island museum. In that same year, Mrs. Burdick became the island's postmistress. She filled that position and ran the store until her husband was transferred to the light at Muskegon, Michigan.

Jim's younger brother, Andrew, who lived nearby on a small farm with his mother and two sisters, occasionally filled in as a substitute surfman at the lifesaving station. He probably would have joined the Coast Guard, but in 1917, when the United States entered the first World War, Andrew was drafted into the army. He unfortunately, succumbed to pneumonia while stationed in Archangel, Russia, just days before the November Armistice. Brought home for burial, he rests today in the island's cemetery.

The schoolhouse, which still stands, was built in 1899 and operated continuously

Relocated Burdick store in Coast Guard Village. Building is now utilized as the island museum

for the next 45 years. This one-room school, containing all eight grades, had its largest number of students in the early 1920s, when the number of young scholars numbered around 30.

It was at this humble one-room schoolhouse that a man who was destined to reach a high position in life received his early elementary education. During his boyhood years, his father served as skipper of the lifesaving station. When the boy reached college age, the father encouraged him to take the entrance exams for the Coast Guard Academy. After graduation Willard Smith rose through the commissioned ranks until he became an admiral. He was at the helm of the Coast Guard as Commandant when sweeping changes were made, revising the operation of that service. The cost of maintaining the many lifesaving stations had become prohibitive and unnecessary. With the adoption of helicopters and faster boats by the Coast Guard, rescue operations could be carried out faster and more efficiently, making these old surfboat stations obsolete. Ironically, Admiral Smith, who had lived as a boy on the stations at both North and South Manitou, was involved in the decisions to close them and the lighthouse. Because of his happy childhood days on the islands, It was a decision he probably found difficult to make. This was a concession dictated by the winds of change, based on practicality instead of emotional ties with the past.

By World War Two, the population of school-age children had almost disappeared. The schoolhouse had outlived its usefulness, and closed its doors in 1944. For many years after its closing, the building still housed desks, books and blackboards. but with time the building was allowed to deteriorate, and all the interior equipment disappeared. In the 1950s,

South Manitou school kids circa 1925
Courtesy S.B.D. National Lakeshore

the last active farmer on the island used the building to store hay. Fortunately, the building has been restored, but its interior , remains empty, leaving to the imagination what it must have looked like when all the tools of that one room-school were still in place.

Much of the knowledge about the island during the first third of the twentieth century comes from two books, written by men who lived on South Manitou at that period. In 1913, when Charles M. Anderson was five years of age, he moved with his sea captain father and family to the island, where he lived for the next 13 years. His book, Isle of View, A history of South Manitou Island, is really not as much a formal history as it is a narrative of his boyhood experiences on the island, and stories about the people he remembered. It is a fond remembrance of his happy boyhood life as an islander. If occasionally the organization of his material is a bit jumbled, and sometimes difficult to follow, his personal stories of his young and impressionable years on the island, give the reader a sensitive insight into the island's social world through the eyes of a child. The other writer, Gerald E. Crowner, served as a Coast Guard surfman between 1926 and 1928, and wrote an affectionate reminiscence of his years in service there in a short book entitled The South Manitou Story.

Both these books mention that the islanders were outstanding in self sufficiency, even when it was against the law. Prohibition bothered them not at all. Crowner comments on the high quality of the home brew he consumed at the home of George and Louis Hutzler. With a ready supply of apples, it was also easy to make hard cider. Charles Anderson relates that his sea captain father, as well as several islanders, were expert distillers of moonshine. If they wanted whisky they added burnt sugar for coloration, or if they desired gin they flavored their batch with the berries of the juniper bushes which grow wild on many parts of the island. Occasionally, there were rumors of an impending visitby a revenue agent, causing a great flurry of hiding the necessary coils and other distilling apparati. The precautions proved to be unnecessary, for agents never came.

At the beginning of the century most of the immigrant family farms were still operated by remaining relatives of the original German settlers. Crop-growing fields were surrounded by fences, allowing much of the island to be used as open range, for the raising of beef cattle. Apple and cherry orchards produced marketable crops as well. But, by the 1920s, it was apparent that the family farms were gradually becoming a thing of the past. High transportation costs made both cattle and fruit farming unprofitable. Cattle disappeared and orchards were no longer maintained, except for the small amount the islanders could use for home consumption. In an attempt to replace these once-profitable endeavors, islanders began raising turkeys and produced maple syrup but it was not enough to stem the tide. The mainland's magnetic pull, with its wider horizons of better educational opportunities, as well as varieties of available occupations and entertainment, constantly drew the second and third generation islanders away from their restricted world. One by one they crossed the straits, becoming permanent mainland dwellers, returning only briefly to visit family or friends remaining on the island. The depression years of the 30's stimulated this exodus from the island. Despite those difficult years, the island had a real moment of agricultural glory.

Prior to and during the twenties, the island played an important part in plant genetics and brought international honors to one of the descendants of the original German settlers. Because of its unique isolation from the mainland, the island became important in developing improved strains of agricultural seed. Since the island was more than five miles from the mainland, it eliminated the possibility of cross-pollination. The Michigan Crop Improvement Association encouraged the islanders to dispose of all types of rye formerly planted on the island and introduce a new strain known as Rosen (Russian) Rye. The nephew of George Johann Hutzler, like his father, George Conrad, was also named George. He and his son Lewis worked hard on this development, and eventually entered a peck of their rye seed in state, national and international agricultural fairs. Their hard work was rewarded, for they received several grand prize ribbons in the competitions. George never used artificial fertilizers, but replenished his soil by using animal fertilizers and rotating his fields every season, allowing each in its turn to lie fallow in clover. To get a winning peck of the Rosen Rye, father and son sorted through about 40 bushels of the grain, Louis picking for color and his father picking for size. The work was arduous and it took weeks of sorting to get that one peck of grain.

A few years later, the Michelite Bean, thought to be especially suitable for the Michigan climate, was introduced to the island. The Hutzlers nurtured this new bean crop with their usual efficient and attentive husbandry. Again they were able to produce beans that won ribbons in seed competitions from the state through the international level. George proudly displayed on his wall over 20 ribbons that he won in the various competitions he entered through the years.

Despite this development of superior seed, the island farms continued to decrease in size and number, especially through the Depression and early years of World War Two. By the 1940s, just one of the existing farms was still operated by the son of one of the original settlers. Only John Hutzler, the second youngest son of George Johann and cousin of George Hutzler of Rosen Rye fame, still operated the original family land grant.

Bertha Peth before she immigrated to the island and married John Hutzler

Although farming on the island was continued (albeit on a more limited scale) until its acquisition by the federal government, the era of the once prosperous German farming community came to a permanent end In 1944. That summer John Hutzler was found dead near his well. He had continued to operate the original family farm until his death at the age of 79. Living alone since his divorce 40 years before, his efforts during his last years consisted mostly of subsistence farming, gaining little more than enough to keep himself and his many household cats alive.

In 1946, Mrs Elvina Beck sold her family farm on the southern end of the island to a group of Detroit Rotarians. This was probably the last farm on the island still in the hands of the original German immigrants, and by 1948 there were only two farms still in operation. During these years several old homesteads were bought up by an absentee landowner named William Boals. He was one of the Rotarians involved in the purchase of the Beck farm. His plan was to use his extensive island holdings for the raising of beef cattle. In 1953, he hired Edwin Riker to be his island caretaker and tenant farmer. Riker, then brought his wife and three sons to the island, and became the last of the island farmers and the last island resident to stay year-round. He remained on the island until 1972, when Mr. Boals sold his holdings to the government. During their 19 year stay, the Rikers also took weather observations, helped with the island summer tourist population and educated their young sons at home.

As long as the Coast Guard Lifesaving Station and the lighthouse continued to operate, there was a small year-round population on the island. In the early 1950s, they consisted of the government personnel necessary to run the lighthouse and the life saving station, the Rikers and the former wife of Johny Hutzler, Bertha Peth. Advanced age finally forced Bertha, then called the Queen of South Manitou, to move to a Benzie County convalescent home. When the sweeping changes initiated by the coast Guard in 1958 closed both the lighthouse and the lifesaving station, their personnel were transferred off the island to other posts. Riker and his family were then the only year-round residents. When Riker's sons reached the age for secondary education, his wife took them to the mainland during the winter so they could attend high school. This left Edwin Riker the sole winter inhabitant of the island. A quiet man, who seldom spoke unless he had to, seemed well suited to this isolated lonely existence. But unlike the former winter inhabitants who were sometimes cut off from the mainland by shore ice for over a month, he could get across the straits when the weather permitted, because he owned and flew a small airplane that he kept on the island.

Although the winter population of the island had been reduced to one man, it was experiencing a surge of summer activity. An example of this turning point in the island's welfare was shown in 1944, when Mrs. Beck sold her homestead on the south end of the island to a Detroit businessman named Lee Barrett. An article in a 1948 edition of the Detroit Motor News stated that the island had been "discovered" by Mr. Barrett who saw the "possibilities of transforming the island into a paradise of peace in which they may escape from the rigors of this modern life." In conjunction with another friend named Joe Harrold, Mr. Barrett formed a corporation which was named the Lee Island Company, and shares were sold to 49 Detroit Rotarians. Their primary purpose was to use the property as a retreat from the intensities of urban life, and possibly later develop it as a resort. The old farmhouse was maintained, and became known as "The Lodge." It did not become a popular rendezvous with the corporation members, and was developed no further. Later it was leased to one of the owners, who in turn rented it out to vacationers as a summer residence on a weekly basis.

Although the Lodge proved to be only mildly successful as a get away place as originally envisioned, it did show that any new commercial direction of the island would be in tourism and in summer homes. Several homesites close to the old Coast Guard Station, formerly used by the families of the lifesaving crews and the lighthouse staff, were rented out or sold to people seeking summer cottages on the island and a small, happy summer community developed. A restaurant and marina, which continued operations through the first years of Park Service ownership, were built along the shores of Crescent Bay.

The Island's Last Entrepreneur

During the 1950s, one more person would attempt to turn South Manitou into an active resort area. Interestingly enough, that person was a great-grandson of Putnam Burdick, the island's first permanent settler. Fred Burdick was born on the island in 1917, during the time his father served as the keeper of the Manitou Light, and his mother operated the small general store nearby. Young Fred lived on the island until 1928, when his father was transferred to the mainland light at Muskegon. During World War Two, when Fred was serving in the armed forces, he thought a great deal about the island of his boyhood. The Burdick family still held property there so a couple of years after his discharge, and an absence of 20 years, this fourth-generation son of an island founder returned for a visit. His love for the island was renewed, but he was disappointed to find there was neither a place to buy food or obtain lodgings anywhere on the island. He then envisioned the possibilities of developing the island as a tourist center.

The Coming of the National Lakeshore

During the 1950s, Fred Burdick began commuting from his home in Lansing on weekends, and started his promotion of the island as a summer resort community. He built three rental cabins along the shores of the island's Lake Florence, reopened his mother's old general store, got the government to donate land for a 2,000-foot airstrip and proposed building a nine-hole golf course. From the tax list, he got the names of island property owners, including a few of the descendents of the first settlers. He was hoping to buy up more land for development, and was surprised to find that most owners were not interested in selling.

He subdivided lots along the main road, where he proposed to build log cabins made from island lumber for prospective buyers. Although a model cabin was begun, the project languished from lack of interest and necessary financing. To attract new customers, he issued a brochure encouraging summer visitors to come to his "Manitou Haven Resort." When the federal government included South Manitou as a part of the proposed new national park, he realized that his dream of building a successful island resort was at an end. Though he now resides in Florida, he intends to return permanently to the island at a later unspecified date. A new light-gray headstone recently placed in the island cemetery bears his name. Upon his death he intends to join the company of his island ancestors forever.

In the 1960s a few modern summer homes were built mostly along Crescent Bay,

One of three modern summer homes built near shoreline of South Manitou Harbor before the acquisition of the island by the federal government. In keeping with the wilderness concept of the island the buildings have been removed

but there was little development of the island's interior. But events were in the wind that would terminate this new phase of building summer residences. In 1958, the same year that the Coast Guard Station and lighthouse ceased operations, a study that would determine the long term future of the island was conducted. Funded by a Mellon Foundation grant, its purpose was to seek out shoreline areas of high scenic value that would be possible locations for future national parks. The Sleeping Bear escarpment naturally attracted the attention of the study group. Their report on the area stated, "by virtue of its outstanding natural features this area is of possible national significance and should be given further study to determine the best plan for preservation." A master plan was initiated, which included South Manitou and the first bill to establish the park was submitted to the Congress in 1961.

Several hearings were held where many local residents voiced their fierce resistance to the establishment of the park. This resulted in a great deal of political maneuvering, in which concessions were made and alternative plans evolved. Senator Philip Hart of Michigan saw early on that the unusual and beautiful natural features of the area would best be preserved as a national park. He therefore became the driving force to accomplish this and was responsible in seeing that various bills to establish the park eventually reached Congress. In 1970, despite strong local opposition, a public law was passed establishing the park which included both North and South Manitou.

Lifesaving Station lookout tower in 1927. The structure has long since disappeared
Courtesy Gerald Crowner & N.P.S.

The Algonquin tale about the mother bear and the cubs, which had given the lakeshore park its name, seemed to have reached its final destiny. Now, the island cubs have been linked together with their shorebound mother in books of law, as well as in legend. Hovering in the water just short of their mainland mother, they are now joined as long as the statutes of our government endure. Myron Vent's book gives an excellent rundown of the up and down proceedings that eventually led to the creation of this national lakeshore. With many readable quotes, it furnishes an impressive brief history of that stormy period, and is recommended to those who wish a more detailed chronological survey of those events.

Today, as the summer population of the nearby mainland seems overburdened with a glut of vacationers, it is nice to think how the roles of the island and the mainland have reversed themselves. In the beginning, civilization traveled from island to mainland. Having fulfilled this useful purpose, its new role was to turn back the clock to the times before its human occupation. Having served in the recent past as a stopover haven supplying food and fuel for lake traffic, and a starting point for a new generation of immigrant Americans, the forests, once denuded, are again allowed to grow unmolested. The crop growing fields are now also returning to nature. Many of the buildings will rot away and the eagles may return to nest. As the island is allowed to partly reclaim this status of wilderness, a limited part of its human history will also be preserved, with the protection of a few important buildings that represent both its nautical and agricultural past.

Although the transfer of ownership of these islands did cause real anguish for a few, in the long run, placing the islands under the protective blanket of the federal government will preserve this island treasure of historical and natural importance from further exploitation. It is now a haven for those seeking to identify with the heritage of its recent nautical, immigrant and agricultural past. The feast of the island's natural wonders, compacted within its insular shores, are now protected from those who would attempt to restrict access to it for an exclusive few or to plunder it for monetary gain.

Chapter VII

Hiking the Trails at South Manitou

Arrival at the island. If you plan to stay overnight or longer your first order of business will be registering for a camp site. When you step off the dock in Crescent Bay Harbor, walk up the ramp leading to the old Coast Guard boathouse which is **Point A** on the island map in this book. When this complex operated as a life saving station the building was raised a few feet above ground level to facilitate quicker launching of boats during rescue operations. Today that building functions as the Park Service Contact Station. If you came on the Leland ferry, a ranger will be there to greet you, answer questions and issue the free backcountry permit which you need if you are camping on the island. If you came by private boat and you find the contact station closed with no way of self-registering, go to the main office found in the Old Coast Guard residence, which is the large building with the big front porch just south of the boathouse. The first decision you have to make is in which of the three island camping areas you wish to stay. Drinking water is always available at either the Bay or Weather Station Campgrounds and occasionally is available near the more distant Popple Campground. All three are equipped with outhouses. However, the three campgrounds are quite different in their physical makeup. A brief description below may aid you in determining which of these camping areas best suits your planned itinerary. If you are staying for more than a couple of days, a good plan to consider is to spend the first part of your visit at the Weather Station Campground enjoying the hikes from that area as well as its unique location, then move to the Bay Campground, which offers a different environment and is much closer to the ferry, eliminating a rush hike on departure day. If you are seeking seclusion and you wish to camp as far as possible from the human traffic of the island, then Popple will be your best choice.

THE BAY CAMPGROUND. This camping area is the closest to the ferry dock, so if your tents and other equipment are not of the light- weight backpacking variety the distance you have to carry your burdensome equipage is greatly reduced. But there are other valid reasons that even gossamer-weighted backpackers might consider for choosing this delightful area. Its western perimeter is less than 50 yards from, and in sight of the sandy crescent beach that runs the length of the harbor from Gull Point in the north to Sandy Point in the south. The only thing that lies between the campsites and the water is a barrier of some low, sandy, easily crossed hillocks. So access to the beach is quite easy. If you don't mind the somewhat cool temperatures of Lake Michigan water, it is a marvelous area for a dip after a hot sunny day of island hiking.

If the weather is cooperating, the beach also is a marvelous place to stroll and walk off any gluttonous overstuffing of supper. The solitude of the slowly darkening evening sky is often enhanced by the light rhythm of wavelets, making their tinkling musical sound as they flatten out on the beach. Such components can make an evening shore walk one of the best tranquilizers that nature can bestow upon us. One can muse upon the bygone scene of a hundred years ago, when as many as 100 ships could have been seen riding at anchor in this harbor. Imagine the population of woodcutters, merchants, farmers and sailors that once

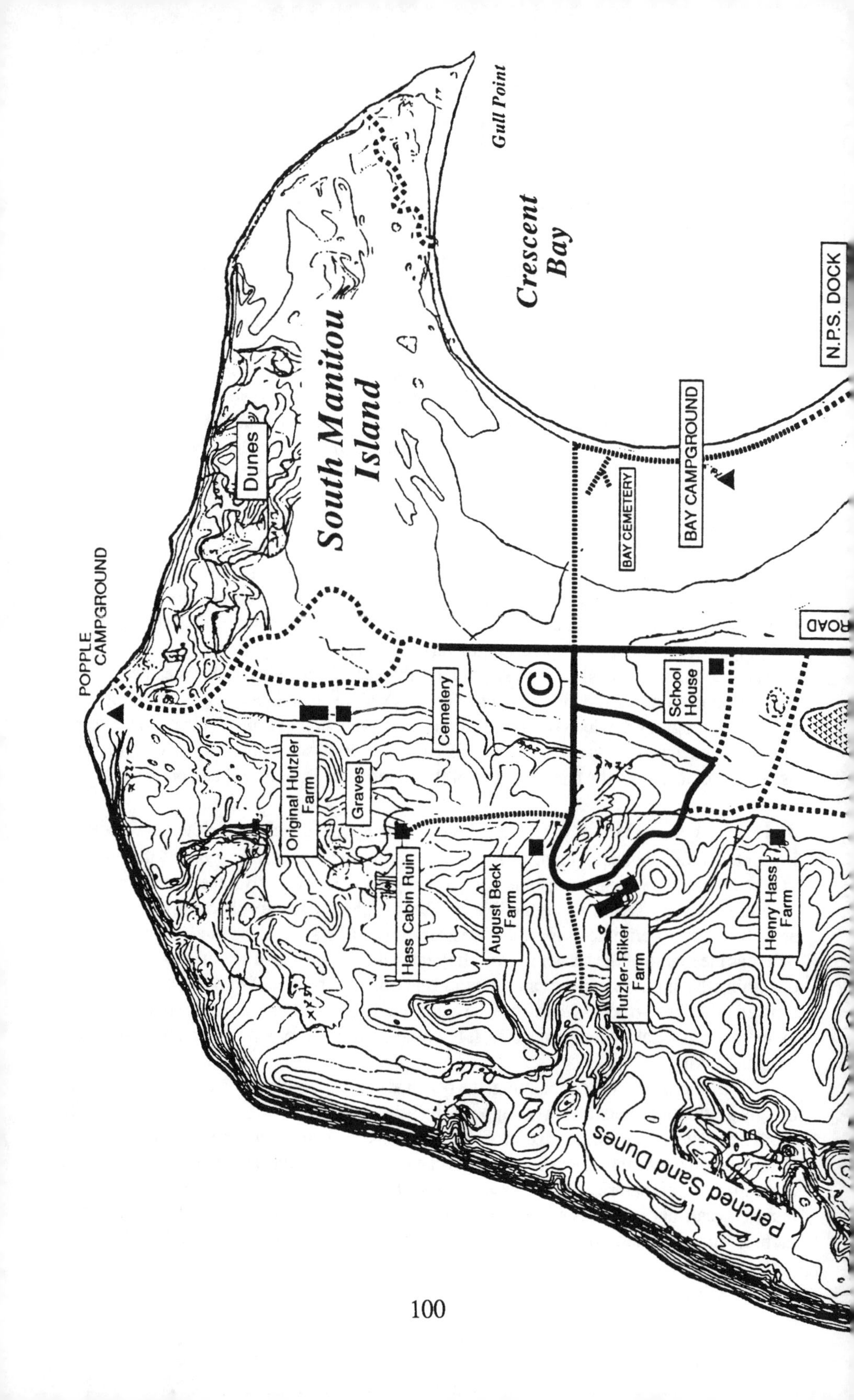
Gull Point
Crescent Bay
South Manitou Island
Dunes
POPPLE CAMPGROUND
N.P.S. DOCK
BAY CAMPGROUND
BAY CEMETERY
ROAD
School House
Cemetery
Original Hutzler Farm
Graves
Hass Cabin Ruin
August Beck Farm
Hutzler-Riker Farm
Henry Hass Farm
Perched Sand Dunes

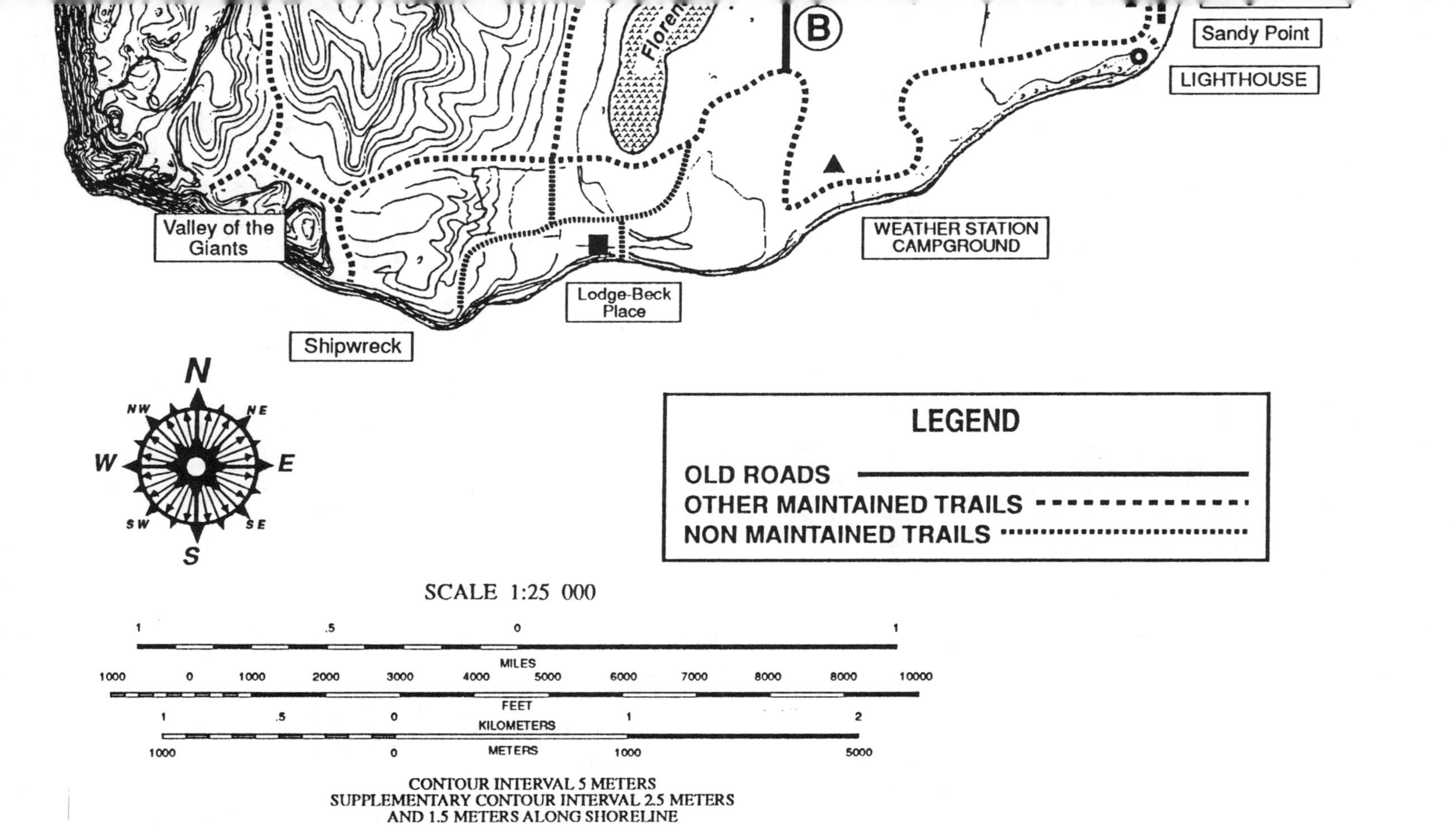

B
Sandy Point
LIGHTHOUSE
Valley of the Giants
WEATHER STATION CAMPGROUND
Lodge-Beck Place
Shipwreck
N
NW
NE
W
E
SW
SE
S
LEGEND
OLD ROADS
OTHER MAINTAINED TRAILS
NON MAINTAINED TRAILS
SCALE 1:25 000
1 .5 0 1
MILES
1000 0 1000 2000 3000 4000 5000 6000 7000 8000 8000 10000
FEET
1 .5 0 1 2
KILOMETERS
1000 0 1000 5000
METERS
CONTOUR INTERVAL 5 METERS
SUPPLEMENTARY CONTOUR INTERVAL 2.5 METERS
AND 1.5 METERS ALONG SHORELINE
SOUTH MANITOU ISLAND

could be found gathered in or near the small hamlet that stood just north of the campground. Or look south to the shadow of the lighthouse, and imagine its darkened cupola again flashing its light, warning phantom ships, buried in the evening mist, of the dangers of the Manitou passage, as it did for almost a hundred years. There is also a fire ring along the beach, making it the one legal place on the island where you can have a bonfire and cook out close to the water's edge.

The camp is found on the periphery of the forest in a partially open area with moderate wind protection furnished by the thin fringe of the forest. Although any part of the island is within reasonable walking distance from the Bay Campground, round trip day walks to the northern part of the island are shorter here, while the hikes to the giant cedars and the high perched dunes in the southwest corner make for a more demanding day. Being much closer to the dock and the ranger station might expose you to more human activity than you usually find at either the Weather Station or Popple Campgrounds. But remember, it is a lot closer to the ferry dock, which gives you the shorter walk on departure day.

FINDING THE BAY CAMPGROUND

It takes about 10 minutes to get to the edge of the campground from the boathouse contact station. When you leave the rear of that building you will see a sign that says:

LIGHTHOUSE
VISITOR CENTER
<—— WEATHER STATION
CAMPGROUND TRAIL

BAY CAMPGROUND ——>

The road in front of you is part of a circle at the end of Burdick Road. Follow the curve to the right, and in a few feet you will hit the point where the circle connects at the end of Burdick Road. Turn right on Burdick Road. About 75 feet beyond this point, there is another road that goes diagonally to the right, with a sign paralleling it facing you which says;

Bay Campground
——————>

Turn right and follow this road, which parallels the bay and takes you to the campground. About five minutes from the Life Saving Complex you will pass a water spigot on the left which has a sign saying: **Drinking Water Only. No Washing.** This is the closest water supply to the camp so you might want to fill water bottles before proceeding. Just beyond this, there is a sign on the left, facing you which says, **Bay Campground 0.4 mi ^.** After a brief walk beyond the spigot you will see a post ahead of you which has a plan of the campground showing the location of the individual numbered sites and the six fire pits. Although a trail proceeds straight ahead here, the better way to find the campsites is to take the trail that goes diagonally to the left into loose sand. Follow it for about 20 feet, then take the trail that goes diagonally off to the left of this trail at that point and follow it into the trees. There you will

Campsite in Bay Campground

pick up the trail that has the site numbers along its side. To the left, there is a small sign which says **Camp Limit**. Turning right on this trail you will see that the site numbers to the left are in the woods and offer more seclusion and protection from the wind. The ones to the right are in view of the bay but are more open and sandy. The trail runs roughly in a straight line through the entire campground, except for a right-left jog after sites 16 and 17. Beyond the camp, the trail continues on to Chicago (Old Dock) Road.

WEATHER STATION CAMPGROUND. This campground does have several distinct differences from the Bay Camp, that may be to your liking. If your overnight equipment load is not excessive, the 1 1/4 mile walk is not difficult. Found in a deep forest at the top of an escarpment overlooking the lake, this camping area often gives one the feeling of being in splendid isolation, miles from other human activity. Most of the sites are buried so deep in heavy forest cover that the camper will often be unaware there is another campsite less than 30 feet away. Unfortunately, a fierce summer storm in July of 1987 wreaked havoc with much of the heavy forest growth, so it is not quite as dense as it used to be. You have two distinct types of sites divided by the path that runs the length of the camp. Those to the north tend to be more isolated, away from the water in a deep woodland setting. To the south are the sites that sit close to or on the edge of the escarpment overlooking the lake, about 50 feet or so above the water. Most of these sites furnish marvelous views of the Manitou Passage and the Sleeping Bear cliffs some seven miles away.

There is one site at the western end of the camp bordering an old farm field which has made a lasting impression on my memory. Its location on top of the escarpment in a partially shaded grassy area gives it an unrestricted view of the mainland expanse of the

"Isle of View Hilton" at Weather Station Campground

Sleeping Bear cliffs and the southern end of the Manitou Passage. I remember sitting there one warm summer afternoon enjoying the company of hiking companions whom I had met on the island, watching the slow progress of a large lake freighter navigating its way through the Manitou Passage, outlined against the mainland's 450-foot Sleeping Bear cliffs. Nowhere on the nearby mainland is there any commercial lodging at any price that gives one such an impressive panorama of sea, sand, sky and an occasional large passing ship. I thought about the name of the Anderson's family farm called "Isle of View" once found on the island at **Point C.** It made me think that here one has an outside view room with an equivalent mainland rate of $150 a night. So I think of this campground as the "Isle of View Hilton." Maybe no showers or T.V., but if you can carry your own portable room to this spot the price is sure right, because this lodging with the million dollar view is free. If you happen to be there during the dark hours, you may also have the pleasure of watching one of the behemoth ships slowly negotiating the Manitou Passage, lighted up like a horizontal Christmas tree.

The Weather Station Campground is an excellent starting point for hikes to the Shipwreck View, the Giant Cedars, perched dunes and the top of the high sand escarpment on the western shore. Lake Florence and the locations of some of the old farms are also within reasonable walking distance from this starting point. The cemetery and the north shore call for walks of longer but not unreasonable lengths. If you plan to spend the last night of your island stay at this camp be sure you allow plenty of time to get to the N.P.S. Dock. It usually takes longer to break camp than expected, so remembering that the ferry does not wait for tardy hikers may save you the unpleasantness of trotting a backpack-laden, huff-and-puff mile to the boathouse, with the real possibility of finding the ferry already a half mile out to sea.

FINDING THE WEATHER STATION CAMPGROUND

There are two ways to get to this destination, and they each consume about the same amount of walking time. The preferred and most used one follows a pleasant woodland path, and gives you your first close look at the lighthouse. The second is mostly a road hike, which is scenically less interesting . If you arrive after a period of heavy rains, you may find the lighthouse section of the first path is under water, necessitating the use of the road. The other drawback to the first trail is a minor one. There are a few brief stretches of open sand where a backpack-carrying hiker may sink in a bit, slowing down the walk and making those with unconditioned legs groan a little. Most hikers will find that it takes a little over a half hour to get to the campground on either trail. Slightly over a mile in length, the woodland path is slower walking than the road, which is a half mile longer. To find the woodland path look for the road curving directly in front of you as you leave the contact station at the boathouse. There you will see a sign that says:

LIGHTHOUSE
VISITOR CENTER
<—— WEATHER STATION
CAMPGROUND TRAIL

BAY CAMPGROUND ——>

Turn left and follow the road passing the new white cinder block toilet facility building on your left. Once you are beyond this building follow the short street that continues straight ahead, which takes you past the Visitor's Center on your right.

This building, which once served as the island's general store, contains the island museum. A few pieces of ancient farm machinery are displayed on its front lawn. There is a boardwalk going past the Visitor's Center in the direction of the Lighthouse that can be used during wet periods, saving the walker much sloshing around. It also helps crossing some open sand, making the walking easier. Make sure you stay on the boardwalk in this open sand area, for it slows down erosion made by the feet of many hikers. If this boardwalk is afloat, a better way to get to the camp is to follow the road route to the campground (see below). When the Lighthouse comes into view, look for a trail that leaves the boardwalk diagonally on the right and soon goes into the trees. There is a sign there which says:

Weather Station
Campground 1.1 mi —>

You step off the boardwalk into the soft sand but the trail gets firmer once you reach the trees. You will encounter a couple of other small stretches of open sand later, but they are brief. In about 10 minutes you will pass a small cabin on your right which is still privately owned. The last time I passed it there was a child's rope swing near the trail that used a tire from a very ancient automobile. Although there are several small pathways that go off to the left, you will eventually arrive at a more prominent one going in that direction at a 90 degree angle. A sign facing you on the left reads:

<—— Weather Station Campgound
↑ Dunes
Cedars
Shipwreck

A left turn here is the quickest way to the campground, but the straight-ahead trail will also get you there by a longer route. Not long after you have made this left turn, you will pass a field on the right which is rapidly being reclaimed by trees. This was once the farm of Putnam Burdick, the first permanent settler on the island, whose family would have close ties to the island for four generations. It still has a few old fruit trees about, indicating its past agricultural use. Toward the end of the nineteenth century, it was purchased by The Garden City Sand Company of Chicago. They planned to develop this area as a real estate investment, selling lots for summer homes. A map made in 1900 shows a series of streets, running north and south and east and west, that were proposed for this location. The plans were not carried out, and the streets were never built.

As the trail swings right around the end of this open area, there is a narrow trail going off to the left, which goes to the escarpment and the lake, but resist taking it, for it does not go to the campground. You will come to a sign on the right showing the location of the group campground and near it, also on the right, is a framed wooden plaque that holds a map of the campground, giving the number and location of the individual campsites. The eastern perimeter of the camp begins at the tree line, and you will see campsite numbers along the trail next to the narrow paths that lead to them. The ones to the left are near the escarpment, which gives the camper easy access to an excellent lakeside view. If you wish to find the drinking water and the toilet facilities, follow the trail through the camp until it reaches a grassy area. There you will find the last of three fire rings found in this campground, complete with wooden benches. Walk toward the open field directly behind this spot, and you will find a road that borders its eastern side. Follow it north, away from the lake, and in just a few feet you will see a solar powered battery operated water pump. Look diagonally to the right and you will see the outhouse which also uses solar power in an effort to reduce the usual stench of such a facility.

If you wish to take the roadside trail to the Weather Station Camp, turn right instead of left when you leave the boathouse. Follow the curving road behind the contact station the short distance to Burdick Road. Turn right on Burdick Road and follow it one mile to the junction with Ohio Road. Turn left there and follow Ohio Road south a short distance until the road forks, the right fork curving into another road going west. This is **Point B.** Follow the left fork of the road, which curves left and becomes less distinct, but is still easily followed. Soon after, there is a division in the trail, but resist taking the path to the left and continue straight ahead. The road begins to border an open field to the right, where the outhouse and water pump for the campground soon become visible on the left. Once beyond them, there is a grassy area to the left which has a large fire ring and a plaque containing a map of the camp, and the numbered locations of the individual campsites. The campground's main trail goes east from this grassy area, and from it begin the smaller pathways identified by their numbers that lead to the individual campsites. The campsites to the right often have the added bonus of a fine panoramic view of the Manitou Passage.

POPPLE CAMPGROUND. This Camping area was closed for overnight stays on my first two visits to the island. After becoming familiar with this location I felt its locale offered hikers some valuable alternatives to the other campgrounds. I was, therefore, delighted to find that this alternatives are again available to island visitors. To some these alternatives will appear to be drawbacks; to others they will be classified as advantages. The first of these is distance. The three and one half miles to Popple is over twice the distance needed to reach Weather Station, and about four times the distance to Bay Campground. There are also some up and down sections beginning about a half mile from the campsite, which make it a testier walk than the level trail hikes to either of the other two campgrounds. For those unaccustomed to carrying backpacking equipment for long stretches, or for others whose camping gear is more of the car camping type and far outweighs the specialized lightweight backpack variety, getting to Popple can be quite a struggle. Experienced and conditioned backpackers with proper gear will find the walk to Popple not much more than a delightful stroll.

Drinking water can also be a hassle. Although the other two campgrounds have a reliable supply of drinking water nearby the closest water pump to Popple is a half mile away and is often disconnected because the water does not meet government purity standards. The next closest source is the schoolhouse pump, about a mile and a half from the campground. It, too, is occasionally shut off because of impurities, but not as frequently as the closer pump. Since Popple is located close to the Lake Michigan shore, the big lake may be the only water source closer than the Bay campground. Lake water should always be treated, either by boiling, chemical treatment or filtering. Even with this precaution, it is not wise to use the lake as a long term drinking water source, for the lake is now polluted by miniscule amounts of mercury.

The camp is nicely situated on a partially open section of hillside which slopes towards the north shoreline. At the bottom of the hill there is about a 10-foot sand escarpment, where you can easily drop down to the nice sandy beach along the lakeshore, offering a view of North Manitou some three miles across the water. Unfortunately, this lightly forested spot also has a fair amount of Poison Ivy. Another drawback for some visitors is that it is further away from many of the more frequented trails on the island. This calls for longer walks to get to many interesting island locations. Then what is the big advantage of this camping area? It can be said in one word. Seclusion. Not only does it attract far fewer campers, but those who come are often the more serious type of hikers. They already have a fair amount of trekking under their belts, and prefer human company only in small numbers. It also offers easy access to the lovely beach along the north shore, and nice views of the southern end of North Manitou.

Finding Popple Campground.

There are two ways to get to Popple from the old Coast Guard Station. The quickest way is to follow the curving road to the right, that is immediately behind the boathouse, to Burdick Road, where you turn right and walk one mile to its junction with Ohio Road. Turn right, following Ohio Road past the Schoolhouse, until its junction with Chicago Road at **Point C.** Then continue with the trail description called, "Hike to the Cemetery, the original Hutzler Farm and the North Shore at Popple Campground from **Point C** beginning on Page **117**. The other route follows the Bay Campground Trail through the camp until its junction with Chicago Road. Turn left there, and walk **to Point C.**

The Trail system

Since there are so many ways to reach the different places of interest on the island, directions to those locales from the boathouse (**Point A**) and the two campgrounds could become endless and confusing. One of the major headaches this author faced was how to avoid endless redundancy in getting to and from the various campgrounds and points of interests that the island offers. With no simple solution to this problem, I've tried to organize the walks in the least confusing manner, but I am sure many readers will occasionally find the text difficult to follow. To partly eliminate this problem, hikes will be described from two major road junctions; the first is just south of the intersection of Burdick and Ohio Roads, which I call **Point B.** The other, named **Point C,** is found at the junction of Ohio and Chicago (Old Dock) Roads. These points are my way of identifying the two most important island junctions on my map. It should be noted that they are not used by the Park Service and the signs at those locations will not contain a point identification. Directions to these points from **Point A** (Boathouse Contact Station), are given below. The directions also include various points of historical and natural interest that occur along these walks, so prospective hikers can read them to see if those walks will appeal to them for trailside interest as well as access to the two points.

Finding Point B from the Boathouse Contact Station (Point A)

As you step out of the back of the boathouse you will see a sign across the road facing you which says:

LIGHTHOUSE
VISITOR CENTER
<—— WEATHER STATION
CAMPGROUND TRAIL

BAY CAMPGROUND ——>

Make a right turn on the road that circles immediately behind the boathouse and follow it the short distance to Burdick Road. You will see small frame houses which are part of a village that developed during the early part of this century. They were used mostly by families connected to the Coast Guard operations. This little village became the center of island activity after the area around the old dock was abandoned. Some of these properties remain in private hands, and are used as summer homes. Of the buildings now owned by the government, a few are being maintained for various Park Service purposes while others are slated to be torn down. Turn right on Burdick Road, and go directly west. Burdick Road is named after the first lifetime family to settle on the island. They remained a prominent island family for three generations. One of its members, James Burdick, held the position of lighthouse keeper for 28 years. His son, Fred, was the last island entrepreneur (See history section).

Fred told me an interesting story that happened along this road that bears his family name. There once was a homemade sign on the right side of the road which announced that this was the site of the "Battle of the Lunch Pails." The school age children of the village walked this road each weekday on their way to the schoolhouse, carrying their metal lunch pails. The pails were not cheap, so the boys and girls were reminded by their parents to take good care of them. A lad, who was somewhat smaller than other boys his age was often intimidated and bullied by them. One day, their teasing made him reach his boiling point, and he took a wild swing with his lunch pail at the nearest offender and scored a hit. When that offender retaliated with his bucket there broke out a melee of swinging lunch buckets, banging and clanging into one another. By the end of this free-for-all, the boys' lunch pails were badly dented. When they sheepishly returned home after school, they received serious parental reprimands, since most of the pails had to be replaced. The new buckets had to come from the mainland at a price which their cash-starved parents could ill afford.

Burdick Road moves in a straight line for a distance of one mile to the junction with Ohio Road. At that junction a sign facing you says:

School house 0.5 mi —>
Farms 1.7 mi —>
Popple Campground 1.7 mi —>

A sign to your left says:

↑ **Camping 0.6 mi**
Shipwreck 1.9 mi
Cedars 2.1 mi
Dunes 2.3 mi

Turn left, and in another quarter mile the road splits with curving forks branching to the right and left. Notice that the right fork curves into a strong east-west road which joins the fork to the left forming a triangle. this is **Point B.** A sign on the right behind the triangle facing you says:

<— Camping
Shipwreck —>
Cedars ———>
Dunes ———>

For hikes from **Point B** see pg.—.

Finding Point C from the Boathouse Contact Station (Point A)

There are two different ways to get to **Point C.** Both have points of historical and sightseeing interest along the way. A loop walk can be accomplished by going out on one and returning by the other. Read the descriptions of each to see which one appeals to you the most. They're both about the same length, but the first one, following Burdick and Ohio

Restored schoolhouse on South Manitou

Road, is a tad faster.

The Inland Route to Point C and descriptions of points of interest along Ohio Road. From the boathouse follow the directions to **Point B** (above), as far as the junction of Burdick and Ohio Roads. Turn right on Ohio Road, but before you make the right hand turn look straight ahead. Although it is less prominent, beyond this junction, Burdick Road continues straight ahead. In a short walk of a quarter mile it leads to one of the last commercial ventures linked to the island's summer tourist trade. There Fred Burdick built three summer cabins for rental purposes. Once equipped with most of the pleasantries of modern living, they are found near the eastern shore of Lake Florence. They were quite popular, and used widely by vacationers right up to the government buyout. Fred told me they were sometimes rented years in advance. Although still standing in 1990, they are slated to be torn down.

If the cabins and a nearby storage building maintained by the Park Service, hold little interest for most visitors, the road does end close to a particularly attractive wooded area along the eastern shore of Lake Florence. From the cabins, one has easy access to the water's edge, where there is a narrow sandy beach. Since the waters of Lake Florence are several degrees warmer than Lake Michigan, I have found this location a handy place for a quick swim, to help remove the grime and sweat of the trail. Its shallow offshore waters are quite pleasant, and since the location is isolated, one will usually share its pleasantries only with his or her immediate hiking companions. Taking a soapy bath here is discouraged, because the lake has no outlet, and the use of soap or shampoo will pollute the waters. In past summers, island mothers sometimes used the lake as a bathtub for small children. It was hard work to draw bathwater from a well, which usually came up at a chilly temperature. It was far easier for a farm mother to herd her offspring to this shore than to heat the water and fill the family washtub for the weekly soap-down.

To continue your walk to **Point C,** turn right on Ohio Road at the Burdick Road junction. Walking northward on Ohio Road, in about eight to ten minutes you will come to a junction with a trail to the left. A sign there paralleling the left side of the road says:

Florence Lake ↑

In less than five minutes, this side trail will take you to the north end of the lake. The trail then follows elevated ground between the lake on the south and a swamp to the north. If you follow the trail for another three or four minutes, past the lake it junctions with the West Side Farm Trail.

When you continue northward on Ohio Road, it will only take you about three minutes to go from this Ohio Road-Florence Lake Trail junction to the schoolhouse. At the schoolhouse, You will pass another trail to the left, which also ends at the West Side Farm Trail. Although formal elementary education was established on the island in 1882, there was no building on the island exclusively used for elementary education until the present structure was built in 1899 or 1890. This schoolhouse remained in continual operation until 1944. In typical rural fashion of the day, all eight elementary grades were taught in this one room schoolhouse by a single teacher. Its most active years were during the first third of this century, and one of its former students became known for his outstanding achievements later in life. Willard Smith, rose to become Commandant of the Coast Guard. The admiral's life is another wonderful example of people who began their education in such isolated rural one room schoolhouses and later rose to prominence (See other Points of Interest Near the N.P.S. Dock). His classmate, Charles M. Anderson, who for many years successfully operated fishing boats from Frankfort, Michigan, is remembered for writing about his happy boyhood on the island in his book, Isle of View.

After 1944, the school population decreased so much that the remaining teacher, Lottie Tobin, taught classes from her home until the closing of the Coast Guard Station in 1958. Public education was then stopped altogether. In the years prior to the government purchase of this property, the island's last farmer used the building to store hay. Restored by the Park Service, the schoolhouse also has a useable comfort station nearby. There is a water pump in front of the building which old timers claim has the sweetest water on the island.

About a half mile beyond the schoolhouse, the forest on the left side of Ohio Road gives way to open fields. Just beyond, when you hit the junction of the prominent Chicago Road, you are at **Point C**. Just before you reach this junction on your left you pass the few skeletal remains of one of the last sawmills on the island. It is briefly discussed in the description of **Point C** below.

The Bay Route to Point C and description of points of interest along Crescent Harbor and Chicago Road. From the boathouse, follow the directions to the Bay Campground. When you reach the post that contains the map of the numbered campsites you have three different ways to proceed. You may take the diagonal trail to the left which leads you to the numbered campground trail. It is the quickest way to get to the Old Dock Road, because it has less open sand areas to traverse, but it is the least scenic. Your second option is to proceed straight ahead from the campground sign, following the obscure remains of a road that once ran between the commercial dock at the original settlement of the island and the lifesaving complex. It goes roughly in a straight line to Chicago (Old Dock) Road, traversing many small sandy hillocks with nice views of Crescent Harbor along the way. But, it is slower going because of the soft sand. The third option is to follow the shoreline beach of the bay itself. As you get close to the former site of the old

Back of old Burdick store in 1987

dock, there is a side trip you should consider.

If you follow the campground trail, once past site #25 and the last group campground, you will notice as the trees begin retreating on the left, there is a smaller trail going off diagonally to the left. It leads to the ruins of the store and post office that operated in the old village complex around Burton's dock. Up until 1989, the front and rear walls of the building were still standing, but now they are on the ground. The store was operated by the Burdick family, but in the 1920s, with the demise of the old dock and the village, they moved their operation to a building in the Coast Guard village which serves as the island museum today. Although the ruins of this first Burdick store front Chicago Road it is partly hidden by a dense growth of trees and underbrush.

This little side trail is also the path you take to the Bay Cemetery. In less than half a minute after you are on the trail leading to the ruins of the Burdick store, there is another faint trail to the left that goes into the trees. This is the path to the Bay Cemetery which you can reach in less that two minutes. Before the creation of the modern cemetery near **Point**

C, this was the main burial place on the island. the island farmers did not use this burial site, but interred their deceased members in family plots near their homes. Those who worked in the village and died there, as well as sailors who succumbed on passing ships or bodies that washed up on shore, were buried in the Bay Cemetery. Once there were many visible graves, but since most were poor itinerant woodcutters and sailors no permanent stones marked their burial sites. The wooden markings have disappeared, for most interments here took place over a hundred years ago. When you approach this burial ground today you will find four picket fences surrounding burial plots. Two of them still have their interesting nineteenth

Back of old Burdick store in 1990

century gravestones in place.

There is an old nineteenth century legend about the Bay Cemetery that says sailors fatally ill with highly infectious Typhoid or Cholera were sometimes taken ashore to die before the disease could spread among other crew members. Often they did not wait until the victims were completely dead before sealing them in hastily constructed coffins and lowering them below the surface of the earth. The doomed men could be heard audibly moaning and protesting by beating against the wooden sides of their coffins. Some say that on misty nights the ghosts of these doomed seamen can still be heard faintly moaning and beating against the sides of their wooden prisons.

If you return to the path you followed through the Bay Campground, you will soon hit a very distinct one-lane road running in an east-west direction. It begins at the water's edge of Crescent Bay and runs westward, more than halfway across the island. Since it once proceeded directly away from what was the island's principal commercial dock, it is often called the Old Dock Road. But it is also known as Chicago Road, named by the Garden City

Gravesite in the Bay Cemetery

Gravestone in the Bay Cemetery

Gravel Company when they began promoting the island as a summer resort. Except for the road itself, and a few pilings of the old dock in the shallow water near the shore, there is nothing in the immediate vicinity to suggest that it is the location of a ghost town that existed here from the mid nineteenth century until the early 1920s. The pier, which was the principle docking facility for the island, was built by William Burton about 1840. It was the island's most important commercial dock until the first quarter of this century. The woodburning steamships tied up to this dock to refuel. Many sailing ships also dropped anchor in the harbor to victual and there were times in the last century that one could look out from this shore and see 50 to 100 vessels lying at anchor in Crescent Bay.

Although the surroundings have returned to sandy hillocks, this was once the

South Manitou's Old dock circa 1900
Courtesyof S.B.D. National Lakeshore

Old Dock today. Former Coast Guard station is in the distance across the bay

center of the island community, and Chicago Road was the island's primary route moving west from the shoreline. The small village included a store, blacksmith's shop and lumber mill. The last island sawmill in the village was located just north of the road. It employed over 50 workmen, and operated here during the first two decades of this century.

Along Chicago (Old Dock) Road

Turn left, and follow this delightful straight-line one-lane road for a little over a half mile to **Point C**. Although the path is the epitome of quiet solitude today, for better than 70 years it served as the main thoroughfare to the island's interior, acting as a lifeline between the island farms and the sea. Admiral Willard Smith remembered in an interview, that when he was a boy how Captain Anderson would pay a visit to his home between lake voyages. The captain, who was the father of Charles Anderson, often tied up his little steamboat the "J.S. Crouse," at the old dock. He then walked along the Old Dock Road the half mile to his "Isle of View" farm near **Point C,** where his family awaited his return. It was also over this road that most of the harvested timber was hauled, either for the hungry furnaces of the woodburning steamers or for the lumber trade.

The dense forest growth of small trees and underbrush lining each side of the road soon gives way to old farm fields, rapidly being reclaimed by nature. The large field to the right, once owned by the Hutzler family, is being taken over by juniper bushes. As you drop down a low rise you will be able to see the road junction at **Point C,** and a large forested ridge lying to the west beyond the fields that runs in a general north south direction. When you reach the junction with the very prominent Ohio Road, you have arrived at **Point C.**

Hikes from Point C.

Arrival at Point C. At the northwest corner of Ohio and Chicago Road there is a large former agricultural field where a Park Service display tells of George C. Hutzler's success in raising seed for Rosen Rye. This is probably not the field he used for that purpose, for his farm lies further to the west (see history section). You will also notice two piles of small fieldstones. They were once part of an entrance way to the Isle of View Farm, the boyhood home of Charles Anderson, who tells about his island life in his book named after this farm.

Near the southwest corner of this junction, you can see the cement foundation and a few remnants of the last island lumber mill. Cutting mostly hardwoods, it operated here during the first two decades of this century.

When visiting his family, Captian Anderson'often tied up his ship the S.S. Crouse at the Old Dock
Courtesy S.B.D. National Lakeshore

Hike to the Cemetery, the First Hutzler Farm and Popple Campground on the North Shore from Point C.

Distance: To cemetery 0.4 mi., to Johnny Hutzler house 0.9 mi., to Popple Campground on the north shore 1.7 mi.

Walking time: To Cemetery 7 to 10 minutes, to John Hutzler House 15 to 20 minutes, to Popple Campground 40 minutes to one hour.

GENERAL REMARKS. This is a level easy hike to the cemetery and the Hutzler house. If you continue on to Popple Campground you will find a few short up and down sections easily traversed by any conditioned hiker. The cemetery contains many graves of the leading pioneer families who died in the twentieth century. The Johnny Hutzler house is on the site of the original George Johann Hutzler farm, and the grave of his father is nearby. There is a lovely small barn there which dates from the days of the original homestead. From the north shore, one gets a beautiful view of the southern end of North Manitou Island some four miles away, including that island's largest blowout, known as Old Baldy. You can also make a loop trip out of this walk by returning to the bay area by walking east along this north shore, then picking up the Gull Point Trail which will take you back to the Crescent Bay shoreline. The one stumbling block to this return is finding the trailhead of the Gull Point Trail, for at this writing there is no sign and it is easy to miss it and walk into the restricted nesting site zone.

TRAIL DESCRIPTION. Heading straight north on Ohio Road from **Point C** the level road is easy to follow to the cemetery since it is included in the motorized island tour. Still surrounded by open fields and out of sight of open water this cemetery fits in well with the serenity of the island's interior. Those familiar with island history will see many familiar family names and stories about them could fill a whole book. For brevity's sake, I will include only a few.

When walking through the gate, the row of graves immediately to the left are those of the descendants of the first German immigrant settler on the island, George Johann Hutzler. The history of this family is beautifully told in Myron Vent's book "South Manitou Island." The farthest grave on the far left of the front Hutzler row is that of John Hutzler, the second youngest son of George Johann, and the last of this branch of the Hutzler family to actively farm on the island. His house, which you may pass on the way to Popple Campground, is just a few minutes walk from here. Immediately to the right are the graves of the Burdick family who were the first to settle on the island. The second grave in from the cemetery's center path is that of Private Andrew Burdick. He was the brother of James Burdick, who served as the keeper of the Manitou Light for 27 years. When I first saw that his death date was 1918, the last year of World War One, I wondered if he had possibly been killed in the trenches in France or by the terrible flu epidemic of that year. I later found out that he had not gone to France but was with a contingent of American servicemen sent to Russia to support the White Russians during the Russian Revolution. He died of pneumonia in the north Russian port city of Archangel. One night, his mother and sisters thought they heard the schoolbell ringing, but could not find a reason why, or by whom it was sounded. The following day, they received the telegram informing them of his death the previous day. His nephew, Fred, who is the son of James Burdick the long-time lighthouse keeper, was active in promoting the island as a summer vacation area right up to the time that it became part of the National Lakeshore. Fred also plans to be buried in the cemetery, for his large double gravestone is already in place further down the lane on the left, where his first wife now rests.

The second row of graves on the left side bear the name Haas and the third row on the right side of the path holds the Becks. They were of two of the important German immigrant farming families on the island. You will pass the original sites of their farms if you take the walk that heads west from **Point C.**

Directly behind the Becks are three graves of a family named Furst. Oswald Furst was a retired bookbinder, who came to the island from Chicago with his wife and children sometime around the turn of the century. Their daughter died when she was in her 20s, and is thought to be the first person buried in this cemetery. Her parents lived to advanced ages, the old bookbinder living into his ninetieth year. As a young man growing up in Germany, he trained for the priesthood, but decided that the religious life was not for him, so he learned the bookbinding trade. Because of his theological background, he was often called upon to perform funeral services on the island. His son, Martin, entered the lifesaving service and served briefly as the keeper of the South Manitou Station. Unfortunately, he died of a burst

Bertha Peth. Photo taken about the time of her marrige to John Hutzler

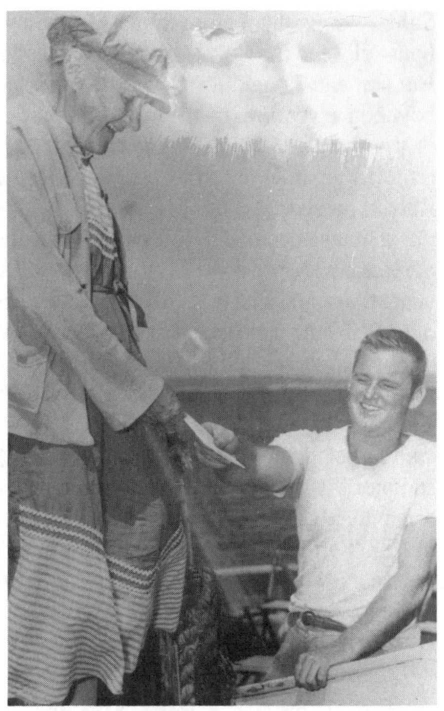

A youthful George Grovesnor delivering mail to Bertha Peth in 1946

appendix when was still a young man, but he lived long enough to marry and have three children. They spent their early years on North Manitou Island where their stepfather, Ernest Hutzler was lighthouse keeper. Oswald Furst's grandson, Glenn recently retired from the Coast Guard after a long and fruitful career.

To the left of the Beck row lies the only member of the other branch of the Hutzler family to be buried in this cemetery. Josie Hutzler was the wife of George C. Hutzler and mother of Louis. This father and son team brought a sizeable amount of agricultural glory to the island with their prizewinning seed crops of Rosen Rye and Michelite beans. The ribbons they won are now on display in the island museum. You will pass their former farmhouse and barns on the walk going west of **Point C.**

This home of the George C. Hutzler family is linked to another grave found on the right side of the path, two rows behind the Becks. It was the boyhood home of Ronald Riker, the youngest son of the last active farmer on the island. Ronald drowned while swimming at the wreck of the ship Francisco Morazon which lies on a shoal south of the island (See Shipwreck on Hikes from **Point B.**)

Immediately to the right of Ronald's grave there is another recent one that aroused my attention when I first saw it, but the name Wayne Shirk meant nothing to me then. Quite by accident, I later met the young man's mother on Beaver Island, where she now lives. Doris

Shirk told me that before South Manitou was taken over by the Park Service she owned a house close to the Coast Guard station and had lived in it during the season for many years. Her son and Ronald Riker, who was six years older, were good friends and shared many boyhood adventures on the island. He and the young Riker often swam out to the shipwreck in warm weather, and Wayne had joined Ronald on the day he lost his life. Wayne had returned to shore ahead of his friend, as he had often done, and was totally unaware that Ronald had become trapped in the bowels of the derelict ship. Wayne loved the island so much that he decided to follow a course of study that could lead to a position with the Park Service, and hoped someday to return to the island as one of its rangers. While pursuing those educational goals he was killed in an auto accident. The two young friends now lie near each other in death on the island that they once had enjoyed so much in their brief adolescent lives.

Another odd and heart-rendering story is connected with the grave of Bertha Peth, found at the right rear of the cemetery behind the graves of the two young men. In 1898, Bertha, a 25 year old German immigrant, arrived from Chicago. She had been hired by a visiting relative of the Hutzler family to look after the lady's young children during a long summer visit. She and Johnny Hutzler, who was then a 35 year old bachelor, became romantically involved and married the same year. All seemed to go well with the couple and in 1900 Bertha gave birth to a healthy baby boy they named Stanley. One day when he was two years old, his mother was distracted by some visiting island women. Stanley got through the fence that enclosed the family bull who trampled on and severely injured the small child. Despite a trip to Chicago for better medical care, Stanley died a few weeks later.

On occasion, Bertha acted as though she was demented. Suffering from what doctors diagnosed as acute hysteria, she would disappear into the woods and lie prostrate on the ground for hours. This irrational behavior made it extremely difficult for the gentle but unsophisticated John Hutzler, for although he tried, he was not well equipped to handle this tremendous emotional problem. For some reason, time did not heal the grief of this loss. Charles Anderson tells in his book that almost ten years after the fatal accident, Bertha would come and visit Mrs. Anderson at her home, which once stood in the field directly north and in sight of the cemetery. Both women were extremely lonely. While Bertha had not adjusted to the loss of her son, Mrs. Anderson, a comparatively new arrival on the island, was not attuned to the solitary existence of the island, which differed so much from the city life she was used to. Often, when Captain Anderson was at sea, the two women would sit together in the evenings sharing their mutual loneliness.

In time, Mollie Anderson adjusted to island living, but the death of young Stanley seemed to have placed a wedge between Bertha and John Hutzler, which widened with the years. Island busybodies made the wound fester, suggesting to John that the accident happened because Bertha had been derelict in her duties toward her son. Some male wags even suggested that Bertha had an affair with a visiting sailor. The combination of his wife's melancholy behavior and the island gossip eventually led John to seek a divorce. Bertha returned briefly to Chicago, but found her life more in tune with the tempo of the island. She came back to lead a lonely existence on the island for many years. Moving to a small house close to the Coast Guard Station, she led a hand-to-mouth existence, seeking out the roots of the ginseng plant which she sold to a pharmaceutical house. Charles Anderson remembered that she had an uncanny eye for finding the plant, and often did so when others could not locate it at all. She also sold a few sundry items, such as candy and gum. Living alone for many years, Bertha's behavior became eccentric. It was extremely difficult for a single woman with no outside financial support to maintain even a minimal standard of living on the island, but this she successfully did for better than four decades.

Knowing that she had a real struggle to exist, Tracy Grosvenor, who ran the island ferry as his son and grandson still do today, would buy the little metal fishnet floats that Bertha gathered walking along the shore. The island children would also gather up the floats and give them to Bertha, for small payments of sweets. Tracy would then buy them from her and resell them to the fishermen, often at a loss to his own purse. When the fishermen began using other methods, Tracy's private welfare program was costing him more than he could afford. He then asked the children to stop supplying Bertha with the floats because he did not want to tell her they no longer had any redeemable commercial value.

As Bertha struggled to exist, so did her ex-husband, for after the 1920s it became harder and harder to make a living on the island farms. About the time of the divorce, John and Bertha agreed that he should supply her with firewood, while she would bake bread for him, an arrangement they both lived up to for many years. They lived alone for the remainder of their lives. Although they apparently preferred the three island miles that separated them, Bertha made weekly visits to the farm.

Outliving John by 12 years, Bertha became known in her later life as the "Queen of the Island." She probably holds the record for a continued stay on the island, for she once went 22 consecutive years without a visit to the mainland. When she did so, she exclaimed that it really wasn't worth the trip. When she reached an advanced age, an eye infection forced her to seek medical help on the mainland. It was soon apparent that she could no longer take care of herself, and was placed in a nursing home in Benzie County. When she died her request to be buried on the island was granted.

There is a small white cross next to Bertha's grave marked, "Howard-Baby 1914." The child was son of a destitute family that lived briefly on the island. Bertha had remarked how lonely this little grave seemed, so she adopted the site as a surrogate grave for her own infant son, who's burial place was in Chicago.

The separation maintained by Johnny Hutzler and Bertha Peth during most of their many years of life is now perpetuated in death, for John's grave is found near the south east corner of the cemetery while Bertha's is on the opposite northwest side.

A rather macabre grave, indicated with the same kind of small white cross as the marking for the Howard infant, is found on the left side of the cemetery near the front. The marker eerily states," Human skeleton found on dunes. 1933."

Shortly after passing the cemetery, the trail enters the woods and curves to the left. There is a fork in the trail here with the right fork heading into a partially open field, where one can see the roof of the Johnny Hutzler house. The best way to that homestead is to follow the left fork, for the path to the right does not lead to the house. The right fork, which has little scenic or historic interest, is easily included in a loop trip on the way back from the north beach of the island.

By following the left fork, you will soon find a small path going off to the left heading into a thick forest. There was a sign there that said "Cemetery," but it was missing on my last visit. Walking about two minutes on this side trail will take you to the grave of George Johann Hutzler, the first German immigrant to settle on the island. In his later years, he made it known that he wished to be buried in an orchard of fruit trees that he had planted many years before. At his death at the age of 74, he was laid to rest there as he requested. His orchard has long been reclaimed by island forest, and the gravesite was lost. Myron Vent

Johnny Hutzler's house in 1987

remembered seeing his great-grandfather's grave on island visits when he was a young boy before the orchard and the grave were swallowed up. Vent rediscovered it, and the grave is easily seen today surrounded by a wooden fence at the end of this brief walk.

A short distance beyond this side path, the trail enters an open area which is the site of the original Hutzler homestead. George Johann Hutzler moved his wife and three children into a log cabin at this location in 1856. Five more children would be born here in the next 12 years. A magnificent barn that was held together entirely by wooden pegs and was a classic of its type, was raised in 1865. This masterpiece of the barn builder's art remained in perfect condition until the 1930s when it was struck by lightning and burned to the ground. There is, however, a beautiful smaller barn here, which is still in good condition. This little barn also built in the nineteenth century, shows the high skill level of the local builders. The original Hutzler home was torn down and replaced in the 1920s by one which is seen today. The building, found near the site of the first home, is known as Johnny Hutzler's house. John, born in the old house in 1865, was the second-youngest son of George and Margaretha Hutzler. Myron Vent related that of all the members of this branch of the Hutzler family, his uncle John most deserved the title of "Islander." Except for a few short trips to Chicago and the nearby mainland, he was born and spent his entire life on the island. Taking over the job of running the family farm from his aging father, he was the last of his family to cultivate it. With the death of his parents and the separation from his wife, Bertha Peth, he continued living on the farm alone. For company, he shared his house with a whole bevy of cats, who ran and hid every time Johnny had a visitor. One of the older felines often would recline in the oven for warmth. One day when preparing to bake some apples, he accidentally baked the cat as well. Although generally quiet and unassuming, he was not a recluse. Well liked by

Small barn built in the nineteenth century by George J. Hutzler

the islanders, he was in demand at social events, for he played the fiddle well and often furnished the music for island dances.

Continuing to work the land into the second quarter of the twentieth century, he found it more and more difficult to earn a living. When he reached his seventies, he began to dread the winters and often thought that if he became ill he would have no one to look after him and that he might die alone. At the site of the original well, located just east of the house and now covered with boards, Johnny Hutzler was found dead in August of 1944.

During the first years of government ownership, the Johnny Hutzler house was refurbished and operated as a youth hostel. It is no longer used for that purpose, and since it is of comparatively recent vintage with no particular historical value it will eventually be torn down. When I first passed this way, the house had recently been painted and looked cozily pleasant. In just a few years, the paint has blackened somewhat. The combination of deteriorating paint and rapid growth of wild shrubbery surrounding the structure has given the house a forlorn and deserted look. It takes on something of the aura of Johnny and Bertha's lives of disappointment and separation, following the demise of their only son, Stanley, who was trampled to death in a nearby field.

From the Hutzler homestead, it should take you less than 20 minutes to reach Popple Campground and the north shore. Heading north beyond the small barn, the trail narrows and becomes more path like through invading juniper bushes, and soon T's into another trail. At that junction you will find the closest water pump to the Popple Campground, which is still about a half mile away. If the pump handle is missing, it means that the water does not meet government purity standards, and has been removed by park personnel. The largest source of this pollution comes from inconsiderate campers, who wash their cooking and eating utensils, and themselves, at the pump, contaminating the water below.

If you make a right turn at the pump, you will find that the trail moves in a sweeping curve to the right, returning you to the junction south of the Hutzler house. You may wish to use this route if you seek a slightly different way to go on your return trip.

To continue to the campground and the north shore, turn left at the well. You will have a gradual climb up a forest-covered dune ridge where the trail turns right. Not far beyond, you begin to descend and soon come to a post with a map locating the seven campground sites. The trail beyond the sign traverses the camp in a big circle, with the bottom part of the circle quite close to the lake. Follow the curve to the left for the quickest way to the shore. You have a rather steep descent through the campground, where the lake is visible through the trees. There is a small sand escarpment about 10 feet high that you descend to get to the beautiful beach along this shoreline. The view from its top gives you a good panoramic look at the southwest shore of North Manitou, a little over four miles away. Its largest blowout known as Old Baldy is quite visible on the southern tip of the island. My first look across this channel immediately produced a strong desire to visit the North Manitou shores, which then was illegal. If you feel the same way you won't have to wait three years to legally do so as I did.

A nice loop walk from this shore, which gives excellent views of North Manitou, is to return to the boat dock area by walking east along this north shore. The problem with this proposed loop hike is getting back to the eastern shore along Crescent Bay without getting into the restricted gull nesting area. There is a maintained trail that cuts through the forest near Gull Point. It takes you to an overlook of the nesting area and on to the bay shoreline, but at this writing it is quite difficult to find the trailhead. The first time I did this loop, I missed the trail and penetrated deep into the nesting area, without meaning to. I have suggested to Park Service personnel that a sign be placed at the trail's northern end like the one existing on the bay side, so it could easily be found by hikers wishing to return to the old Coast Guard complex from this direction. The island ranger I talked to thought that this would be a good idea, for it would make an invasion into the nesting area by unsuspecting hikers far less likely. The sign therefore, may now be a reality.

Hike to the Hass Cabin, Beck Farm, the Hutzler-Riker Farm, the Hass Farm and the West Side Farm Trail from Point C

Distance: to the Beck Farm 0.7 mi., to the Hutzler-Riker Farm 1 mi., to the Hass Farm Florence Lake Trail 1.5 mi., to junction with the Dunes Trail 2.4 mi.

GENERAL REMARKS. This inland hike, taking you within sight of several homesteads of the German settlers, follows well-established farm roads over almost continual level terrain. Although the scenery is never of the spectacular variety, hikers find walking these old farm roads often brings on a reflective and nostalgic mood. Reminding one of an active rural mode of living so prevalent at the turn of the century, it has now passed into history. This can often produce a wave of quiet contemplation, especially if you walk them alone. One can imagine the scene of perhaps 60 years ago when autos of the Model-T vintage chugged along these one lane sand roads, or see a perspiring farmer in a nearby field using farm machinery pulled by a team of horses. Some of these reapers, planters and plows are still on the fields silently rusting away where they once were used. Others have been gathered and placed in front of the last Burdick store which now serves as the island museum. Along with the deteriorating farm buildings, they are reminders of a different less nerve-wracking, albeit a hardworking, lifestyle that seems to elude us today. Most assuredly these homesteading farm families toiled daily for long and difficult hours in their mostly self-sufficient insular community and their history relates that they suffered the usual trials and tragedies that life always brings. But, I feel that this close-knit bucolic community of German immigrants enjoyed a sense of detached security on their island that is lost to most of us in this restless atomic age.

TRAIL DESCRIPTION. As you proceed west on Chicago Road, you will be walking toward a forested ridge, which runs generally north and south. On your left you will soon pass the remains of a large apple orchard, that was planted and operated by a man named Thomas Foster. A former real estate agent from Grand Rapids, he and his family left that city before the turn of the century to try his hand at fruit farming. He soon found that pears were too perishable to withstand the trip to Chicago in the holds of the lake steamers, but several different types of apples held up well and remained a moderately successful crop for him during the first two decades of the century. Mr. Foster also became island postmaster in 1889, and held the job for several years. With the Anderson farm directly across the road on the north, young Charles knew the Fosters. In his book, "Isle of View," he tells the story of how Mrs. Foster could never get her husband to build her a proper kitchen, so she ordered the necessary tools from the Sears catalogue and built it herself. Unfortunately, time has eliminated her handiwork. She must have been a lady of some stamina for during the severe winter of 1917 she made three round trips across the ice to Glen Haven on the mainland, some six miles away.

You will notice a well-used road that goes diagonally to the left from Chicago Road and passes through the Foster's old orchard. It is used for the island motor tour, passing through the middle of the old orchard completing the farm loop back to Chicago Road. A sign that parallels the right side of Chicago Road placed at that junction reads:

Historic Farms
<— Loop Road
2.3 mi-Total

Following this side road part way down takes you into a section of the old orchard where edible apples can still be found in season. The island's airplane landing strip was to the north of Chicago Road, close to and paralleling the treeline below the ridge.

Once Chicago Road passes into the trees, you have an easy climb up the ridge. About ten minutes more walking in the forest will take you to the open fields surrounding the August Beck farm. Just before the road passes out of the forest, there is another faint road on the right hand side heading north. Although not maintained, the first part of it is easy to follow. Today the small ruin near the end of this side road has little scenic interest to attract the visitor, but it once was the site of a large homestead of one of the more important German families on the island. Originally coming from Bavaria, George and Maria Hass met and became friends of the Hutzlers in Buffalo, New York. After the Hutzlers established themselves on the island, they encouraged the Hasses to emigrate to the island with their sons. About 1860, the Hass family arrived and settled on this farm. They soon built a large house on the location of a now derelict cabin. It was not far from the Hutzlers, for the eastern part of their land abutted the Hutzler farm, and the friends remained congenial neighbors for many years. Later a Hutzler girl would marry a Hass boy, uniting the two families in blood. Since the main island cemetery was not established until the first decade of this century, George and Maria Hass were buried in the family orchard as was George Johann Hutzler. The site of George Johann Hutzler's grave is easily found today but those of the senior Hasses are more

Bill Hass' cabin in 1987

difficult to find.

Their youngest son Henry established another farm near the west side of Lake Florence, which is described later on this walk. Their oldest son, John married, and with the help of his younger brother Bill took over the original family farm. John lost his wife and only child to illness, and he never remarried. He and his brother William remained on the farm as bachelors the rest of their lives. Bill did most of the field work, while John looked after the animals and did the cooking. Bill was also the island blacksmith, and maintained a forge complete with large bellows in a side building near the house. There he shaped the shoes for the island horses and repaired farm machinery. Since parts had to come from the mainland at a great time delay, Bill was often able to make temporary repairs to worn parts, so the farmer could continue work until replacements arrived. One day, as he looked out of the farmhouse window during lunch, he saw his blacksmith shop aflame. Despite the help of many neighbors, the shop which was some distance from the nearest well, was a total loss. It was the end of blacksmithing on the island.

From their orchard, the brothers could press enough juice from their apples each year to nearly fill two 55-gallon barrels. Sugar and raisins were added to top off each barrel. The barrels were then stored in a pit, where natural fermentation took place. After six months of aging, the brothers had 110 gallons of first-class cider to brighten the long and lonely winters.

John died in 1924, and shortly thereafter the large family house was struck by lightning and burned to the ground. This left his 65 year old brother homeless and alone. Several island neighbors helped Bill build a one room log cabin, where the bent old man lived out the remaining years of his life. This ruin is all that is found at the former site of the original Hass homestead. The building is now surrounded by small trees growing both inside and outside of the remaining log walls. Although I did not know the story of the Hass family when I first visited it, the now-desolate location and deterioration of the ruined building left me with a strong feeling of loneliness and isolation.

If you wish to see this ruin, it should take you about ten minutes to walk back to it. Follow the side road to the right, which is still in the forest but parallels a large open field on the left. You will come to a small open area that is easily crossed before returning to the woods. As late as 1987, you could follow this side road almost to the old cabin but today the latter part of this road is so clogged with deadfalls and underbrush that it is better to continue on the field to the left. If you look north up the hill, you will see a treeline crossing the field at the top of the hill. Walk towards a break in that treeline, which once served as a border between the Hass and Beck farms. Once beyond the break, start walking diagonally to the right in this field. Keep your eye peeled for the walls of the old cabin, mostly hidden in small trees near the eastern border of the field. If you are not used to doing off-trail walks you won't miss anything of spectacular interest if you skip this side trip.

When you continue on the main trail, you almost immediately enter a large field, where a substantial well-maintained house is easily seen. This is the homestead of August Beck, who was born in Germany and came to the island with his two older brothers, Theo and Albert. The three teen age boys arrived about 1860, shortly after the Hasses. The oldest, Theo, established his own farm on the southern end of the island. The Hass and George Johann Hutzler farms to the northeast and the farm of the other branch of the Hutzler family adjoining the Becks to the southwest formed the nucleus of the German community, which would dominate farming and the social life of the island for better than 70 years.

These families were often linked together by marriage. Eligible young women were usually in short supply. The 1880 census showed that only three young ladies were available for the 12 youthful bachelors living on the island. This meant that men sometimes married girls considerably younger than themselves, or spinsters who were a great deal older than their prospective husbands. The early death of some married men saw their widows remarrying other available island bachelors, making genealogy of the island a confusing hodgepodge of inter-related families.

The Beck house was to become the longtime home of one of these young couples. Their marriage linked two of the island families together. 19-year old August Beck married Elizabeth, the daughter of the nearby Hass family, when she was only 16. The marriage thrived and was fruitful, for when Mrs. Beck was 24 years old she was already the mother of four children.

During the early part of this century, August Beck was the most influential farmer on the island. Energetic and resourceful, he was instrumental in introducing new and better

August Beck Farm, circa 1920
Courtesy of S.B.D. National Lakeshore

August Beck Farm in 1990. Note foundation of barn in foreground

farming machinery to the island. Other farmers looked to him for leadership in dealing with cattle buyers and other off-island salesmen in commercial farming matters. He also organized a cooperative, which was responsible for bringing and operating a large threshing machine on the island. One islander suggested that he should have been known as King of the Island.

The house is used today as an occasional residence for Park Service personnel on an as needed basis and is being maintained for that purpose. Several farm buildings are still standing across the road from the house, but are not being maintained, and are rapidly deteriorating. The large barn was still standing on my first island visits, but since the structure was in danger of total collapse, it was torn down and only the mortared ceder log butt walls of the foundation stand today.

Family cemetery above Beck Farm

On a rise behind the west side of the house, you can see the picket fence surrounding a small family cemetery. A modern stone indicates that Elizabeth and David Beck, parents of the three Beck boys are interred there. Some ten years after August Beck had established his farm, he arranged to have his aging parents immigrate from Germany. They shared his new island home with him until their deaths.

Once beyond the buildings of the Beck farm, the road curves to the left at the bottom of a hill on the right. If you leave the road momentarily and climb partway up that hill, you will be rewarded with a pleasant panorama of the Beck Complex and the surrounding countryside. Once beyond the hill there is a large field to the right. About a hundred yards beyond the hill, you will see that the road returns to a narrow stretch of forest. But well before reaching the trees, there is a path that goes to the right, leaving the road crossing that field. This unofficial trail may be of interest to the more adventurous hiker, for It leads up to the top of the island's largest blowout, where one can drop down through its open sand to the edge of the escarpment some 350 feet above Lake Michigan. This area is usually approached by following the important South Island Dunes Trail, on the southwestern end of the island.

If you have the time and the energy and decide to take a look at this blowout from its top, it will take you about a half hour to reach the ridge top, with some very tough climbing through loose sand. If you do not want to take this side trail, skip the next two paragraphs.

While crossing the field, you will pass the rotting hull of an old wooden boat in the open field, which now has small trees growing through its bottom. Shortly after you enter the forest, you have your first climb. This is an easy warm up, for the real climbing test still lies ahead. A short level stretch follows, which gives you time to catch your breath before you hit the steep slope, where you slide back in the sand with every forward step. This ascent takes you out of the trees to the top of the ridge, with the blowout lying below. From there, you can make your way down to the summit of the escarpment which runs the entire length of the western side of the island. When you reach its edge, approach it cautiously for it is an angling 350 foot drop down to the shoreline. If time allows, you can turn right and follow the escarpment to the northwest corner of the island, giving you interesting views of North Manitou. A more adventurous and time-consuming walk is to turn left and follow the escarpment south, finding your way to the Southside Dunes Trail and return by that southern route. Both of these cliff walks are difficult and time-consuming so do not attempt them unless you are in good hiking condition and have plenty of time.

If you decide on an escarpment walk with a return to the eastern part of the island by using the South Island Dunes Trail, turn left and walk along near the top of the escarpment. As you proceed south with the lake on your right, you will see two small rounded tree covered sandhills ahead of you. As you get close to them you will see the treeline to the left of these hills retreat, opening up a large dune area. Do not turn, but continue walking south past the two hills keeping them on your left. When you pass the furthermost one almost straight ahead but slightly to the right you will see a very high ridge with trees on its top. Walk behind it where you should see the dunes trail coming down a high ridge on the left.

If you are continuing your walk along the farm road, you will soon walk through a narrow border of trees between two fields. Once past this tree line, another historic farm complex comes into view. This is the original home of George Conrad Hutzler, the half brother of George Johann Hutzler who had encouraged the younger man to leave his Bavarian home of Oberkrumbach and emigrate to the island. George Conrad Hutzler supported himself by working as a fireman on lake steamers until his farm was productive enough to support his family.

Almost 60 years after establishing this farm, his son and grandson would make agricultural history on the island with their prize seed crops of Rosen (Russian) Rye and the Michelite bean. In 1919, representatives from the Michigan Crop Improvement Association and Michigan State College encouraged the island farmers to grow the improved Rosen Rye for seed, because the island was far enough away from the mainland to prevent cross fertilization. George and his son Louis were the most active islanders in this endeavor, and continued growing the seed crop long after other island farmers lost interest. Entering their prize seeds in several international agricultural exhibitions, the father and son team won a whole series of first prizes.

An even more important innovation in seed growing happened in 1923. A new bean hybrid was developed, known as the Robust type. The Hutzlers, working with the Crop Improvement Association agreed to grow this new pea-bean hybrid on the island. The success of this new type of bean was overshadowed in 1937, when Dr. E. E. Down from Michigan State College developed an improved variety of pea bean known as the Michelite

Farm road leading to the Hutzler-Riker Barn

bean. The Hutzlers then stopped planting the old Robust variety and concentrated exclusively on the new Michelite variety. By 1946, it was estimated that 80% of the pea-beans grown in the United States were descended from the stock that had been nurtured by the Hutzlers in their island plantings. In that year, most of the 600,000,000 pounds of beans grown in the state of Michigan were descended from the original Hutzler plantings.

George also played an important role in one of the island's social functions. Each Saturday night during the snowy season the islanders enjoyed a square dance. George did the calling while his cousin Johnny helped furnish the music playing his fiddle.

The road turns to the left in front of the house, but if you do not turn and walk straight ahead keeping the house on your left you will see a path going uphill on the right. The path takes you to the grave of George Conrad Hutzler. For some reason, the modern stone placed to mark his grave does not have his first name on it.

This Hutzler farmhouse was destined to play another important role in the twentieth century history of the island. In the 1950s, the Hutzler farm was one of several bought up by a Detroit citizen named William Boals, who wished to establish a cattle raising enterprise on the island. Previously, most island farmers raised cattle and let them roam the island as open range, protecting their crop-growing fields by enclosing them behind fences. As many as 60 head from various farms freely roamed the island during the warmer season, returning to the individual owner's barn to be fed and sheltered during the winter months. By mid-century, economic conditions ended profitablity of the traditional field crops on the island. Since South Manitou offered a large area enclosed by water, which was void of natural predators, an opportunity for specializing in cattle raising seemed to offer a favorable climate for reasonable profit. To look after and nurture this project William Boals hired a college-educated professional farmer named Ed Riker to be his tenant farmer on the island.

Arriving in 1953 with his wife and three sons, Ed Riker moved his family into the Hutzler house, which served as their home for the next 19 years. It was the last house on the island to be occupied by a working farmer and to be lived in year round. Besides running the farm and maintaining over three miles of fences, the Rikers busied themselves maintaining the island's telephone lines, the county roads, taking weather observations and chauffeuring tourists around the island during the summer season. When the Rikers, came they shared the island with about 10 people who lived around the still-operating Coast Guard Station. After the closing of that station in 1958 Ed, and his family became the sole year-round residents of the island. When the government purchased the land from Mr. Boals, the Rikers were forced to leave, which they did reluctantly. Eleven boat loads of household possessions, farm machinery and livestock were shipped to their new home on the Upper Peninsula. In the Rikers' eyes their almost 20 years of residency in the old Hutzler house had changed the building into a real home. Ed and Esther had raised their sons and spent the most productive years of their lives here. When they were forced to leave, they left not only this house but their youngest son, who was drowned on the island's shipwreck and is buried in the island cemetery. Although in the long run what the government was forced to do was essentially correct and in the best interests of what the island was destined to become, it didn't make the evacuation any less painful for the Rikers.

The one-lane road curves to the left as it passes in front of the Hutzler-Riker house, and begins moving in a southeasterly direction across a large open field. Sometime before you reach the eastern tree line, turn around and look back at the house. The view down the rutted road that leads to this farming complex can be a nostalgic reminder of backroad rural America during the early age of the automobile. A couple more minutes walking in this southeasterly direction brings you to a trail junction. A sign which parallels the road on the left reads:

School
house
———>

If you wish to return to the Bay Campground or the N.P.S. Dock you can take the left fork east at this junction and walk to Chicago Road at **Point C,** or to Ohio Road at the schoolhouse some 6/10 mile away. If you decide to follow this left fork, you will see that in a short distance, the road curves to the left and goes off diagonally across the remains of the Fosters large orchard. It dead ends at Chicago Road near **Point C.** The road is quite distinctive, because it is used by the island motorized tour. If you wish to pass the schoolhouse, do not follow the left curve of the road, but proceed straight ahead following the less distinctive path which ends at Ohio Road.

The right fork at this junction heads due south in a straight line, following a row of trees on its left. This path, which I call the West Side Farm Trail, once linked the farms and fields on the south end with those in the central part of the island. It can be followed past the junction of the South Island Dunes Trail, stopping just short of South Manitou's southern shore. The distance from this junction to the junction with the South Island Dunes Trail is 1.2 miles.

If you decide to follow the West Side Farm Trail, a short walk will return you to a stretch of woods, before entering another large field on the right. This field is less prominent,' because it has largely been taken over by juniper bushes and clumps of small trees. You will soon come to another junction with a sign paralleling a trail on the left which reads:

Path leading to schoolhouse and Ohio Road

↑ Florence Lake

A left turn on this trail will take you past the northern end of Lake Florence and ends at Ohio Road.

If you look carefully on the right side of this junction, there is a faint trail almost obliterated by juniper bushes. A short walk in that direction will soon take you to the rapidly deteriorating homestead of Henry and Margaret Hass. Born in 1860, Henry was the youngest of George and Maria Hass's four sons. If you took the short walk back to the cabin ruin of Henry's brother William before arriving at the August Beck farm, you visited the original home site of this important German immigrant family. It occupied the ground of the family home which was destroyed by fire. Since two of Henry's elder brothers stayed on the original Hass farm, Henry moved to this southern location and established his own. Henry and his wife not only raised the usual island crops of corn, oats and rye, but also produced the island's best maple syrup.

Charles Anderson recalled that as a boy he liked visiting this house, because Mrs. Hass always offered the children delicious candy made from the syrup. He also remembered how spotless Mrs. Hass kept her house, even scrubbing her hardwood floors with white sand taken from the beach. Henry and his wife Margaret tried to grow ginseng in a shed they designed and built for that purpose, but they had only marginal success in growing this wild plant. Henry also became an expert in extracting diseased teeth from the domestic animals on the island. When the need was urgent enough, he occasionally brought relief to human sufferers as well. He did most of the shoeing of the island's horses. After dressing the hoof and getting the measurements, Henry had his brother Bill shape the shoes to size in his blacksmith shop before he replaced them.

Henry's son Harrison, who was born and raised in this house later joined the Coast Guard. He returned to the island in 1934 as the keeper of the life saving station, where he remained for three years before being transferred. Although many men born on the island served the station as surfmen, Harrison was one of two native sons to hold the job of "Skipper." His Uncle Joseph, who was the eldest of the four Hass brothers, served as mail carrier until he was accidentally drowned in 1912. His wife Florence immediately took over

Henry Hass Farm, circa 1920
Courtesy S.B.D. National Lakeshore

Henry Hass Farmhouse in 1990

the job of running the mail between the island and Glen Haven. She had obtained her pilot's license only the year before, and is thought to be the first woman to be so licensed on the Great Lakes.

Henry, by reaching the age of 86, outlived all his brothers by a wide margin. His wife Margaret followed him in death six years later, the same year the Rikers moved to the island. She and the four Hass brothers all are interred in the island cemetery. Although maintained and lived-in until recent times, the well-constructed Henry Hass house is of no particular historical value, and will eventually be torn down. Because of its unsafe rotting condition hikers should inspect the building only from the outside.

If you continue to follow the West Side Farm Trail south from this junction, you should arrive at the South Island Dunes Trail in less than 20 minutes.

Hikes from Point B

Arrival at Point B. Located at the southern end of Ohio Road it is the first important junction the hiker reaches south of Burdick Road. Hikers from the Bay Campground arriving from the north and those from the Weather Station Campground coming from the south will arrive at the trailhead of one of the most important sightseeing paths on the island. I call it the South Island Dunes Trail. The junction is at a small triangle of roads, and is easily recognizable by the signs. Directions to **Point B** from **Point A** are given on page 108. A sign on the west side of the roads says:

<— Camping 0.4 mi
Shipwreck 1.7 mi —>
Cedars 1.9 mi —>
Dunes 2.1 mi —>

Interior of Henry Hass House in 1990. Collapsed roof shows the danger of entering these derelict buildings

The South Island Dunes Trail

Distances from **Point B**: To the Lodge-Beck Place Side Trail 0.3 mi.; to the Shipwreck View Side Trail 1.4 mi.; to the Valley of the Giants Side Trail 1.8 mi.; to the top of the Perched Dune 2.3 mi.

Walking Times from **Point B:** To the Lodge-Beck Place 15 to 20 minutes; to the Shipwreck View 30 to 40 minutes; to the Valley of the Giants 50 minutes to 1 hour; to the top of the perched dunes 1 to 1 1/2 hours.

GENERAL REMARKS. The South Island Dunes Trail is the starting point for proceeding to the old Lodge-Beck homestead, the shipwreck overlook, the giant cedars, the perched dunes and the walk along the top of the sand bluff escarpment that runs along the western edge of the island. If you plan to extend your hike to include walking along the high sand escarpment above this western shore, possibly making a loop trip of the walk, you might want to split this south adventure into two hiking days. Crowding all those worthwhile features into a single day's hike may be exhausting for many hikers, and will leave little time for savoring these island highlights. One of the two hiking days can be devoted to a leisurely walk, using the side trail destinations to the Lodge, the Shipwreck View and the Valley of the Giants. You can use the second day's hike for the dunes and a walk following the top of the high bluff northward, with all its marvelous panoramic views.

Remember that except for the path that crosses the perched dunes that leads directly to the edge of the escarpment, hiking across the dunes themselves is discouraged. Hikers wandering across the dunes cause much ecological damage to the fragile erosion-controlling plant life. Except for the very steep climb made in loose sand up to the perched dunes, the walking is not demanding. Your path is over mostly level ground, along easily-followed former island roads. Be aware that the distances and times given are from **Point B,** and consideration should be given to the extra mileage and time needed to get to and from the campgrounds or the N.P.S. Dock. All the side trails except the Lodge-Beck Place are included in the general description of the South Island Dunes Trail. The Lodge-Beck Place walk is found at the end of this trail description.

TRAIL DESCRIPTION. Proceeding west from **Point B,** this well-defined farm road remains mostly in the trees all the way to the dunes. In a little over five minutes, you will come

South Island Dunes Trail near western bluffs

to a fork in the road where a sign to the right facing you says:

↑ Shipwreck
Cedars
Dunes

The left fork is the road to the Lodge-Beck Place (See Pg.143). As you proceed west along the Dunes Trail in less than ten minutes beyond this junction, the south end of Lake Florence becomes visible on the right. If your hike happens to coincide with a period of heavy rains, this part of the trail may be quite soggy and possibly impassible. Lake Florence, like so many of these island lakes, has no natural stream to carry off rain waters, so the low ground around the lake absorbs the excess water. If you find the trail disappearing into a big pond there is a way to avoid sloshing through these saturated surroundings. Retreat to the last road junction, and follow the directions to the Lodge. Although longer, this route will give you a high ground passage back to the South Island Dunes Trail, where it junctions with the Westside Farm Trail. It skirts around the soggy area at the southern end of Lake Florence. If you pass Lake Florence in dry weather, about five minutes walking beyond the lake brings you to the junction with the West Side Farm Trail. A sign on the right side of the road facing you says:

↑ Shipwreck
Cedars ^
Dunes

Just west of this junction, the trail parallels a large field on the left. This was one of the last fields on the island to be actively used by the island's last farmer for producing hay. From here you have about 3/4 mile to cover before arriving at the next fork in the road, which takes you to the view of the shipwreck. A sign between the fork facing you says:

<— Shipwreck 0.3 mi
↑ Cedars 0.5 mi
Dunes 0.7 mi

A brief walk on the left fork will take you to the escarpment view of the Francisco Morazon. The fate of this vessel followed a pattern that is all too common on the Great Lakes. Usually the last navigable month for the big lake is November, but this month has the greatest number of violent storms. More ships have been lost during November on the Great Lakes than any other time. Gambling on the late season, The Francisco Morazon sailed from Chicago on November 29, 1960, bound for Holland via the St. Lawrence Seaway. With a crew of 13 and the captain's pregnant wife aboard, this freighter of Liberian registry encountered heavy weather the following day. A 40 m.p.h. northwest wind put the decks of the ship awash and, as the ship approached the Manitou Passage, she was further hampered by fog and heavy snow. The 28 year old captain incorrectly assumed that his ship was at least 70 miles further north than his real location, and turned east, heading for the Straits of Mackinac. By turning too soon the ship ran aground on the southern shoals of the island at almost the same place the steamship Walter L. Frost was wrecked in 1903. The island's lifesaving station had been deactivated just two years before the Morazon mishap, but helicopters from the Traverse City Coast Guard and three other ships effectively rescued all hands and the pregnant lady. The only loss of life connected with the ship happened eight years later. Ronald Riker, the youngest son of the island's last farmer, swam out to the wreck with his younger boyhood companion Ronald Shirk. Although they had done this swim together several times before, somehow Ronald became entrapped in the ship's hold and drowned.

Among the ship's cargo were several thousand empty plastic shampoo bottles. As the hull deteriorated the bottles began washing up on the shore. The green bottles broke into thousands of small plastic pieces that glistened like emeralds along the beach, and for years they continued washing up on the sand. A good deal of the ship's hull and superstructure have fallen victim to the winter ice through the ensuing years. At this writing, there is still enough of the derelict left to make the side trip worthwhile, but how long it will take before the wreck will be entirely claimed by the lake, as it most assuredly will be, is anybody's guess.

After returning to the main trail, it's about a quarter mile before this trail T's into another. A sign on the opposite side of that road facing you says:

<— Cedars
Dunes —>

The Francisco Morazon shortly after she ran aground in 1960
Courtesy S.B.D. National Lakeshore

The Francisco Morazon in 1987

By turning left, a walk of less than five minutes ends in a small loop trail at the Valley of the Giants. Just off that loop, you will see a large white cedar with a wooden fence around it. This tree is the biggest of the island's virgin cedars, and is thought to be the largest of its type in the world. Although it is over 80 feet high, some visitors are disappointed in first viewing the tree because the name suggests to many that they will see something nearer the size of a California Redwood. There are many trees of different species found on the island that are a good deal higher, but the great interest in this tree and several other White Cedars

The "Walter L. Frost" wrecked in 1903 within yards of where the Francisco Morazon met the same fate 57 years later

Courtesy of Ethel Furst Stormer

nearby is that they are record holders of their species in both size and longevity. The tree is over 17.5 feet in circumference, and was probably over a hundred years old when Columbus began his fateful voyage to America. A nearby fallen cedar that approached the size of its still-living companion was found to contain 528 growth rings, which means these trees were probably saplings when the English longbowmen helped decimate the French Cavalry at the Battle of Agincourt.

At one time, there were many thousands of giant White Cedars in Michigan, but the ruthless timber boom in the nineteenth and early twentieth centuries obliterated all known virgin stands of the species except this small group of trees, tucked away in this southwest corner of South Manitou. Because of the cedars rot-resistant quality, the wood was in great demand for roofing shingles and for other applications where a high resistance to water was desired. One of the last two operating lumber mills on the island specialized exclusively in cutting and processing cedar. Fortunately, the loggers apparently did not know this grove existed. It apparently escaped notice, and was not discovered until a 1940 survey of the island was made by the Cranbrook Institute of Science. The director of that institute, Dr. Robert Hatt, then had to wage a bitter campaign to save this historically-significant grove of trees from timber interests.

If you are proceeding on to the dunes from the T junction, less than 10 minutes of walking will bring you to a turnaround at the end of the road. In the early years of the park, the motorized island tour included this south trail, with stops at the shipwreck and the giant cedars. This was the turn-around for the concession vehicles and those who wanted to see the dunes walked from here. This south end of the island now has a wilderness classification which prohibits the use of any wheeled vehicle, so at this writing, the motor trip is restricted to the central and northern sections of the island.

Bark of the giant white cedar

At the end of the circle, a narrow but quite distinct path continues through a thick forest on level ground. Then you run into a steep uphill section on the lee side of the dune, where the trail surface has loose sand that buries your feet as you climb. Often you slide halfway back in the sand for every step forward. It's slow, ex-hausting going and is not for everyone, but any seasoned hiker in good health should experience no serious difficulty. Once you are above the tree line the climb is less steep,ut just as sandy. Although it is easier to walk on the foliage growing alongside the trail please do not do so, for you can help destroy that delicate groundcover and add to the erosion of the dune. When the path reaches its highest level, stop and look around you, for you are close to the highest point on the island, standing in the middle of a perched dune, surrounded by a marvelous panorama of spectacular scenery. The sand around you was not laid down by the glacier. It was torn off the surface of the large bluff below you to the west and deposited here by prevailing winds which created a perched dune (see Dunes in Natural Setting chapter).

If the weather favors you with clear, non-misty skies, you will have one of the most spectacular panoramic views found on any of the islands. You can see Lake Michigan in almost every direction. Looking east, the lighthouse and Gull Point are usually visible far below you, and the Sleeping Bear escarpment some 10 miles away is seen on relatively clear days. To the north is the sister island of North Manitou and its large blowout known as Old Baldy is easily seen. If you happen to reach this island high point on a particularly clear day, by looking straight west, faint mirage-like forms may be seen, which suggest shimmering trees that seem to dance vaguely on the horizon. You are looking all the way across Lake Michigan to the Wisconsin shore. A hiking companion told me it was Washington Island, but after looking at a map I believe the area is south of that island, and is actually part of the Door Peninsula that forms Green Bay some 40 miles away. This high point is the only place that the distant Wisconsin shoreline can be seen from the trail, for if you continue following the path down to the edge of the escarpment top, the faint low Wisconsin shore disappears

Giant white cedar, the largest in the world, thought to be 500 years old

from view as it drops below the curvature of the earth. The brush covered dune in front of you and slightly to the left is the highest point of the island. High foliage growing there blocks

Looking east from high point on the South Island Dunes Trail

any outstanding views from its top.

As you stand looking at this high point, you can easily see the trail descending in front of you before it ascends again heading westward. You can also see how it turns right and skirts the edge of a huge sand bowl. If you follow the trail down, you will find that once beyond this sand depression you can turn left and walk to the edge of the high sand escarpment. The view from the top of this angular cliff is spectacular. Although about a hundred feet lower than its big brother cliff on the mainland, it still places the viewer about 350 feet above the water level of Lake Michigan. This sloping cliff runs without serious breaks for almost three miles. To me, a walk along the edge of this magnificent slope, with the panorama of sand and what seems like unlimited sea, is one of the most exhilarating walks a person with romantic inclinations can take. You have a wide natural cornucopia of sights restricted only by the distant horizon to the west to delight your eyes. While still earthbound, you may experience a sensation of being lifted almost like a soaring bird into a different plane of existence. If you can't fly off the escarpment or duplicate hawks riding the thermal uplifts of the cliff, you can mentally soar with the freedom of a flying bird unshackled from the usual scenes of a plundered earth. The greatest humiliation this natural area was ever subjected to by the hand of man happened in the 1920s, when ships from the Great Lakes Naval Training Center used the cliff for ship-to-shore artillery practice. Fortunately, no such folly has taken place for years.

If you wish to walk along the bluff's edge, it is easy walking. You can make a loop hike out of it, but it is more demanding. If you opt to return by the loop, follow the escarpment for a little over a mile until you arrive at the island's biggest blowout, where wind has torn out the vegetation and exposed the sand up to the crest of the ridge. Climb to the top of the blowout where you will find a trail that takes you downhill through a thick forest before it levels out and crosses an open field. The trail dead ends at the road that lies between the

Looking west over perched dune from high point on the South Island Dunes Trail

August Beck and the Hutzler-Riker farms. If you wish to return via Chicago Road, turn left here. The distance to **Point C** is about 3/4 mile, but the Beck homestead is less than a city block away. If you want to return to via Ohio Road, turn right. You will soon pass the Hutzler-Riker farm on the right with the junction of the Schoolhouse and West Farm Trail less than a half mile beyond it. By continuing straight ahead at that junction, you will soon arrive at the schoolhouse and Ohio Road.

Trail to the Lodge-Beck Place

Distance from **Point B**: 0.7 mi.
Walking Time from **Point B**: 20 to 30 minutes.

GENERAL REMARKS. Although the remaining buildings at this location are not unusual enough to warrant special attention, nor are the natural attractions there so vivid as to classify them in a "must see" category, many will find that the combination of human history and the panoramic overview from this location make this short hike to the southern shore a delightful side trip. Standing in front of the old lodge, taking in the vista of the lake at the beginning of the Manitou Passage and the distant Sleeping Bear escarpment, or following an easy access down to one of the most delightful sand beaches on the island, will attract those visitors who wish to spend some unhurried time in amiable surroundings. Isolated from the busier sections

On top of western escarspment. Back cover of book is a panoramic view of this high bluff

of the islands, it is a nice place to pack a book and a lunch for a pleasant, unhurried, get-away-from-it-all type day. You can enjoy the view from its low bluff, or spend a lazy afternoon stretched out on that pleasant expanse of beach, and possibly take a swim. This side trail can also be used for a detour around the soggy end of Lake Florence during extended periods of heavy rain.

TRAIL DESCRIPTION. In seven to ten minutes walking time from **Point B** you will arrive at the first fork in the road along the South Island Dunes Trail. A sign facing you says:

↑ Shipwreck
Cedars
Dunes

Follow the left fork at this junction. In about seven minutes, the trail makes a sharp left turn near an old wooden fence on the left, and goes up a small rise. Shortly beyond the rise, the trail breaks out into an open field. If you keep a sharp lookout to the right, you will see a small break in the trees, where another road comes in from that side. If you are only interested in taking the detour around the south end of Lake Florence, turn right on that road and follow it a brief distance until it junctions with another road near the corner of a large field. This is the southern end of the West Side Farm Trail. Turn right there, and take the road that follows the eastern border of the field. In about 0.2 mile you will junction with the South Island Dunes Trail.

Shoreline view from the Lodge-Beck Place. Sleeping Bear Bluffs in the distance

If you want to go on to the lodge, don't turn, but keep walking straight ahead in a southerly direction towards the shore. On your right there is the fallen ruin of a barn, and just beyond it you will see what looks like a cozy little hideaway cottage. It might have been used for that purpose, but it also functioned as a small tenants' house for the lodge. If you walk over and examine it closely, you will see that it has not been maintained for several years, and is in dilapidated condition. Viewing it from a comfortable distance, it still maintains some of the charm of a honeymoon cottage. You also can see the Beck home and lodge in front of you. It is in far better condition than the other buildings found here, for it was maintained and occupied right up to the date that South Manitou was absorbed into the National Lakeshore.

The buildings and surrounding acreage were originally owned and farmed by Theo Beck, who was born in Germany in 1841. About 1860 when he was 19 years old, he immigrated to the island with his two younger brothers, Albert and August. He and August both established and successfully operated farms on the island well into the twentieth century. Their respective farmhouses are still standing, but August's home is the only one that is being maintained and is easily reached in a short walk from **Point C**. Both raised families and were a part of the vibrant German community, the most powerful social force on the island during the last quarter of the nineteenth century. All three of the brothers are buried in the island cemetery today.

After Theo's death in 1910, his widow Elvina was able to keep the farm going with the help of her son Willie, and her brother-in-law Albert. Some years later she began an on-again, off-again affair with an immigrant Norwegian fisherman named Beneth Johnson.

Both of them were well along in years when they married in 1920, and apparently both were set in their ways. They quarreled so much that they seldom lived together for any extended period of time. With the onset of winter, the wry old fisherman usually established domestic peace with Elvina and stayed in the comfortable farmhouse, while his boat was laid up through the cold and lonely freeze-up months. Once the breakup of the lake ice occurred and Beneth could start his seasonal fishing activities, he would let a small domestic quarrel develop into a major row and move back to his own place near the Coast Guard Station. Although he would visit her occasionally during the warm season, he conveniently delayed his cohabitation until the onset of the winter season.

In the 1940s, two Detroit business men, J. Lee Barrett and Joe Harrold, saw possibilities developing this section of the island as a resort, partly as an investment and partly as a pleasant island retreat. Being members of the Rotary, they interested fellow Rotarians in forming a corporation to promote such a venture. Forty-nine Rotarians became members of the corporation, and the Beck farm was purchased and became known as "The Lodge." Although this very ordinary farmhouse was refurbished and maintained by the corporation it was little changed. The expected enthusiasm for such a project never materialized, and further development ceased.

Standing on the front lawn with the marvelous lake vista in front of you today, you might imagine how the building behind you could have looked if the idea had taken hold. There a large building of country club proportions might have stood, possibly in the tradition of an English half-timbered manor house, complete with verandas, swimming pools, lawn chairs and umbrellas, with a putting green between the building and the bluff. A smaller building in the same architectural tradition might have stood nearby for stabling the horses. But the island was never really "discovered" by the fashionable elite, and behind you remains only the modest Beck farmhouse. The lodge members used it very little, and eventually Joe Harrold, who had other summer interests on the island, leased it from the corporation. He rented it out to vacationers on a weekly basis during the season. The place was used for that purpose right up until the year it was purchased by the federal government. Although the house is in excellent condition at this writing, there are no present plans to save the building, and it will probably be torn down.

If you want easy access down to the beach there is a little ravine a short way east of the house which allows a non demanding descent down to this delightful shore.

Another house that lies not far away might be of interest to a few visitors. It is a modern A-frame structure situated on a higher escarpment found near the southernmost tip of the island, and was still standing when this author visited it in 1987. The land had been inherited by relatives of an island family. They built a pleasant modern A-frame summer home on the inherited land. Unfortunately, for the owners, the house was built after 1964. Federal law stated that all property built after that date must be sold to the government. Reluctantly the owners were forced to sell.

Beside the A-frame, there is an attractive one-room side building with a large picture window and an attractive interior fire-place. Since the location is on a high promontory, the view from the window was grand. Recent tree growth has restricted this view considerably. The escarpment there is especially steep and descent to the beach is hazardous.

Since few are interested enough to hike to this isolated corner, the trail is unofficial, and in 1987 was already difficult to follow. The hike may only be rewarded by viewing the remains of the foundation, for eventually the building will be demolished. If you would like to make this side hike and you are at the lodge, retrace your steps north until you reach the road on the left that is just beyond the small cottage. Turn left there, and walk until the road passes into another field and junctions with the southern end of the West Side Farm Trail. Turn left at that junction, and follow the road south the short distance into the trees. Once into the trees, the road makes a direct right turn and briefly parallels the field to the north. If the trail is not too difficult to follow, you should reach the location of the A-frame in less than 15 minutes. Although faint, the trail is easy to find in the forested sections, but becomes almost non existent across the open fields. By following the left edges of the fields you should be able to find your way. If you are uncomfortable with pathfinding situations, I advise you not to go. The scenic rewards are hardly worth the risk of losing your way and spending hours wandering through field and forest.

Other Points of Interest Near the N.P.S. Dock

The Coast Guard Station Complex. The building at the high end of the ramp that leads to the dock and the larger building with an ample porch to the left behind it were the two most important buildings of this rescue station. The main function of this complex, which was in operation from 1902 to 1958, was to aid stricken ships that ran afoul of the reefs in the Manitou Passage and the north and south ends of the island. The primary purpose was to save the lives of these stranded crews and passengers, and if possible the cargo and ships themselves.

The large house with the porch housed the keeper and his crew. It now functions as the ranger station and a residence for park personnel. A stairway in the middle of the building divides it into two separate halves, the Skipper or Keeper occupied the right side, often with his wife and family, while both floors of the building's left side were utilized by the surfmen, usually six to eight in number. The side to the left of the stairway of the upper floor served as the crew's dormitory. At the rear of the main floor under the dormitory, there is a large kitchen and the crew had a "loafing room" in the front.

Behind this building, you will see a small round building with iron walls. It originally was located near the lighthouse, and served there as a paint locker. Sometime between the closing of these government facilities in 1958 and the island becoming part of the National Park System, a local contractor had himself deputized as island constable. He felt that to carry out his newly assumed responsibilities a proper jail was needed. Since the paint locker was made of iron he thought it would make a suitable hoosegow and had it moved from the lighthouse to its present location behind the ranger station. No one was ever incarcerated within its metal walls, and someday it may be moved back to its original location near the lighthouse complex.

The boathouse, which now serves as the contact station for visitors, contained two large boats, one powered by oarsmen and the other motorized. The boats, mounted on iron wheeled cradles, sat on iron rails that ran down into the lake. In 1916, this boathouse was raised an additional four feet above its original foundation, so the boats could be more speedily lowered into the water. The complex also had a lookout tower, which since has been torn down located about a quarter mile south of the main building. There, a 24 hour watch was maintained. On a clear night, the watch could easily see the mainland's Point Betsie light some 20 miles to the south, and the North Manitou light five miles to the north. In addition to this surveillance, surfman also conducted walking beach patrols, that ran along the island's eastern shore and part of the north and south shores during the navigation season.

Island headquarters in former Life Saving Service complex. Building on right, once the keeper's residencs and crew dormitory is ranger station. Boathouse building on left is contact station

This was the boyhood home of Willard Smith, whose father served as Keeper of this station during World War I. Willard later went to the Coast Guard Academy, and during his active career rose to the rank of Admiral and Commandant of the Coast Guard. It was under his leadership that vast changes were made in Coast Guard procedures. With the advent of radar, helicopters and other newer techniques, such stations as this one became obsolete and were closed.

Those interested in the history and operation of these stations should not miss visiting the old Coast Guard Station located on the mainland at Glen Haven. Once an active life saving station like the one at South Manitou, it has been preserved by the National Park Service as a museum. Two interesting recorded messages made by the retired admiral may be heard there. In them, he has given an engaging history of these stations and the Coast Guard. he also included a narrative of his personal career, which include reflections of his happy boyhood experiences in growing up on South Manitou. Another interesting personal account is found in a book entitled The South Manitou Story. It was written by Gerald Crowner, who served a two year hitch as a surfman at the South Manitou Station.

Many buildings seen behind the Coast Guard complex were originally built as private residences for people who were in some way connected to the activities of the station. The first island hamlet was north of here, around the old dock on Crescent Bay. Here ships once docked to take on fuel and other island commodities, but with the demise of those commercial activities during the first quarter of this century the center of human activity moved south, and clustered around the station. Surfmen assigned to this station had only one

Surfmen launching lifeboat at South Manitou, circa 1910
Courtesy of Ethel Furst Stormer

36 foot self-righting motor lifeboat on South Manitou Island boat ramp
Courtesy of S.B.D. National Lakeshore

Admiral Willard Smith, U.S.C.G.Ret.
Courtesy of S.B.D. National Lakeshore

day off in every eight, making it almost impossible for those with families to spend any time with them. By having their families living in this little island community, it was possible for the surfmen to have almost daily contact with wives and children. It is also a good reason why several surfmen were native islanders. When the station was closed, many of these buildings were bought by persons who used them as summer homes. When the island became part of the National Lakeshore, most of these residences were sold to the government. Some of them have been torn, down while others are maintained for various Park Service purposes. Two are still privately owned, and used as summer homes.

The Lighthouse. Easily found south of Sandy Point just off the trail to the Weather Station Campground, this building is one of the most aesthetically pleasing of the historic lighthouses on the Great Lakes. Standing 104 feet high, it was the third lighthouse built at this location, and one of the highest to be built on the Great Lakes. Although the Lighthouse Service was combined with the Coast Guard in 1938, the Keeper of the lighthouse and his assistants functioned separately and independently from the rescue station. Constructed in 1871 it replaced two former lights at this location that had operated here since 1834.

This location was extremely important to nineteenth navigators. Sailing up or down the middle of the lakes and having little more than a compass for navigation, made it difficult for the sailors to know exactly where they were. They used a technique known as coasting. By keeping the shoreline in view, they could locate their position from prominent landmarks along the coast. Going through the Manitou Passage instead of passing the islands on their western side also cut about 60 miles off their journey. From the 1850s through the 1880s, this was Michigan's nautical super highway. During this period, a third of all U.S. commerce was on the Great Lakes, and over half of it passed between this shore and Sleeping Bear Point, some six miles across the straits. This light continued to help guide ships through the Manitou Passage until 1958. It also guided ships into South Manitou's Crescent Bay, the last natural harbor between this point and Chicago, some 220 miles to the south. Here ships could take on fresh supplies of cordwood for their woodburning boilers sequestered in a harbor that protected them from periods of nasty weather.

South Manitou's Coast Guard Village in 1990

South Manitou light and Keeper's house

To further aid navigation through the treacherous Manitou Straits, a lightship was anchored between South Manitou and the mainland. It was anchored at the end of a shoal that runs from North Manitou southeastward for over three miles into the Manitou Passage. This was considered particularly hazardous duty for Coast Guard crews, for in times of decreased visibility, ships were guided past the shoal by a radio beacon from high up the lightship's mast. If pilots steered a direct course toward the signal, it would run them right into the lightship.

In 1935, the lightship was replaced by a permanent facility built at the end of the shoal in 26 feet of water. Known as the North Manitou Shoal Light, crew members served on this tiny cement island for three weeks, followed by one week's leave on shore. At the beginning of one season, a coastguardman brought a puppy to the station that was less than a month old. The puppy did not come off the station until the shipping season closed in late November. The first few weeks on shore, the dog would only walk in circles about the size of the shoal light's perimeter. Today the facility is totally automated.

North Manitou Lightship
Courtesy of S.B.D. National Lakeshore

North Manitou Shoal light

For navigational purposes, the strategic location of the shoal light was an improvement over the site of the South Manitou light, which now seemed to duplicate a service better performed by the shoal light. Manmade harbors along the lake shore also decreased the importance of the island's harbor as a refuge. The lighthouse was decommissioned the same year as the Coast Guard Station, and for over 10 years the complex remained deserted and unattended.

Although boarded up, vandals broke in and did extensive damage both to the lighthouse and the Keeper's residence. Hoodlums not only smashed many holes in existing walls, but wrecked the doors and broke the windows as well. One group even built a bonfire on the hardwood floors of the three story residence. The covered passageway connecting the residence and the lighthouse was severely damaged when hoodlums carried large fieldstones up to the top of the parapet of the lighthouse and dropped them through the roof of the passageway below. Windows in the lighthouse cupola were shot out by passing pleasure boaters with high powered rifles. During this time of abandonment wave action ate away at the surrounding bank. The building was dangerously close to following the fate of her sister lighthouse on North Manitou which was swept into the lake.

When the island became part of the Sleeping Bear National Lakeshore, the lighthouse was restored, and a patch up job on the other buildings was carried out. The retaining sea wall was reinforced as a holding action, until a more permanent wall could be built. A new costly but effective sea wall has now replaced the old one, ensuring the safety of this historically important building for the next 100 years.

Damage to interior of Keeper's house done by vandals during the 1960s

As you approach this small cluster of buildings, the little white structure that you pass on the left was the fog signal station. In the days before radar, ships were warned of approaching nearby fogbound shores by sound. In the early years, this was simply carried out by a gargantuan bell weighing a thousand pounds. In 1875, this little building was built to enclose a steamdriven basso-profundo foghorn of ear-shattering capacity, which replaced the bell. For many years, islanders bid on the yearly contract to supply the wood for the steam boilers, and pictures taken during its active years show a huge, neat, long row of wood cut and stacked to be used to fuel the furnace. Later the steam engine was replaced by a diesel-powered unit, but oldtimers swore that the newfangled diesel motor never produced the mellifluous subterranean roar of the steampowered horn.

Before the present lighthouse was built the yellow Keeper's house behind it served both as the home of the Keeper and the lighthouse itself. Erected here in 1858, this building replaced the island's first lighthouse which began operations in 1839. Like its successor, it combined the dual functions of beacon and living quarters, for a round wooden tower, six feet in diameter, once extended upwards from the eastern side of its roof. At its top was placed a kerosene lantern of the fourth order. The original lantern used in this tower was designed by a young army officer who's name was Lt. Meade. Civil war buffs will recognize his name, for he later rose to the rank of general during that war, and commanded the union forces at Gettysburg. The residence was large enough to house both the Keeper's and the Assistant Keeper's families, as well as workrooms and an office. Although it served as the lighthouse for only 13 years, the building was in continual use as a residence until the complex closed 101 years after its completion. Despite the heavy damage that occurred after the complex closed, the building was so well built that it is still structurally sound. It is hoped that at some later date money may become available to restore and refurnish the interior of the Keeper's residence as it looked about the turn of the century.

When viewing the lighthouse, which is 99.6 feet high up to the cupola, few are aware that its underground pinnings extend down below the surface for over 70 feet. In 1870, a

George Hutzler, Fred Burdick and Glenn Furst in front of fog signal building. Both George and Fred are great grandsons of the island's first settlers. George and Fred's fathers and Glenn's stsepfather all served as keepers of the South Manitou light

floating pile driver was anchored here and began sinking white oak beams into the ground. 100 of these beams, measuring a foot square and 60 feet in length, were driven into the ground until they were below the water level. Since white oak does not rot when wet, the engineer, who's name was E. M. Poe, knew he was supplying the tower with a permanent base. 15 feet of limestone blocks were placed on top of the beams, and became the platform for the tower. When they began building the tower the following season, the builders did not use scaffolding, but the latticed round iron steps inside the structure that serve as the stairway to the top today. The outside diameter of the building at its base is 18 feet, which tapers to 10 feet at the top. The structure was built with an inside and outside wall, with an air space between them. This gives the building flexibility to bend slightly in heavy winds. The thickness of the wall at the base is five feet 2 inches, with an air space of three feet between the inner and outer wall. Since the interior wall is cylindrical, the thickness of the wall at the top is a little over two feet, with only four inches of air space between the inside and outside walls. 12 lighthouses of similar design were built on the lakes during that decade. It is a testimony to the builders that all of them are standing today.

During busy seasons, the Park Service conducts tours through the lighthouse. Check with the rangers to see if and when tours are being given during your island stay. During the tour, you can climb the spiral staircase consisting of 125 latticed iron steps all the way to a glass-enclosed platform. On your way up, you will pass through two trapdoors, spaced at different elevations, which served a very important purpose. During the hours the lantern was lit, the immense heat created by the burning wicks would cause a strong sucking updraft of colder air from below. A floor, sealing off the upper parts from the lower prevented

Latticed iron steps in lighthouse interior

this updraft. However, every time the trapdoor in that floor was opened when the lamp was burning a strong surge of cooler air would again be drawn from the bottom. To make it possible for the Keeper or his assistants to go up and down during hours of operation, a second floor and trapdoor were added. In this fashion, authorized personnel could go up or down while the lamp was lit, for it was necessary to have only one trapdoor open at a time. Between the trap doors, there is a room with windows on three sides. Known as the watchroom, the Keeper could observe ships approaching the passage. Until the life saving station was commissioned in 1902, the Keeper and his assistants were also responsible for carrying out rescue operations for any grounded ship. They were also required to paint the tower every other year.

When you reach the platform encircled by windows, you can see a large circular iron track embedded in the floor. On that track stood a large kerosene lantern of the third order, encased in a fresnel lamp housing. It was capable of projecting a light visible for over 17 miles at ground level. Because of the tower's height, the visibility of the light was extended, and on clear nights could be seen from the Point Betsie light, 45 miles to the north. The lamp contained three large wicks of different heights. Every morning, the lamps were refilled with kerosene, their chimneys cleaned and their wicks trimmed. The lens was polished with a chamois cloth. Although the lamp housing has been removed a similar third order light can be seen at the mainland Coast Guard Station Museum near Glen Haven. From this 360-degree glass enclosure, magnificent views of the island are seen, especially its eastern shore.

Existing records are unclear whether It was from this window or one in the watch room that a tragedy was witnessed by those whose lives it would deeply affect. In 1878, on a beautiful unseasonably warm March day, the Keeper and his wife accepted an invitation from a friend to take a sailboat ride. They were still in sight of the lighthouse when a violent squall unexpendedly hit, quickly swinging the boom of the sail to its opposite side. It struck the Keeper on the head with such force that he was knocked into the water and the boat capsized. The Keeper quickly disappeared. but his wife, holding her baby in one hand, desperately held onto the side of the boat with the other. Their friend, who had been steering the craft, looked for a rope so he could tie the poor lady and her child to the side of the capsized craft. Before he could reach them, the mother and baby also slipped below the surface of the water. The skipper of the sailboat had a difficult time saving his life, for he clung to the side of the boat through the rest of the day and night. The following morning the boat finally drifted close enough to North Manitou Island, where it was possible for him to walk ashore and become the boat's only survivor.

Apparently the Keeper's two older children had climbed up the lighthouse to watch Mama and Daddy take their pleasant sail, only to witness the accident that made them orphans. Louisa Hutzler, the youngest daughter of George Johann, who would later become the mother of Myron Vent, was ten years old at the time. Mr. Vent relates the strong

South Manitou Harbor and Crescent Bay from lighthouse balcony

impression this tragedy had made upon his mother. She recalled how the two newly-orphaned children walked the beaches wailing for their lost parents, hoping that they would return to them from the sea. As far as I know, no one has reported hearing eerie ghost-like voices of these long ago children still searching for their lost parents in misty twilight walks along this beach, but it is from such situations that apparitional voices are sometimes imagined.

If you visit the interior of the lighthouse, the climb up the 125 stairs is not particularly spooky, since the solidly built curving stairway takes up most of the interior space and does not permit a straight downward view. The glass-enclosed light platform also lends a sense of security, but the outside balcony that circles the tower just below that platform is a different matter. Although the railing and deck are substantial, there is 90 feet of nothing between you and the ground. If you suffer from acrophobia you may prefer to view the island below only from the security of the glass enclosure. If you do venture out, and are blessed with a day with high visibility and little wind, the view is spectacular.

Of the 35 listed keepers of the Manitou Light, one was a woman and a least five of them were native islanders. Two of them were from the Hutzler family, and two from the Burdicks, both among the island's original settlers. James Burdick, the grandson of the first lifetime settler on the island served as Keeper from 1908 to 1928, the longest period the job was held by one person. If you walk to the lighthouse from the Coast Guard Station, you will pass the island museum, which once was a store run by his wife. His son, Fred, who is still is an island visitor, lived many of his boyhood years there, and reopened the store a few years before the island became part of the seashore.

The last civilian to serve as Lighthouse Keeper was another islander named John Tobin. His wife, Lottie, was a granddaughter of George Johann Hutzler, and the island's last schoolteacher. In 1939, the lighthouse service was incorporated into the Coast Guard, and the Manitou Light was maintained by enlisted personnel from that time until its closing in 1958.

Gull Point. At the northern end of Crescent Bay a sand spit known as Gull Point forms the easternmost land protrusion of the island. This area is literally for the birds, for it is off-limits for humans. The point, and a similar long sand spit on High Island, were once two of the largest nesting colonies for both Herring Gulls and Ring-Billed Gulls on the Great Lakes. The active nesting season is between May and July, and up until the early 1970s, as many as 5,000 Ring-Billed Gulls and 500 Herring Gull nests had been counted at Gull Point. By August, the colony diminishes in size, for many of the parents and fledglings disperse to other areas for their fishing and scavenging livelihoods. Although nesting activities are over by late summer, there are enough gulls and other shore birds who remain there for the rest of the season that hikers should not venture out on the spit. This makes for much needless anxiety among the remaining birds. The Park Service originally planned to build an observation tower near the spit so visitors could watch the mating and nesting habits of the gull colony at a distance and not fluster the birds. But shortly after the acquisition of the island by the government, the number of nesting gulls began to decrease. The decline in nests continued until the active nests of the Ring-Billed Gulls fell to about 900 and the Herring Gulls less than 250. part of the decline is due to a strange paradox.

Since the island has become a part of the National Lakeshore the gulls are totally protected, but so are other living creatures, particularly foxes. In previous times, the fox population was kept in check by trapping and hunting by the island residents, but now, protected from human molestation, the number of foxes on the island has increased dramatically. They have been observed not only devouring a great number of chicks, but also killing others for the pure hell of it. It was proposed that an electric fence be erected to isolate the spit from the rest of the island. The power of the electricity would be low enough that an intruding fox would suffer no permanent harm, but would get enough of a jolt that his wish to get to the other side would be seriously diminished. The idea of the fence was not carried out, because it wouldn't fit in with the natural environment of the island. Possibly in ensuing years, nature will be able to work out its own balance. Gulls at this time are far from becoming an endangered species, and there is a good chance the foxes could swim around the fence anyway. The decreasing gull population had become enough of an environmental concern that the government scrapped the idea of the observation tower.

Several contributing factors, such as other predators, pesticides, pollution and human molestation of nesting sites probably all contribute to this dropoff to some degree. Damage to the rookery is still an area for further research. Ornithologists from the University of Minnesota have been conducting research about such problems on High Island for several years. They found that the most active predators raiding nests on that island are not the small carnivorous mammals as originally expected, but snakes. It has also been well documented that various species of shore birds in the Great Lakes area will mysteriously disappear from an area for no known reason, only to return in abundance many years later. During the last half of the nineteenth century, when Crescent Bay was an active harbor for commercial shipping, sailors from the many ships anchored there often ate the gull eggs, but such activity probably had little effect on the colony's size, and the decrease in colony numbers happened long after such egg stealing was over. Nonetheless, the decreasing number of active gull nests is a matter of some concern.

Anyone saying there are too many pesty gulls around anyway should be reminded of the fate of the American Passenger Pigeon. As late as the last two decades of the nineteenth century island residents reported that the sky was often covered with a spotted cloud of thousands of pigeons that was so dense that the light of the sun was almost blotted out. Island farmers seeded fields with grain where meshed nets were concealed. When the feeding birds alighted the nets entrapped hundreds of live birds, which were then shipped to Chicago for 50 cents a bird. A former islander who hunted the birds on the nearby mainland wrote that a single shotgun blast in 1873 would often bring down six to eight birds. In one season he killed 9000 birds and shipped them to Chicago for which he received a dollar a dozen. He also reported that just seven years later there was a serious decline in the Passenger Pigeon population. By 1910 the birds were entirely gone from the island and in 1914 the last living Passenger Pigeon died in the Cincinnati Zoo. Of course, the islanders were not directly responsible for making the Passenger Pigeon extinct, but it does show that species, even when they number in the thousands, should be of great environmental concern when there is a noticeable decline in their numbers.

If you wish to closely observe this large nesting site without invading their sanctuary you will find a marked trail beginning near the spit which turns west away from it but still provides you with a good overall view of the colony. This trail leads up to an overlook then enters the woods and continues on to the North Shore in about 20 minutes of walking time. If you wish you can make a loop walk out of it by following the north shoreline west to Popple Campground then south past the Johny Hutzler place and the cemetery back to **Point C**. It will take the average walker about an hour from the boathouse following the shoreline of Crescent Bay to this trailhead. Much of the walking is in open sand so it is often slow going. The trailhead that takes you to the overlook and to the north shore is easily found for it is marked with a prominent sign which says:

Gull Rookery
CLOSED AREA
Follow marked trail inland to viewpoint overlooking
Gull colony and the north shore of the island.

After reaching the sign, the trail turns left, diagonally away from the shoreline and heads inland crossing loose sand. This section of the trail would be extremely difficult to follow, but the park service has inserted wooden posts about every 50 feet or so to show you the way. You will soon have a dune climb, which takes you to an overlook that gives an overview of the active nesting area which lies between you and the sandy spit. At this writing, there is an old non-government sign at this overlook which is mostly unreadable. I could only make out the words "NOTICE" on the top and "KEEP OUT" on the bottom. From this point, the trail drops down into the woods, where it meanders back and forth a good deal, and in about 15 minutes of walking brings you to the sandy beach along the north shore. There you have a nice view of North Manitou and its large blowout known as Old Baldy, about four miles away.

The West Island Shore Walk. Unless the Lake Michigan water level is very high, there are almost no obstructions along the shore for the hiker to worry about for the entire circumference of the island. Determined young hikers have covered the 14-mile shoreline in a single day. For most of us, doing half of the circumference is a more reasonable day hike. Although all the islands have worthwhile shore hikes, South Manitou offers one section of beach walking around the western side of the island that cannot be equaled on any of the other four islands discussed in this book. The shoreline walk along the bottom of the sloping 350 foot escarpment isolates one between its sloping walls and the lake. The grandeur of the huge wall on one side and the voluminous volume of water on the other may give walkers a feeling of seclusion, and remind them how tiny and insignificant they are on the surface of the earth. This walk also places you on the same level of the wreck of the Francisco Morazon. Passing so close to that deserted derelict may bring on a closer identification with the perils and mysteries of the sea. The first time I did the beach walk, the site of the doomed ship brought forth in my head the descriptive melodies of Rimsky-Korsakov's "The Sea and the Shipwreck" from his Scherazade Suite.

Your plan should be to cover the whole western half of the island along the shore. The high bluffs make any other return route highly impractical. If you are on the southern side of the island, a good place to begin is to drop down to the shore at the Lodge-Beck Place, turn right and follow the shoreline around the western shore until you get to Popple Campground. Take the inland trail from Popple to **Point C,** and from there to your campsite. The only tricky part is finding Popple, for it is not easily seen from the beach. You have to keep your eye peeled for the short climb up a ledge of sand about 10 foot high which places you at the lower end of the campground. Or you can start at the Popple end and do the hike in reverse. Once you pass the shipwreck it takes about a half hour more to get to the Lodge-Beck Place, or you may want to continue on to Weather Station. Estimating the time for such a loop hike is difficult, but it will be a good day's hike for even a conditioned hiker. I once took this hike starting and returning to **Point B.** Dropping down to the beach at the Lodge-Beck place, I returned across the island from Popple. A few stops were made along the way for lunch and to drink in the scenery. I am a reasonably fast walker and it took me 4 1/2 hours to complete the loop.

The Sweetwater Trail. I learned about this little unofficial path in an unusual way. During one of my stays in the Bay Campground, a man approached me and asked if I was the person writing a guidebook on the island. After I answered in the affirmative, he said he knew of a little-known trail nearby which had an unusual history which I might be interested in hearing. After assuring him that I was, he told me the following story.

During the first year that the island became part of the National Lakeshore he had made regular camping visits from his home in Traverse City. Since he usually stayed in the Bay Campground, he found the old camp water pump left several things to be desired. First, the water did not taste very good. Second, the pump's handle was often removed by the government because the water had become polluted by inconsiderate campers who washed themselves, dishes and clothing at the well. This necessitated two less-desirable options in obtaining drinking water. The first was to take the water from the bay. This source has two undesirable features. It needs purification before consumption and the accumulated amount of mercury in the water makes it a health hazard when one drinks it repeatedly. The other was to walk back to the Coast Guard station which then had water that didn't taste any better than the Bay Campground well.

Old timers had told my informant that the sweetest water found on the island came from the well in the schoolhouse yard, but that source was over two miles away by road. But if one walked through the woods from the Bay Campground, the schoolhouse is only a half mile away. He then began to hack out a little trail directly connecting the two locations. Each time he camped at the Bay Campground he surreptitiously cleared another section. It took him several years to complete the trail, but he told me it served him well on his many visits. Today this walk to the "sweetest water" is no longer as necessary as it once was, for water found both at the Bay Campground and the Coast Guard Station no longer comes from nearby wells. It is purified and piped in from an always-reliable and good-tasting inland source. Nonetheless, this little meandering woodland trail does exist, and you can use it as an alternate way to reach Ohio Road from the Bay Campground. The trail begins at the back of Bay Campground's Group Campsite #1 and will take about 15 minutes to walk to Ohio Road. Once the trail breaks out of the woods into a field which parallels Ohio Road, the trail disappears, but you continue in a westerly direction across the field and in about another two to three minutes you will hit the road just south of the schoolhouse. Since it is an unofficial trail, and meanders more than government regulations allow, it will probably not be officially maintained or recognized, and use of it may also be discouraged. Since the trail's engineer wanted to remain anonymous, fearing some sort of government retaliation for his unauthorized handiwork, I didn't bother to write down his name. I knew I would conveniently forget it, which I have.

Part III
NORTH MANITOU ISLAND

Chapter VIII
Introduction and General Remarks

The reader should be aware that much important information on visiting North Manitou is in the chapter entitled "**Making Plans for Island Hiking; Which Island to Choose.**" To avoid redundancy much important information on the island is not repeated in this section. Read both sections to gain necessary information that will greatly aid you in planing a visit.

What the Island Has to Offer

There are few places in America that offer the backpacker-hiker as many exciting and different possibilities as are available on this 7-1/4 mile long, 4-1/4 mile wide island. It provides a different type of hiking experience than South Manitou, for the loop hikes on this larger island are much longer, and one is not restricted to spending nights in designated campgrounds. Not only does this spread out the hikers, but far fewer visit this island, which often gives one a feeling of splendid isolation. In the Lake Michigan Archipelago, it is second only to Beaver Island in size, and the largest that is entirely government owned. All except 27 of its 14,753 acres are designated as wilderness, and the self-propelled outdoorsman has over 30 miles of easily followed wide trails from which to choose. One may wish to leave the trails and go crosscountry through many heavily forested areas, which can more easily be done than on the other islands because the forest bottom is almost entirely clear of underbrush. Tracing out old timber roads, rapidly returning to nature is another option. One can also tramp along the island's 20 mile shore line, mostly on pristine sand beaches, in relative isolation. With only a few minor restrictions, you can make camp where you want to, often quite close to marvelous panoramic views, where hundreds of square miles of the deep cerulean-colored waters of Lake Michigan are often visible. All this is just an 11-mile ferry ride from the busy little resort town of Leland. What a change one feels between the summer's traffic laden streets of that once active commercial fishing port and the quiet and deserted, ghost-like village of North Manitou, a little over an hour's ferry ride away.

The island is especially well suited for the novice backpacker, for the main trails are wide and easy to follow, with only the gentlest of climbs. But the loop hikes are long enough to test your skill in carrying your portable backpack house, complete with kitchen and bedroom to your various bivouac locations. If you are the type of hiker who prefers not to be burdened daily by that weight but who likes long day hikes, if you land at the village N.P.S. dock, you can carry your camping gear a half mile to the village campground and set up a base camp. If you land at the southern end of the island, you have about a five mile walk ahead of you to reach the island's only campground. But once there, you can choose from a variety of shorter loops that allow you to return to camp nightly.

At this writing, the plan is to maintain a six foot wide hiking trail along a major old Manitou Island Association dirt and sand road about 20 miles in length, which roughly forms a figure 8. The road from the village to Lake Manitou will also be maintained. This trail system gives the hiker access to most of the major points of interest on the island. For the more adventurous, there are many secondary roads and trails not being maintained but often are still easily followed, and I have included descriptions of the more interesting ones. With the passing of time, these secondary paths will become harder to follow, for the trees that fall across them are not being removed as the island returns to wilderness. There are other roads and trails that appear on older island maps which have nearly disappeared. One can also find others still fairly visible, leading to less interesting points on the island. I have left out descriptions of them, to keep this book down to a manageable size, but more adventurous explorers may wish to try them.

The hiker will notice many roads and trails that are not marked on any maps. Often these are remnants of old logging roads or deer trails that go off into the woods without a landmark destination. Most cleared areas on North Manitou were once farms. Old cellar holes and well holes exist in abundance. Often remnants of fencing, fence posts and gates give clues to where old roads traveled to farms and through fields. Use caution and common sense when walking through clearings and around old buildings.

Those who wish to try the faint trails or leaving the trails altogether to go crosscountry, will find that the heavy browsing of the large deer population has kept the island's underbrush down to a minimum. This makes boondocking far easier than in most wilderness areas. If you are undertaking such off-trail adventures, make sure you carry a reliable compass.

Name places used on the island today come largely from a map made over 50 years ago by a long time resident of the island. He was asked by the major landowner of the island to mark down the names he knew for island locations on a supplied map. He did not live on the island at that time and was not particularly interested in the job but he did as requested and wrote down from memory the names he could recall. With no further historical justification, these names became the traditional names that are in use today.

Fishing on Lake Manitou

If you enjoy fishing from the shores of an inland body of water, the 1 1/4 mile-long Lake Manitou offers the possibility of hooking some very large Smallmouth Bass and a variety of pan fish. If you feel up to hauling a boat the 2 1/2 miles from the village to the lake it is legal to use one, but motors are verboten. Most anglers will find the shallow and sandy shore areas quite suitable for wading out into the lake and can manage very well without a water craft. A Michigan fishing license is required.

My Personal Introduction to North Manitou

Some years ago, when I was vacationing with my small children in this northern section of Michigan, I became casually aware of North Manitou from its obvious presence on Michigan road maps. Later, when the island was mentioned for inclusion as part of the proposed Sleeping Bear National Lakeshore, I put it on the back burner of my mind as a possible location to practice my new found hobby of backpacking. But a strong wish to visit did not develop until I took a hiking trip to its smaller sister island, South Manitou, during the summer of 1981. From the high point of the trail that goes to the top of South Manitou's perched sand dunes, one has a magnificent panoramic look at its north island neighbor. I thought then that it must be a big gorgeous, hunk of wilderness real estate. Wouldn't if be fun to explore. A day or two later, while standing at the waterfront near Popple campground

Ferry heading toward the Manitous

on the north shore of South Manitou, the distance between me and North Manitou had shrunk to just slightly over three miles. From this close observation point, I could see several miles of sloping sand escarpment between the beach and its green forest topping. The huge blowout known as Old Baldy could be seen in detail, cutting right through the forest line to the sky. Engulfed with a strong desire to go, I felt as though that nearby shoreline was mocking me, for in 1981 it was like a forbidden China closed to the foreign white devils. I had to wait until The Angell Foundation, which then owned the island, and the federal government agreed on an acceptable price for that sumptuous hunk of real estate. The sum was finally determined by court action and the first hiking visitors under Park Service auspices were permitted on the newly acquired island in 1984. Two more years had to pass before I could arrange my own schedule for my first passage to this exquisite isle.

I remember the excitement I felt just before my first trip to the island. It happened on a somewhat chilly September morning in 1986. Standing at the edge of Leland harbor, I waited for the Manitou Island Transit Ferry to take me across the eleven-mile stretch of open water. Brisk, unseasonably cold winds rolled low gray clouds towards us from the lake,

Southern shoreline looking east from near Old Baldy. Dimmick's Point and former location of Lighthouse in distance

suggesting that my first hiking day on this new island might be done in anything from dreary overcast skies to cold drenching rain. Suddenly, the whole island burst into sunshine and glistened alone in the surrounding watery gloom, which I took as a good omen. I had just left a dandy little restaurant in Leland called the Early Bird where I indulged myself with hash browns, lightly fried eggs and what seemed like a gallon of first-rate black coffee, a farewell to our cholesterol laden world, soon to be changed to the freeze-dried fare of the modern backcountry hiker. The sweaty summer already seemed far in the past, and an invigorating temperature in the high forties suggested weather perfect for hiking. As I waited impatiently to cross the waters and begin this new island experience this hiker felt not unlike Robinson Crusoe. As it turned out, there were only two other hikers on the island and for my first three backpacking days I saw not another human being. The weather smiled on me, for my first two and a half days on the island were filled with sunshine. Then I got what we all should prepare for, three days of bone-chilling torrential rain. The day of my return to the mainland, the weather was again warm and filled with sunshine. It seemed as if some force from beyond had ordered this winsome and seductive day saying, "Come back, come back. See how lovely everything is here." I knew then, like General Douglas McArthur, I would return.

RULES AND REGULATIONS

Upon arrival at the island the leader of each group must obtain a free backcountry permit. If you cross over to the island on the Manitou Ferry, a park ranger will meet you wherever the ferry puts you ashore, to issue the necessary backpacking permit. If you come by private boat, and plan to stays overnignt on the island you should go to the ranger contact station where information will be available (found on the front porch of the ranger station in the village at this writing) for registration.

A postcard sent in 1906 showing life saving station
Courtesy of Leelenau County Historical Society

The village campground has designated sites, with communal fire rings which are the only places on the island where that open campfires are allowed. Once out of the village area wilderness camping regulations are in effect. One can set up camp where the spirit moves with the following exceptions: campsites may not be within sight or sound of a designated trail, building, another camp or the island's two inland lakes. Camps must be set back at least 300 feet from Lake Michigan's high water mark and any other water source. All drinking water obtained outside the village should be purified. Since open fires are prohibited, all cooking must be done on portable stoves. Sanitary facilities are found only at the ranger station and the village campground. Toilet paper and human waste must be buried in the soil at the depth of at least six inches. All trash must be carried out of the back country and may be deposited in specially designated trash containers in the village area. Except for the official visitor contact stations, one may not enter any of the island's buildings, either in or out of the village. Many are, dangerous because of their advanced state of deterioration. There are no stores or overnight accommodations available on the island, so come prepared, especially for adverse weather conditions. See ''WHAT TO BRING,'' in the general introductory chapter entitled "**Making Plans for Island Hiking; Which Island to Choose.**"

ARRIVAL AT THE ISLAND
Coming by the Leland Ferry.

On my first two visits to the island, the Manitou Island Transit ferry landed passengers at a short temporary wooden dock, close to the village. In even mildly blustery weather, getting on and off the smaller of the two Manitou Island Transit Company's ferries was an adventure in itself, sometimes bordering on the precarious. Quite often the trips had to be scrapped altogether, for rolling swells made any type of landing quite unsafe.

Landing At the N.P.S. Village Dock

Realizing the inadequacy of this dock, the Park Service constructed a new and much longer metal pier close to the location of the original town dock, south of the temporary dock. Partly completed and first put in service during the summer of 1987, it was hoped that the new facility would allow the larger of the two Manitou Island ferries to land passengers there. The larger boat, the "Mishe-Mokwa" was able to make the trip once. Then nature played one of its unending tricks, putting the best-laid man-made plans asunder. After the new dock was completed, the lake level dropped and a natural sand bar accumulated at the deep water end of the dock. This made it unusable for either of the two ferries. If the dock remains unusable for larger boats, the ferry will be using one of two landings at the southern end of the island described below. Wherever the ferry lands, a ranger will meet you there. If you have been able to land at the village dock, after you have received your backcountry permit you can proceed to **Point A.**

Finding Point A from the N.P.S. Dock. Unless you need to fill out a camping permit or seek information at the ranger station, you will probably want to walk to the village crossroads at **Point A.** To find **Point A** from the N.P.S. Dock follow the road that leads directly away from the dock. Shortly after passing a white house on the left, this road T's into another. A left turn here will take you to the ranger station where drinking water is available (look for garden hose type faucet alongside the building). To get to the crossroads, turn right at this junction, where you will find the road Y's into another very close to a cement block building. Turn left, and walk past a small field stone building on the right. Just beyond it you will find another road coming in from the right. This is the village crossroads and **Point A**. A sign at the **Point A** junction says:

West side
via
Pole bridge 6.5 mi —>
<— Centerline Trail 6 mi
<— Fredricksons 8.5 mi
Village Campground—>

At Point A. The road proceeding due east is the take-off point for the Figure 8 Loop Trail and the trail to Lake Manitou. The road heading north will lead you to the Pole Bridge and the Maleskis. This is also the road you take to the village campground. To find it, follow this right hand road past the large village barn on the right and the old airfield on the left until, you come to a place where you find trees on both sides of the trail. A sign there that says: **Village Campground** is found on the left side of the road. This campground is in the middle of an old apple orchard. For those who do not want to use the official campground, other good camping locations in open areas on the eastern side of the island include the Schoolhouse Field, The South Cherry Orchard, the old Stormer Dock Area and the Maleskis. On the west

North Figure 8 Loop Trail from Point A leading to Village Campground. Eastside barn on right

Rangers assisting backpackers departing from Miller Beach

side, Fredricksons, the Big Field and Crescent City are also pleasant. One note of warning. The island has many hungry and nervy raccoons. These little bandits were introduced to the island many years ago, and they have adapted well to island conditions. They are notoriously bold camp robbers, especially at the Village Campground. All food should be suspended from trees when you are not in camp.

Landing at the Southern End of the Island

If a southern landing is used, as it was during the 1990 season the smaller ferry named "Manitou Isle" will land passengers on one of two beaches near Dimmick's Point. Weather determines which of the two landing sites will be used. When the lake is calm or the winds are westerly, the ferry runs its bow close to the beach along the southeast, shore north of Dimmick's Point. The boat can get close enough to the beach to allow hikers to use a long gang plank to disembark on dry land.

When there is a strong easterly wind, the smaller ferry goes around the western end of Dimmick's Point and lands its passengers at Miller Beach, on the south coast of the island. The water there is a bit shallower, so the boat cannot get as close to the shore. When the gang plank is lowered, it drops into the water about six feet short of the beach. Hikers then are required to wade in not quite knee-deep water the short distance to the beach. Rangers are always there to help the passengers disembark.

I originally wrote the important trails descriptions of this island with the general idea that most hikers would begin their hikes from **Point A** in the village near the new N.P.S. Dock. These new landings near the island's south end place you over four miles south of **Point A.** Unless you begin your exploration along the beach, your first contact with the Perimeter Trail will be at **Point C** on the southern half of the Figure 8 Trail. By using your map and the trail notes, you can alter your itinerary accordingly. These southern landings makes the ranger's job more difficult for they have close to a 10 mile round trip hike from the ranger station every time the ferry arrives.

Finding Point B and Point A from the South. If you land on the southeast side you follow the trail north for about 1.5 miles, past the Bourniques and the cemetery to **Point C.** If you come from Miller Beach, the distance is about 1.3 miles to **Point C.** It is not necessary to walk all the way to the Bourniques on the Miller Road Trail. When the trail enters a very large field, walk a few steps back into the woods where you will see another trail heading north. It will take you through an old farm homestead. It then goes behind the cemetery, where it meets the trail to the Bourniques. Turn left, and in a few minutes you will be at **Point C.** If you wish to do the southern loop of the Figure 8 Trail, turn left and see the trail description for the South Loop. If your first goal is the North Loop, the village campground or Lake Manitou, turn right on the Figure 8 Trail at **Point C**. The East-West Centerline Trail begins at **Point B** in 1.8 miles. For **Point A**, continue north on the Figure 8 Trail from **Point B** for another 1.1 miles.

Coming by Private Boat. If you are coming by private craft, you may have a draft shallow enough to use the new metal National Park Service dock. Vessels however are not permitted to tie up at the dock for more than 15 minutes. Private boats may not be left unattended for any long period of time at the dock, for this landing point has no natural harbor for protection. A strong east wind could seriously damage both boats and dock, or drive water craft up on the beach. So if you intend an extended hike on the island, don't come by private boat unless you can pull it up on shore, or have someone who will stay with the vessel. Then see Finding **Point A** from the N.P.S. Dock on page 166.

HIKING SUGGESTIONS AND VARIATIONS

There are enough interesting trails and variations on North Manitou to offer the hiker walks that can last from two days to two weeks. When laying out plans for your hiking activities, consider whether you wish to backpack the larger loops, pack in to specific points and day-hike from them, or day-hike only from the village campground. These must be determined by your general hiking ability, the time you have for your island stay, and the points of interest you wish to see. For those wishing to take extended hikes and visit a variety of the island's sightseeing possibilities, the Figure 8 Loop Trail offers the best path to follow. This trail system takes you to, or close to, almost all the most accessible and desirable points on the island. One can take a 17-mile hike using only the exterior of the Figure 8 Trail, or if time is too short, follow either the top or bottom half of the Figure 8 Loop. Check the General Remarks for the two loops, and their side trails, to get an idea of the ground you would

Along the Figure 8 Trail. Lack of under brush due to heavy deer population

like to cover in the time you have to spend on the island. Also, read the descriptions of the walks from the village.

When planning your trip, you should also be aware that even during the height of the summer season, high winds can make boarding to or landing from the ferry too dangerous to risk. Since air service to North Manitou is prohibited, occasionally people must spend a couple of extra days island-bound. I remember one day being surrounded by the dour faces of several hikers around the dock area who had just been told by the ranger that blustery weather conditions had extended their island stay by two more days. In contrast to the generally gloomy expressions, one young man's face blossomed at the news. He announced, "When I was young and heavy snow made it necessary to close the schools, I had an enjoyable snowday vacation. I now have a wonderful two-day snow vacation in the middle of the summer. Returning to civilization like returning to school can happily wait."

If the ferry is picking up passengers on the southern end of the island on the day of your departure, it is a good idea to spend your last island night somewhere near the Bourniques. From the Village Campground, you will have about a four-mile walk to the Bourniques. If you are departing via the N.P.S. Dock, you only have about a ten-minute walk from the campground. After loading the departing passengers, the ferry leaves, for it does not wait for late arrivals. If you are camping at another location, a miscalculation in time or a wrong turn may mean that you have extended your stay until the next ferry arrives. Be sure to be at the Bourniques or the dock at least a half hour before departure time, for sometimes weather conditions will force the ferry to arrive and leave a bit early.

WHEN TO COME

At this writing, North Manitou is open to hikers from mid-May through mid-November. For practical purposes the backpacker should consider that the nominal hiking seasons ends in early October and regular ferry service is available from late May until that time. The late October and early November extensions are for the island's deer hunting

Coast Guard Station and Cottage Row in snow, circa 1910
Courtesy S.B.D. National Lakeshore

season. In an effort to control the island's excessive deer population, deer hunting is permitted on the island during specified periods starting in October and continuing through November 15. The island is not reserved exclusively for hunters during that period, but it is a wise time to be hiking elsewhere (See Deer Hunt below). Since October is a beautiful if somewhat nippy hiking month, you can still go hiking on the island if you want to. But be forewarned. Because of the smaller numbers going to North Manitou the cost of the ferry ride to the island increases considerably and the ferry does not run on a regular schedule. Be sure to check with the Manitou Island Transit before any trip for either the regular or deer hunting seasons, since available times tend to vary from year to year.

The Deer Hunt

This hunt has assigned times for bow, primitive and modern weapon hunting. Those interested in the hunt may write or call the Sleeping Bear Dunes headquarters for a pamphlet on the hunt. The following is a direct quote from that pamphlet.

> "Please note that the North Manitou hunt is not for everyone. The wilderness camping conditions, the cold wet weather, and the difficulty of the hunting makes this a serious challenge. Hunters should travel light and take only necessary equipment; they must be in excellent physical condition and prepared for a challenging experience."

Address

Sleeping Bear Dunes National Lakeshore
P.O. Box 277
Empire, Michigan 49630   Phone. (616) 326-5134

Chapter IX

A Short History of North Manitou Island

For the earlier historical development of this island see the chapter entitled **"A Brief Early History of the Lake Michigan Archipelago."** To aid hikers interested in the history of specific places, much of the detailed information about those island locations is given with the trail descriptions. For reasons of brevity, much of that information is not in this short historical sketch, or only briefly mentioned. Readers of this narrative wishing to find out more about a particular location, should turn to the trail description for that locale in the trail guide chapter.

When ambling along the eastern beaches of the island, the hiker might wonder if the large voyageur canoes of the seventeenth century French fur trappers ever touched these shores, and if so, did they stay for any length of time. Such musings are entirely speculative, but from the scant evidence available today it is generally assumed the earliest white inhabitants staying for any extended period on either of the Manitous were itinerant fisherman and trappers who might have been on the islands as early as 1820.

The first steamboats appearing on Lake Michigan were wood burners, that usually followed the eastern shore. The close proximity of large supplies of suitable timber with easy access to sufficiently deep offshore water meant that this natural resource would soon lead to successful timbering operations on the islands. These early woodburning ships consumed enormous quantities of wood, making it difficult if not impossible to carry enough fuel for an entire voyage, without using large areas of precious cargo space. Unlike South Manitou, North Manitou does not have the advantage of a natural harbor. This delayed the first woodcutting on North Manitou for five or ten years after such activities began on her neighbor to the south.

The first recorded name of a wood dealer operating and owning land on North Manitou was Nicholas Pickard. He was born in 1817 in Madison County, New York. As a young man, his uncle hired him as an agent for supplying wood for steamboats, which brought him from Buffalo to North Manitou. He and several other woodcutters were probably taking wood from land they did not own as early as 1843. By 1847, when there was still no settlement on the nearby mainland, there were 40 woodcutters and one family living on the island, delivering wood to the ships along the eastern shore. In 1849, Pickard purchased land and enlarged his operation by building the first dock on the east side of the island, near its southern end, close to where Peter Stormer would build a dock 60 years later. With the increase of steamboat traffic on the lake, Pickard enlarged his operation in 1855 by buying up more land for his expanding timbering business.

Although North Manitou lacked the natural harbor that gave South Manitou an advantage in suppling wood to the passing ships, the larger island had one geographical feature that her immediate southern neighbor did not possess. The whole western shore of South Manitou is taken up by a spectacular high bluff, which rises 350 feet above the water. This made any proposed docksite on that side of the island highly impractical. Although there are also bluffs on North Manitou's western side, they are not as precipitous, and there is one area almost in the center of that western shoreline which lies only a few feet above the lake.

Chrsistian Alstrom's barn, 1905

Courtesy George Grosvenor

It furnishes an excellent site for a dock. When strong winds blow in from the east, even South Manitou's harbor offers little protection. Ships approaching North Manitou from the west during a period of strong easterlies, would be protected by the wind-breaking barrier of the island. Not only was this low lying area on the western shore a prime area for a docksite that could be used during times of calm weather and eastern storms, it also was handy for those ships that wanted to avoid the Manitou Passage. Pickard apparently realized this, and had a dock built on this western shore. The site that he choose would play an important role in the twentieth century, for it became the location of the largest town the island would ever know.

Not only did Pickard own the eastside and westside docks, he also held title to more than 1,200 acres, making him the island's largest landowner. In addition, he probably had stumping right agreements with other owners for considerably more acreage.

The 1860 census showed that Pickard's was the largest but not the only business on the island. Along with supplying wood for the lake steamers, there was a real attempt to establish general farming on the island by residents who came as homesteaders. The revolutions of 1848 had precipitated a wave of immigration from Europe which reached its heaviest momentum in the 1850s and 60s. Many of the homesteaders came from Norway, Sweden, Denmark, Switzerland, England, Ireland and France, but by far the largest numbers of these northern immigrants were from Germany. In the antebellum year of 1860, the island's census counted a population of 50 families, with 269 inhabitants occupying over 50 dwellings. It was the highest number of inhabitants that would live on the island in the nineteenth century. At least nine of the family units were entirely devoted to farming and one employed no less than seven hired hands.

During the Civil War period, both North and South Manitou had significant numbers of homesteading German families involved in farming the traditional crops. The German farms and families on South Manitou would remained remarkably steady into the

Family members in front of Maleski island home, circa 1920
Courtesy Paul Maleski Jr.

Maleski house in 1990

first decades of the twentieth century, whereas the ones on North Manitou began to seriously decline by the 1870s. By the late 1880s, general farming on North Manitou was almost non-existant, but this was followed by an upsurge in general farming on North Manitou with a new wave of immigrant farmers who were of Scandinavian origin. By the turn of the century, these farmers too, were either leaving the island or seeking livelihoods in other fields.

There are two reasons often given for the failure of general farming on North Manitou, while it continued to flourish on its southern neighbor. One concerned the general condition of the island's topsoil. North Manitou's is reputed to be sandier and not as adaptable to the usual farm crops as South Manitou's. The other is that South

Farming family reunion, circa 1900
Courtesy George Grosvenor

Manitou's harbor made it easier for the farming community to sell their products to passing ships, or to have them shipped to Chicago. Whatever the reasons, the population of the bigger island was far more transitory that its southern neighbor's.

Only one family name listed on the 1860 North Manitou census was found on on such lists in the twentieth century. Even that name disappeared from island records in the 1860s, and did not reappear until the twentieth century. Henry Stormer was a German immigrant who arrived on the island and set up a farm in 1859. His oldest son Peter, was born the following year at the site of the original farm, which is known as the Carson Place. The Carlsons were part of the second wave of island immigrants, mostly from the Scandinavian countries. Although Henry Stormer left the island and relocated his family near Empire, Michigan in 1864, his son Peter returned to the island during the second decade of the twentieth century, and operated a successful island logging business and sawmill for several years.

The large island population of the 1960s indicated that other commercial activities were commencing. A small lumber mill and the very first ferry service available between North Manitou and Leland and were both in operation by 1860, but neither endured for an extended time. Commercial fishing was the only other occupation of any consequence that occupied islanders.

As his wood business increased Pickard, apparently realized that trying to operate docks on both sides of the island was more than he could handle. Shortly before 1860, he decided that he would keep his business interests on the island's busier east side, and sold his west side dock to George F. Aylsworth, from nearby Empire, Michigan. Aylsworth was

Farmers at work at Sweede Anderson's Farm, 1905
Courtesy Geroge Grosvenor

married to a daughter of George Hutzler, who was the first German settler on South Manitou. A small village grew up around the dock and was named after its new owner, but through misspelling, its name survived as Ailsworth. The small town prospered for better than ten years, but when the dock closed in 1873, this small hamlet soon withered away. The location of the island's first-named ghost town came to life again during the first decade of the twentieth century, for it was here that the largest town in North Manitou's history would be built.

The decade of the 1860s saw the first of a series of non resident land speculators who bought large parcels of the island. This early speculator was Albert Bacon, of Grand Traverse County. Gaining title to most of his island holdings by using Military Bounty Land Grant certificates issued to the veterans of the War of 1812, he escaped a direct cash outlay. Apparently, he could get the certificates from the veterans quite cheaply, and used this method to buy up almost half of the island. He did nothing to develop his holdings, and through the years he sold them piecemeal to others interested in island property.

By 1870, the island population had declined to 91. Of those residents, 70 were foreign-born. Even though general farming had seriously declined, the strong demand for timber fuel continued. Nicholas Pickard's lumbering operation was still the largest and most successful business on the island. He prospered well enough for his family to winter in New York State, escaping the isolated and lonely rugged island winters. His timber fuel business continued to prosper up to the time of his death in 1876.

By 1880, there was a further decline in the island's population until it reached a low of 71. As lake boats turned to other types of fuel, a gradual decrease in the timber business followed, until there was only one wood merchant left on the island. Some slack was made up by a slight increase in general farming, mostly caused by the new Scandinavian farmers.

Wreck of the Josephine Dresden, North Manitou 1907
Courtesy S.B.D. National Lakeshore

But not all of them were Scandinavians, for among the farmers was a family named Malechiska, later simplified to Maleski. They had migrated from the vicinity of Oswicim, then part of Prussia but now in Poland, and better-known today as the dreaded Nazi Auschwitz. Arriving in 1875, Adam Maleski first worked for a wood merchant, but later bought land on the north east corner of the island. There he farmed, fished and raised a family, who were a part of island life for three generations. Since the affiliation of his family with the island lasted until 1955, the Maleski's had the longest continuing year round island family. Remains of some Maleski farm buildings are still visible and their former homesteads are often visited by hikers today (See Figure 8 Loop Trail).

With this new immigrant influx, general farming again became a significant way of life. By 1890, 713 acres were under cultivation for both crops and pasture. Commercial crops included corn, oats, rye, wheat, potatoes, flax and peas. Dairy products, pork, beef and wool were produced, mostly for island consumption. It was in this decade that fruit farming increased to a level of commercial importance, including over 33 acres of apple orchards. Yields of pears and grapes were still too small for export, and were used for island consumption only. In 1894, an agreement was reached between an island resident named Betham and a large fruit tree company in Wisconsin to greatly expand commercial fruit farming. Over 1,500 pear trees and 2,500 apple trees were shipped and planted in various sections of the island. With the heavy lake steamer traffic, the fruit growers had easy access to the wholesale markets of Chicago, and orchard crops had become an important export.

Introduction of Federal Government Nautical Stations

Two years before Pickard's death, the Treasury Department of the U.S. Government leased from him a parcel of land on the eastern shore, for a dollar a year. The Manitou Passage is one of many places on the globe that deservedly has received the name "graveyard of ships." Despite the heavy traffic of both sailing and steamships passing through this treacherous stretch of water, the only aid to navigation in the early 1870s was the impressive new lighthouse on the southern end of South Manitou. Although the new light could be seen for a distance of over 40 miles on clear nights, ferocious winds often drove ships unto the shoals surrounding the islands where sailors and passengers sometimes drowned within sight

Early photograph of completed North Manitou Life Saving Station, circa 1900

Courtesy of S.B.D. National Lakeshore

of land. In 1871, after a series of seacoast disasters both on the ocean and the lakes received wide newspaper coverage, the Congress authorized a new organization of professional life saving crews. It was named the U.S. Lifesaving Service, and placed under the jurisdiction of the Treasury Department. In 1877, the Treasury Department began construction of a lifesaving station on the island on the land Pickard had leased to the government. It was the first of three such stations that would be built bordering the Manitou Passage. The other two, at South Manitou and Sleeping Bear Point, were not built until after the turn of the century, so the North Manitou station was the only life saving station in the area for over 23 years.

The first lifesaving station of the Archipelago was probably established here instead of South Manitou, because a new 100-foot lighthouse had been built on that island just six years before and the new lifesaving station would give each island a part in the role of aiding ships. The overworked lighthouse keeper and his assistant on the southern island were also supposed to conduct rescue operations along their shores. The first structure completed for the North Manitou station was a single frame building, which included a watch tower. The

Looking south towards Lighthouse complex at Dimmick's Point
Courtesy Leelenau County Historical Society

Lighthouse and fog signal building
Courtesy N.P.S.

facility was gradually enlarged, and by 1897 all the buildings found in the complex today had been built. Reorganized as part of the Coast Guard in 1915, this station remained in active operation until World War Two (see A Walk Through the Village).

Another complex of government buildings for the island was authorized by Congressional action in the last decade of the nineteenth century. Although the attractive lighthouse that can still be seen on South Manitou Island had been operational since 1871, there was no such beacon on its northern neighbor. In 1895, Congress appropriated funds for a similar complex for North Manitou. First, a site on a high bluff on the northeast end of the island was considered, and for utilitarian purposes this would have been far superior to the place that was eventually chosen. This high elevation would have extended the visibility of the light for several extra miles. Furthermore, a light at this northern location would nicely overlap the illumination of the South Manitou Lighthouse 13 miles to the south and the South Fox Island light about 17 miles to the north, which had been in operation since

1867. This location would not only have furnished a stronger light on the northern end of the Manitou Passage, but also for lighting the passage between North Manitou and South Fox Island. Finally a site was chosen at the opposite southern end of the island at Dimmick's Point, with an elevation of just a few feet above the water level. This site placed the newer and smaller lighthouse only seven and a half miles from the south Manitou light. The choice was probably influenced by the North Manitou Shoal which runs almost due south from Dimmick's Point for a distance of three miles. Brick buildings to house a steam-operated fog signal and a home for the lighthouse keepers were constructed in 1896, but authorities could not make up their minds on the type of structure they wanted for the light itself. First a cylindrical steel tower was considered, but this was downgraded to a smaller clapboard-covered wooden light house, that was built and put into operation in 1898.

From the point of longevity, the site for the lighthouse was a poor choice, for the low, shifting sand spit has no protection from the lake's wild winter storms. In 1910, a light ship was anchored at the end of the North Manitou shoal near the present North Manitou Shoal light making the North Manitou light even less important. Two years later, the lake currents had eroded the sand away until the water was lapping at the foundations of the fog signal building. Engineers hurriedly built five spur cribs to help stabilize the rapidly eroding shore. The cribs worked well, for a new beach began to build up until the lake shore was more than 50 feet from the signal building. This complex, having seven buildings, was operated and maintained by a keeper and crew up through the 1930s, when new technology made it obsolete. In 1938, the government declared the complex as surplus, and sold the land to William Angell who apparently had no interest in saving the structures. With no further attempt to stabilize the beach, continuous erosion ate at the shore, undermining the lighthouse which fell into the lake during a ferocious storm in 1942. Today nothing remains of the original seven buildings except a collapsing wooden barn, a few bricks at the base of what was once the Keeper's house and oddly enough, two outhouses that stand side by side next to the barn. One of the little buildings was for the exclusive use of the keeper and his family. The other was for the assistant keeper (see Figure 8 Loop Side Trails).

The buildings of the Coast Guard Station fared much better, for most of them are standing today. But, like the lighthouse, the lifesaving station itself was looked upon as no longer essential. In the financially difficult depression year of 1933, the federal government, looking for ways to economize, transferred all except two of the island's Coast Guardsmen to other posts. The remaining two men operated the station as a skeleton crew until World War Two, when the station was permanently closed and sold to the Manitou Island Association.

The Development of a Resort Area

With the building of the two government complexes, the rejuvenation of farming and a growing horticultural business, the 1890s also saw the beginning of an entirely new activity that would bring a summer population to the island. The area behind the coast Guard Station was developed as a community of summer homes. Getting away from the city was as much a wish of vacationers at the end of the last century as it is today. In the late 1800s, air conditioning was a thing of the far-off future, so the easiest way to evade stifling urban summers was to escape to cooler northern climes. Travel, however, was far more restricted, since the automobile was in its infancy and paved roads outside urban areas were rare. The

S.S. Missouri arriving at North Manitou from Chicago, circa 1898
Courtesy S.B.D. National Lakeshore

availability of passenger trains far exceeded present miniscule offerings, but once off the train, those seeking lakeside serenity far from the madding crowd had to rely on horse-&-buggy transportation over dirt or at best, gravel roads. If one lived in or near a large lake port like Chicago, the frequent sailings of comfortable lake steamers put islands such as North Manitou within easy reach, with a minimum of discomfort and time.

The beginning of what is now known as Cottage Row can be traced back to a retired Chicago banker named Silas R. Boardman, who was looking for a healthier environment in which to live. In the early 1880s, he moved his home to the island, bringing with him his wife, his son and two daughters. To occupy his time, he began raising Percheron horses and took some part in the farming activities of the island.

His daughter named Carrie, was married to George Blossom and made her home in Chicago. She enjoyed paying summer visits to her parents on the island, and wanted to share the experience with a few of her personal friends. She asked some of her married acquittances to join her in spending part of the summer with her family at her parent's home. In 1893, two families did so, arriving by lake steamer. They became enchanted with the island and all three families decided that they would like to have summer residences on the island.

In 1890, Silas Boardman had purchased a slightly elevated strip of land near the eastern shore, along the edge of what was known as the Beech Woods. This area, behind the lifesaving complex, seemed an ideal location for summer homes and with this in mind, Boardman subdivided this land into ten equal lots, running parallel to the eastern shore. Measuring 102 feet in width, they become part of North Manitou Village, and appeared on many real estate deeds of the time as the "W.O. Green Plot."

In 1894 Boardman either sold or gave a lot to his daughter Carrie Blossom, and had a cottage that stood nearby moved to the site. In the same year, he also two of the lots for $75 each to the other two families. They drafted a covenant for the subdivision, which stated that the western 300 feet of the lots should be used for residences and servant quarters, while the area between the cottages and the lake was designated as a private park. Each lot owner would

Post office and boardwalk that once ran in front of cottage row, circa 1918. Stacked logs were part of the Newhall operation
Courtesy George Grosvenor

also have the right to build a boathouse along the shores of the island's Lake Manitou, called the little lake by the islanders. The two families began construction of almost identical cottages in 1894.

Two carpenters were brought from Chicago to build the cottages. One of them, Nickolas Feilen, who was an immigrant from Bavaria, liked the island so well that he decided to stay. He later was able to persuade his brother John, who was also a carpenter, to join him on the island. These lifelong bachelor brothers remained on North Manitou for the rest of their working lives. Nickolas died on the island in 1939 at the advanced age of 87.

Direct descendants of one of these original families still own a house on a cottage row lot, which today is the only land on North Manitou that remains in private hands.

The year after putting up the first cottages, the Feilen brothers were hired to build what would be the largest building on Cottage Row. It was built for a Mrs. William Shepard and her daughter, Katherine, following a design similar to their former home in New Orleans, Louisiana. This two-story structure was designed with a large open porch running the entire length of its eastern and southern sides. From the size of the structure, it might have been envisioned by Mrs. Shepard from the start as a place to take in summer boarders, with the dining facilities open to other island visitors. Such operations did begin around the turn of the century. The cottage, unofficially known as the Shepard Hotel, was operated for many years by Katherine, whom the islanders affectionately called Miss Katie.

Although the original ten lots of the subdivision were all sold in the ensuing years, a few never had cottages built on them. At this writing, several structures along cottage row are still standing (see A Walk Through the Village).

One of the most interesting and unusual buyers of island property for recreational purposes at the beginning of the twentieth century was Alvar L. Bournique. In 1903, this instructor of dancing and owner of several dancing studios in the Chicago area decided he

The German immigrant Feilen brothers making maple syrup.
Courtesy George Grosvenor

wanted to build a summer home for his family. He probably became acquainted with the island by visiting his brother-in-law, who owned a summer home in the village's Cottage Row. But unlike his relative by marriage and the other summer residents, he did not buy land in the W.O. Green plot in North Manitou Village, but purchased acreage three miles south of the village, just north of Dimmick's Point. There he built an elaborate summer home complex, much of which is still standing (see Figure 8 Loop Side Trails). During the years he occupied this summer home, he increased his real estate holdings on the island, and by 1920 he owned several parcels of land with a total of over 435 acres. In 1939, some years after his death, his daughter sold the property to the Manitou Island Association. The eastern village area and the Bournique property are the only locations where summer homes were ever built on the island.

Formation of an Island Association

The Cottage Row Subdivision was only a small part of a larger plan that Boardman was involved in, to develop other holdings of the island for agricultural and horticultural purposes. It had become apparent that the soil of the island was far more suitable for fruit growing than general farming. A wholesale fruit merchant from Chicago named Frank Newhall apparently realized this, and in the last decade of the nineteenth century began buying large amounts of property. In 1900 he bought out Silas Boardman. He eventually became the largest landowner on the island, with over 8,000 acres under his control. It has been alleged that by some questionable court decisions, Newhall became owner of tracts that by tradition had belonged to some of the island's small landowners. Because of his interests in the fruit business, apple, pear and cherry orchards were planted, with encouraging results. Because of the heavy outlay of funds to promote these activities and the buying of land, Newhall obtained a mortgage held by a group of investors mostly from the Chicago area.

These mortgagees included some very large companies like the Monarch Food Company, and eventually became known as the Syndicate.

Newhall's eastside operations also included growing corn, oats, rye, wheat and potatoes. The second largest landowner then was an island resident named Gottlieb Patek, whose 4,000 acres represented another 28% of the total area of the island. Patek was one of the earliest to establish and operate a ferry and mailboat service to the mainland. He sold his land to a large lumbering firm named Smith and Hull at the beginning of the twentieth century.

Rear of the Bournique summer home in 1990

Frank Newhall's son John took over the operation of the land his father owned. In 1908, he began to promote the island as a summer resort. John insisted on a change of policy that would hasten the demise of the last remaining small independent farm on the island. During the early part of the twentieth century, there was a general policy of using the island as open range for grazing cattle by any farmer. Paul Maleski Senior, who in 1910 began a long tenure as the island's mailman, was the last independent farmer of the island who still relied on cattle as the major source of his income. Much of his monetary profit was gained by maintaining a large herd of open range cattle which, at opportune times, could be rounded up and shipped by steamer to the markets of Chicago. For years he had an easygoing and friendly relationship with the Newhalls, but at the insistence of John, the agreement for use of the island as open range was terminated. Since the acreage held by the Maleski family was far too small for extensive cattle grazing, Paul and his children then had to scale down their operation to truck farming, mainly for home consumption. This brought on real economic hardship and left the senior Maleski with an embittered feeling toward the Syndicate.

Some felt that Newhall had closed the range vindictively in an effort to ruin the small farmers, but he had a sound reason for doing so. He know that the bulls of the herd posed a real threat to the well-being of any walker, even within the limits of the village. There were many incidents where the lives and safety of the cottage row summer residents and their children were jeopardized by the action of the bulls. Many of the island's activities and social events had to be rearranged or cancelled because of the free roaming herds. Anxious to promote his resort ideas, he knew such conditions would ruin any chance of further developments of the community. He also had the wholehearted support of the cottage row families in closing the open range.

John Newhall continued to buy up property hoping to make the island into a great plantation of fruit orchards which were strongly favored by the moderating temperature of the lake and the general soil conditions of the island . Although he increased the acreage devoted to fruit farming until he controlled over three fourths of the island he could not keep up his mortgage payments, and lost his land to the mortgage holders. They hired an island manager, and it is at this time that the name "Syndicate" was commonly used by the

Cattle round-up during open range days, circa 1905

Courtesy S.B.D. National Lakeshore

mortgagees. Not long after this, the Syndicate found an anxious new buyer for most of their vast acreage. He turned out to be no friend of the remaining island homesteaders or the summer cottage owners, but was a great benefactor in keeping the island from further malicious exploitation.

At the beginning of the twentieth century, the island's year round population was increasing. By 1906, the school district officers of Leland Township decided there were enough permanent resident families on the island with school age children to warrant a small grammar school. A schoolhouse was built south of the east side village, and began operating the following year. All eight grades were held in a single classroom school, and taught by one female teacher. Continuing in operation until 1941, the population of the school fluctuated a great deal during its 41-year existence, with 25 students being the highest number ever reached. For a brief time, there was a second grammar school on the west side of the island at Crescent City during the short active years of that community's existence (see Figure 8 Loop Trail).

Revival of Island Timbering

Although lumbering declined in the nineteenth century until it was no longer the dominant commercial enterprise of the island, it again become the most important business activity in the first decade of the twentieth. If the wood for the lake boats was being replaced by coal, the demand for lumber used in construction was ever increasing. When this century began, most of Michigan's large mainland forests had been depilated, but North Manitou still

Postcard of westside schoolhouse at Crescent City, circa 1910
Courtesy George Grosvenor

had thousands of acres that could be used to furnish that hungry market. To exploit that possibility, in 1906 the Smith & Hull Lumber Company of Traverse City, Michigan bought more than 4,000 acres of prime forest on the island's west side from Gottlieb Patek. By 1909, when that company began cutting hemlock trees, they also contracted to build a sawmill that could process 40,000 board feet a day. It was built at the same location as Pickard's old westside dock in the earlier hamlet of Ailsworth, along the western shore. Further improvements included a dock large enough to handle lake freighters, and a standard-gauge steam railroad. The location became known as Crescent City, and with a population of over 200, it became the largest town the island would ever know (see Figure 8 Loop Trail). Lumbering was the town's sole raison d'etre, and when the Smith and Hull company stopped operations in 1917, the community quickly withered away. Since the logging was carried on with no thought of any type of reforestation, some present day naturalists feel that the ecological damage done to the western side of the island by the Smith and Hull operation was the worst of any timbering done there. During the period of the Smith & Hull operation, another large lumber company, under arrangements with the Newhalls, was loading harvested timber at the east side village dock, just north of the lifesaving station.

Another smaller logging operation, which continued to operate after the demise of the Smith & Hull mill, was conducted on the eastern side of the island by a man who had connections with North Manitou. Peter Stormer, who was born on the island in 1860, had left for the mainland with his family when he was five years old. He returned about 1908, working as a logging contractor on the southern end of the island for a firm in Empire, Michigan. He later began logging operations under a contractual arrangement with the Newhalls, cutting wood in both the north and southern sections of the island. The division line between the two

Main Street, Crescent City, circa 1910
Courstesy S.B.D. National Lakeshore

White's Sawmill at Crescent City, circa 1910
Courtesy George Grosvenor

major lumbering operations of the Newhalls and Smith & Hull, was somewhere between the clearings named the Davenport and Stormer Camps on many modern maps. About the time Smith & Hull closed down their operation, Peter Stormer who had established a year-round

Logs harvested from Newhall properties being loaded aboard ship from the island's eastside, circa 1910

Courtesy S.B.D. National Lakeshore

home on the island in 1913, built a dock and sawmill on the southeast side, possibly buying his machinery from the defunct Crescent City mill. Before 1917, all wood cut by Stormer had been shipped to the mainland for milling but that task was now carried out on the island. Stormer finally ceased operations during the early 1920s. The remains of the family homesite, which was abandoned sometime before 1928, is an interesting place to visit today (see Figure 8 Loop Side Trails).

In 1910 the Smith & Hull company hired a sawyer named George Grosvenor, who brought his wife and young son to live with him on the island. When his son Tracy reached manhood, he briefly served as the island manager for an organization called the Manitou Island Association. But more important he would continue the active ferry service between the port of Leland and North Manitou, which was an important occupation for him for many years. He later added service to South Manitou as well. Tracy's son George, who grew up on North Manitou, continued to run the ferry service. Later he incorporated the service, which is officially known today as the Manitou Island Transit Company. George, at this writing, is still busy piloting ferryboats between Leland and the two islands. His son, Mike, with the aid of his wife Beth, now manages the company, and is the third generation of Manitou Island boatmen and the fourth generation of that family to have close ties with the island.

The Angell Era

It was in the early 1920s that North Manitou was first visited by a man who would

Island ball club made up of Indian workers, circa 1910

Courtesy George Grosvenor

have a more profound effect on the island's continuing history than anyone who ever lived. An executive and one-time president of the Continental Motors Company in Muskegon Michigan, William R. Angell, accompanied by a party of fellow business executives, first came to the island in 1926. The party came by air, arriving on the island in a Ford Tri-motor airplane. Impressed with the island, he envisioned it as a possible haven of natural and unspoiled beauty, isolated from the hubbub of the mainland. He could see how ruthless timbering had decimated much of the island's natural loveliness. But he also saw that most of the island was undeveloped, without any industrial or urban areas, no large farms of any consequence, and only a handful of summer homes. Most of the syndicate as mortgage holders of the vast Newhall properties seemed little interested in developing North Manitou, for they apparently felt their island holdings offered little possibility for quick financial gain. Since many of them were anxious to sell him their shares Angell was able to buy over 13,000 acres of the island from these absentee mortgage holders making him the major shareholder of the Syndicate. These transactions gave him control of over 92% of the island's 14,753 acres.

The years 1926 and 1927 were landmark years in determining the future of the island, for as long as Mr. Angell held onto his large acreage no further large scale exploitation of the island was possible without his approval. He purchased this extensive acreage just before the famed Stock Market crash of 1929. The Great Depression which followed the crash, made investment capital almost non existent, and land speculation was at an all time low. Angell decided that he wanted to save the island from further exploitation. But unlike today's environmentalists, he envisioned the area more as a personal Valhalla than a public one. It was his private game preserve where he could entertain friends and corporate guests.

Almost from the beginning of his tenure as the major landowner on the island, Mr. Angell essentially closed the island to all except invited guests. He even made it as difficult

Looking north from near Dimmick's Point in 1990. All that remains of the lighthouse complex is ruined barn on left. Telephone post is one of the 1927 telephone line still upright.

as possible for other legitimate landowners to have access to the island. Finding that he could not keep the remaining landowners from access to their property, he made it known that he was willing to buy up all existing properties, whenever the title holders wished to sell.

At the time of the large land purchases by Mr. Angell, most of the farms mentioned on recent island maps, such as the Fredricksons, Johnsons, Armstrongs, Swensons and Carlsons, had long been abandoned, and were part of the Syndicate land holdings. Besides the federal government lighthouse complex at Dimmick's Point, the only other non-Syndicate property owners south of the village were the Bourniques, the two bachelor Feilen brothers, who also owned property near the schoolhouse, and a family named Anderson. Landowners closer to the village included Tracy Grosvenor, who was now operating the mail boat between Leland and the island, several summer home owners in North Manitou Village, a fifty-acre site along the east shore of Lake Manitou owned by the Fiske family, the Maleski farm on the northeast corner of the island, and the government Coast Guard complex. Except for the federal government employes at the Coast Guard station and lighthouse and Paul Maleski, everyone employed on the island worked for the Syndicate, either part or full-time. In the late 1920s, as many as fifty people stayed on the island throughout the winter.

The years 1926 and 1927 saw innovations that had lasting effects upon the island. The large eastside village barn, built by the Syndicate in 1927, was used continuously until the island was purchased by the federal government, and is being maintained today (see A Walk Through the Village). The village sawmill, whose operating machinery may have come from the defunct Stormer mill to the south, was also put in operation in 1927, primarily to produce lumber for the new barn. It also produced the lumber used in building the fruit pickers dwellings that still stand alongside the North-South Road, just north of the village. Its capacity was small, and it operated sporadically during the ensuing years. The older equipment used in the mill predated 1927 by a good many years, making it difficult to operate competitively. It was fired up briefly during World War Two to harvest trees that were the victims of a ferocious storm in 1940. Because of the antiquated age of the machinery, much of which is still in the building, the site has high historical interest (see A Walk Through the Village).

That same year, the island's primitive telephone line was replaced by a two-wire system that ran south along the eastern shore, then westward across the island, where it was linked with South Manitou and the Coast Guard station at Sleeping Bear Point. There were sixteen miles of #12 copper wire strung on poles along the North Manitou shore. Most of the construction was done by the Coast Guardsmen stationed on the island, and much of it is still standing (though inoperable) today. A Coast Guardsman named Giles Merritt who brought to the island not only a strong background in maintaining electrical equipment but also a 1917 Harley Davidson motorcycle, took on the job of maintaining the line. Since he visited many of the island's residents on his inspection runs, he knew almost everyone on the island well and his remembrance of that period has been an excellent source of information about island life and attitudes of that day.

At the time of the Angell land acquisitions, farming activities on the east side of the island included most of the fruit orchards and limited crops of potatoes, corn and hay. On the island's opposite side, using the existing westside barn next to the old Crescent City site, a cattle-raising operation was carried on. At the suggestion of his employees, Angell increased farming activity on available cleared land, which included an expanded hay crop and adding oats and barley. Farming remained at this level until the mid 1950s, when crop growing was stopped altogether.

Ironically, it was at the beginning of Angell's stewardship of the island that an event occurred which would have the largest and most negative ecological impact on the island in this century. Although there were various cash producing economic endeavors carried out on the island by Mr. Angell's employees, it was apparent that he never invested in the island with a profit motive in mind. A few cash-producing endeavors were simply allowed to help defray the expense of maintenance and upkeep of his island properties. It was also true that from the beginning of his stewardship he wanted to maintain the island's natural beauty. But unlike a modern environmentalist's wish to preserve it for future generations, his purposes were different. His actions through the years would suggest that he looked upon the island as his private hunting and fishing club. It was to be maintained in its pristine condition for the enjoyment of himself and his personal guests, to the exclusion of everyone else. The largest and one of the most popular game animals in Michigan are deer. But deer were not found on any of the Archipelago islands. If deer were introduced to the island Mr. Angell and his guests could enjoy the presence of these beautiful herbivores on one of the largest deer preserves in the United States. What better way to play the role of the Grand Seigneur.

With that idea in mind, in 1926 or 1927 a few deer were released on the island. Giles Merritt remembered that the new herd numbered six does and two bucks. At first, the deer had a natural enemy in household dogs, who apparently ran some deer to their death. An order was then issued that any dog caught chasing the deer would be shot, eliminating a check on the growth of the deer population. The proliferation of the deer was not long in coming. This also showed that Angell and his associates could issue general island ordinances, which the

Mr. and Mrs. Paul Maleski Sr. in front of car used to deliver the island mail. The Model T Ford, owned by their son Paul Jr. still runs and is in show-room condition

Courtesy Paul Makeski Jr.

smaller landowners had to abide by, whether they liked them or not. It reminds one of Elizabethan England when a Lord of the Manor looked upon his deer herd as private property, and woe unto any yeoman who caused it harm.

It also brought on more undue stress for Paul Maleski. Not only had his income been seriously strained by the elimination of the open range for cattle, he now found the new brand of cloven footers, which freely browsed the entire island, helped themselves to the produce he grew on his truck farm. Since he could not legally shoot the intruding deer, he erected fences around his fields, but the deer easily leaped over them decimating much of his crop.

Year round island life at that time had other risks than financial to cope with. They included a lack of quick medical attention especially for emergencies. Paul Maleski's appendix burst before he could receive adequate medical attention. Although he survived and lived to the advanced age of 93, the aftereffects of the burst appendix permanently undermined his health. The combination of loss of the open range, inadequate defence against the browsing deer, and a serious permanent set back to his health left Paul Maleski a financially ruined and bitter man. In 1940, when he left his farm for the mainland, the era of the independent farmer on North Manitou was over. His son Paul Junior, who had joined the Coast Guard in 1939, realized that it was impossible to make a living on such a small island holding, and sought his future destiny on the mainland. The Maleski family, however, did not sell the old farm property at that time (see Figure 8 Loop Trail).

Mr Angell decided sometime in the early 1930s to organize his island holdings as the Manitou Island Association, for purposes of managing the island and handling such matters as controlling the deer herd. This all but eliminated the old Syndicate, but a fraction of it existed until the federal buyout, for one original Syndicate member refused to sell out to Mr. Angell.

The Manitou Island Association (hereafter called the M.I.A.) was established as a non-profit trust corporation, with the ownership divided between two partners. The minor partner, Mr. Avery T. Wing owned 5% of the M.I.A. and Mr. Angell owned the remaining 95%. This detached the island from his personal estate, so in case of his death it would not be tied up in probate or possible litigation by his heirs. After his death, his family did not claim any ownership of the island for themselves, for they were well aware that he had decided to use it in some charitable endeavor and they respected that wish.

By 1937, the deer population had proliferated on the island for over ten years, growing so large that these herbivores could no longer exist exclusively on the island's foliage. Artificial feeding of the animals was begun, to avoid mass starvation. The M.I.A applied for and was granted hunting rights to the entire island, including property held by others. The Association also obtained a "breeder's license" to be used for herd management. It was during the decision-making year of 1937 that the first hunting of deer took place, and eighteen of the herd were shot. Between 2,000 and 3,200 bushels of feed consisting of oats, apples and hay raised on the island were fed to the herd during the winter months. A few permits to hunt on the island were also sold to outsiders, to offset the expense of the artificial feeding program.

In 1938, the deer kill increased to 41, and a steady rise of the number harvested was allowed until it reached 256 in 1944. Despite the artificial feeding program and the killing of does, winter starvation of the animals was increasing. A Department of Conservation expert brought in to evaluate the situation estimated that the size of the herd had almost doubled in four years, reaching a population of at least 1,600. Since the M.I.A. was realizing a profit from hunting fees, it was proposed that the deer population be allowed to increase. The larger herd could be maintained by augmented artificial feeding, paid for by permitting more fee-paying hunters on the island. There were two serious drawbacks to this proposal. Since the deer browsed the island's ground foliage clean, there was little or no regeneration of plants or trees which caused extensive damage to the island's ecosystem. Because of this severe browse line, the under-structure of the forest is still so sparse that today the heavily wooded lands have an open park-like feeling. It was also estimated that the number of hunting fees necessary to pay for the artificial feeding would lead to an army of gun-toting hunters who might end up shooting each other. The situation was probably at its worst during the years of negotiation between a foundation established by Mr. Angell and the federal government for purchase of the island. No hunting or artificial feeding was carried on for this period which lasted several years. Since the herd exceeded 1,500, the yearly starvation of the animals numbered in the hundreds.

In October of 1984, after the island was bought by the federal government, an effort was made by the Department of the Interior to bring the population to a manageable number. A controlled deer hunt was held in which over 600 deer were shot and dressed. Even this large number of harvested animals did not reduce the herd's size enough to end serious starvation, so another hunt was permitted the following year, when 350 deer were killed. The policy at this writing is to allow enough deer to be taken during an annual hunt in October and November, to maintain a herd of about 200. It is hoped that this number can maintain itself without serious winter starvation and allow some recovery of the forest floor from the severe

Stormer house in 1987

browse line caused by overpopulation of the herd.

In the period of the 1940s, the Association realized a healthy financial return from hunting revenues, but increased costs of artificial feeding kept the island managers aware that other sources of income were necessary. Mr. Angell was still strongly in favor in keeping it in as natural state as possible, but the proliferation of the deer herd and the financial drain it created forced him to look about for some way in which revenue from the island's resources could offset the expense.

The most obvious source of revenue were the island's forests. Despite the large clear cutting carried out on the northwest and west side of the island by Smith & Hull, which ended in 1917, and the smaller Newhall and Stormer operations stopped in 1923, there were still significant amounts of timber found on Angell's vast acreage. Much of the island's forests had rejuvenated during the years following the disappearance of the wood-burning lake steamers. The westside barn, built in 1927, was constructed mostly from island trees cut for that purpose, and turned into lumber at the village sawmill. Although most of the forests were second or third growth, there were significant enough numbers of trees that a professional forester was hired in 1942 to do a timber survey. His recommendation included setting up a twenty-year cycle, which would allow a cut of a million board feet of lumber each year.

Since Mr. Angell never wanted to exploit the island for personal profit, and wished to keep the island as naturally beautiful as possible, strict rules were included in this plan for cutting operations. Only selective cutting was allowed. Trees had to be at least eighteen inches in diameter or larger at the stump before they could be marked for cutting. No trees were to be cut near the roads of the island. Dead and hollow trees were to be left for the benefit of wildlife. Neither oaks nor American chestnut could be cut; the former for their inherent value and the feed they produced for wildlife, the latter because of the blight which decimated chestnuts throughout the United States. After 1927, only small-scale sporadic timbering was carried out for almost thirty years. This plan of 1942-43, calling for larger timber operations, was not implemented until 1956, when hunting fees were falling further and further behind the cost of the artificial deer feeding program. The plan was enacted by Tracy Grosvenor, who was then the island manager and continued by his successor Marvin Fluelling, for the next twenty years. It helped keep the island operation solvent during that period, without doing serious damage to the island's ecology or natural appearance.

Beginning of the Charitable Foundation

Six years before this timber management plan was utilized, an important change in island governance and ownership was adopted. In 1949, because of changing trust laws, Mr. Angell established a foundation that bears his name. Organized as a non-profit organization, the Angell Foundation was created to promote and finance certain charitable and educational aims especially in loans to needy young students seeking professional careers, and to aid the handicapped, aged, sick and underprivileged. By creating this foundation, Mr. Angell could use the island and other investment properties he owned for these philanthropic purposes. The trustees of the Association could run it as a business, but could take no personal compensation for services rendered beyond a just payment for their services. Some trustees also served on the board of directors of the Manitou Island Association which the new foundation would oversee. The following January, while crossing a street in Detroit, Mr. Angell was struck by a bus and killed.

Since the foundation had been in existence for such a brief time before the death of William Angell, the trustees were left in an awkward position. Precedents in policy had not yet been firmly established. The trustees were well aware of Mr. Angell's philanthropic aims, but how these aims were to be accomplished was, more or less, in limbo. Since there was some doubt in the trustees' minds whether the island could be run at a profit, one plan proposed during the early years of their stewardship was to turn the island into a liquid asset by selling it outright. Advertisements for buyers brought diverse prospective purchasers whose plans for the island included private vacation resorts for employees of various corporations, a Catholic retreat and two which could be labeled as environmental disasters, oil drilling and using the island as a federal prison. Fortunately, the idea of turning North Manitou into a Great Lakes Alcatraz or carving up its interior with oil exploration rigs never materialized. Since all the prospective buyers would have used the island for purposes that deviated at least in part from Angell's basic philosophic goals, this may have influenced the trustees into not pursuing further negotiations for the island's sale.

Because of the charitable nature of the foundation, the trustees felt a far stronger desire to make a profit from the island than Mr. Angell ever did. To attract wealthy sportsmen and give island managers easier and faster year-round access to the mainland, landing lights were added along the runway of the airfield, and it was lengthened to double its former size. Deer were not the only animals introduced to the island. During these later years, an effort was made to turn North Manitou into a type of Disneyland for hunters and fishermen. Game birds such as wild turkey, partridge, guinea hens, pheasants and ducks were released during the 1960s, to attract the wing shot hunter. Trout were introduced to Lake Manitou adding to the bountiful supply of small mouth bass, for the benefit of the angler. Most of these new species did not thrive and soon died, out but the island turned out to be an ideal habitat for another animal that had been introduced earlier, the raccoon.

Deer hunters were guaranteed that they would shoot a deer. This was be accomplished with very little physical effort on the part of the hunter. During the season a guide would drive four or five hunters to a likely spot on the island that deer were known to frequent. There they were positioned on tree stands, to wait to wait for a passing deer. In the meantime, the guide would try to herd the deer in the direction of the tree sitting hunters, who apparently felt that it was great sport to shoot a deer as the animal passed under him. The Association also built outhouses nearby for the convenience of the hunters, in case the wait took long enough to bring on a natural call. Several of these outhouses are still found in various locations on the island. It seems as if they were trying to duplicate the mass slaughter of game birds on the great English estates, when the titled hunters stood in a line waiting as the game beaters drove the birds in the direction of the shooting line. I do not know whether or not tea and sherry were served and guns loaded by the island guides in the best English tradition. The organization continued the operation for the sportsmen in season well into the 1970s.

From the time of Mr. Angell's death, the Trustees continued to follow his policy of buying up island property when it became available. With the passage of time, original owners of island property, who loved the island and had resisted any offer of Mr. Angell's to buy their land, were aging and dying. Often the heirs to these properties were in a more receptive mood to sell. When opportunities arose, the Foundation was anxious to negotiate, for they did not want new landowners on the island. At the time of Mr. Angell's death, the largest holdout landowners included the home and 17 acres of the original holdings of Paul Maleski on the northeast end of the island, and the summer home of the Bournique family on its southeast side. In 1955, Paul Maleski's wife sold the family farm to the Foundation, which ended the longest continuous association of a family that had made its year-round home on North Manitou. Some Bournique acreage was sold to the M.I.A. at the death of the old dancing master in 1939. The rest of the Bournique properties were not acquired until 1958 or 59. Through the years, Mr. Angell and later the Angell Foundation, were so successful in buying island properties that when the National Park Service began land acquisitions the Foundation owned all except 22 acres of the island.

Through the years, William Angell's and the Manitou Island Association's attitude toward other islanders and curious uninvited visitors had remained heavy-handed. Summer residents with long-standing ties to the island who had previously rented cottages for island vacations that were not owned by the M.I.A were made to feel unwelcome. This policy was more-or-less continued for the rest of Mr. Angell's life, but eased up somewhat after his death. According to one still-living former long time resident of the island, Mr. Angell held himself aloof from other islanders and seemed to be very parsimonious with hired laborers. But Angell's concept of excluding new property owners, and of maintaining the island, not for personal monetary exploitation, but to protect its natural environment, did prevent ruthless timbering and preserved its loveliness. His buying up all available property also prevented any major real estate developments, which could have resulted in a plethora of new summer cottages. It also ended the possibility of other exploitative commercial, industrial or governmental operations, which might have blighted the island's natural beauty. North Manitou's large and excellent airfield also could have encouraged another type of scenario. Surrounding an interior devoted to large orchards of apple and cherry trees, the periphery of the island might have turned into an area of expensive summer homes and condominiums for the wealthy, with private Airplanes replacing the passenger lake steamers of the past. A pleasant environment to be sure and not entirely negative, but so much of Upper Michigan has been used this way that having this small parcel of land in its natural setting lends a

Swenson's Barn and Crescent City barbershop, 1987

balance, in contrast to the increasing urbanization of the mainland.

Although Angell's introduction of deer to the island later created serious environmental problems, knowledge about such problems was almost nonexistent in the 1920s. In the climate of that day, many looked upon that introduction as being a favorable environmental move. His decision to establish the island as a trust to be used for philanthropic purposes, instead of dividing it piecemeal among his heirs or friends in his will, for later sale or exploitation, was the largest single factor in preserving the pristine quality of the island. It also prevented much bitterness toward the government by small landowners forced to sell their recreational property as happened both on south Manitou and the mainland.

North Manitou Becomes Part of the National Lakeshore

When Congress authorized the Sleeping Bear Dunes National Lakeshore in 1970, North Manitou Island was included in the overall plan. The first order of priority for the Park Service was to establish the mainland part of the park as a functioning reality for the expected wave of visitors. After many on-shore problems were solved and the park was operating, the federal government began purchasing the island. Since The Angell Foundation owned all but a fraction of the island, agreement between the National Park Service and the Foundation would essentially put the island under government control. Yet the agreement was a long time in coming. The Angell Foundation had no objection to seeing the area become part of the National Lakeshore. They favored it, because this concept would keep the island unexploited and its natural beauty protected, as Mr. Angell had wished. It also meant that the island could be turned into a liquid asset, and the Foundation could concern itself with its charitable goals, and no longer be concerned with the management of the island. The fly in the ointment was price. The Foundation, naturally wanting to realize as large a sum as possible for use in its charitable work, felt the government's offers were too low. After five years of litigation, in September 1983, a federal judge set the price of the island at $12,200,000. The following spring, North Manitou rangers welcomed the first seasonal visitors to the island.

CHAPTER X

NORTH MANITOU TRAILS

INTRODUCTION TO THE TRAILS SYSTEM

Caution to Hikers: The hiker will notice many faint roads and trails that are not marked on the map. Often these are remnants of old logging roads, farm roads or deer trails that go off into the woods without a landmark destination. Most cleared areas on North Manitou were once farms. Old cellar holes and well holes exist in abundance. Often remnants of fencing, fence posts and gates are clues to where old roads traveled to farms and through fields. Use caution and common sense when walking through clearings and around old buildings, so you can enjoy the island without mishap.

Organization: This chapter is divided into four subchapters listed below. The first of these sub groups, called the **Figure 8 Trail** introduces the hiker to the major trail system of the island. The description begins at the village settlement area at **Point A** heading south around the lower half the island, returning along the East-West Centerline Trail or continuing northward around the upper half of the island. The second sub chapter, **Figure 8 Loop Side Trails** covers those trails that lead to interesting points of the island from the Figure 8 Trail. The last two sub headings, **Short Loop Hikes from the Village** and **A Walk Through the village** also use the village as a starting point. A permanent campground with latrines and fire rings is located near **Point A** on the map. The campground is only a few minutes walk from **Point A**, the village, the N.P.S. Dock and the ranger station where fresh water is available. To aid the hiker in finding a particular trail's description the page numbers are listed below.

Read the General Remarks for each section to see which ones interest you the most.

FIGURE 8 LOOP TRAIL

Distance: South Loop 12.1 mi.; North Loop 12.3 mi.; Perimeter Trail 15.5 mi.
Walking time: South Loop 6 1/2 to 7 1/2 hours.; North Loop 6 1/2 to 7 1/2 hours.; Perimeter Trail 9 to 10 hours.

GENERAL REMARKS. Until 1987, the Figure 8 Loop Trail was a maintained but not paved primitive road allowing access to most parts of the island. Although the trail is often a good distance from the lake shore at its northern and southern ends, the exterior sections of this imperfect figure 8 roughly follow the perimeter of the island. The middle section of the Figure 8 Trail almost cuts the island in half as it travels in an east and west direction and is called the East-West Centerline Trail. This figure 8 configuration is the foundation of the island's trail system. It is used by many hikers as either a long loop trail hike or as a way to get to other areas of the island they wish to explore. With one exception, it is the only trail system on the island maintained and signed by the Park Service.

One may wonder why more of the other interesting trails are not either signed or maintained. Under federal law, the island has a wilderness designation. This act specifies that trails are not to be maintained unless there are good reasons to make exceptions from the intent of this legislation. Exceptions have been made for this long-established old road, to aid hikers in getting to the more remote wilderness sections of the island, including some better-known historical sites and viewpoints that lie some distance from the village. Since the outside parts of the Figure 8 Trail do roughly follow the outlines of the island, and the East-West Centerline Trail ties the north and south sections of the Figure 8 Trail together, it is the dividing point between the north and south loops and are called by those names in this trail guide.

Many of the trail names, including the ones used to designate the side trails, are not official names but used by this author to aid the hiker. Designation points **A, B, C, D** and **E** are also mine, and not the government's. Since it was once the major road system of the island, the Figure 8 Trail is wide, easy to follow and almost never steep. Not only is it used as access to interesting side trails, but also for those hikers wishing to get to a certain point where they can go cross country penetrating the more remote trailless areas of the island. If you plan to hike one or both loops, read the descriptions of the side trails to see which of those trails would be the most rewarding. Most of the side trails are not maintained, and many are becoming more difficult to follow. Even though most of the side trails are not maintained, the more important of them are walked enough during the hiking season that, except for the time it takes to go over or around fallen trees, they are often as easy to follow as the main trail system.

Like the Figure 8 Trail, the side trails are also divided into two sections. Their placement is determined by where their trailheads are found. The walking times given above consider only the loops themselves, so hiking one or both loops with the inclusion of some or all side trails means that the time frames you should consider will be in days not hours.

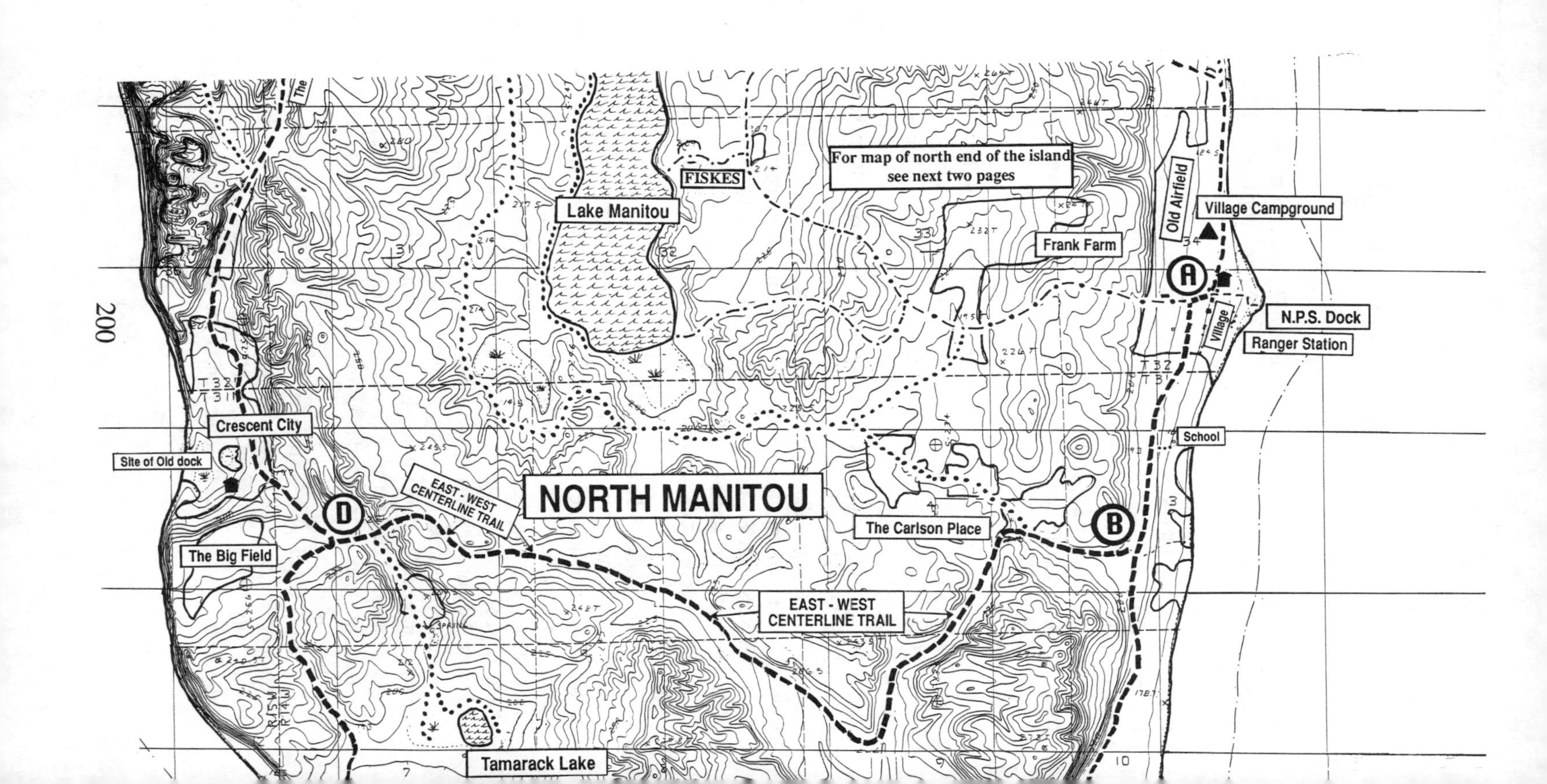
The
Lake Manitou
FISKES
For map of north end of the island
see next two pages
Old Airfield
Village Campground
Frank Farm
A
Village
N.P.S. Dock
Ranger Station
School
Crescent City
Site of Old dock
D
EAST - WEST
CENTERLINE TRAIL
NORTH MANITOU
The Carlson Place
B
The Big Field
EAST - WEST
CENTERLINE TRAIL
Tamarack Lake

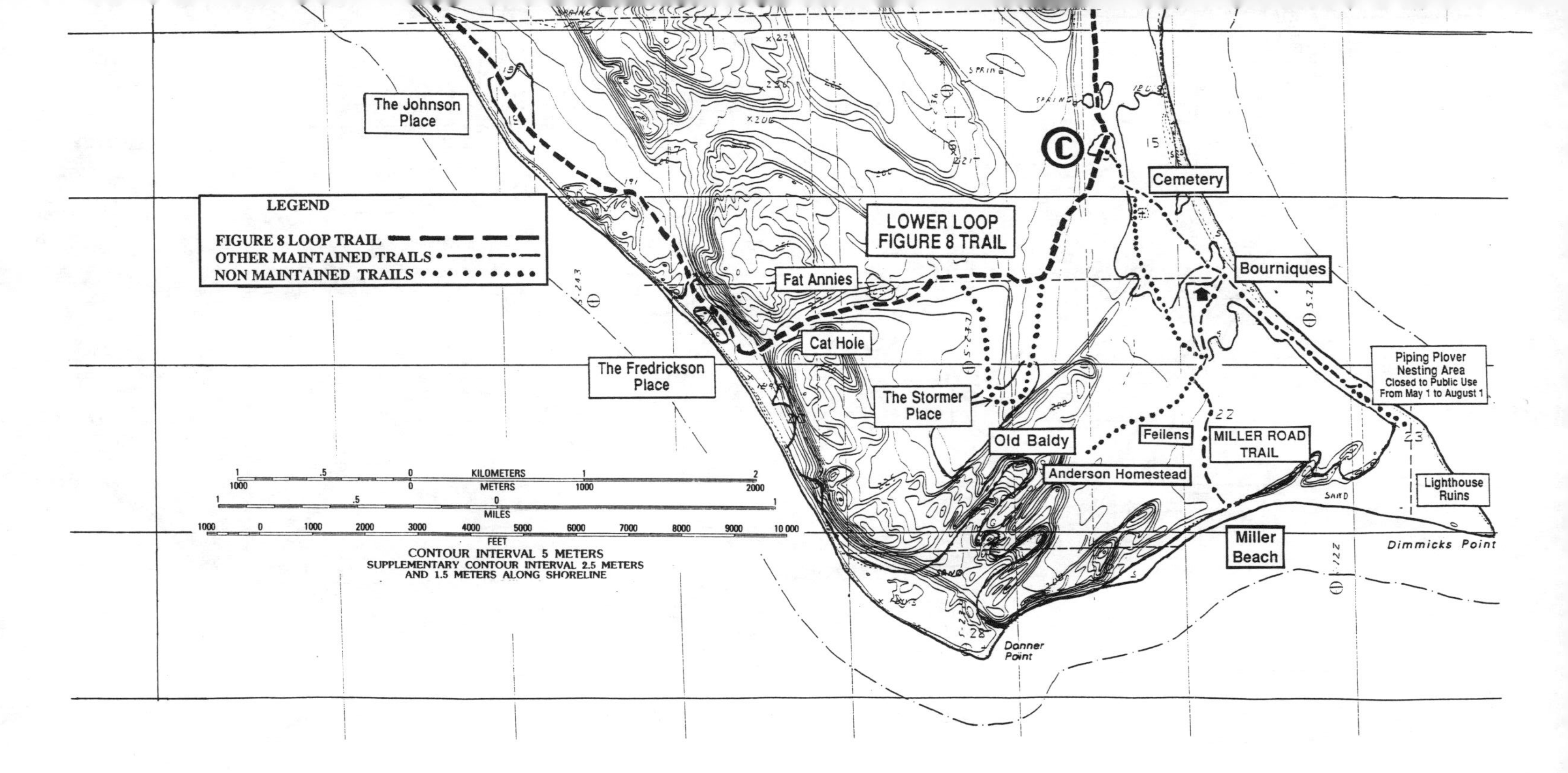

NORTH MANITOU ISLAND, SOUTH SECTION

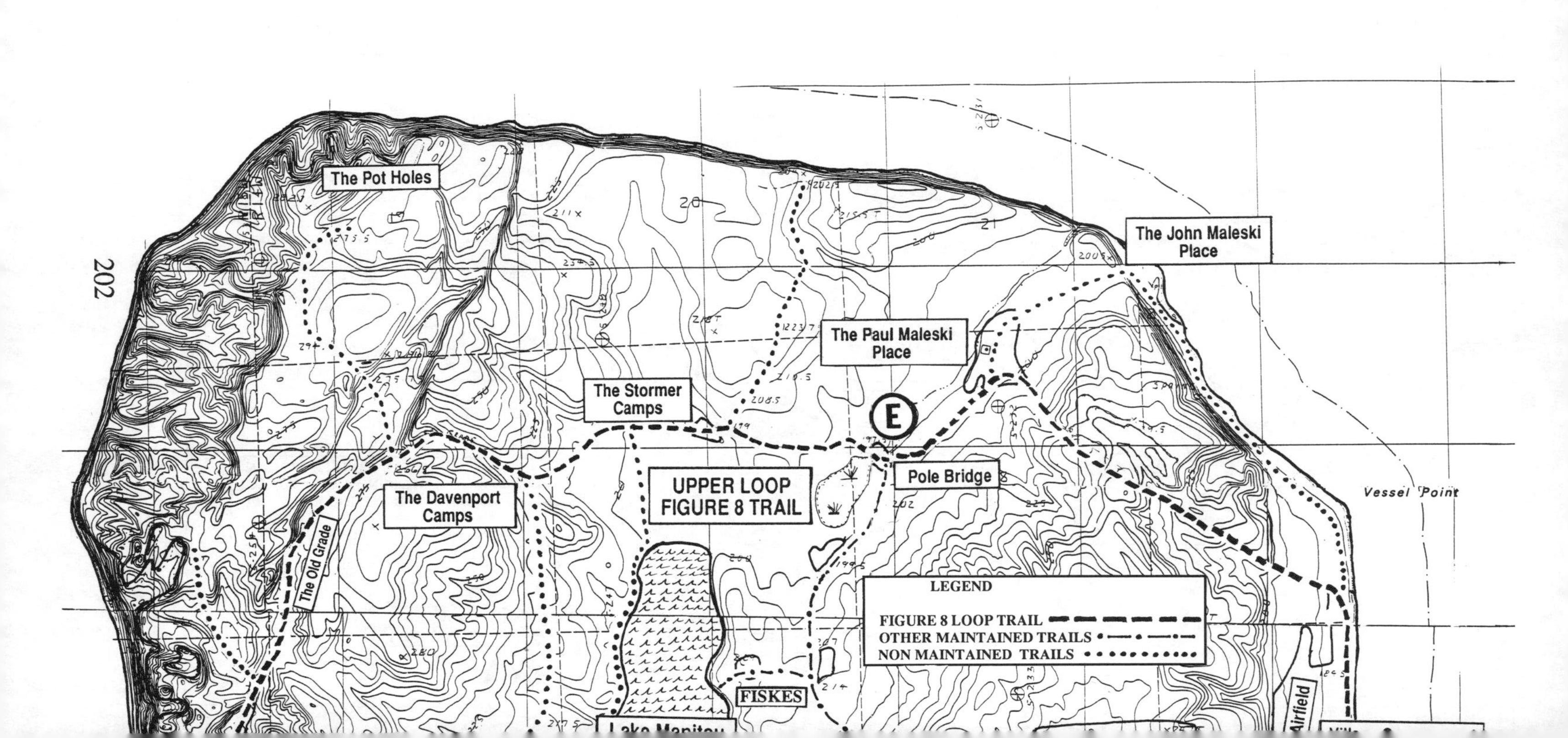
The Pot Holes
The John Maleski Place
The Paul Maleski Place
The Stormer Camps
E
Pole Bridge
Vessel Point
The Davenport Camps
UPPER LOOP
FIGURE 8 TRAIL
The Old Grade
LEGEND
FIGURE 8 LOOP TRAIL
OTHER MAINTAINED TRAILS
NON MAINTAINED TRAILS
FISKES
Airfield

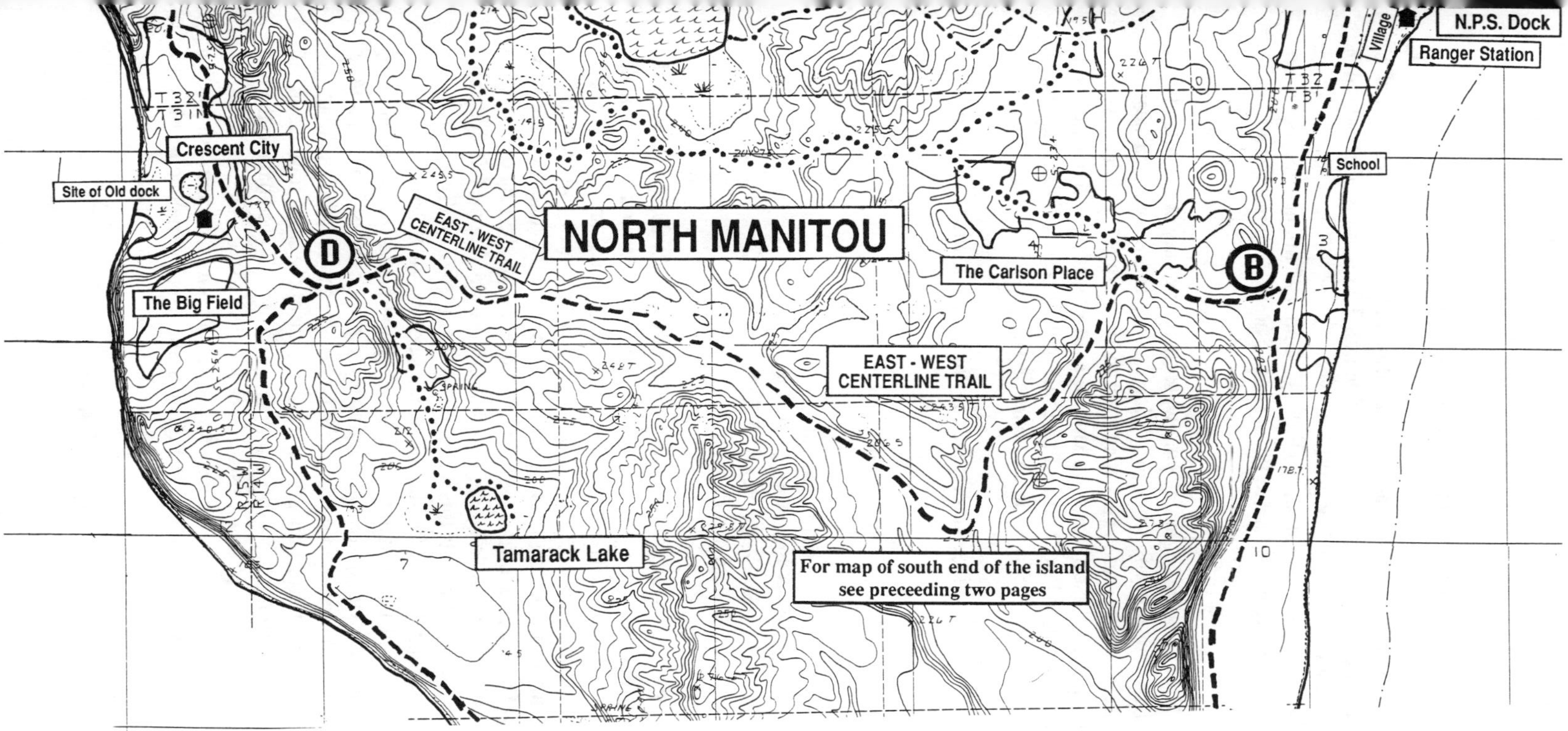

NORTH MANITOU ISLAND, NORTH SECTION

South Loop of the Figure 8 Trail

Distance from **Point A**: to junction with the Centerline Trail at **Point B,** 1.1 mi.; to Dimmick's Point side trail at **Point C**, 2.9 mi.; To Stormer Place side trail 3.5 mi.; to Fredricksons 4.7 mi.; to **Point D** 8.2 mi. Complete South Loop, 12.1 mi.
Walking time: To **Point B**, 20 to 30 minutes.; To **Point C**, 1 hour 20 minutes to 2 hours; to Fredrickson's, 2 hours 20 minutes to 3 hours; to **Point D** 4 to 5 hours. Complete South Loop, 6 to 7 1/2 hours.

GENERAL REMARKS. If you are beginning your walks in the vicinity of the village, one of the most popular first day hikes is from the village to the shore line area near the Bournique's. The walking is easy and the distance from the vicinity of the village is short enough that it only consumes a couple of hours walking time. Most visitors will find that both the Bournique-Dimmick's Point and the Stormer Place side trails are well worth the time, and the view from the upper fields at Fredrickson's is marvelous.

TRAIL DESCRIPTION. At the village crossroads at **Point A**, you will see a sign facing you on the right that says:

West side
via
Pole Bridge 6.5 mi —>
<— Centerline Trail 6 mi
<— Fredricksons 8.5 mi
Village Campground —>

From this crossroads, the Figure 8 Loop Trail briefly proceeds straight ahead in a westerly direction, before curving left, away from the road that leads to Lake Manitou. As you make this turn to the south you will see an old orchard to the right with the road paralleling the back yards of several former summer homes to the left. A couple more minutes walking will take you into the forest. You are only in the forest about a minute when the road forks. Follow the right fork. The left fork leads to one of two private residences on the island.

In a few more minutes of walking you will find the trail skirting the left side of an open field. Old stumps show that formerly this was a fruit orchard. About halfway across the field, there is an old sign along the trail facing you which says <—— **SCHOOL.**

Those hoping to find the nostalgic equivalent of the Little Red Schoolhouse, conjuring up mental pictures of long-ago children sitting at their wooden desks, will be sorely disappointed. Unlike the well preserved schoolhouse on South Manitou, this building has been reduced to a wasted heap of broken boards and the outline of the stone foundation. If you feel that viewing these remains are worth your time, an easily followed path to the left leads you on a brief walk which drops down a small embankment to the shattered remains. When you reach the deteriorating boards, walk a few feet further north and you will see the fieldstone outline of the original foundation. The Feilen brothers had a small house close to the lake not far from this site which has totally disappeared. Although they farmed a clearing

Farmers such as the ones pictured here have used the Figure 8 Trail as farming roads for almost 100 years. Picture circa 1900
Courtesy George Grosvenor

which still bears their name on island maps near the southern end of the island, they lived here near the schoolhouse.

Built in 1906, the building held its first class of young scholars in 1907. Functioning as a one-room schoolhouse for all eight elementary grades, it was one of two island grammar schools that operated during the early part of this century. The other school was located on the west side, at the Smith & Hall's Lumber Company town of Crescent City. Although the dates are uncertain, the Crescent City school was believed to have functioned from 1909 until 1917. With the demise of the large lumbering operation, that school was closed and its few remaining students were transferred to this eastern shore location. The school population varied widely, once reaching a high of 25, but the numbers began a serious decline in the 1930s. During the last year of operation, only four students attended. The decline can be mostly attributed to the policy of the Manitou Island Association preferring to hire staff that were single or married couples without children. Teaching here must have been a tough and lonely job for one teacher. The large number of female school marms shows no one stayed at the job for many successive academic years.

When you return to the trail and continue south, you will have about another five minutes of woodland walking before you come to **POINT B.** As you approach this cross-roads, you will see a sign facing you to the right of the trail which says;

West Side 5 mi —>

Just beyond the crossroads, a sign to the right facing you says:

Dimmick's Point 4 mi ↑
West Side via
Fredrickson's 7.5 mi ↑

There is another sign on the left side of the trail facing the opposite direction which tells you that the ranger station is now 1.3 miles away. This is the junction with the East-West Centerline Trail. If you wish to visit the old Carlson place, Tamarack Lake, Crescent City or the entire North Loop without doing the southern loop turn right here (see East-West Centerline Trail on pg. 225).

School kids at eastside village school, circa 1930
Courtesy Paul Maleski Jr.

If you are going to Dimmick's Point or doing the South Loop via Fredricksons, you proceed straight ahead at this junction. If you are doing only the south loop of the Figure 8 Trail, you will return to this Centerline Trail junction on your way back to the village.

Slightly beyond **Point B** on your way south, you hit a short downhill section which is the only one you encounter between the village and Dimmick's Point. You will now have a woodland walk which will consume the better part of an hour, before you see a group of small open fields to your left. These fields will let you will know **Point C** is not far away.

You may want to stop at a spring near here. As you approach the point where there are no trees between the trail and the left clearing, look for a faint trail going off to the right. If you follow it, you will soon be in a small clearing at the foot of a ridge. There you may find an old road that goes diagonally up to the left. Just to the right, there is an iron pipe coming out the side of the hill which has pure spring water flowing from it. You might want to stop and replenish your water supply. If you are not sure of the whereabouts of this turnoff, and it is easy to miss, there is a simple way to find it. When you reach the junction at **Point C**, turn and retrace yours steps for three to four minutes, keeping a sharp eye out for the very faint road to the left.

Just before the junction at **Point C**, there are low-lying hillocks with their surfaces covered with lichens, near the right of the trail. As you approach this **Point C** junction, you will see a spur road angling off to the left. You will pass a sign on the left hand side facing the opposite direction which says the ranger station is now 3.3 miles away. A sign on the right facing you says:

Fredrickson's 2 mi ↑
Westside via
Fredrickson's 5.3 ↑

When you look down the road to the left, a sign facing you on the right side of that road says:

Dimmick's Point 2 mi

This side trip is one of the best that can be taken from the southern loop. It leads you to the only easily-found cemetery on the island, the Bournique home and Dimmick's Point. It also leads to the southside beaches used for ferry landings when the N.P.S. Dock cannot be used. Although Dimmick's Point is closed to hikers between May 1 and August 1, the other features of this walk make it well worthwhile (see Bournique House Dimmick Point Trail on pg. 227).

Figure 8 Loop Trail South from Point C.

From the Dimmick's' Point junction to **Point D** at the western end of the **East-West Centerline Trail** junction.

Distance: To Stormer Place side trail 0.6 mi.; To Fredricksons 1.8 mi.; to **Point D** 5.3 mi. Walking time: To Stormer Place side trail 10 minutes; to Fredricksons 40 to 50 minutes; to Point D 2 1/2 to 3 hours; to Fredricksons including the Stormer Place side trail, 1 hour 20 minutes to 1 hour 30 minutes.

GENERAL REMARKS. If you're a bit of a romantic and your imagination can let physical surroundings help you piece together an imaginative story of the past, you'll enjoy the Stormer side trip. When you reach the eastern shore at Fredrickson's, you are high enough above the water that you will find rewarding panoramic views of the vastness of Lake Michigan including views of South Manitou.

TRAIL DESCRIPTION. Following the forest-covered road south from **Point C,** in less than ten minutes you will come to a short uphill section elevating you up to a new plateau. The climb is brief and easy, and happens just before the trail junctions with the side trail to the Stormer place. This side trail begins on the left after you negotiate the rise. This side trip

Southeast shore looking north from the site of the Stormer Dock. Life saving complex is on distant point

is highly recommended, but for totally different reasons than the walk to the Bournique's and Dimmick's Point (see Stormer Place Side Trail on pg. 237).

If you do not take the Stormer Place side trail, you will junction with its return trail in about ten minutes. About five minutes beyond that point, the trail skirts the bottom of a hillside open field that lies to the right. Known as Fat Annies, it was named after a very large woman whose name was Annie Buckner. One legend has it that this was the site of a brothel during the Crescent City days. If so, the lumbermen had a walk of almost five miles, which might have cooled their sexual appetites a bit. Since this information came only as hearsay, this myth is probably maligning the character of a perfectly respectable heavyset lady. One knowledgeable person who is steeped in island history informed me that this myth was a complete fabrication.

When I first passed through this location, I noticed a red fox sunning himself about fifty yards up the hill. Since I thought he had not seen me, I quietly walked along the road wondering if my presence would spook him. He looked in my direction, and there was no way in the world this crafty hunter could have missed seeing me. Instead of bolting for the woods, I swear his face took on a look of utter boredom, and he yawned. If not quite as tame as the foxes on Isle Royal, where I have seen them follow backpackers down the trail like pet puppy dogs, the foxes on this island sanctuary are beginning to lose their fear of man.

Just beyond The Fat Annie Clearing, the trail begins a gentle climb and soon arrives at a second clearing called the Cat Hole. I could not find how this clearing got its name. Just a short distance beyond the Cat Hole, you reach the hillcrest at the edge of the open fields of the Fredrickson farm. From here, where you can see the path rapidly drops down to a lower plateau, both Lake Michigan and South Manitou are visible dead ahead.

It is known that the Fredricksons were possibly among the earliest white inhabitants

Overlooking westside bluff at Fredricksons. South Manitou on horizon. Old table once used by islanders for an annual "All-Island Picnic"

of the island, for Hendrick Fredrickson bought this land during the 1830s or 1840s . None of the former islanders still living can remember anything about them, it is assumed the family must have moved off the island shortly before the turn of the century. There were two different farming homesteads in this large clearing.

As you descend to the level part of the field, you will see that the trail turns right and continues northward behind a tree-covered dune between the trail and the lake. On your way down, look left and you may be able to locate the approximate site of one of the houses that existed here. Although the buildings have long since disappeared, there are remnants of lilac bushes and an old orchard near where the house once stood. If you don't immediately follow the trail to the right, and instead, walk directly toward the lake, you will soon come to the top of a steep sloping sand escarpment. With the tree-covered dune on your right, this point is high enough above the water level to give you a marvelous panoramic view of the lake and South Manitou Island. The cliff at this point, however, is steep enough to make a trip down to the water's edge difficult,and the climb back up exhausting. If you wish to get down to the lake, there is a far easier place to descend about a hundred yards south of here, near the location of the old homestead. It leads to a beach, where you can see the old cable box that was the connecting point for an underwater telephone cable to South Manitou.

I was surprised to find a few weathered wooden benches scattered about near an old rickety kitchen table almost at the edge of the escarpment. I later learned how they got there. At least once every summer during the 1960s, there was an "All-Island Picnic," when summer residents and the employees of the Association drove to this clearing in the early afternoon. The benches and table were placed there by one of the managers of the Manitou Island Association. With loaded picnic hampers, lawn chairs and other accoutrements of outdoor recreation, the islanders came to spend a leisurely day playing softball, throwing Frisbees, walking the beach, swimming or just catching up on island gossip. In the evening Clark Fiske, whose family owned one of the cottages in the village, accompanied the picnickers on his guitar as they sang well-known songs. He also told the gathered ensemble that he had visited the place as a young boy in the early 1900s, when it was easy to walk on the roof of the deserted Fredrickson's house. Located near the cliff edge, most of the house was buried in the sand by westerly winds leaving only the roof still visible. Today the remnants of the house have been completely covered by the encroaching sand, and like the ghost forests, it may reappear if the prevailing winds unearth it at some distant future date.

When you begin to take the trail northward, on your left you will pass two tree-covered bluffs that lie between you and the lake. Just beyond this second one, there is a sign telling you that this is the possible site of the buried Fredrickson homestead. Just beyond the sign, the trail returns you to the woods, and except for the open field at the Johnson place about a half hours walk away, the trail stays mostly in the forest and out of sight of Lake Michigan all the way to the former site of Crescent City. At the Johnson clearing, only a small orchard still producing edible if not particularly succulent apples is left, to suggest that people once made their home here. It is assumed the Johnsons were farming homesteaders, but when they came, when they departed or their major occupation on the island, is unknown. You will find it far easier to get down to the lake at this homesite than it was at the Fredricksons.

Returning to the woods, you will encounter a couple of easy uphill sections in the middle of a dense forest, occasionally relieved by a glimpse of the lake though the trees. In about twenty minutes, the trail moves further inland away from the lake, going diagonally to the right and slightly downhill. A few more minutes after this turn, where the trail curves sharply to the left, another less defined trail continues straight ahead. This side trail once was an easily followed loop trail around Lake Tamarack. Although at this junction the side trail is easily visible, it becomes harder and harder to follow, and soon becomes lost in the general forest growth. A much easier way to get to that small body of water can be found in the Tamarack Lake Trail.

About a half hour further on the trail, you may see a small shed on the right side of the path. It probably was one of the many outhouses placed at various parts of the island by the M.I.A. for the convenience of their paying hunting guests. It is found just before the junction at **Point D.** The first sign you pass here will be on the left side of the trail, facing the other direction, telling hikers moving south that the ranger station is eight miles from here via Fredrickson's. Just beyond, you T into another trail at **Point D.** Look right and you will be able to see a sign on the right side of the trail that says:

Ranger Station 5.5 mi. ↑

If you are taking only the southern loop of the Figure 8 Trail, you turn right and follow the East-West Centerline Trail until you rejoin the east side of the Figure 8 Trail at **Point B**. If you want to see Tamarack Lake, its trailhead begins less than three minutes from here on the East-West Centerline Trail (see pg. 239). If you follow the Centerline Trail eastward beyond the Tamarack Lake junction, you have about three and a half miles to cover from this junction before reaching the old Carlson farmhouse site. **Point B** is about ten minutes beyond the Carlson Farm.

If you are planning to hike only the south end of the Figure 8 Loop, you may still want to consider walking the short distance north to the site of Crescent City before turning east. It will add about a mile to your round-trip distance.

To continue north on the Figure 8 Trail, turn left at the junction where you will see a sign on the right side of the trail facing you which says:

West Side Clearing 0.5 mi ↑
Ranger Station via
Pole Bridge 7.3 mi ↑

If you are going to complete the North Loop of the Perimeter Trail or go the short distance to the site of Crescent City, you will find that the distance to the field at the edge of that former town is less than ten minutes walking from the junction.

North Section of the Figure 8 Loop Trail

Distance from **Point D**: To site of Crescent City 0.3 mi.; to Pot Hole cut off 2.6 mi.; to Pole Bridge 4.5 mi.; to Maleski Side Trail 5 mi.; to North Manitou Village 7.3 mi.; Complete North Loop 12.3 mi.
Walking Time: To Site of Crescent City less than 10 minutes; to Pot Hole cut off 1 hour 15 minutes to 1 hour 30 minutes; to Maleski side trail 2 hours 30 minutes to 3 hours; to North Manitou Village 3 1/2 to 4 hours. North Loop round trip 6 1/2 to 7 1/2 hours.

GENERAL REMARKS. Except for the walk across the large field where Crescent City was located, the entire loop is out of sight of the lake and mostly in the forest. Besides the shoreline near Crescent City and the walk up "The Old Grade," its most rewarding features will be found in the side trips, which include an old railroad spur, the Pot Holes and the Maleski homesites.

If you are starting from **Point D**, continue on below. If you are starting the North Loop from the village, take the Figure 8 Trail south from **Point A** to **Point B.** (see pg. 199). Then follow the Centerline Trail west across the island to **Point D** (See pg. 225)

TRAIL DESCRIPTION. A very short walk from **Point D** brings you into the island's second largest open area, known as the West Side Field. The trail goes northward across this large crescent shaped clearing for 0.7 mile. Once the site of the largest town on the island, the only two structures still standing are almost immediately on the left. One of these, a large barn still in an excellent state of preservation, is often referred to as the "West Side Barn," to differentiate it from the other large barn in the village. Its other name is "Swenson's Barn." A man by that name farmed the fields where Crescent City would later be established, around the turn of the century . "Swenson's, Barn" is a misnomer for it was built many years after he farmed here. During the 1920s, The Manitou Island Association kept a resident foreman here to raise hay and livestock that organization, to supplement feeding the small resident

Swenson's Barn on left. Center building was the Crescent City barber shop, the last remaining structure of that former town still standing in 1990

population. Animal stalls that can be seen through the open doors are still well preserved.

One hiker who had visited the island during the worst years of deer overpopulation, told me that he had seen over a hundred deer carcasses in the barn. In a weakened condition, they had huddled in the building during the winter for shelter and warmth and died there of starvation. Just to the northeast of the barn is the only other standing structure. Unlike the barn, this building is near the point of total collapse. It once served as the village barbershop, and later as an ice house. A few hundred feet further northeast, one can find the concrete foundation of the once-large saw mill. Another wreck of a farmhouse lies just within the tree line, near the south east corner of the field.

There is another large open area, known as the Big Field, just south of the West Side Field. Once an area of cultivation and grazing for Crescent City and later for the Island Association, it is about one third the size of the Crescent City area, and lies on a higher terrace directly south of the Big West Field. It may originally have been cleared and put under cultivation by Mr. Swenson. If you wish to see it, climb the low wooded ridge directly south of the barn. At the crest, you will break out into the Big Field.

As on South Manitou, one would logically assume that any significant town that would spring up on this island would be located on the more accessible eastern shore, only 11 miles from the Michigan mainland. Although there is over 50 miles of open water between the western shore and the Wisconsin side of the lake, this west shore location was the site of two towns, which both functioned as centers of large lumbering operations. There are two reasons for this. Unlike South Manitou, which has an excellent harbor on its eastern shore, North Manitou has no sheltered anchorage. It was far easier and more profitable to load fuel for woodburning steamers or to ship lumber directly to major lake ports like Chicago and Milwaukee by lake freighter, than haul it south overland to those southern markets. Since

Building the dock at Crescent City, 1907. When completed this structure extended 600 feet out from the Lake Michigan shore.
Courtesy George Grosvenor

White's Mill and lumber yard at Crescent City, circa 1908
Courtesy S.B.D. National Lakeshore

there is no harbor, the eastern shore offered no advantage, and it was just as easy to load fuel or cargo bound for Chicago on the west side.

Shay locomotive, Manitou #1
Courtesy S.B.D. National Lakeshore

Gearing on the power drive wheels of a Shay locomotive. This photo was taken from an historic locomotive on display in a Cadillac Michigan public park

The early island entrepreneur, Nicholas Pickard, built a dock here in 1857 to supply wood for the boilers of lake steamboats. Some time after the Civil War, his holdings here sold to George Aylsworth. A village that bore his name, sometimes corrupted to Ailsworth, grew up around the dock. As the woodburning steamboats were replaced by more efficient coal burners, this type of operation became less and less profitable. The dock operation was closed in 1873, and the village of Aylsworth withered away with it.

A new lumbering operation began on the island sometime after the turn of the century. By that time, most of the mainland forests of Michigan had been decimated by the timber barons. There were still hundreds of untouched forest acres on the island that now became economically interesting to large-scale harvesting operators. Because of the lucrative prospects of turning out finished lumber instead of fuel, the Smith & Hull Lumber Company of Traverse City purchased over 4,000 acres of forest land in 1906. Company officials established a lumbering center at the site of the old Aylsworth village and dock area. They built a sawmill, boardinghouse, hotel, school, general store, saloon and post office. They shipped two 28-ton Shay steam locomotives to the island, and had six miles of standard-gauge railroad track laid, beginning in a marshalling yard. The main line had four miles of track, with two spurs of about a mile each.

This was the largest single enterprise the island would ever know. The town soon had a population numbering close to 300. The inhabitants were engaged in cutting and moving as much as 40,000 board feet of lumber a day. To expedite this large scale movement, a long dock was built eventually extending 600 feet out into Lake Michigan. In the heyday of the village, an average of one ship a day stopped at the dock. If you walk along the beach on days when the waves are rolling well, you can still see a few of the dock's wooden pilings.

By 1917, the timberlands needed for such large scale operations were used up, so the Smith & Hull Company closed down operations. The population scattered, and Crescent City, like Aylsworth before it, became a ghost town. The huge emptiness of the location is the only easily seen evidence that this was once a noisy, vibrant but short lived community.

Hotel at Crescent City
Courtesy George Grosvenor

If you enter the field on its southeast corner via the Figure 8 Trail, you will notice that to the northwest near the lakeshore the land falls off into a swampy area, with a very small pond which is sometimes dry. A pleasant short excursion that can be taken from here is to the narrow area that lies between that pond and Lake Michigan. From there, the lake shore is easily reached by dropping down a ledge only about six feet high. This places you on a beautiful long stretch of beach, where one may walk uninterrupted by obstructions or people for miles in either direction. It is also a nice place for a dip in the lake, if you arrive when the weather is sunshiny warm. I like to camp as close to this spot as is legally possible, for in the evening as the sun sets, a walk along the beach with the high sand cliffs behind you can be an experience long remembered.

Getting there can be a bit of a problem. Don't attempt to walk directly to it, for crossing the swamp would not only be frustrating, but also use up a tremendous amount of time and energy. There is a much easier way to get there. After working your way to the back of the barn, follow the southern edge of the forest line in the direction of Lake Michigan. The weeds are very high, and will really slow you down. There is a road of sorts just inside the tree line that goes part way. By following it, and other paths through the weeds, work your way to the tree line that borders the southwest corner of the field. Once you reach the trees, turn north, and with the lake on your left, it's an easy walk down the hill to the open area near the small pond and the swamp surrounding it. You can easily find the access to the lake in the open area that lies between the trees to the north and south.

If you make the trip down to the beach and wish to return to the Figure 8 Trail, there

Main Street, Crescent City, circa 1912
Courtesy S.B.D. National Lakeshore

Looking across the Big West Field, the former location of Crescent City. Note--hill in background is the same in both pictures

is no need to retrace your steps. You will see a tree-covered high dune paralleling the beach, just north of the swamp. Walk north on the beach, until you pass the dune. Not far beyond it you will see a sandy break in the escarpment. Climb to the top and go east across the field until you hit the Figure 8 Trail.

When continuing on the north loop, you will find that the trail has an easy rise as it crosses the open Crescent City area. You will become even more aware of how large this field is, for it will take the average hiker almost 20 minutes to cross the 0.7 mile of trail that leads to the forest edge in the north. When you are about halfway across this open area, it is a nice idea to turn and look back, for the gentle rise gives you a panoramic view of the swamp, the small pond and South Manitou in the distance. On my first September walk up this rise, I saw a flock of Canadian geese circle and land on the pond. It reminded me very much of a scene you might see on the front cover of an outdoor equipment mail order catalogue.

When you reach the northern tree line, you have already begun the longest, highest and steadiest climb of any trail on the island. You are now following the rail bed of the Smith & Hull timber railroad, which comes close to the highest point on the island. A little over a mile and a half from here, you reach the top of the "Old Grade," but the rise is steady and moderate. Although the tracks and ties were taken up over 60 years ago, the gradual rise of the old track bed is quite evident.

Author looking north along western shore from former site of the Crescent City Dock

Along these tracks, this rise was negotiated by an engine named after its famous designer, Ephraim Shay. This Civil War veteran engaged in large-scale timber harvesting in Michigan, and found that the methods of getting logs from cutting sites to sawmill were extremely costly and inefficient. He worked out and patented a unique design for operating the drive wheels of a steam locomotive. This invention proved to work well for hauling timber from remote backwood areas. He continued to make improvements, and contracted with a locomotive plant in northern Ohio to build his engines. Their success made him a wealthy man, for better than 2,700 engines of various sizes and designs were built and sold. They remained a vital part of lumbering in Michigan, until replaced by huge trucks and tractors during the second quarter of the twentieth century. One of these remarkable old engines is now preserved and displayed in a city park in Cadillac, Michigan. Shay's unusual octagonal shaped home, which he designed, is also preserved in Harbor Springs, Michigan.

You are only in the woods about a quarter-mile before the trail breaks into a smaller narrow field and proceeds another quarter mile lengthwise through it. This is the last open area of any size for over a mile and a half. If you are carrying a heavy pack, it may take you the better part of an hour to reach the top of the grade. Fortunately, the grade is never steep, and is gradual enough that hikers in good shape should reach the top as easily as the old Shay engines used to.

About a half hour's walking in the woods will bring you to a well- engineered spur of the old railroad. Going off diagonally to the left, it soon rises above the main line then curves left and goes through a cut in a sand ridge. If you follow the spur, you will find that it tops out as it goes through the break in the ridge. It then goes straight as a ruler downhill

Shay engine backing down the "Old Grade" with a load of logs
Courtesy Lawrence Wakefield

for almost a quarter-mile to a small clearing, which was once a center for log loading and possibly other short spurs. If you follow the spur to this point, you will notice on your way back to the Figure 8 Trail that the grade is much steeper than the main line. This gives you some idea of the ability of the Shay engine to climb steeper-than-normal railroad grades, even when pulling flat cars loaded with logs.

Not far beyond this junction, the Figure 8 Trail levels off for a long stretch, and one might assume the crest of the "Old Grade" has been reached. But the top-out point of the grade is still about ten minutes farther up the trail. When you have reached that point, at an altitude of just under 900 feet, you are about 300 feet above lake level and have reached the highest point of any trail on the island. This is about 60 feet below the absolute highest elevation on the island, which lies about a quarter-mile south of here.

Shortly after you reach the top of the "Old Grade" and begin the downhill section, a second major railroad spur goes off to the left. This is the one you follow if you want to hike to the Pot Holes (see Pot Hole Hike on pg. 242)

The first part of the downhill section is still on the main line of the timber railroad, and you will find the gentle grade soon leads you to a small open area known as the Davenport Camp. Once the site of a lumber operation, the presence of apple trees suggests that the site also served as a homestead at an earlier time. Just a couple minutes beyond the Davenport Camp, there is a major island road which goes off diagonally to the right. This trail, which curves around the southern end of Lake Manitou, joins the Manitou Lake Trail at the southern end of the Frank Farm. Although not maintained and never in sight of the lake, it is fairly easy to follow and can be used as another way back to the village (See North Perimeter Frank Farm Linking Trail on Pg. 243).

Proceeding straight ahead on the Figure 8 Trail, another half mile brings you to a slightly larger clearing, which is called the Stormer Camp on maps. The Stormers did use this camp during the early 1920s even though their homestead is more than seven miles from here and the sawmill they operated on the south east shore of the island, is almost that far. This shows that their timbering operations were widespread over the island (See Stormer Place Side Trail).

In the 1950s, the Lake Michigan Hardwood Company constructed and operated a sawmill here. When they first set up this mill, they cut over the north end of the island, and this location served as their main area of operations for years. One of favorite memories of the children who summered with their parents on the island was the year the huge sawdust pile adjacent to the mill caught fire. It continued to burn all through the summer and fall months, and was not extinguished until the deep winter snows smothered it.

There is still a trace of a building left here, and some wrecked trucks dating from this operation. The Park Service plans to remove the vehicles eventually.

Just past the clearing on the northeast corner, there is a faint road that, in about a mile, takes you to a high cliff area on the north shore of the island (see North Cliff Trail on pg. 245). There is another trail that follows the western shore line of Lake Manitou that begins just west of here (see Lake Manitou West Shore Line Trail on pg. 244). The last two times I visited this open area, there was an ancient wooden wagon with three of its wooden spoke wheels still intact.

If you continue eastward on the Figure 8 Trail towards the Pole Bridge, you will pass a square area that is enclosed by an eight-foot wire fence on the right side of the trail. I had been erroneously told that it was constructed as a corral to hold deer for a population study. It was used for a deer study, but the high fence was put up, not to keep the deer in, but to keep them out. By comparing the interior of the enclosure with the surrounding land, it can be determined how much damage these browsing animals are doing to the island's vegetation. Because of overpopulation, the regeneration of new forest is practically at a standstill since the deer eat all the shoots of new saplings when they can get at them. A National Park Service naturalist told me that he counted 121 maple seedlings within the enclosure that grow unmolested from the hungry deer.

Just beyond this old enclosure, you can see a forest of dead trees off to the right. As you proceed, you will find that the trees are in the middle of a large swamp, which is the drainage from Lake Manitou. There is a causeway built across the end of the swamp for the north section of the old road. Run-off water from the swamp passes through two culverts placed in the causeway. This is the Pole Bridge, which seems a strange name, since there are no poles in evidence. My first inquiry about the origin of the name netted me what seemed to be a plausible answer. The name I was told, came from the fact that the causeway caused the backup of water, creating the swamp and subsequently killing the trees. The dead trees look like a forest of poles, in the swamp, hence the name. I later learned that the name came from an old corduroy road made of logs, or "poles," that once aided both wagons and walkers across the swamp. The name stuck, long after the more permanent roadway and culverts in use today were constructed.

After crossing this causeway, you will see another small path which comes in from

Enclosure on north loop of Figure 8 Trail used for studying ecological damage done by browsing deer

the left. This junction is **Point E.** If you continue straight ahead, this more prominent trail takes you to the Bennon Place clearing, with easy access to Lake Manitou, then through the south end of the Frank Farm and back to the village. But if you want to stay on the Figure 8 Trail, with a possible side trip to the Maleski farms, take the trail to the left. Since most people either come or go on the trail heading toward Lake Manitou, the Figure 8 Trail is far less prominent, and is not much more than a diminutive path to the left.

As you walk toward the Maleski farms, you can see swampy areas to the left that run alongside the outlet draining Lake Manitou. When the trail gradually swings right, and you are approaching a large open field to the left, you may be able to see the remains of the Paul Maleski homestead to the left, through a light covering of trees. There is a road to the left that takes you through this small copse of trees directly to this old homesite, but sometimes it can be hard to find. If you miss the side road, walk to a point where the large open field that was once part of the Maleski farm is easily seen on the left. By looking back on the left side, you can see the family orchard which is quite close to the remaining buildings. Historically this location is interesting, for it is the homestead of the last independent farming family on the island. If the homesite is not as romantically situated as the Stormer Place, the Maleski's tenure on the island was continuous for over 70 years making it the longest uninterrupted surviving homestead of a single family on the island.

With his wife and one daughter, Adam Maleski, a Polish immigrant, arrived on the island in 1875. Settling as a squatter, his first employment was as a woodcutter for a company supplying fuel for the woodburning steamboats of the day. He also worked as a commercial fisherman. The northeastern point of old island maps are marked "the fish shanty" where

Swamp by the Pole Bridge

Adam and later his son John kept their fishing boats and equipment. After buying this northeast corner of the island sometime after 1880, he began general farming as well. Four more daughters were born on the island to Adam and Mary Maleski before the arrival of their first son, Paul in 1884. This was followed by the birth of his brother John in 1886. These first seven children lived to maturity, but two daughters born later died in infancy.

Adam gave the farm to his oldest son Paul, who continued to farm it with his mother and father staying with him until their deaths. Adam died in 1921, preceding his wife in death by nine years. After living on the island for 55 continuous years, Mary died in November, 1930. To move his mother's body to the mainland for burial, Paul used two teams of horses, one pulling a snowplow to clear the way over the ice and another pulling a sleigh carrying his mother's remains. It was soon determined that the ice was not yet solid enough for a safe crossing, so after he returned to the island, he placed his mother's body in a vacant house until she could be safely transported to the mainland in the spring of 1931.

Beside crops planted in the surrounding fields, a big part of Paul Maleski's livelihood was gained by the raising of beef cattle. Much of the eastern half of the island was used as open range, and since both fish and beef cattle could easily be exported by lake steamer to Chicago, both Paul Maleski and the Manitou Island Association raised many head for that purpose. An informal and easy relationship existed between Paul, who now was the

Mary Maleski with her grandson Paul Jr. standing in front of their island home, circa 1928

Courtesy Paul Maleski Jr.

The Maleski House in 1987

only independent farmer on the island, and the Association, until the island's largest landowner, a man named Newhall, insisted that the open range concept be stopped. Since the Newhall's chief interest was in developing the island orchards, cattle would have had very little detrimental affect on such an operation. Some felt the action was taken to drive the small farmer from the island. The loss of the open range severely curtailed the island's small farmers possibilities for income. But the Newhalls did have a very good reason for wanting to do away with the open range concept that had nothing to do with vindictiveness. They were interested in further developing the island as a summer resort. Bulls on the loose presented a real danger to any walker in the vicinity of the village. Children who summered there with their parents in the early part of this century and are still living, remember vividly being chased by bulls. Events often had to be altered for grownups and children alike because of the free-ranging bulls. Since his farm was not large, it killed the opportunity for Paul to make any real profit and was the death knell of any commercial operation independent from the large land holders on the island.

Now forced to do only truck farming, where little profit could be made, the relationship between Paul Maleski and the island's major land holders deteriorated. When deer were introduced to the island, they invaded his land and did extensive damage to his truck farming activities. He constructed fences to keep the deer out, but they simply leaped over them. His major source of income was reduced to the small amount he received for serving as the island's postman, a position he held for many years.

If you follow the road the brief distance back to the homestead, you will find that, although the house is still standing, the roof has partly fallen in and it will not be long before it becomes a total ruin like the barn nearby. Paul Maleski Junior fondly remembered the neat and ordered beauty of his boyhood home. The grounds were kept trimmed, with the house surrounded by a beautiful and extensive flower garden maintained by his grandmother. His father brought a Model T Ford to the island which he used in delivering the mail. It was kept in a small garage which still stands near the house The Ford too, is still running. Paul Junior has kept it in showroom condition, and still drives it on occasional Fourth of July celebrations in Traverse City. He was kind enough to share his family photographs with this author allowing me to pick the ones I wanted to have reproduced in this book.

Paul Senior continued to live in his island house until the 1950s, when advanced age forced him to move to the mainland. His wife sold the property to the Manitou Island Association in 1955. Commenting on the sale In later years, his son told a long-time summer resident, "It broke my heart, but $2000 was a lot of money to her and she needed it." Paul Senior lived on to the advanced age of 93. This was probably the only home built for year-round occupancy on the island that was continuously lived in for over 70 years by three generations of the same family.

I had a memorable experience the first time I viewed this homesite. It was the third day of what seemed like a continuous and particularly depressing drizzling rain. As I walked towards the house, a small and very young bird, who was about four inches high, landed on my elbow. At first, I thought the young fledgling had fallen from a nest or was just learning to fly and my arm happened to be the nearest landing point on an early, unsteady solo flight. But this was the second week in September, long after the nesting season, and the bird's neophyte flying days were already a couple of months behind him. At this close range, I could see that the bird, although young, was fully developed. The fledgling while looking straight at me, began a steady stream of unhappy and melancholy chirping. I thought the bird had sustained some sort of debilitating injury, and in desperation was asking for my help. What could I do with an injured bird far from any civilized place where he might be nursed back to health? After his unhappy chirping continued for well over a minute, I thought of a plan that might solve this dilemma. I was about 30 feet from the Maleski house, and I knew that the roof was still keeping one corner of the building dry. If the bird was only stunned, I reasoned that placing him in that dry corner might give him time to recover. I talked to him explaining my plan, but he paid no attention to my conversation and kept up the disconsolate

The Degan Cottage in 1987. This house is located near the southwest end of the former airfield

chirping. I turned, and to keep the bird from being unduly alarmed, began to move toward the house as slowly as I could. Immediately after I moved, the young bird took off with such power and speed that I realized there was nothing physically wrong with him. Why did he land and sit on my elbow for well over a minute, staying put even after I had talked to him long enough for him to realize that I was not a tree? Because he looked directly into my face while he was chirping, he knew that I was some sort of living thing. Possibly I was the only human being he had ever seen or been close to and he had not learned to fear man. All that joyless chirping may have been nothing more than bitching to another handy living thing about the continuing lousy weather.

In my estimation, the best way to complete the loop back to the village is not to follow the Figure 8 Trail, but to continue to the homestead of John Maleski, the brother of Paul Senior. From there, a shoreline trail takes you back to the village area. To get to this former homestead, just follow the faint trace of a road that passes the Paul Maleski house, moving away from the Figure 8 Trail until it joins the woods at the eastern end of the field. Once you hit the trees, the road to John Maleski's homestead is easy to follow (see John

Maleski Lakeshore Trail on pg. 246).

If you choose to take the Figure 8 Trail back to the village, it follows along the southern end of the Maleski farm until it reaches the southeast corner of the field. There the trail makes a sharp turn to the right. The path begins a moderate uphill grade that will continue for about ten minutes. Once you've topped out, it's downhill all the way to the old airstrip clearing, and it will take you less than a half hour to hike it. The trail crosses the north end of the airfield before turning right, paralleling its eastern side. As you walk along its edge you will be aware that the length of the field is extensive. The original field was 1,700 feet long, but its length was increased almost three times the original distance in the 1960s to a length just 700 feet short of a full mile (see A Walk Through the Village). Diagonally to the right, you can see the remains of a white summer home built in 1902. Known as the Degan Cottage, it sits on a little rise near the southwestern edge of the field.

The trail proceeds straight ahead along the left side of the field. It is near the upper edge of a small bluff which parallels Lake Michigan below. Soon you will pass four small bunk houses on the left side of the trail. They were built by The Island Association for migrant workers brought to the island to pick the cherry and apple crop. When you come to an area where there are trees on both sides of the trail, you are near the village campground. If you look right, you may see the top of the privy and many little side trails that lead to individual campsites. Another few minutes takes you past the barn and to the junction at **Point A.**

EAST-WEST CENTERLINE TRAIL

Distance: from Point B to Point D, 4.5 mi.
Walking time: 1 1/2 to 2 hours.

GENERAL REMARKS. This trail forms the middle part of the Figure 8 Trail. In the east-west direction it may be used as the bottom section of the North Loop of the Figure 8 Trail, or the top section of the South Loop. It can also be used for shorter hikes to the site of the Carlson Farm, with a possible return hike through the Frank Farm, a visit to Tamarack Lake or the quickest route from the village to the former site of Crescent City on the west shore. This old island road is easy to follow and has no serious climbs or descents.

TRAIL DESCRIPTION. (Westerly direction From **Point B** to **Point D**) From the village junction at **Point A** to the beginning of this trail at **Point B**, the walk to the trailhead along the Figure 8 Trail will take you between twenty minutes and a half hour. At the trailhead at **Point B,** the sign on the right facing you which says: "**West Side 5 mi.—>**" indicates a turn on the road to the right. The five mile distance shown on the sign is the mileage to the former site of Crescent City. The junction with the Figure 8 Trail at **Point D** is about a third of a mile closer.

After walking a minute or two, you will see that the forest on the left side thins out but is not clear cut, leaving the moderate hillside's grassy slopes partly exposed. This is the beginning of the "Carlson Clearing" which is in fact four individual fields that at different times were farmed by three successive families. The first of these, the Stormers, were early German immigrants who settled here in 1859 and left the island in 1864. Their oldest son

Peter was born here. He returned to the island during the second decade of this century and established a homestead and a sawmill near the southern end of the island. This partial clearing on the left may have been the location of the first homestead in the vicinity.

You will soon begin to see a large field through the trees on the right, which is the second of the four large fields that make up the Carlson Clearings. It is not long before that field reaches the right side of the road, which is about ten minutes walking from **Point B.** There a derelict building is easily seen. It appeared to me that it had once been a small residence, but I was later told that it served as an ice house in comparatively recent times. Although the roof has fallen in, the four walls are still standing.

There was a 15 years interlude between the time the Stormers departed for the mainland and the Carlsons arrival. Nels J. Carlson was born in Sweden in 1853. He, and his wife, Sophia came to the United States, eventually arriving at North Manitou in 1879. They had a large family of 12 children, some of whom were born on the island. Many years after the family left the island, one of the Carlson sons recalled the tremendous amount of work it took to be the wife of an island farmer. His mother not only kept house and cooked for the family, she also had to feed the hired hands. It was common to have 17 people sit down for every meal. Mrs. Carlson also sewed, carded and spun wool which she knitted into socks and mittens as well as doing all the baking. This included bread, coffee cakes, and pies. In the summer she canned fruits and vegetables in quantities large enough to keep the family and extra hands fed through the long, isolated winter.

It was during these long winter months that island families often got together. Six or seven families would gather at one of their homes on Saturday nights. After eating a huge pot luck supper, they would play games, sing and dance until midnight. Then, before facing the wintery blasts on their homeward journey, they would sit down again and have a second large supper.

When the Carlson family left the island on St. Patrick's Day in 1903, they crossed the lake on the ice, with three teams pulling loaded sleds followed by six milk cows. It took them eight hours to cross to the mainland, where they settled on a farm near Leland. One of their daughters named Hulda, stayed behind as the island postmistress. She unfortunately succumbed to a diphtheria epidemic which swept the island in 1805. She was only 20 years old at the time of her death, and her grave can be seen today in in the island cemetery.

If you are doing the loop from the village called **The Carlson Farm-Frank Farm loop Hike** you leave the Centerline Trail here (see pg. 248).

Continuing on the Centerline Trail about a half hour beyond the Carlson Farm, you will see that this old road takes a definite right turn and goes up a rise. At this point, another distinct trail goes off to the left. This is another old road heading almost due south, which eventually connects with the southern end of the Figure 8 Trail. Known as the Center Island Road, it was heavily used by the Lake Michigan Hardwood Company for many years. I have never walked it, but since It has not been maintained for several years I had assumed that, in places, it would be difficult to find your way. However two friends of mine hiked it in 1990 and said that it is still easy to follow.

Another half hour on the Centerline trail you will see that the dirt trail has changed to a grassy bottom. In another quarter hour you will begin a long easy downhill section which ends in a wide ravine with a big forested dune to the left. An ancient and barely readable

Manitou Island Association sign to the right of the trail and facing you says:

<—TAMARACK LAKE

(see Tamarack Trail on pg. 239).

Just two or three minutes more hiking time will take you to the **Point D** junction. You will pass a sign on the left side of the trail facing the opposite direction which says: **"Ranger Station 5 mi ^"**

As this trail curves slightly to the right, a sign facing you on the right side says:

West Side Clearing 0.5 mi ↑
Ranger Station
via Pole Bridge 7.5 mi

The grass covered trail coming in from the left is the southwest section of the Figure 8 Trail. A sign to the right of that trail facing you says:

Ranger Station via Fredrickson's 8 mi ^

You will find that the walk to the south end of the large clearing that was once the site of Crescent City is less than a ten minute walk from here. (For the trail description of the north section of the Figure 8 Trail see pg. 240) If you are going south from this junction, the site of the Fredrickson Farm is 3.5 miles from here.

FIGURE 8 LOOP SIDE TRAILS

Southern Figure 8 Loop Side Trails

GENERAL REMARKS. All the trailheads in this section begin along the south loop of the Figure 8 Trail, so you may use that trail description to guide you to the side trails you wish to explore on the island's southern end. Before starting on the trail walks, you might want to read the descriptions of the individual walks to see which ones interest you most.

Bournique House, Dimmick'S Point, Miller Beach Trails

Distance from **Point C**: To Bournique House 0.5 mi; to Dimmick's Point 1.5 mi; to Miller Beach 1.3 mi; to Old Baldy 3.3 mi.

Walking time from **Point C**: To Bournique House 10 to 15 minutes; to Dimmick's Point 35 to 45 minutes; to Miller Beach 40 to 50 minutes; to foot of Old Baldy 1 1/2 to 2 hours.

The Nyrland Farmhouse or Bournique Tenant House in 1990

GENERAL REMARKS. This is one of the most interesting side trips that one may take from the entire Figure 8 Trail, and when the ferry lands on the southern beaches of the island, its an absolute necessity. Although visiting one of the best parts of this walk is not always legally possible, it still offers a unique combination of contrasting things to see in a short distance. The small cemetery has little to detain one for very long, but a few minutes' walk beyond it brings you to a former summer home complex of a resident who had an unusual profession. Beyond it, you can go to the southeast corner of the island, where a large sand spit called Dimmick's Point juts out into Lake Michigan in a south easterly direction. This point, which contains a large sea bird population and the former location of the North Manitou Lighthouse, is also the nesting site of a pair of Piping Plovers. Because this bird is now on the endangered species list, Dimmick's Point is closed to visitors during the nesting period from May 1 to August 1. If you would like to continue around the southern end of the island and take the lovely shore walk to Donner Point and the biggest blowout on the island, called Old Baldy, you can successfully bypass Dimmick's Point by taking the Miller Road Trail to the beach. This excellent shoreline hike also affords excellent views of South Manitou Island, some three miles away.

Trail Description. This side trail begins at **Point C** on the southeast section of the Figure 8 Trail, about three miles from the village. From the Figure 8 Trail you follow an old road to the left in a south easterly direction and soon leave the woods.

This open section will always be impressed in my memory because I once encountered a fat old mama raccoon and her offspring waddling down the trail in front of me. They were blissfully unaware that I was following them about twenty feet in the rear. When

Kitchen in the Nyrland House

I unintentionally made enough noise for them to turn and discover this unwelcome human intruder, mama ambled off the trail, more in annoyance than in fear. She had some trouble convincing Junior that I was not to be trusted, for he had taken a curious interest in this tall stranger and did not retreat. Mama then vigorously nosed him away to what she thought was a safe distance.

You may notice that shortly after you break out of the woods two other old roads branch off to the right and left. The one to the left heading towards the eastern shore, is the road to the former site of the Stormer sawmill and dock. The one to the right is not a direct route to the Bourniques or Dimmick's Point, but passes behind the cemetery and takes you to a junction with the Miller Road Trail about a mile away. In a little more than ten minutes of walking, this side road will also take you to the ruins of a farm complex which has a small house and ruined barns. The first time I saw the dwelling through the trees it reminded me of Grandmother's house in the Grimm fairy tale. On close inspection, I found that the wolf of time has torn up the house pretty badly. The walls of both the house and the barns are made of large squared logs. When I first walked through the complex, the substantial timbers suggested to me that the house might have been built as early as the Civil War period. I later learned that it was probably built as a homestead by a blacksmith who had immigrated from Norway. Matt Nyrland arrived on the island in 1887, and supported himself, his wife and three daughters by fishing and farming. While fishing on Lake Michigan, he was drowned while trying to lift his nets. All three daughters eventually married island residents, but their mother returned to the mainland and remarried.

The place was later purchased by Alvar Bournique, and it became known as the "tenant house," for he used it as a dwelling for his caretaker. It only takes a few minutes to walk to it, but if you are going to the Bourniques and/or Dimmick's Point, you can make a small loop hike from the Bourniques and pass this complex on your return to **Point C.**

If you continue straight ahead, avoiding the right turn at this junction, you almost immediately come to the cemetery on the right. Some graves are enclosed in wooden picket

Bournique House in 1990

fences. None of their readable grave markers are particularly old, but at least two of them have readable death dates of 1905-06. This was a year of high mortality, caused by a diphtheria epidemic that swept the island.

One easily read tombstone marks the grave of John Anderson, who once owned a farm near here. Its clearing can be reached today by a path that branches off the Miller Road Trail. His thirteen year old daughter lies beside him. Many burials here predate the twentieth century, and through lack of maintenance their markers have disappeared. No one has been permanently buried here in the last 50 years because the Manitou Island Association encouraged burial on the mainland.

In another five to six minutes of walking, you will come to a small copse of trees, where the old road forks. The left one will take you on to Dimmick's Point but follow the right one, for almost immediately the Bournique homesite appears on the right. There is a sign there that says: **Bourniques.** Another sign alongside it, saying **Ferry Departure,** is used to aid hikers during times when the ferry leaves from the island's south end. On it, rangers will place another sign which say **East Side** or **South Side** on departure day, showing which of the two beaches the ferry will use.

When I first viewed the Bournique complex, I knew little of the island's history. The buildings suggested to me that it was probably the home of a well established family of professional farmers, fishermen or loggers, who might have indulged a bit in all three activities and inhabited the house on a year-round basis. But despite it's farmlike appearance, this solid story-and-a-half building, with three gables across its front, historically identifies more with the summer homes in the village than a homestead of the island yeomanry. Although the house was constructed solidly enough to be a year-round residence, it was built

Interior of the Bournique House, circa 1920
Courtesy Leelanau County Historical Society

and used as a summer home for many years by a dancing instructor, whose name was Alvar L. Bournique. In 1903, he purchased several acres of land and increased the acreage in the next few years to 152 acres. He formulated the plans for the present house and several supporting buildings, which included a horse barn, a garage, a wash house, privies and several small sheds used for various purposes. Made of vertical cedar logs in the French Canadian 'Post on Sill' construction the house is a rare example of this type of architecture. Despite its architectural uniqueness and excellent state of preservation, it is not being maintained and unless there is some change in present governmental policy, it will eventually fall into ruin or be torn down. In 1990 all except the roof of the house was in excellent condition. Unless something is done to make roof repairs, the entire building will quickly fall to ruin.

Since Mr. Bournique choose an isolated area, away from the village, for his summer home, one might assume he was a recluse avoiding the company of others. Island residents who knew him well testified that just the opposite was true. He was a jovial man, who thoroughly enjoyed the company of all islanders, regardless of their stations in life. For many years, the Bournique family occupied this home from May through October. He and his family are remembered fondly by ex-islanders who worked for or had close contact with him, his spouse and children.

The Bourniques operated a ballroom dancing studio in Highland Park, Illinois. Apparently they were quite successful, for like an early midwest version of the Arthur Murray Studios, they developed other successful branches in Waukegon, Lake Forest and Chicago as well as Milwaukee, Wisconsin. Bournique later bought more island property, until his holdings exceeded 400 acres. In 1939, shortly after his death, his daughter sold these holdings

Miller Beach departure

to the Manitou Island Association.

The garage that you can see to the left of the house once held Model T Fords the family used for many years. One of them was a rare 1926 wood-sided station wagon. It apparently was well looked after for it is said that this same Model T is now part of the famous collection of automobiles at the Ford Museum in Greenfield Village, Michigan. If you wish to continue to Dimmick's Point see below.

Hike to Miller Beach, Feilen & Anderson Homesteads and loop return to Point C. If you want to go to any of the above places from the Bourniques, or to the Old Baldy Blowout when Dimmick's Point is closed, follow the trail that heads southwest, left of the Bournique buildings, and crosses the field. If you wish to do the loop return to **Point C,** shortly after the trail returns to the woods, look for another trail on the right that heads north. This path takes you through the old Nyrlend farm complex and rejoins the main trail just below the cemetery. Turn left there, and in about five minutes you will be back at Point C.

If you want to go on to Miller Beach don't turn, but proceed straight ahead on what is now known as the Miller Road Trail. In 1921, there was a ferocious storm which may have involved a twister that resulted in a tremendous windfall of downed trees. They were so thickly crisscrossed that it was almost impossible to fight your way through the woods to the southern shore. In the 1970s, an Indian named Archie Miller who worked on the island cleared out the deadfalls that lay over the former road. Islanders began calling the new path "Miller's Highway" as a tribute to his work. It ends at the southside beach which now now also bears his name. Used as a boarding site for the southern islanders when strong easterly winds prevented boat landings along the southeast shore, it is used today for the same purpose by the Manitou Island Ferry.

When you have been on the Miller Road Trail for about two minutes, you will see that it bears to the left. At that point there is a faint trail that branches off the Miller road Trail and proceeds straight ahead. This side trail will lead you to the Feilen and Anderson clearings. If you follow this faint trail, about a five minute walk will bring you first to the Feilen Clearing. Two German immigrant brothers who worked as carpenters on the island, also had a house near the east village schoolhouse. Both are buried in the island cemetery. About another five minutes brings you to the Anderson Clearing, where the trail dead ends. Anderson is also buried in the island cemetery next to his thirteen year old daughter. Both these clearings are in deep woods without any remaining structures. If you continue on the Miller Road Trail you will find that Miller Beach is an attractive one, and is a good starting point for the shore walk to Donner Point and Old Baldy.

North Manitou Lightship

Continuing to Dimmick's Point. From the signs on the east side of the Bournique house, follow the road south. You will see that the road parallels a small forested ledge on the right. You will not proceed very far before you come to a sign facing you on the left, which tells you that Dimmick's Point is a restricted area between May 1 and August 1. You will reach the turnoff to the eastside beach landing site before you reach this sign. The sign explains that one pair of the endangered Piping Plover nests here annually. In 1984, there were only thirteen pairs of this bird known to exist in the entire Great Lakes region. Human encroachment near the nesting site might prove disastrous for this rare nesting pair. If you are here during the restricted season and wish to take the lovely walk on to Donner Point and Old Baldy, take the Miller Road Trail down to the beach as it nicely avoids the restricted area.

If you are hiking in this area either before or after the restricted season, you may be interested in going out far enough on Dimmick's Point to the former location of the North Manitou lighthouse. Remember, please do not walk through the Dimmick's Point before August 1. As you proceed southeast, crossing some open sandy areas, you will see part of a collapsed wooden building, which sits near an elevated sand ridge. This derelict structure, two small outhouses and a crumbling brick foundation nearby, are all that is left of this complex. Its location, just three miles northeast of South Manitou Island, strategically overlooks the channel between the two islands. The light also helped mark an underwater sandbar that runs over three miles into the Manitou Passage, southeast of the island. This is a particularly dangerous sea lane when navigation is hampered either by severe winds or restricted visibility.

After a recommendation from the Light House Board, Congress authorized the building of a fog signal and lighthouse for North Manitou in 1893, but did not appropriate the money for construction until the following year. In 1896, a brick building containing a steam-operated fog signal and a lighthouse keeper's home were built, but the lighthouse was

North Manitou Lighthouse complex, circa 1910
Courtesy Ethel Furst Stormer

Lighthouse barn in 1987, only surviving building of the lighthouse complex

not completed and in operation with a fourth order, ten-second flash lantern until 1898.

Because the reef jutting out into this sea lane made passage here particularly dangerous during severe weather or times of poor visibility, a light ship was anchored in the passage in 1910. It was replaced in 1935 by the present North Manitou Shoal Light, in 27 feet of water. With the addition of the light ship and later the shoal light, the importance of the North Manitou Lighthouse complex diminished significantly. Nonetheless, operation of the light was continued until 1938. Because this location is exposed to severe winter storms, the buildings rapidly deteriorated after its closing, and were consumed by violent action of waves and wind.

In the fall of 1990, I was fortunate enough to visit this former lighthouse location with Glenn Furst. In 1919, when Glenn was six years old, his stepfather Ernest Hutzler became the keeper of the North Manitou Light. Previously, he had served as assistant keeper on South Manitou and was a direct descendent of the first German settler on that island. Glenn pointed out to me that the sands of Dimmick's Point had shifted westward; the former location of the fog signal building now was under water, and the lighthouse today would be found on the present beach, almost at the water's edge. The deteriorating wooden building had been the barn. One of the two existing privies near the barn was for the exclusive use of the keeper; the other for the assistant keeper. Glenn remembered that the first year the family lived on the island, his mother decided that the nine-mile round trip to the school in the village was too much for a six year old especially with the severe blizzards the area is subject to, so only his two older sisters were allowed to attend. His stepfather had considered buying a car, but there was no way to get the car across the sands of Dimmick's Point to the lighthouse complex. This problem was eventually solved by placing cedar boughs in the sandy wheel ruts all the way to the barn.

Glenn's halfbrother, George Hutzler, later told me an interesting story involving that car. The only other auto on the island was owned by the Stormers. One day, when young George was a passenger in his father's car, it passed a blind curve and collided with the Stormer vehicle going in the opposite direction. Several years later, when George was a young man living on South Manitou, he was driving the family car on that island and had a collision with another auto. Although in both accidents the cars sustained substantial damage, no one was hurt. George recalled that although the swearing was heated enough to be heard for quite a distance, it did not quite come to blows. George has the dubious distinction of being the only person involved in auto accidents on both islands, with the added oddity that the first collision happened between the only two cars on the island.

Unlike the stationary light at South Manitou, this North Manitou Light was a revolving red one. Glenn Furst recalled that as a young boy the reflection from the red bull's eye lens moved rapidly across the sand. The children would chase the reflection as it moved in its circular pattern, but its pace was so rapid they could never catch it.

You may notice some old telephone poles still standing, a few posts still strung with wire. This is part of an old phone network that crossed from South Manitou by underground cable and ran near the eastern shoreline, terminating at the Coast Guard complex in the village.

If you are not continuing a walk along the Figure 8 Trail but plan to return to the village, as an alternative route, you can follow the eastern shoreline all the way back to the ranger station. It's an open beach walk most of the way, with only an occasional retreat into the trees to get around deadfalls. The four-mile distance is a much slower sand walk than returning by the Figure 8 Trail, but a much prettier way to return. If you go that way, you will pass many of the old telephone poles and one of the two houses on the island that still are private residences. Don't trip on the wire, for much of It is lying on the ground and is sometimes hard to see.

Painting of the Stormer Farm done by Alvar Bourniques' daughter
Courstesy of Ethel Furst Stormer

Modern view of the same area. Small orchard on right side of painting is same as the left one in photograph

If you decide to continue to Donner Point and Old Baldy, you will find that it is a very pleasant beach walk, with no obstructions to hamper your progress. The walk offers nice views of South Manitou Island and its lighthouse along the way. If you can find the beginning of the Miller Road Trail on your return, you could shorten your walking distance back to **Point C** considerably.

Stormer Place Side Trail

Distance: 1.2 mi
Walking Time: 25 to 30 min.

GENERAL REMARKS. Since the second part of this side trip returns you to the Figure 8 Trail, it only extends your total loop distance by less than a mile. This occurs because the not particularly interesting part of the Figure 8 Loop that you miss is about a half mile. The walk is easy and the historical setting is very interesting, not only for its attractive setting but also because we know a great deal about the family that once lived there.

TRAIL DESCRIPTION. To get to this trailhead, follow the Figure 8 Trail from the village to just beyond **Point C.** An easy woodland walk of about a half mile along an old road will bring you to the clearing of the former homesite of the Stormer family. It is best not to enter it at this point. You will be able to see from its fringes that to the left of you a rise cuts across the field dividing it nicely into a high upper field on your left and a lower field in front of you. You can see the remains of an old orchard along the left side of the ridge, and to the left of the orchard are the remaining walls of the Stormer house. Take the road which follows the edge of the forest, skirting alongside the left side of the field. While still in the forest, the road climbs the ridge, and passes the Stormer house on the right. It then turns right, bringing you back into the open field in front of the remains of a log barn. There is still a large piece of farming equipment within the confides of what were the walls of that building. You may wonder who the people were who occupied the house to the right of the barn with the four walls still standing.

Migrating to Milwaukee from Germany in 1857, the Stormer family arrived on the island in 1859. They were the first to establish a farm at the location which is now identified on modern maps as the Carlsons, along the East-West Centerline Trail. During this period, many German families were settling in various parts of the Great Lakes. Several also homesteaded on South Manitou. Whereas their farmer neighbors on the southern island prospered, the Stormers did not, and they returned to the mainland in 1864. Probably the difference in the success of these German immigrants on the two islands was not due to negligence or laziness, but to the availability of customers and the quality of the soil. The usual farming crops thrived more readily on the smaller island. With the excellent harbor at South Manitou, it was also easier to supply the many ships that dropped anchor there.

So might have ended this family's connection to the island. However, the island must have been remembered favorably by their oldest son Peter. Born in 1860, he was the first of their nine children born on the island. He returned to the island in 1908 as a logging contractor. In 1913 Peter Stormer bought this property, and moved his family to the island.

Approaching the Stormer House, 1987

Farm machinery found in the ruins of the Stormer Barn

His logging operations were extensive, and were carried out on many parts of the island. He also built and operated a sawmill and a large dock on the eastern shore, north of Dimmick's Point. The road to his mill and dock can still be seen. It begins near the cemetery, branching off the trail to the Bourniques. The logging operation was carried on until 1923.

This farm was used, not as a place to grow commercial crops for resale, but to support the family lumbering business. Aside from the immediate needs of the family and hired hands, the crop raising was to raise fodder for the draft animals needed in the logging camps. More than forty horses were kept for use at the various lumber operations. After the demise of Crescent City, this was the center of the logging operations on the island, and this farm must have been a beehive of activity, supplying many of the requirements of the lumber camps and the sawmill. An old combine that was once used in this activity, can still be seen in the ruins of the log barn.

Today this land, enclosed by forest on every side, has a pleasant feeling of quiet isolation from the rest of the world. Although less than a mile from Lake Michigan, there is no suggestion that a great body of water is nearby. My first visit here was on a warm and beautiful September afternoon, and there was no sound or suggestion of the lake or the busy world beyond. Although I much enjoy human company on my hikes, I was glad that day to be alone. There was no one to intrude upon my thoughts and imagination as I sat in silence among the decaying buildings, the skeleton of the old orchard and the deserted fields around them. The enclosing forest walls on every side left me with a feeling of isolated but not unpleasant loneliness, which would have been quite different if another human had been nearby. For a long while I sat near the shattered house, where I could see both the upper and lower fields, and felt the presence of that logging family as though they were still working the farm. Sixty years ago, I would have been in the midst of teamsters and farmhands, of household women going about the hundreds of necessary daily chores, while keeping an eye on the next generation, of older ones who now only watched and enjoyed the warmth of the September sun. A marvelous cacophony of rural farming activity. On this day, except for the occasional song of a bird, the only sounds I heard were the ghost voices of those past active years.

The return trail to the loop, if not readily apparent, is easy to find for it heads north, cutting directly across the field from the old barn. At this writing, three old fenceposts mark the road line across the field. If the posts are missing, the road becomes very distinct once it comes under the canopy of trees, and is not hard to find. From there, your progress along the easily-followed road will be slowed somewhat by several deadfalls that you must negotiate around or over before reaching the Perimeter Trail.

Tamarack Lake Trail

Distance: 0.8 mi.
Walking time: 20 minutes to 1/2 hour one way.

GENERAL REMARKS. Tamarack Lake is so named for the abundance of tamarack trees that grow in the swampy area. It is a classic tamarack swamp, and the open water is gradually silting up and filling in. In the 1960s, one lone beaver lived on the lake for several years, constantly gnawing down trees and building a dam at the northeast corner of the lake. He must have come over to the island on winter ice and lived out his life on Tamarack. Unlike the much larger Lake Manitou to the north, Tamarack is not good for fishing, but islanders often hunted bullfrogs here and enjoyed the frog's legs which were tremendous.

Formerly, there were four different trails that led from the Figure 8 Trail, but I found three of them so grown up that they are now impractical for anyone except the most dedicated of pathfinders. If you wish to see this tiny isolated body of water, which is more like a large pond, and is almost completely surrounded by swamps, there is one way that is easy to follow.

TRAIL DESCRIPTION. This side trail begins on the East-West Centerline Trail about a two minute walk east of **Point D** (see Centerline Trail on pg 225). When you head south from the Centerline Trail junction, in less than five minutes you will enter a large field with a ridge running across it to your left. Cut across the corner of the field roughly paralleling the ridge on the left. There you should easily see the place where the trail returns to the woods. There is a large spring found near here and in about five minutes further down the trail, you will see a narrow wet area to the left which sometimes is a small stream. Look for a not-easily-seen trail that cuts off to the left of the main trail, which will take you across the wet area. You will know you have taken the correct left turn if you cross a small culvert bridge about 25 feet

An old photo of Tamarack Lake taken at the turn of the century.
Courtesy George Grosvenor

from the main trail. This trail will lead you to a much larger swamp at the north end of Lake Tamarack. When the trail swings to the right, you will see the trail is paralleling the eastern bank of the lake, about fifty yards from it. Once past the southern end of the lake the trail soon peters out, and unless you want to go boondocking, it is best to return the way you came.

In returning across the culvert, I was in hopes that a left turn on the main trail would take me to a junction point with the southeast section of the Figure 8 Trail as is clearly shown on earlier maps. I found, however that although the trail follows alongside the swamp on the west side of Tamarack Lake, the lake itself is never visible, and the trail seems to stop at what looks like a dry stream bed. If you have a compass and don't mind jumping over or detouring around many downed trees, the Figure 8 Trail is less than a half mile away due west.

Northern Figure 8 Loop Side Trails

Introduction. Although many of these side trails will be reached by hikers following the Figure 8 Trail in the clockwise direction, many will wish to approach these side hikes by going north from the village and using the Figure 8 Trail in a counterclockwise direction. Although this segment of the Figure 8 Trail is easy to follow, to help hikers in finding the trailheads on this North Loop from the village this section begins below with a description of that trail in reverse as far as the Pot Hole cut-off. If you are starting at **Point D** skip to page 242 for the individual trail descriptions.

Figure 8 Trail
Counterclockwise (Northwesterly) Direction from Village

Distance: To Maleski Lakeshore Trail cutoff 2.2 mi.; to the Pole Bridge 2.8 mi.; to the North Cliff Trail 3.5 mi.; to Lake Manitou West Shore 3.7 mi.; to Frank Farm Linking Trail 4.2 mi.; to the Pot Hole cutoff 4.6 mi.
Walking Time: See individual hikes for estimated walking times.

GENERAL REMARKS. To aid those hikers wanting to do one or more of these north loop side trails from **Point A** or the village campground, a description of the last 4.6 miles of the Figure 8 Trail in the opposite direction is included here. The trail described may be used as a linking trail for the following side trail and day loop hikes from the village. The Pot Holes, North Cliff Trail, North Permitter Frank Farm Linking Trail, Lake Manitou West Shore Trail, North Cliff Trail and the John Maleski Lakeshore Trail.

TRAIL DESCRIPTION. From **Point A**, take the trail north past the large barn. Shortly beyond the barn, the trail enters woods on both sides, which is the location of the campground. You will also soon pass four old bunkhouses on the right that once were used as housing for migrant fruit pickers. The trail parallels the old airstrip to its end, where the path turns and crosses the north end of the runway before entering the woods. From here, you will have a long but gentle uphill grade that should take you about a half hour before you start downhill. About ten minutes beyond that crest, the trail will turn left in front of the right hand corner of a large field. This is part of the Paul Maleski farm, and you may be able to see a faint road that goes straight ahead from this corner across the field. If you are making the John Maleski Lakeshore Trail, It will take you to his homesite, but the better way to go is to make the left turn, and walk about a hundred yards further. When you see a little copse of trees that juts out into the Maleski field, look for a faint road on the right that passes through that copse. By following it, you will soon pass the Paul Maleski house and go on to the homestead of his brother John (see John Maleski Lakeshore Trail on pg 246).

As you continue toward the Pole Bridge, the trail swings left at the end of the Maleski farm. Through the trees on your right, you will be able to see open swampy areas created by the run-off from Lake Manitou. After you have hiked twelve to fifteen minutes beyond the Maleski field, you will approach a junction where this trail T's into another. You are almost at the Pole Bridge, and a left turn at this junction would take you in the direction of Lake Manitou and the Frank Farm. Turn right, and in a few feet you will be on the causeway that crosses a large swamp and contains the two culverts that is the Pole Bridge.

Just beyond this point, you will pass a high fenced-in area. If you compare the many maple saplings in the enclosure that the deer can no longer reach to the somewhat bare surroundings outside the fence, you have some idea of the intensive damage the deer do to the island's foliage.

In another ten minutes you should reach the Stormer Camp clearing. The trailhead for the North Cliff Trail can be seen on the right just before you enter the Stormer Clearing (see North Cliff Trail on pg. 245). If you cross the clearing, you will be able to see along its fringes remnants of old trucks used during the last days of lumbering activities on the island.

A beautiful old wooden wagon sits in the middle of this field but, I fear it is only a matter of time before it falls prey to some reckless hiker.

If you are looking for the cutoff for the Lake Manitou West Shore Trail, five or six minutes beyond the Stormer Camp clearing you will arrive at a place where the main trail makes a decided right turn with a fainter trail continuing straight ahead. The path that continues straight ahead is the one to Lake Manitou (see Lake Manitou West Shore Trail on pg 244).

About ten minutes beyond this junction, there is another easily-seen trail on the left side. This is the beginning of the North Figure 8-Frank Farm Linking Trail (see pg. 243). It will only take you about a minute beyond this junction to reach the small Davenport Camp Clearing. Beyond the clearing, the trail begins a gradual climb which, in about ten minutes, will take you to the top of the Old Smith & Hull railroad grade. This is the highest point on the Figure 8 Loop Trail, but the cutoff for the Pot Holes hike is just before you reach the summit. By looking right, you will be able to see an old railroad side spur that climbs up and cuts through the right-hand ridge. That is the beginning of the walk to the Pot Holes (see Walk to the Pot Holes below). If you are continuing west to the field where Crescent City was once located, it's nice to know that it is downhill all the way.

Walk to the Pot Holes

Distance: From the Perimeter Trail 1 mi.
Walking Time: Difficult to estimate.

GENERAL REMARKS. If you are not used to doing off-trail hiking and such thoughts make you nervous, you might want to skip this otherwise exciting side trip. But if you are an experienced boondocker or ready to try your first trip heading into the boonies, this is an easy one to do. The hungry deer have devoured the underbrush, which makes the crosscountry walking here far easier than in most wilderness areas. Since there is no established trail over the last part of this walk, it is highly recommended that you have a compass along and know how to use it. Some old maps show the Pot Holes as being round enclosures that the geologists call kettles. They are really narrow steeped walled valleys, reaching depths of over 200 feet, with open ends on the lakeside. These valleys were largely made by wind erosion before the ground was stabilized by plant growth. The bottom of the Pot Holes contain stands of virgin timber and springs. Once there, you have two options as possible return routes. One is to go back the way you came, which isn't nearly as easy as getting to the Pot Holes. If you decide to return this way, the use of a compass could save you from walking around in circles in the woods for hours or days. The other is to drop down to Lake Michigan for a shoreline return, which also can have some unpleasant surprises for people not used to boon-docking, including deadfalls which force detours into the water.

TRAIL DESCRIPTION. The first part of this walk is easy, for it follows a side spur of the old lumber railroad. You may either use the North Loop Trail description in the easterly direction or the Perimeter Tail Northwest Direction description to get you the this spur off the old main line. From the point where this side spur leaves the Perimeter Trail, It parallels and rises above the main line, before curving left where it goes through a cut in the ridge. Then you have an easy downhill section of fifteen minutes or less before this trail fades to nothing. There are a couple of other very faint spurs that branch off this one, but I think it is best to follow the center one as long as you can. From there you begin an off-trail walk of about a half mile. Take a compass reading and head straight north. You will probably have to climb a steep dune or two before you top out on one of them, where you will be able to look down into one of the Pot Holes below you.

Once there, you have the choice of two ways to return. You can turn back and see if you can connect with the side spur as I was lucky enough to do. Otherwise, you will have a longer crosscountry walk. If you miss the spur, continue to head straight south and you should junction with the Figure 8 Trail in a little over a mile. In either case, use your compass.

The other option is to get to the lakeshore and take a beach walk of just under three miles to the John Maleski property on the northeast corner of the island. At that point, there is an easy path that will take you up the sand escarpment, and you can follow the John Maleski Lakeshore Trail back to the village. I intended to return that way the only time I visited the Pot Holes, but I made one major mistake. I decided to stay on the ridge top until I could see the lake. By staying on the high ridge, I reasoned I could proceed to its end where I could more easily find a passageway down to the shore. Instead, I got embroiled in the most horrible snaggle of downed trees where movement of any kind in any direction was painfully slow, extremely difficult and exhausting. This maze of tangled trunks and branches limited my view and I came very close to falling over a 70 foot clay cliff. After that narrow escape I decided to return the way I came. Before I made that trip, I had talked with hikers who had successfully made it to the shore, and since they had not mentioned any difficulty in doing so, I figured there must be an easier way. By this time, however, I was exhausted and since I had made the hike alone, I felt another mishap might mean my early demise from the planet. In talking with the island ranger the next day, I learned that the best and possibly only sensible way to the lake shore is to look for a beach approach from the bottom of the Pot Holes instead of the top as I did. Once there you have a shore walk which sometimes can be difficult, for much of the shoreline is rocky and rugged.

North Figure 8, Frank Farm Linking Trail

Distance: 3.9 mi.
Walking time: 1 1/2 to 2 hours.

GENERAL REMARKS. Although this walk, which curves around the southern end of Lake Manitou, is a pleasant one, it is a far less interesting way to return to the village than remaining on the Figure 8 Trail. Although once an important island road, it had not been used much in the last years of foundation ownership. In some sections, the old road is a bit vague but generally it is not hard to follow. It skirts swampy areas on the west and south side of Lake Manitou, but is never in sight of the lake itself. This is a woodland walk, for there are no clearings before the Frank Farm area.

TRAIL DESCRIPTION. If you are moving east from the Crescent City area this trailhead is the first prominent road to the right, which is reached almost immediately after leaving the Davenport Camp Clearing. If you are traveling west from the village area, this prominent road to the left is about a half mile beyond the Stormer Camp Clearing. The first part of the road has had recent maintenance, so you will encounter remarkably few deadfalls. As you head south, away from the Figure 8 Trail, in less than ten minutes of walking you will come into view of a small white clapboard building about 50 feet from the right side of the trail. It once served as an outhouse for pampered hunters, who paid for the privilege during the association days. This road is quite distinct for the first half mile or so, then you will find it suddenly becomes far less concise. It wanders up, down and around little wooded hillocks before the first swampy area appears below you on the left. After this, the trail takes a gradual swing to the left heading east around the bottom of Lake Manitou. Again, a large swamp materializes, but this time the biggest part of it is on the right, and you cross this low area on a slightly raised section of the trail that apparently is an old fill, put there many years ago so logging vehicles could cross this boggy section. As the trail climbs above this drainage, you again will have several short up and down sections over and around small wooded hills before the trail levels out. Soon you should be able to see the open fields of the Carlson farm through the trees some distance away on the right. When you break into a narrow south section of a huge open field, you have come to the Frank Farm. Keep heading north and in about a hundred feet you will junction with the Lake Manitou Trail. If you want to return to the village, which is about a mile away, turn right. A left turn takes you to Lake Manitou in about a mile and a half (see pg 249).

Lake Manitou West Shore Trail

Distance: To Lake Manitou north end 0.4 mil.; to south end 2.8 mi.; to Village 5.4 mi.
Walking Time: To Lake Manitou north end 10 to 15 minutes; to south end 1 to 1 1/2 hours; to the village 3 to 3 1/2 hours.

GENERAL REMARKS. Some sections of this walk are more like a route than an established trail, and might prove more than some timid walkers want to take on. It calls for walking through high weedy areas whose bottoms become boggy and swamplike during long periods of wet weather or cyclical high lake levels. But the walk on higher ground, along the old road that follows the west shore, is delightful, and is the easiest long path along the entire shoreline of this beautiful lake. From this road, one has marvelous views of this pristine body of water that appears to be untouched by the hand of man. The walk to the lake may be done as a side trip from the Figure 8 Trail, or as a way to return to the village. If you don't feel adventurous enough for the swamp and shallow lake walking, but still want to see this lake, the eastshore loop hike described in the **Short Loop Hikes from the Village** section is on easy, dry trails all the way. The introduction to that walk, found on page 249, also has some interesting comments about the lake itself which you may wish to read.

TRAIL DESCRIPTION. The trailhead for this walk is just west of the Stormer Camp clearing. When traveling westward, once you are beyond the clearing take the first road to the left. If you are traveling in the eastward direction on the Figure 8 Trail, it is easiest to walk to the Stormer Camp clearing then turn around, retracing your steps to the road to the left. After the turnoff from the Figure 8 Trail, this side road is easy to follow, despite the many small deadfalls you must get around. You will follow this road about ten minutes before it breaks out into the swamp at the northern end of the lake. The road is now impossible to see, for it is buried in long grass which comes above the knees. The walk from here to the lakeshore can be irritating and taxing for the high grass hides most of the many deadfalls you have to overcome in getting to the shore. Though in dry weather you will find the bottom is not soggy, you must proceed slowly and carefully. Follow the west side of this swampy clearing until you approach the tree-covered shoreline. There, by turning right, you should soon pick up the old road that remains in sight of the shoreline its entire distance. It will probably take you about 30 minutes of easy walking along this well-defined old road to reach the south end of the lake, which is also a big swamp. The road once circled the lake's southern end, but the high grass and deadfalls make it nearly impossible to follow. I struggled about halfway around this southern end before retreating to the shoreline. With its many roots and stumps, the shoreline is almost as bad to walk as the swamp. I then found a far easier way to reach the eastern shore. The southern end of the lake is quite shallow with a hard sand bottom. The best way, I concluded, is to take off your footwear and wade the shallow sandy end of the lake around to the small building on the southeast shore that is misnamed the boathouse. From there you can see the beginning of the trail that in 2.2 miles takes you back to the village, passing through a corner of the Frank Farm on its way. From the lake you have about 20 minutes of uphill hiking, but once you reach the crest, it is either downhill or level the rest of the way to the village.

North Cliff Trail

Distance: 1.1 mi. one way.
Walking time: 20 to 30 minutes.

GENERAL REMARKS. This walk, which leads you to the high rugged bluffs of the north shore, gives you spectacular views out across the northern reaches of the lake, including South Fox Island. The accessibility of the lakeshore from this point, however, would have to be considered quite treacherous, for the bluff is very steep with an overhanging drop at the top. The trail follows a faint road that was used for logging as late as the 1950s, and since it is not walked very often, is sometimes quite vague. If you keep a sharp eye on its whereabouts, you should have little trouble in following it.

TRAIL DESCRIPTION. When you are on the Figure 8 Trail at the Stormer Camp clearing, just east and in sight of the northeast corner of that clearing you should be able to see this road's faint beginning, heading north. After you proceed for about three or four minutes, you will come to a place where the main trail curves to the right, with a tempting, less prominent road continuing straight ahead. Follow the right turn. There are no serious up and down sections or bluffs to climb. Although there are many dead falls across the road, most of them are trunks of smaller trees and are easy to climb over or scoot around. Watch the trail at curves, especially on the way back, for often there are spur roads which might lead you astray. When you arrive in an area that once served as a logging collection point, with a few old logs lying about, you are just a few feet from the edge of the bluff. Approach it carefully, preferably where you can use a tree to hang onto, for much of the cliff edge is on an overhang making the drop off quite sudden.

John Maleski Lake Shore Trail

Distance: To John Maleski Homestead, 0.6 mi.; to **Point A,** 2.8 mi.
Walking Time: To John Maleski Homestead, 10 min.; to **Point A,** 1 hour.

GENERAL REMARKS. I much prefer returning to the village by this lake side walk, for it is in sight of the water most of the way, and there is nothing of outstanding interest on the remainder of the Figure 8 Trail. There is little of interest at the homestead clearing of John Maleski, for all that remains of the former buildings is one collapsing wall of the house. But there is a marvelous cliff view nearby, which gives you a sweeping vista of the lake and South Fox island about 20 miles to the north.

TRAIL DESCRIPTION. The faint trace road that passes alongside the Paul Maleski house will take you to the opposite end of the field in less than five minutes. An alternate route is found at the southeast corner of that same field. Another trace road, found where the Figure 8 Trail makes a sharp turn to the right, also crosses the field. Once you reach the trees, the old road is easily seen, and another five minutes of walking will bring you to the much smaller clearing of the former John Maleski home. There are still many fruit trees in the clearing.

John Maleski worked as a commercial fisherman for many years. Later he became an orchard manager for the Manitou Island Association. He then converted his old home into an icehouse, to store ice cut from Lake Manitou in the winter. The building is no longer standing.

If you continue to the tree line on the opposite end of the clearing, you will see that you are on top of a high bluff. By turning left and following the edge of the bluff north, a walk of less than five minutes brings you to the northeast corner of the island where a marvelous panoramic view awaits. Looking straight north from this bluff high view, South Fox Island is plainly visible some 20 sea miles away. If you would like to go down to the shore, there is a steep path on the east side of this sloping sand cliff, which drops diagonally south, taking you close to the shore. If you walk part of the shoreline west across the top of the island, it is not far before you reach a small waterfall which is the outlet from Lake Manitou.

I remember sitting on the high bluff one evening, when South Fox Island was a dark shadow on the lake and the lights along the mainland near Leland began to appear. I wondered what it would have been like to be raised on the island as the Maleski children were for two generations. What were their feelings on seeing those mainland lights just a few miles away, but almost as remote to them as a distant planet. Paul Maleski Junior related to a National Park historian some of those feelings. Although father and grandfather seemed to be mesmerized by the island's overall serenity, his own view was a mixed feeling of curiosity and loneliness, which bordered on despair. He remembered as a boy walking to his uncle's place, and sitting on this bluff watching the mainland's blinking lights. They suggested to him contacts with interesting people, a wider choice of possible jobs, entertainments and vanities, meeting and enjoying the company of many young ladies. The blinking lights made him feel that this insular island life cut him off from an exciting world of wider social contacts, better education and wider occupational opportunities. He very much wanted to explore the mysteries of the blinking lights over an extended period of time. His first opportunity to live

High bluff on northeast corner of the island near the John Maleski Place

in that outside world came when he joined the C.C.C. in 1938. With the coming of World War Two, he enlisted in the Coast Guard. Returning to the island after the finish of that war, he found that the ways of making a living on a year round basis on North Manitou, which were possible during his father's and grandfather's day, had disappeared. In 1955, he moved his ageing and ailing father to the mainland. The old man lived on for another 21 years. At his death at the age of 93 an age of North Manitou island died with him. This island had become the personal fief of a single member of the industrial aristocracy. But this new phase, like the age of the Maleskis, the Stormers and the Bourniques before it, would soon pass.

If you are on the bluff and want to return from the John Maleski Place to the village, the trail along the lake is not only easy to find and follow, but also a delightful scenic way to go as well. It was once an old road, which begins near the clearing for the house. This trail stays in the forest all the way to the end of the airfield. Follow the top edge of the bluff south, and just after you pass the clearing, you will see where the old road angles diagonally down toward the lake level. Once down, you can see a large sand bank that cuts off the view of the lake, with a lagoon in front of it. This was the site of "the fish shanty," where Adam Maleski and later his son John operated their commercial fishing boats.

The trail soon takes you partway up the bluff on the right to a ledge, which is still a good deal below the top of the bluff. You will have one very sloshy section, made damp most of the time by a spring that is found further up the side of the bluff. There is also a short side road to the left that takes you down to a small sandpit, quite close to the shore at Vessel's Point. This point is exactly one mile from the village, and the Coast Guard erected a "mile post" there. The surfman on beach patrol stuck in a key here to show he had made his rounds.

The offshore waters are quite dangerous here and several ships have been wrecked off this point. One of them, a brig named the "Supply," carried a load of smooth bricks which still occasionally wash up on shore.

Soon you will find that you have risen to a second ledge, with the lower one still visible a few feet below you on the left. The once high bluff to the right has deteriorated to your level. When you enter a quasi-open area, with many small scattered trees, you are almost at the end of the old airstrip. After negotiating a small rise about six feet high, you will join the continuation of the Figure 8 Trail, with the airstrip behind it. By turning left, you will soon walk past four old bunk houses that were used by the M.I.A. for housing seasonal migrant fruit pickers. A short distance beyond them are the Village campground and **Point A.**

SHORT LOOP HIKES FROM THE VILLAGE

The **Carlson Farm-Frank Farm Loop Hike** and the **Lake Manitou East Side Loop Hike** are moderate ones that can easily be completed in a half day. They also may be considered as pleasant full day excursions at a relaxed and dreamy tempo, with plenty of time for sight seeing and letting the imagination wander. Three other longer loop hikes may be made from the village, using side trails from the Figure 8 Trail. Two that return to the village along the east shore line of Lake Michigan are the **Bournique House, Dimmick's Point Trail** and the **John Maleski Lakeshore Trail.** Another inland loop can also be walked by using the **Lake Manitou West Shore Trail.** Any one of these three can be covered in a single day, but the amount of time and energy expended is increased considerably. The descriptions of these last three loops are given in the Figure 8 Loop Side Trails section. Descriptions of the first two mentioned loops follow below.

Carlson Farm-Frank Farm Loop Hike

Distance: 4+ mi.
Walking time: 1 1/2 to 2 hours

General Remarks. This makes a pleasant loop hike from the village. If you are planning to stay in the village campground the first night but would like to stretch your legs a bit after the ferry ride, you should have plenty of time to set up camp after your late morning arrival, then take this walk, leaving you enough time to cook supper by daylight. It will take you through a typical farm site and the largest orchard on the island. If you are new to the island, this walk will give you experience in both designated maintained trails and some non-maintained island paths. Some sections crossing the open fields are quite faint so you can test your route-finding skill without any danger of really getting lost.

Trail Description. Starting at the village crossroads at **Point A**, follow the Figure 8 Trail south to **Point B**. Then turn right and follow the East-West Centerline Tail west. In about ten minutes you will come in sight of the remains of an old Carlson shed on the right.

Walk around the right side of the building, then turn left. There you should find a faint road heading in a westerly direction through a short corridor that connects two large open fields. This road follows along the left edge of the second field until it turns right and begins cutting across it at almost its widest part. As you walk towards the tree line, you will notice a large pile of rocks. They were probably removed from the surrounding field in order that plows and other farm machinery would not be damaged. When almost across the field, the trail goes left, following fairly close to the edge of the forest. The old road briefly enters the forest, and quickly comes into the third field of this Carlson farm complex. Briefly paralleling the trees on the right, the trail then heads for the northwest corner of that field. Once into the trees, the road is easy to follow and in about a minutes' walk, you will find that it T's into another. Turn right on this road, which is also easy to follow but at a slower pace, since it has many deadfalls to skirt around.

You have about ten minutes of walking before the road enters another large field, which is on the southern edge of the Frank Farm fruit orchard. The trail is almost non-existent here, so proceed straight north, and in about a minute, you will see a well-defined trail that crosses the narrow southern end of that field and moves in an east-west direction. This is the main trail between the village and Lake Manitou.

If you are running late or are tired, turn right and take the easy-half mile walk back to the village. If you wish to continue the loop hike through the Frank farm, make the right turn. But just before you get to the tree line, look for a very faint road to the left that heads north paralleling the trees. If you can't find this faint road, walk north paralleling the tree line and you will soon see how large this old orchard was. As the field widens to the east, you leave the tree line and walk downhill into the heart of the orchard. Keep your eye open for a faint road that goes to the right, up an easy grade, heading for the far eastern side of the old orchard. It eventually curves right, entering the trees, and starts downhill where the road is again easy to follow. In a short distance it T's into another road, which is the Lake Manitou Trail. Turn left and in less then five minutes you will find yourself back in the village clearing.

Lake Manitou East Side Loop Hike

Distance: to boathouse 2.2 mi.; to Fiskes 2.5 mi.; round trip by walking eastern shore between the boathouse and the Fiskes, 6.8 mi.
Walking Time: To boathouse 45 minutes to 1 hour; to Fiskes, 1 hour 20 minutes; round trip, 3 hours 30 minutes to 4 hours.

General Remarks. To differentiate between this delightful inland lake and Lake Michigan, long-time islanders referred to Lake Manitou as the "little lake.' With a length of 1.3 miles and a width of 0.4 miles, this smaller body of water is often the major goal of enthusiastic fishermen. This is not surprising, for I have seen smallmouth bass pulled from its waters that could be classified as "whoppers" without any exaggeration. Other species of fish in the lake include perch, white suckers and sunfish, but the smallmouths seem to be its major claim to fame. No motors of any kind are permitted on the lake, and although there are no boats on the lake, you may use one if you feel like hauling it the 2.5 miles from the village dock to the lake and back again. Most ardent fishermen do not find this much of a hindrance, because the bottom of the shoreline waters are almost entirely of firm sand with the water depth shallow enough that walking securely quite a way out from shore is easily accomplished.

But fishermen are not the only ones who enjoy Lake Manitou. I remember the first time I walked along its shores, it seemed to me that there was something wrong with this beautiful isolated body of water. There was some ingredient that was not quite right. At first I was at a loss in trying to figure out what it was. After spending a few minutes along its shores, I realized the uneasiness was not that something was wrong but exactly the opposite. Having spent my boyhood summers along the shores of a popular lake in Minnesota, and seeing many similar lakes in Michigan, my mind was programed to see many summer cottages close to the water's edge. My subconscious was not ready to accept a pristine lake with no sign of human habitation. Once I became aware of what was bothering me, it was an easy matter to turn my thinking around and thoroughly enjoy this unspoiled lake. So even if one does not fish, the shoreline can offer the hiker a pleasant and peaceful view of a forest enclosed lake that has largely been unscarred by the hand of man. Although you might feel that camping along its shores would add to the serenity of a peaceful night, remember that camping is not permitted within sight of the lake. This seems very wise, since the great numbers of people that camp near the lake would soon turn ideal locations of the shoreline into trampled muddy bare spots. This rule also states that one may not camp within sound of the lake, but since sound can travel several miles, it is a difficult rule to interpret.

For many years, this easily accessible lake served another valuable purpose for the island's summer residents. The long winter insured that ice would freeze to a depth of several inches and would not be piled up by wind and wave action like the big lake. It furnished an ideal location for cutting the needed summer supply of ice, and its closeness to the village made it easy to transport and store the ice.

Lake Manitou was the scene of a tragedy during the winter of 1986. A sergeant of the Michigan State Police, who was a licensed private pilot instructor, was on a training flight on December 16, with a student pilot from Northern Michigan University. Encountering severe fog, over Lake Michigan which might have been complicated by unknown problems of the aircraft, they tried to make an emergency landing on Lake Manitou in their Piper Cherokee. Since they made no radio contact just prior to the crash, their whereabouts and the reasons for their attempted landing were unknown. When they failed to return to the airport an air search was initiated. With improved weather conditions, the plane wreckage in the lake was easily spotted from the air. No one is in residence on the island during the winter months, so the rescuers had to come from the mainland. They found the sergeant had managed to reach the shore but had sustained injuries serious enough that he died shortly after. The body of the student, however, was still in the plane under water and was retrieved by state police divers two days later. Ironically the old island landing strip is a mere two miles to the east, but weather and possible mechanical failure prevented them from reaching it. The plane could not be removed until the following spring.

Hiking to and around Lake Manitou can be done in several ways but only two of those possibilities are discussed in this book. There is a west shore hike discussed in the Figure 8 Loop Side Trails section. Although many hiker-fishermen will want to camp in the vicinity of the lake, hikers who wish to keep their campsite at the Village Campground can easily complete a loop hike in a single day using either the east or west shore walk.

The trail to the area identified on the maps as the boathouse is the easiest and quickest way to the lake, and leads you to the southeast corner of the lakeshore. The area around the Fiskes is more open, in pleasanter surroundings.

TRAIL DESCRIPTION. From **Point A,** the trail moves directly east in a straight line away from the village. As you approach an old orchard to the left you will see where the Figure

View of Lake Manitou from the Fiskes

8 Trail turns left in front of that orchard while you proceed straight ahead, passing the old Degan house and an old lumbermen's bunkhouse behind it on your right. After reaching the forest, in about five minutes of walking, you will notice a less defined road coming in on your right. This side trail goes to the northeastern end of the large orchard known as the Frank Farm, and is used as a return for the Carlson Farm Loop Hike described in the book. By proceeding straight ahead in another twelve to fifteen minutes of walking, the main trail will lead you into the south finger of the Frank Farm. When the trail hits that opening, you will see that it cuts across this narrow south corner, with the large existing orchard at some distance on your right. The island was once an active location for commercial fruit growing, with the crops transported to Chicago by boat. The Frank Farm is the largest of many orchards on the island, and was operated by the Manitou Island Association. Only the orchards alongside the airplane landing strip compared in size.

When you reenter the woods, another three to four minutes will bring you to a fork in the road. The right fork will lead you to the Fiskes, and the left to the boathouse area. If you want to go to the boathouse area first, you can later proceed along the shore line north from the boathouse to the Fiskes, covering the somewhat uneven terrain near the bank where a trail of sorts can be followed. This will not be much of a handicap for day hikers, but those carrying backpacks may find it a bit rough, and it might be a better idea to go to the Fiskes by the trail that is not along the lakeshore and, after dropping your pack, explore this stretch without that heavy burden.

If you continue in the direction of the boathouse, you will have a steady climb of about ten minutes, then a steady downhill section lasting about twenty minutes, taking you almost to the edge of the lake. When you arrive, you will find that the name "Boathouse" is a ghost name. Of the lake's east shore, only this southern corner was owned by Mr. Angell. There was a lovely post-Victorian two story boathouse at this location that stood here well into the 1950s. It is no longer in existence, and may have been destroyed by fire. You will see a small white building on the right, with two deteriorating outhouses nearby. You can easily see from the small size of the building that it never was a place to store boats. Its two small rooms served the dual purpose of changing rooms for swimmers and storage for outboard motors, oars and other paraphernalia for fishing and boating excursions on the little lake. A few posts of an old dock are still visible in the shallow water.

You will be able to see that the south end of the lake is a fairly swampy area. There never was a road along this east shore, but you can hike along the bank northward to the Fiskes. About halfway, the walking becomes much easier, for there is a path made by fishermen which is neither demanding nor difficult to follow. Just before reaching the Fiskes, you will pass a very low boathouse that was used to store a rowboat and was built by the Fiske family. The rotting hulk of the boat that it once held is half buried along the shoreline

If you decide to go directly to the Fiskes via Bennon's place, without going first to the boathouse, once you have passed the Frank Farm clearing, take the first fork to the right. You have a short easy climb and then about 20 minutes of easy downhill trail through the woods before breaking out in the Bennon's Place clearing. The turnoff trail to Fiskes is at the far north end of this field. About five minutes after you begin walking toward the lake, you will come to a clearing which is in sight of, but not directly on the lake. As you approach the lake you are in an area known by summer residents as Fiske's Landing.

The Fiske family were long-time summer residents of Cottage Row, where their home still stands (see a Walk Through the Village). This area of Lake Manitou was called Fiske's Landing, because Mr. Fiske owned 100 acres along the eastern shore of Lake Manitou, which he obtained in a trade. He owned a similar size tract of land with a valuable spring in the center of the island that the Newhalls wanted. They traded him this very desirable land along the shore of the little lake in exchange for the the center island property.

Since this shoreline area is an idyllic location, it doesn't take a lot of imagination to see that it would make a wonderful place for a small get-away summer home. I had originally assumed that the Fiskes purchased this land for that purpose, but apparently that was never their plan. I wondered if there had ever been any buildings larger than the the Fiske's small green boathouse which stands nearby. Susan Wasserman, a lady of tremendous knowledge about the island has supplied me with valuable information on many aspects of island history. She is a great-granddaughter of Howard Foote, who was one of the original participants involved in forming the summer community which eventually became cottage row. She told me the original deeds for the cottage row lots specified that each lot owner would also have the right to build a boathouse along the shores of the little lake. In the 1890s, Mr. Foote had the Feilen brothers build a two-story boathouse close to the water in front of the grassy knoll north of the path. A few years later, after the building was destroyed by fire, Mr. Foote had a second one built. It was used for many years by the Foote descendents, but apparently it fell to ruin during the World War Two period, and there is no sign of a building there today.

If you wish to complete the loop hike, return to the Bennon Place clearing and turn left. In less than ten minutes, you will enter another open field and be able to see through the trees on the right what looks like another open field. It is not a field, but part of the large swamp that lies northeast of Lake Manitou, with the Pole Bridge at its far end. Once across this clearing, you will soon be approaching the Pole Bridge at **Point E.** If you have not previously walked the Figure 8 Trail, be aware that the Pole Bridge has no poles in evidence, and is really two culverts bisecting a causeway that passes across the end of the swamp. As you approach the bridge, look for a trail to the right. That junction is **Point E.** The path to the right is the continuation of the Figure 8 Trail that will take you past the Maleskis and back to the village (see pg.220).

A WALK THROUGH THE VILLAGE

Writing this section is done with a great deal of ambivalence and uncertainty, because there is the real possibility that, soon many of the buildings described here may no longer be standing. A 1987 Park Service Draft Development Concept Plan under consideration stated, "Most village structures outside the lifesaving station complex will be removed, except for one building for maintenance and storage, one building for a shelter hostel, and a historic sawmill." At this writing, the statement is not yet official policy, but it might become so. I feel that from the historical perspective, this policy may not be the wisest and alternatives for saving three or four of the other existing buildings might be considered.

In the last decade of the nineteenth century, there was an active attempt to promote the present village area as a small affluent summer resort. The largest number of the village's summer cottages were constructed then. Most of the people involved were friends and acquaintances from the Chicago area, who built these summer cottages before the turn of the century. In 1979, shortly after the island was proposed for inclusion in the Sleeping Bear National Lake Shore, a student from Michigan State University did a study of existent structures to determine which should be proposed for nomination to the National Register, and thereby be saved from further destruction. His incredible report suggested that none of them, including the Coast Guard complex, warranted such a classification. Since then, a more sensible reclassification has been made. It is a vast improvement over the first report, but seems to have been influenced more by utility than significant historical worth.

Although my major concentration in the historical field has been in the European area, I was born in this country and maintain an intense interest in many facets of our history. Though I claim no great scholarly expertise in architecture, my own opinions sometimes differ from the official view. I am fully aware that my thinking has been emotionally influenced by the happy seasons I spent during my boyhood in a similar summer community on an island in a Minnesota lake. But I am also old enough to be acutely aware that so many delightful summer residences built around the turn of the century in these northern Midwest lake states, once so common, are rapidly disappearing. There is a chance, unique on this island, to save a delightful reminder of this small segment of moderately well-off Midwest Americans enjoying themselves. The Development Concept Plan for the island includes a wilderness recommendation for the entire island excluding only 27-acres within the village to be developed as a possible historic zone. In the opinion of this writer it would be much desired if such a policy could be adopted, at least in part.

With the serious problem of our huge federal deficit and the limited, miniscule allotment of funds the Congress allows the Department of the Interior to operate our national

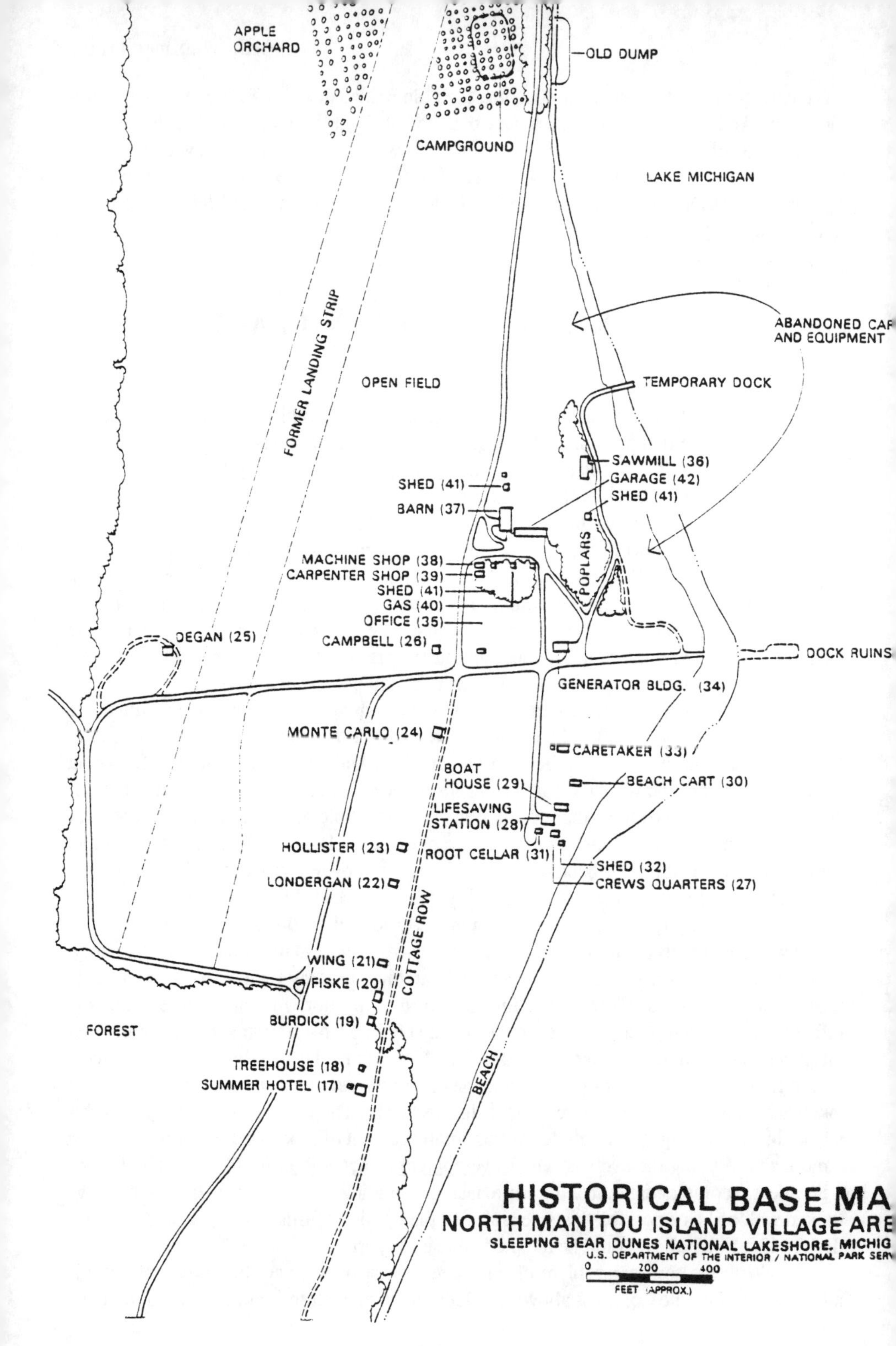
APPLE ORCHARD
OLD DUMP
CAMPGROUND
LAKE MICHIGAN
FORMER LANDING STRIP
ABANDONED CAR
AND EQUIPMENT
OPEN FIELD
TEMPORARY DOCK
SAWMILL (36)
GARAGE (42)
SHED (41)
SHED (41)
BARN (37)
POPLARS
MACHINE SHOP (38)
CARPENTER SHOP (39)
SHED (41)
GAS (40)
OFFICE (35)
DEGAN (25)
CAMPBELL (26)
DOCK RUINS
GENERATOR BLDG. (34)
MONTE CARLO (24)
CARETAKER (33)
BOAT
HOUSE (29)
BEACH CART (30)
LIFESAVING
STATION (28)
HOLLISTER (23)
ROOT CELLAR (31)
SHED (32)
LONDERGAN (22)
CREWS QUARTERS (27)
COTTAGE ROW
WING (21)
FISKE (20)
BURDICK (19)
FOREST
TREEHOUSE (18)
SUMMER HOTEL (17)
BEACH
HISTORICAL BASE MA
NORTH MANITOU ISLAND VILLAGE ARE
SLEEPING BEAR DUNES NATIONAL LAKESHORE, MICHIG
U.S. DEPARTMENT OF THE INTERIOR / NATIONAL PARK SERV
0 200 400
FEET (APPROX.)

parks, it would be difficult for this underfunded branch to assume the costly restoration of a few summer homes on an island that is largely designated a wilderness, and few would see. But there are many precedents for this type of action that have been taken by the Park Service in the past.

A good example of this procedure was followed at the mountain farm complexes at Cades Cove in the Smokies. The first plan for the cove was to allow it to return to wilderness and remove the farms. Then it was realized that these mountain farms represented an important part of our Appalachian heritage. So the plan was changed and the farms are now maintained by the Park Service. But Cades Cove is easily accessible by automobile, and open to thousands of visitors each year. North Manitou is far less accessible and if accessibility became easy, the increase of visitors would seriously alter the wilderness concept of the island, something that most hikers, including this author, would deplore.

North Manitou's small summer community was never large in number nor does it approach anywhere near the role in the romance of American history played by the Appalachian farmers of Cades Cove. Some island's summer residences have been changed so much that they no longer have visible historical identification with the period, or they have deteriorated beyond the point of sensible economic reconstruction. There are still a couple of uniquely American summer home structures, however, close to a hundred years old that have suffered only minor structural changes. Could there possibly be some historical group that might raise funds to save the more important of these summer homes, if such a policy could be worked out? My own suggestions for choosing a few of these buildings for stabilized maintenance to keep them from further deterioration and for later possible renovation are included in this Chapter, following the walk down cottage row.

If you have read the history section of this chapter you are already aware that the largest and oldest named villages on the island were on its opposite side along the west shore. From the time of the first white settlers, there were settlements on the eastern side, but they remained small until just before the turn of the century. Aside from its closeness to the mainland, two other factors aided in the growth and survival of a small eastern shore village, while the west shore settlements disappeared entirely. Since most ships traveled through the famous Manitou Passage, the Lifesaving Service, which eventually became a branch of the Coast Guard, built a rescue station here. It was also in this vicinity that the island's only resort area was built.

In using this guide of North Manitou village you may find the National Park's **Historical Base Map** reprinted on the opposite page useful in locating the buildings. Not all buildings on that map are included in this discussion, for many are in an advanced state of deterioration or have no particular interest for the average visitor. The numbers enclosed in parentheses in the text identify the numbered buildings found on the map.

THE COAST GUARD LIFESAVING STATION.

The winter of 1870-71 was particularly stormy, resulting in many deaths and shipwrecks, with over 214 fatalities on the Great Lakes alone. Because of such carnage along the coasts, Congress authorized money to be spent in establishing the first professional life saving crews along the shores of the oceans and Great Lakes. Of the 214 deaths reported on the Great Lakes that year, over half of them happened on Lake Michigan. Since most of the shipping on Lake Michigan passed through the hazardous Manitou Straits, it became a prime location for one of the early stations. This complex, which had its beginnings in 1874, was the first lifesaving station established in the Manitou Passage and the Lake Michigan Archipelago Islands. Records of when each of the existing buildings was constructed are sketchy. It is even unclear whether this is the original site of the station, but accounts do indicate that an important building of the station was built at this location in 1877. It is also known that most of the existing building were constructed during the 1890s, and all the present buildings were built before the turn of the century. Of the remaining government buildings on either of the Manitous, only the lighthouse complex on South Manitou is older.

North Manitou Coast Guard Life Saving Station, circa 1930
Courtesy George Grosvenor

Some of these buildings in the North Manitou complex are among the oldest structures that have not become derelicts on either island.

The complex was under the charge of a keeper, often called the skipper, and manned by six to seven surfmen. At the beginning of the twentieth century, two new stations were added at South Manitou and Sleeping Bear Point. In 1915, the Lifesaving Service was incorporated into the Coast Guard, and the North Manitou station continued to be manned by a full crew until 1933. During that most difficult of the depression years, it was felt that having three such stations in such close proximity was a bit of overkill, so the North Manitou crew was reduced to two. This skeleton crew was maintained until shortly after World War II, when the base was shut down and the property sold to the Manitou Island Association.

To better understand how such a station functioned, a visit to the restored Sleeping Bear Point Coast Guard Station just north of Glen Haven is worthwhile and highly recommended. This mainland station is now a Maritime Museum maintained by the National Park Service and is designed to show the visitor how such a facility operated.

The present main building of the North Manitou complex (#28), which functioned as the residence of the commanding officer, the crew's dormitory and the headquarters for the station, was not the original building used for that purpose. The first building known to house the skipper was called the Buss House. That building was later moved nearer Cottage

Row, and eventually destroyed by fire. The present Keeper's house was probably not built until the 1890s. This solidly constructed building is smaller, older and stylistically quite different from the resident headquarters found on South Manitou and Sleeping Bear Point. Since the building had been well maintained and conveniently located near the docking areas, the M.I.A. first used it as a residence for a family that worked for them. In 1953, when the lodge located next to the Monte Carlo House burnt down, the Keeper's residence was

Surfmen launching lifeboat from boathouse, circa 1910
Courtesy S.B.D.National Lakeshore

remodeled. It then became the new home for their island manager, and remain so until the M.I.A. discontinued operations. When the complex became government property for a second time, this building was adopted as the headquarters and residence for the park rangers. There is a strong possibility that one of the other remaining buildings of the complex will be refurbished for a new ranger residence. Except for one important exterior change made in this century, the outside appearance of the main building has not been altered significantly since its construction. This major change was made in 1932, when the Coast Guard added the large front porch on the east side facing the lake.

Directly to the south of the main building stands a one story structure listed as the crews quarters building, which might have been the original dormitory for the surfmen. Housing for the crew was probably changed to the present keeper's house when it was completed, for its second floor with its large individual lockers, was obviously designed for that purpose. This smaller structure did contained the "loafing room" for the off-duty men. It is occasionally used today for lodging Park Service personnel.

Just to the north of the main building is the old boathouse (#27). The earliest record in existence indicating the construction of an actual building in the complex dates from 1877. It describes a single-story building with a watch tower on top. Since this building originally had such a watch tower, it might be the structure mentioned in that document. If this is true, the boathouse was built about 25 years before the ones on South Manitou and Sleeping Bear Point. Except for the lighthouse complex on South Manitou, this building would then be the oldest remaining government building on either of the Manitous. It once had huge doors on the east side to accommodate large lifesaving boats. This furnished a quick and easy way to get the boats down to the water for both rescue and drill. Under the first years of M.I.A. ownership, it was used as the island post office and for storage. In 1953, when the M.I.A. began refurbishing the Keeper's House, it was decided to convert this the old boathouse into a residence. The cupola on top of the building, which functioned as a lookout tower during the lifesaving days, was found to be in an advanced condition of decay and was removed. The massive front doors were replaced with a wall containing a spacious picture window. It recently has undergone extensive interior renovation by the government, and is now an attractive residence for Park Service personnel.

The next small white building to the north Is the Beach Cart house which was undergoing extensive renovation during the summer of 1990 (#30). The Beach Cart stored in this building held paraphernalia for rescuing victims, who were stranded out in the water on their wrecked ships, but close enough that they could be rescued from the shore. The cart, which had very large metal wheels, would be pulled by the surfman to the closest land point to the shipwreck. This building may become a contact and orientation station for visitors, and might also include rest rooms. This entire complex has been nominated for inclusion in the National Register and will be maintained by the Park Service.

Just north of this complex is a white house known as the Halstead House, or the caretakers residence (#33). Located just south of the road to the new N.P.S Dock, it was once part of a row of three similar structures that lined the road between The Coast Guard complex and the East-West Road. They might have been part of the government complex, but official inventories do not mention any of the three. It is most likely that these residences were built by private individuals as rental property for the families of the surfmen. Nothing is known about anyone named Halstead, and the name is only known from a 1953 insurance map. In more recent times, the dwelling was occasionally used by the M.I.A. as a caretaker's residence, and is known by that name as well. It is now being considered for refurbishing, to act as the main residence for the Park Service rangers.

Just north of the Halstead House, facing the south side of the East-West Road, is the generator building. This unsightly cinder block structure with a fieldstone section on its west end (#34) houses a small garage, and the island power generator. If you turn east here and follow the road to the shore, you can still see posts that were once part of the old village dock. In its heyday, this dock extended out far enough to facilitate lake steamers of considerable size. It also served as one of two main loading areas for wood products during the lumber boom of the early part of this century.

By following the road north, walking past the front of the cinder block building, you will pass through a small copse of lovely tall Lombardy Poplar trees. You will soon be alongside the old sawmill building (#36) on your left. Although the structure is now boarded up, preventing an inside view, most of the mill machinery is still within the building. We think this mill apparatus was previously used by Peter Stormer at a site south of here, near his dock about a mile north of Dimmick's Point. In 1927, a few years after Peter Stormer shut down his operation, the syndicate bought his mill and moved it to this site. First the mill operated without the shelter of a building, but the following year the mill was enclosed in the present structure. This mill certainly never matched the large scale operation once carried on at Crescent City, but was used primarily to supply lumber for various island building projects, instead of for the mainland market. It was fired up when needed, and used sporadically for many years.

One of the first jobs the mill accomplished at this new location was to produce most

First dock used by the Park Service for arriving and departing hikers. It has since been dismantled

of the lumber used in constructing the large eastside village barn. The last time the mill was put into operation was during World War ll. A furious storm on Armistice Day 1940 leveled thousands of island trees. During the winter of 1942-43, the steam powered mill was fired up to save the aged fallen wood for lumber. It has not been in operation since that war period, because modern technology had made this mill so archaic that it no longer could be run profitably. Members of the Northwest Michigan Engine and Thresher Club believe that the engine might have been manufactured as early as 1875, and no later than 1905. Since very little mill equipment of this age has survived, this machinery is of high historical value. The park service is in hopes that someday the mill can be restored and open for public view.

A little way northeast of the mill is the site of the first dock used by the Park Service. The short temporary wooden dock that once was found here served as the major landing point for the Manitou Island Transit Company until 1988. Certain weather conditions often made landing backpackers here a chancy thing, and a bit of an adventure all by itself. If you walk to the site where the dock once stood, you will see strewn about this vicinity several rusting automobile bodies of various ages and states of deterioration. These unsightly hulks will eventually be removed by the Park Service.

If you turn around and walk back until you have passed the mill you will see a wide path to the right that heads toward the large eastside barn. By turning here, you will pass a very long garage shed on your right (#42), which is still used to store government vehicles and heavy equipment. Although the large shed itself is of no particular interest, in 1990 it

Old gas station at East Village

sheltered a marvelous old threshing machine that is in excellent condition. It would be a prime candidate for inclusion in a museum of farm equipment.

Directly across from this large shed is a little jewel of the past, a one-pump filling station, with both the pump and the small building behind it (#40) in excellent shape. Although this station was never the equivalent of a mainland commercial station, it is reminiscent of a time 60 to 80 years ago when such one pump facilities were common throughout rural America. It would be only one of the services offered by an adjacent hardware, grocery or general store, when autos were more of a luxury than a necessity. This little station is a beautiful nostalgic reminder of that era. Every time I pass it, I think of what it must have sounded like when Alvar Bournique putted in from the south end of the island or Paul Maleski came from the north, in their Model T Fords for a fill up. The mellifluous chugging of those old four-cylinder engines produced a type of early mechanical music now lost in our fast paced jet age. I know that from a historical viewpoint, this little station has little to recommended it, but I know of nowhere else where such a station has survived. Because of its rarity and as a reminder of a gentler, slower-paced automotive past, how I wish it could be saved.

As you walk west covering the short distance to the North-South Road, you will see there are several buildings on each side and behind the gas station, which were once part of the maintenance facilities needed to carry on the routine operations of the M.I.A. They are not particularly interesting, and will not be maintained. But alongside and facing the North-South Road, one could hardly miss the very large eastside barn (#37). Built in 1927, this barn is unusual because it has four distinct working levels within. It has served as a shelter for farm animals, the storage of fodder used in feeding both domestic animals and deer, and as a holding and collecting point for the island's fruit crop. Although the outside design of the barn is not uncommon today, it still is an excellent example of such buildings constructed in the earlier parts of this century. Recently it has been used as a place where deer killed during the annual hunt are dressed and packed. Because it can still be used for this latter purpose, its excellent state of preservation, its large and convenient storage facilities, and a proposal to adopt part of it as a shelter hostel, it is likely that this building will be maintained. Its excellent condition, its role in local history and its architectural distinctiveness add to the strong possibility of its continued existence.

I particularly remember passing by the barn one pleasant sunny evening in early September, after filling my water jugs at the ranger station. As I passed the barn on my way back to the village campground, I felt a distinctive warm feeling toward the romance of the independent American farmer of past generations. Although the barn was never owned by an independent farmer, it still suggested a bucolic scene of the earlier part of this century, so nostalgically American. The scene, which seemed almost too perfect, stirred within me romantic visions of an utopian agrarian past, where all the parts of this world seemed to be in harmony with each other.

If you follow the road south from the barn to **Point A**, before you reach that junction, you will see a diminutive white cottage to the right (#26) facing the North-South Road, and a small fieldstone building on the left (#35), which faces the Old Dock Road. When I first passed the little fieldstone building, I, like many other visitors, assumed that from the size and location it probably functioned as the village post office. Not so. Built in 1939 to serve as an office, it functioned as an administrative center for the Manitou Island Association for many years. Despite its obvious charm and good condition, it is not considered important enough to be saved.

There once was a large home behind this small building that was known as "the farmhouse." It was an important island residence from the 1890s until it was destroyed by fire in the 1920s, for it served as the island home of both Silas Boardman and Frank Newhall, who later bought out Mr. Boardman's property and eventually owned over 8,000 acres of island land. It also served as the island headquarters for the Syndicate until its destruction.

The small white frame house on the northwest corner of **Point A** is usually known as the Campbell Cottage. Joe Campbell and his wife lived in the house during the 1950s, and the name stuck. It is also occasionally remembered as the Kinnucan House. Mr. Kinnucan, who managed the Syndicate in the 1930s, also made the cottage his home. During the 1940s, his son became the island manager for the M.I.A. and he too used the house as his island home. When it was built sometime between 1895 and 1898, it occupied the ground on the southeast corner of this junction, just north of the little fieldstone office. The Campbell Cottage was moved from its original site across the road to this northwest corner of **Point A** sometime before World War II.

By looking west from this point in the direction of Lake Manitou on the East-West Road, you can see another white house that sits about 100 feet north of the road (#25). Named the Degan Cottage, after a family from Manistee, Michigan, it was one of two summer rental cottages built along that road in 1902 by the son of Frank Newhall. Mrs. Degan loved the existing island's Lombardy Poplar trees, and was responsible for planting others in the village area. The construction of the two cottages was carried out by Benjamin Newhall as a real estate venture to expand the island's resort area. If you walk west on the road to the fringe of the forest in the direction of Lake Manitou, you can see that the house sits just west of the lengthened airfield. Its somewhat larger companion house was found on the east side of the extended runway, just south of the Degan cottage. In 1956 the east side structure was struck by lightning and consumed by flames, leaving the Degan house in what seems like lonely isolation along the deserted airstrip.

Cottage Row

If you look directly south from **Point A**, you will see a grass covered lane that fronts a series of buildings which is Cottage Row. When you cross the East-West Road at **Point A** and proceed south, there is a large empty lot between the road and the first house along Cottage Row. Up until 1953, this empty lot was the site of another building, originally called the Buss House. Its first location was close to the Life Saving Complex, and had served as the home of its first captain. After the house was moved to this northeast corner, it was remodeled and used as the island dining room. It also was utilized as a small store, which included the island post office. When William Angell bought this property, he adopted the Buss House as the center of his island operations. It then became known as the Lodge, and was attached to the existing cottage south of it (the Monte Carlo House) by a roofed wooden passage. The Lodge became the home and office of Mr. Angell's resident manager. Rooms for Mr. Angell's guests and a dance hall were also found in the building. In 1953, the building was struck by lightning and destroyed. The firefighters had a difficult time saving the Monte Carlo House next door.

Cottage Row is perched on a ledge that parallels Lake Michigan and overlooks the Coast Guard complex. The idea for these cottages came into being during the summer of 1893. Sometime during the 1880s, a retired banker from Chicago named Silas Boardman moved to the island for "reasons of health." He bought extensive acreage on the island, and became involved in farming and raising Percheron horses. His married daughter, Carrie Blossom, invited two other married couples to spend part of the summer with her at her father's spacious house on the island. This summer party included a lawyer named Mr. Fredrick Trude, and Mr. Howard W. Foote, who was in the musical instrument business. Since all of them were from the Chicago area they arrived by lake steamer from that city and soon became enchanted by the island. All three families expressed a wish to have their own island summer homes.

To encourage the young couples, Mr. Boardman subdivided a strip of land near his own home into ten lots, on the edge of what was then known as the Beech Woods. He sold the Trudes and the Footes a lot for $75 each, and gave his daughter Carrie another. Apparently, Mr. Boardman's idea for the resort was never to promote it widely, but to develop it for this coterie of his relatives and Chicago friends. They drew up a covenant for the subdivision which stated that the western 300 feet of the lots should be used for residences and servant quarters, while the 18 acres between the cottages and the lake was designated as a private park. The lot owners also had the right to build a boathouse on Lake Manitou, which the islanders referred to as the "little lake."

The general area of the village was briefly promoted as a resort area to outsiders by Frank Newhall and his son, after the senior Newhall bought the Boardman properties. Extending this promotion for any appreciable length of time was handicapped by their own serious financial problems, and they were forced to turn their interests in other directions.

The S.S. Missouri. Many summer residents came from Chicago to the island aboard this ship during the decades just before and after the turn of the century

Courtesy S.B.D. National Lakeshore

For reasons not known today, this subdivision later became known as the W.O. Green plot, and was so named on some legal documents. The earliest cottages built here were of a like design. This is not apparent today, since so many changes were made by later owners, adding such things as porches and woodsheds through the years. All the early cottages were built without kitchens, the occupants using a nearby dining hall operated by Mr. Boardman for various island employees. Kitchens were added to the cottages some years later, when this dining facility was closed. Many accouterments for the first cottage, such as stained glass windows and mouldings, came from display booths in the Manufacturer's Building, which had been part of Chicago's great Columbian Exposition of 1893.

One might wonder why people would want to build summer residences so far away at a time when overland transport was restricted to trains and horse drawn vehicles. The answer is that it was quite easy to get to the island with a minimum of fuss In those days aboard passenger lake steamers. Passenger carrying ships departed from Chicago on regular schedules twice a week, with stopovers at the island. In that less hurried age there were excellent accommodations on the ships, where island bound passengers would spend about a day and a half, either in snug cabins or weather permitting, ensconced on deck chairs, enjoying an effortless ride to their island destination. In 1904, the one-way cost of the overnight journey from Chicago to North Manitou, including a cabin and meal, was $8.00.

With the improvement in passenger train service, the coming of the automobile and better roads, lakeboat passenger service decreased, making the island less easily accessible for Chicago residents. World War l brought on a further decline of Passenger service, and

The Monte Carlo Cottage in 1987

by the 1920s there no longer was any scheduled passenger service. This made the island less attractive to would-be vacationers resulting so very few summer homes were built on the island after the first decade of the twentieth century. Also, by the late 1920s, the major landholder of the island discouraged any building of private residences on the island. This helps explain why a few of the ten original lots were never used to build summer homes. None-the-less, many early members of this developing summer community held and used their property for many years. Not only did they develop ties of personal friendship, there were some marriages among the eligible younger members. This tended to mold together a happy summer community that did not completely dissolve until the 1940s. A granddaughter of one of the early summer cottage owners, Josephine Alford Hollister, wrote:

> "It was a very simple life. The only activities were hiking, fishing, and picnicking with an occasional boat trip hayride or dance. The chief attractions were the beauty of the island itself and the opportunity to spend time with old friends and their families. There was no concentrated effort to bring in new people and as the years passed, the summer population diminished."

In the 1950s, only two of the village cottages were still owned and occupied by families that were not associated with the M.I.A. Both families kept their properties until the government purchased the island, and one of them is still privately owned. In this same period the M.I.A. periodically rented out the cottages they owned to summer vacationers.

As you walk south along this cottage row, the first summer home you come to is, in this writer's opinion, the architectural gem of all the cottages. Known as the Monte Carlo

Cottage (#24), it was built by a relative of Mr. Boardman between the fall of 1893 and the spring of 1894, to be used by its owner as rental property. That first summer it was rented by Howard Foote, and occupied by his family while they waited for the completion of their own cottage. In later years, male college students, who had summer jobs working in the fields and orchards, often rented the house. It became known as the Monte Carlo Cottage because these students held evening card games far into the night.

With its large screened-in front porch and the interior made bright and airy by the oversized front windows, the building expresses the feeling of easy summer gentility as experienced by the upper middle classes at the turn of the century. For many years, this type of summer home was common through the lake areas of the Middle West, but through alterations, destruction by fire, demolition and changing tastes, these beautiful summer retreats are getting scarce. The Monte Carlo house, at this writing, is still in excellent shape. Its superb condition possibly resulted from the fact that William Angell used it as his residence when he stayed on the island. Since he had the house connected to the lodge next door by an enclosed wooden corridor, he had easy access to his manager and his guests during inclement weather, but still had the privacy of his own residence nearby.

If any building outside the Coast Guard Station complex can be saved, I sincerely hope it can be this one. There is a chance that this might happen, for the Development Concept Plan now being considered has suggested that it might be used as a shelter hostel financed privately, for primitive overnight accommodations. It also would make an excellent island museum.

The empty lot south of the Monte Carlo house is the first of the numbered lots you reach in the W.O. Greene Plot (Lot 10). Although it was sold to and owned for several years by a man named Fox no building was ever constructed on the site.

The next building you pass along cottage row is distinguished from the others in two ways (#23, Lot 9). One can see that the architectural style identifies it as being built at a much later period than the other structures along this row. It is a Sears Roebuck prefabricated cottage that was assembled here in 1935. The first house that occupied this lot was put up in 1901 by Howard Foote, one of the original party that had stayed with the Boardmans in 1893. He had built his first cottage on the island on Lot #8 in 1894, and it still stands on there. He sold it seven years later to build a second cottage on this property. When his wife died around 1912, he deeded the property to his children and it was most often used by his daughter Shirley Foote Alford. When it was destroyed by fire in 1934, Mrs. Alford replaced it with the Sears building the following year. Its other distinction is that it is still owned by Mrs. Alford's grandchildren, the only property on the island that remains in private hands today. Although it has had many names through the years, it is known today as the Hollister Cottage after one of its present owners.

The next structure (#22, Lot 8) is known as the Riggs-Londergan Cottage. The first two owners of the lot, who also were from Chicago, did not build on it and sold it in the early 1920s to Miss Margaret Riggs. She had spent previous summers with her mother and two sisters boarding at the Shepard Hotel. About 1924, she hired two brothers named Feilen, who had originally come to the island to construct earlier summer homes, to build her cottage. She used the cottage as a summer home for herself and her aging mother for better than 20 years. In 1947, she sold it to Margaret Londergan, who also used the cottage for over 20 years. In 1958, she sold it to the M.I.A. This structure looks less cottage-like than the others, resembling more a typical suburban house that might have been built in any midwestern city during the 1920s or 30s. In 1990, the roof covering the southwest corner was falling in. Otherwise, the house is still in good shape.

There are two empty lots directly south of the Riggs-Londergan House. Both lots had been sold for summer homes, but a cottage was never built on the first one. The second lot once contained one of the earliest cottages built along the row. Mr. and Mrs. Herbert Keating built a summer home here in 1895. It stood on this lot until World War ll when it was moved to a site north of the present Campbell House. Placed upon an inadequate foundation. it fell apart a few years later.

After passing the vacant lots, you come to at a cottage with a large screened-in front porch. Known today as the Wing Cottage, it was the first dwelling that Howard Foote built on the island in 1894 (#21, Lot 5). He brought two carpenters from Chicago to erect it. One of them, a German immigrant named Nickolas Feilen, liked the island so much that he decided to make it his year-round home. He persuaded his brother John, who was a cabinet maker, to join him. The two bachelor brothers continued to live on the island the rest of their working lives. They constructed many buildings on the island, including at least three of the row cottages. Nick was buried on the island, apparently in a makeshift fashion, for an islander who assisted in the burial said in later years, "We buried him like a dog." His brother John, who was now an old man, was taken to Leland were he remained until his death. His body was returned to the island for burial.

In 1900, when Howard Foote was preparing to move to his new cottage on lot #8, he sold this house to S.W. McMunn. Mr. McMunn was probably responsible for introducing the island to Alvar Bournique. Mr. Bournique, who in 1903 began the building of the largest single summer home complex that the island would ever know, happened to be married to Mr. McMunn's sister and probably learned about the island on a visit to his brother-in law's cottage (see Figure 8 Loop Side Trails). Mr. McMunn later sold the cottage to a Missourian named William Stark. Mr. Stark probably also learned about the island through marriage, since his wife was a member of the Newhall family.

When Mr. Angell bought the cottage in 1928, he sometimes used it as his personal island home, and it became known as the Angell cottage. In 1942, when he apparently moved his island residence to the Monte Carlo House he allowed Avery Wing, his junior partner in the M.I.A., to use it as his summer home. Mr. Wing did use the cottage for several years, which accounts for its present name. Although this is the original building built by Howard Foote, it has undergone many changes during the ensuing years. The back porch is now a ruin, and the front porch is also rapidly deteriorating but the basic structure is still sound.

The next building south (#20, Lot #4), which is known as the Fiske cottage, was built in 1894 by Fredrick Trude. He and his wife had been one of the house guests of Mr. Boardman and his daughter, Carrie Blossom in 1893. A young man who was a good friend of the Riggs was, in part, responsible for the cottage's present name. After visiting the Riggs family on the island, Fredrick Fiske got his parents George and Mary Fiske interested in having a summer home there. They later bought the Trude cottage, and it remained in the Fiske family for two more generations. It was still owned by them in 1979 when the federal government purchased it as part of the lakeshore project. If it is still standing during your visit, a look though the windows will show that it has a beautiful pine-paneled interior.

The Fiskes also owned a lovely piece of lakeshore property on the east side of Lake Manitou, where they had a small boathouse and boat. Both were still there in 1990, but in deteriorating condition. Mentioned in the trail section of this guide, the Lake Manitou

The Burdick House or Tanglewood, circa 1920
Courtesy George Grosvenor

Burdick House in 1987

property would have made an idyllic location for a summer home, but except for a few large boathouses with changing facilities, the little lake never had a substantial residence built along its shores.

The next cottage, known as the Burdick House or Tanglewood (#19. Lot 3) is the oldest of the summer homes. According to one source, it was originally built near the present power plant building by the wife of Silas Boardman, to serve as a summer home for two of her elderly aunts. Another states that it was an old farmhouse, which may have been taken over by Mrs. Boardman for her maiden aunts. When the resort area was organized in 1894, the house was moved to this location by Mr. Boardman for his recently married daughter Carrie Blossom. She and her husband named it Tanglewood. It was later sold to an owner who's name was Burdick which makes one wonder if they were any relation to the Burdicks of South Manitou.

Persistent island rumor has suggested that the original plans for the Burdick house were drawn by Frank Lloyd Wright. At one time or another, almost every house along the row has been attributed to that great American architect, but it is highly unlikely that he designed any island building. These rumors probably grew up because Mr. Wright was actively involved around that period in Chicago projects where most of the cottage owners had their permanent homes. There is not a single thread of supporting evidence known to this author or other people knowledgeable about island history that would identify Mr. Wright's name with the design of any of the island's buildings.

After being acquired by the M.I.A., the Tanglewood property apparently was not maintained. The house is in the poorest condition of any of the cottage row structures. For all practical purposes the building is beyond saving, and had already reached this very advanced state of deterioration when the island became federal property.

The Treehouse (#18, Lot 2) lot once contained a cottage that was built about 1896 by an English couple named Hewett. Some years later the property was sold to a Dr. and Mrs. Rhodes, who were responsible for the building of a childhood fantasy come true, the existing treehouse. Built for his daughter Margaret by Dr. Rhodes, its very uniqueness suggests a carefree, pre-adolescent world. The treehouse, however, was built for her as a sort of honeymoon cottage when she married a geologist from Ohio State University. Margaret inherited the property from her parents, but sold it to the M.I.A. in the 1920s. The original cottage was not maintained by the association and was torn down in the 1950s. The remaining treehouse is in an advanced state of deterioration, and not considered historically important enough for restoration. Although the expense of reconstruction of the treehouse is beyond any practical consideration, some of us who remember the magic of those Winnie-the-Pooh fantasy years, wish that it was within sensible financial limits to save it. Margaret's brother Jack, met his wife on the island. She was the sister of Margaret Riggs. Their mother Mrs. Riggs, had originally brought her three daughters to the island and boarded at the Shepard Hotel.

The last building at the southern end of the cottage row is the largest of all the surviving resort structures (#17, Lot 1). This building, which has a substantial second story and a wide porch running along its left and front sides, is known as the Shepard Summer Hotel. It was built in 1895, by the bachelor Feilen brothers for Mrs. William Shepard, and her daughter Katherine. Although the Shepards lived in Chicago at the time of its construction, it was patterned after a house they formerly owned in New Orleans. It contained neither a kitchen or dining room, for these rooms were in a separate building behind the house.

The Treehouse in 1987

It is not known whether Mrs. Shepard originally intended to use it as a summer boardinghouse, but the size of the house and the dining room would suggest that she had this in mind from the beginning. When the island dining hall was closed by Mr. Newhall, residents of the summer cottages, which had originally been built without kitchens, often took their meals there. Among her first resident guests was Mrs. Riggs. She was a close Chicago friend of the Trudes and the Fiskes who encouraged her to summer on the island with her three daughters. They boarded at the Shepards for many summer seasons until her daughter, Margaret, built the Riggs-Londergan cottage (#22,lot 8).

Katherine Shepard, who became known to the islanders as Miss Katie, inherited the property from her mother and continued to operate it as a summer boardinghouse until 1935. It remained closed until the late 40s, when an elderly couple rented it for a number of years and used it for a summer residence. In the 1950s, the property was sold to the Continental Motor Company, the firm that the now deceased William Angell had once headed. They apparently planned to use the property for corporate entertaining, but the plans were never activated. Owning the property did give them leverage for access to the island and use of the lodge for their executives and corporate guests. Except for a couple of summers during the late 50s, when it was rented to an employee of the M.I.A., it has remained unused. The main house is now boarded up and is in excellent condition, but the attached kitchen-dining room is in a state of ruin. These rear appendages were recently demolished even further by a huge beech tree that fell across one side of the deteriorating structure.

If you stand in front of this building and look northward along the grassy lane, you can speculate on how that path must have appeared around the turn of the century. At that time, there was a boardwalk along this entire lane that was lit at night by gas lanterns. At the

The Shepard Hotel in 1987

road crossing just beyond the Monte Carlo house, the gas-lit boardwalk turned right and continued down to the lakefront.

The buildings outside the Coast Guard complex that the previously mentioned government's Draft Development Concept means to save are probably the barn, saw mill and one of the existent maintenance buildings. I would like to see that list extended somewhat. My primary list would include, first the Monte Carlo House, then the Shepard Hotel and the Fiske Cottage. All three played an important historic role in the early years of cottage row and are presently in an excellent state of preservation. Buildings of lesser importance that might be placed on a secondary list would include The Riggs-Londergan and Wing Cottages, the little gas station, the small fieldstone office of the M.I.A. and the Campbell Cottage. It would not be a great loss if any of the structures on the secondary list were destroyed, but losing the gas station and the fieldstone office would greatly decrease the romance of the village.

The Landing Field

If from **Point A** you walk the East-West Road toward Lake Manitou or along the North-South Road passing the barn in the direction of the campground, you will be aware of a very large and quite long open field. You can rightly assume it was once the airfield, and if you follow the North-South Road to the northern end of the field, you will be aware that it seems long enough to bring in a 747 jet. Originally 1,700 feet long with each end closed in by a fruit orchard, the short field forced planes to make rapid ascents and descents. Its length was adequate for the old Ford Tri-Motor planes, for they can land and take off safely in less than 1,500 feet. It was in this fashion that an important passenger, concerned with the later history of the island, arrived in the late 1920s. In 1926 and 27, the Tri-Motor "Tin Goose" landed executives of the Continental Motors Company of Muskegon, Michigan on this field. Among them was William Angell, who later became president of that company. He was so impressed with the island that he began buying up parcels of land, until he owned most of it (see history chapter).

Up until the 1960s night landings on the short strip at night were accomplished by parking a truck at one end of the field and turning on its headlights. During that period, when commercial sports hunting was being promoted on the island, the field was enlarged to 4,000 feet, and landing lights were added. The field is no longer in use or maintained, and landing on it is forbidden. Even crippled aircraft trying to land under emergency conditions would find doing so somewhat hazardous today, for many small trees have grown up in widely scattered patterns on many parts of the field.

The Romance of the Village

If you have romantic inclinations, you might find yourself indulging in some fantasies as I have, reconstructing a not-too- distant age. After walking through and approaching the environs of the village on several occasions, I have woven an unconscious fabric of the past within the back channels of my imaginative mind. It seemed to blossom out one pleasantly warm summer evening as I returned from Lake Manitou and entered the large village clearing from the west. As I walked out of the forest and passed the Degan Cottage approaching Cottage Row in the quiet and ghost-like village, I thought of what I might have seen and heard if I had been there during a summer of the early 1920s. I might have heard popular songs of that post World War I period such as "Stumbling Along" or "K-K-K Katie, Beautiful Katie" sounding from a windup victrola in the Degan Cottage. There might have been three or four ladies, young mothers perhaps, catching up on the gossip of the summer community as they promenaded graciously along the lane towards the center of the village. They might have been garmented in those ankle-length gossamer frilly summer dresses in soft pastel shades, wearing wide-brimmed floppy hats and carrying small summer parasols in their hands. As they heard the sound of a Model T Ford chugging northward entering the village clearing they might have looked up, expecting the arrival of Alvar Bournique, who was coming in for an evening visit with one of his friends staying at Miss Katie's. Perhaps they would also see a bevy of college age young ladies dressed in those ridiculous skirt-burdened, neck-to-knee bathing suits racing from one of the near-by cottages towards Lake Michigan. The promenading women might also have heard the young ladies' mild protesting screams. For behind them, an eager group of young men, attired in their straw hats and stripped bathing attire, were pouring out of the Monte Carlo House noisily pursuing the young ladies to the water's edge.

Standing in the doorway of the cottage where the young women were staying, a prim spinster, their dour chaperone watched the young people racing to the beach. As she held open the porch screen door, a look of distaste formed on her persimmon face and disapproval showed in her eyes. The disapproving look was a mask of envy, for time and circumstances had taken from her the chance of ever again participating in such youthful charades.

A short distance down the beach, a young surfman might have watched the young college group as they neared the water. A wave of bitter envy swept over him. It made him think of a young lady from his mainland home town who had decided not to wait until his enlistment ended. He was about the same age as the frolicking college group, but he felt entirely different and separate from them. Their worlds seemed isolated from one another by education and social position.

And so I could let my imagination carry on until I had a whole romantic novel. But this is not our purpose here, and you can create your own story if the surroundings have the same magnetic effect on you as they have had on me.

PART IV
GARDEN ISLAND

Chapter XI
Introduction and General Remarks

Lying less than two miles northeast of Beaver Island, Garden is the northernmost island of any size in the Lake Michigan Archipelago. It is the only one of the four hiking islands in this book that does not have high perched sand dune escarpments along its western shore. Lying further east than the other islands, is more protected from the full force of the prevailing southwest winds, because it is partly shielded by Beaver and smaller islands of the group. Existing hills on the island are diminutive in size, and there are many flat areas . Poor drainage in these flat areas results in Garden having the largest acreage in swamps of any of the four islands.

Because of comparatively shallow water around much of the periphery of the island, especially on the southern end, its offshore waters are excellent for bass, making them attractive for sports fishermen. The island has abundant wildlife, which includes both deer and coyotes. Neither animal is native to the island, but gained access to the it by either swimming the channel or walking across the ice between Beaver and Garden. The deer population of the island has never gotten out of hand as it did on North Manitou, for the coyotes and hunters keep the herd in reasonable numbers. Anyone having a great fear of snakes might best choose another island for his hiking adventure, because Garden Island has a large reptile population of several varieties, and High Island has almost as many. Any summer hiker will probably encounter a dozen or so on a walk of any distance. This need not trouble anyone who does not clutch up at the sight of even the smallest snake, because there are no venomous varieties on this or on any of the other islands in this group. The collection of wildflowers is incredible and will delight the enthusiast, particularly during the spring and early summer.

Because of its closeness to Beaver, Garden is the only island that is sometimes reachable during the severe winter months, for the ice may become solid enough to cross even when Lake Michigan does not entirely freeze over. Safe passage between the two islands is usually possible for a month or two each winter. It also is the closest island of the group to Michigan's Upper Peninsula, some 17 miles to the north. Its area of 7.8 square miles places it as the fourth largest island of the Archipelago, and the second largest of the Beaver Group. The distance from its southeast corner to Northwest Point is about five miles, and its width from Graham's Point east is about three miles. Better than 90% of the island is owned by the State of Michigan, and is administered today by the Department of Natural Resources as part of the Beaver Island State Wildlife Research Area. Under present plans, the state intends no further human development or harvesting of timber on the island. It is open for recreational use by hikers, backpackers, fishermen, hunters and cross-country skiers. Except for summer research activities, no one has lived on the island for over 40 years and nature is rapidly reclaiming its acreage. There are only three maintained structures on the island, which include a D.N.R. cabin and utility building in the southwest corner of the island. In the other maintained cabin which is found near the northeast shore, research about the island's herbal plants and native American herbal medicine is carried on. During the summer months, an Indian lady known as Kee, trained in science, carries on these studies. Kee is an abbreviation of her full Indian first name which is Keewaydinoquay.

Unlike the two Manitous, Garden Island's geographic location did not place it in a strategic position for capitalizing on the nineteenth-century nautical commerce of the Great Lakes. Her diminutive size and relative closeness to the larger and more strategic Beaver Island meant that she was destined to play a satellite role to the larger island in the commercial development of the region. Although Garden has the best-protected harbor in the entire archipelago, it is small and shallow, making it unusable for large commercial sail and steam vessels. But the harbor is a favorite anchorage for moderate-sized cruising sailboats, that sometimes anchor there for days at a time.

My first evening spent on this island convinced me that the rewards for visitors here would be strikingly different but as equally rewarding, as on the other islands. The low-lying western section is one of the features that helps create this difference. The shore of the main harbor along that western bank is a particularly beautiful location for watching the setting sun and offers possibly the best location on any of the islands for sunsets. Looking due west, less than a quarter mile away one sees the diminutive and appropriately named Little Island. Other islands also visible a few miles in the distance seem to almost hang on the horizon. As the sun disappears behind a group of these small islands and the open lake, the viewer has a panorama of beauty in an aquiline wilderness which is unspoiled by the hand of man. The view suggests unhurried tranquility, and can bring upon the viewer a peacefulness that is welcome and delightfully alien to our hurried urban existence. I can still vividly recall the first night I spent on Garden Island for, I was privileged to watch a particularly brilliant performance of the setting sun, as it moved downward through shreds of scattered clouds and silhouettes of the wooded islands.

This would have been reward enough, but nature presented another phenomenon for me to view, which did not contain the tranquility offered by the sunset. The sun was almost down, when thousands of mayflys that had just hatched, began moving from the island over the waters of the harbor. Possibly a million of these diminutive insects with their long tails dragging downward, dotted the sky above. Suddenly, a great number of seagulls flew in and began acrobatic gyrations, as they scooped the helpless mayflys into their beaks. Over a hundred gulls took part in this frenzied eating spree. It seemed miraculous that these tightly-packed diving and turning birds maneuvered batlike, without ever colliding, as they devoured the long bodies of the mayflys. I watched this air attack for 10 or 15 minutes before the gulls flew off and left me totally alone on the beach. I stood again in silence as the evening moved toward twilight.

Besides this often-brilliant display of sun and inland sea, another of the island's unusual attractions responsible for drawing many visitors, is the Indian cemetery. Although there are over 3000 native Americans buried on the island, most of the internment sites are unmarked. What the visitors come to see are the few remaining spirit houses erected over some graves. Many of them are in an advanced stage of deterioration but several are of recent enough vintage to be in an excellent state of preservation. These small wooden structures

Author on D.N.R. Dock in Garden Island Harbor. Little Island is to the left

built over the graves maintain the spirit of the departed much as the ancient Egyptians pyramids preserved their Ka. All the existing spirit houses are of comparatively recent origin.

Hikers wishing to visit the island may feel tempted to cross the two-mile channel between Beaver and Garden Islands in a small boat or canoe. Such boats are really not suited for big water, as this author found when he attempted his first crossing in a 12-foot runabout. Although the day was relatively windless and the water was almost at a dead calm along the shore, once my five-horsepowered boat was clear of the shoreline's protection, I found rolling swells developing that moved from west to east and hit my little craft sideways. The lake here, sandwiched between the two islands, was like a wide and mildly turbulent river that existed in the channel. The swells were large enough that my boat might easily have swamped, so I wisely turned back. I later learned from local boatmen there are often strong currents between the two islands, so I hired a Beaver Islander who was better equipped to take me for my first visit to Garden Island.

For hikers who have boats sea worthy enough for the big waters and wish to do extensive hiking, lasting for several days, Garden Island, has an advantage that is not shared by the other three hiking islands. Garden Island is the only one of the four islands in this book which has an adequate harbor, where one can leave a well anchored boat in relative safety despite the wind direction. Both South Manitou and High Island have deep harbors with adequate protection except for a strong easterly wind. The shallower Garden Island Harbor takes more cautious maneuvering to get into without running aground, but once your boat is in the harbor, sequestered and secured behind Little Island, you have good wind protection from all directions.

CHAPTER XII

A Short History of Garden Island

Although Garden Island has had no recent scholarly archaeological investigations of prehistoric Indian settlements using the latest technical advancements, it can logically be assumed the two-mile expanse of water between the two islands was easily navigated by ancient Indians who resided on Beaver. But if these prehistoric people made that crossing, they probably came for short seasonal stays, not remaining on the island for any length of time, because there was no compelling reason for them to do so. From archaeological evidence found on other islands of the chain, the earliest penetration of the islands by prehistoric Indians happened during the Late Archaic Period, about 3000 years ago. The islands were occupied sporadically during the late Woodland Culture, which is the last archaeological period before the coming of the white man (See chapter entitled "A Brief Early History of the Lake Michigan Archipelago."

All this radically changed when white settlers in northern Michigan pushed the Indians out of the more desirable areas of the mainland. Looking for areas where they could maintain their culture and remain relatively undisturbed, the Indians needed places that the white man had not occupied, and considered economically unimportant. These Native Americans also wanted places where some physical barrier would limit contact between the opposing cultures, allowing them a major share in determining their own destinies. The Lake Michigan islands that lay outside the mainstream of commercial lake traffic offered such refuges. When the Ojibwa and Ottawas surrendered their lands to the United States In 1836 the Beaver Group of islands was included, but a proviso was added that the Indians already on the islands could stay for a minimum of five years. After that period had elapsed the federal government withheld land occupied by Indians from public sale and allowed the native Americans to stay, but denied them direct title to the land.

Beaver Island is the largest island in Lake Michigan and has an ample harbor capable of handling large commercial ships so white traders established businesses along the shores of that harbor during the late 1830s. With further intrusion of the white man many Indians began leaving Beaver to settle on Garden and High islands. An 1840 census placed the Indian population of the Beaver Group at 199. A high percentage of that number probably resided on Garden Island, and by 1847 most of the purebred Beaver Indians had migrated to the smaller island, where they could maintain their native inheritance. To recognize this arrangement, in 1855 the federal government worked out a new treaty with the Indians. Both High and Garden islands were withdrawn from public sale. Parcels of land on those islands were awarded to Indian families residing on them, but the islands themselves were not given to the Indians as a whole nor were they looked upon as "Indian Reservations." It is not surprising that of all the islands in the entire archipelago, Garden Island is the richest in recent Indian lore. Little documentary evidence exists to support this aboriginal, past but much has been pieced together from fragmentary knowledge, folklore and oral history.

Its original Indian name, Miniss Kitigan, translates into English as Garden Island. This name was derived from Indian tradition, which suggests that in times past, in large areas of the interior, both corn and squash were successfully raised for generations. An important shipping lane used during the early nineteenth century by sailing ships and steamers was the narrow passage between Beaver and Garden Islands. The island became known by white men as Little Beaver. But with time, the island gradually became known by the English translation of its Indian name, which survives today.

Whites, familiar with this Indian tradition, began using the name Cornshokers, to distinguish the Garden Island Indians from those living on other islands of the archipelago. The similar name of Cornstalk was also used. Some island residents who migrated to the mainland adopted these names as useable surnames in English. They have survived in active use today as last names of some Indian descendants of the Garden Islanders.

By the 1830s, the fur trade, which had dominated the commercial activity of the Great Lakes region for over 200 years was rapidly disappearing. But other trading activities were increasing, and new trade products were replacing pelts. Fishing, at which the Indians were particularly adept, was carried out. Garden Islanders often transported huge amounts of fish to the distant uninhabited Gull Island, for large-scale drying of their catch, later to be brought to Beaver Island for barter. They also made maple syrup in amounts exceeding their own personal needs, because it was a desirable trading item. Balsam fir proved to be quite marketable for its medicinal properties. As early as 1837, trade with the Garden Island Indians was extensive enough that a white man from Fairport, Ohio, named Alva Cable, established a trading post on Whiskey Point. This is on the northeast end of Beaver Island Harbor near the present site of the harbor lighthouse. The location was handy for both the Garden Island red men and the commercial vessels entering the harbor.

Cable operated the trading post successfully for ten years, then turned it over to a business associate, also from Fairport, named Peter McKinley. His oldest daughter, Sarah, moved with her family to the island when she was eight years old, and remained there for the next five years. The family fled the island in 1852, in fear of the growing number of Mormons who were under the spell of their proclaimed messianic King, Jessie Strang. Years later, she wrote memoirs of her Beaver Island experiences, which include interesting anecdotes of the relationship that existed between the McKinleys and the Garden Island Indians.

She reported that the Indians often crossed the 1.5-mile open stretch of water in canoes when weather conditions were such that this passage seemed impossible. The canoes would frequently disappear from view in the trough of waves, only to rise again on the crest of the wave, with the Indian seamen in perfect control of their small open vessels. She wrote of the amazing skill of Indian boys in spearing fish. Standing motionless like magnificent young statues, they would suddenly move so fast that the quick plunge of their spears into the water was almost too rapid to be followed by the human eye. The young fishermen were so skilled, that their barbed spears always brought back an impaled fish. Walking across the ice on winter visits to Garden, Sarah reported that the Indians lived in comfortable log cabins which were warm, well-kept and snug. According to her account, many regularly attended church services. The island was often visited by a mission priest named Father Zorn, who was responsible for converting many of Garden's Indian residents to Catholicism.

Despite the apparent friendliness between Garden Island Indian Chief Peaine and McKinley, the Indian trader was probably involved in a popular swindle of the day that was in common practice among Indian traders in northern Michigan. The location of McKinley's business may have gotten its name, Whiskey Point, from his habit of selling what was known as "Indian Whiskey" to the local red men at exorbitant prices. Two gallons of raw whiskey were diluted with 30 gallons of water. Red pepper was added to make the mixture taste fiery, plus enough tobacco to add color and taste to the mixture. This watered-down booze cost about five cents a gallon to produce, but the Indians paid fifty cents for a gallon, twenty-five cents for a quart, or six cents a glass.

Garden Island Indians were still friendly toward the traders, and apparently thought highly of them, unaware of the inequity in the real worth of goods and the prices paid for them. This is borne out by an incident that happened during the winter season of 1850-1851. At that time, McKinley, his family and employees were the only Caucasians left in the harbor area of Beaver who were not followers of James Strang. McKinley apparently felt that the Mormons were going to resort to violence, to rid the harbor area of non-Mormons. The power struggle between the increasing number of Mormons and the non-Mormon whites almost resulted in a shootout that season. Thirty Indians led by four chiefs, complete with war paint, came to the aid of the traders. Probably all of this defending group of Native Americans came from Garden.

According to Sarah Mckinley, her father felt that his family and post were in imminent danger, and asked the Garden Island Indians for help. They responded immediately. She remembers that Chief Peaine, who was a friend of the family and the most important of the chiefs, wanted to drive King James and his followers into the lake but Mr. McKinley felt that this was too drastic a measure. The well-armed Indians stayed with the family for two weeks and did not leave until they extracted a promise from James Strang that the McKinleys would not be molested. Chief Peaine and a group of his men left the McKinleys and marched toward the Mormon settlement carrying a white flag. The chief then told Strang and his followers that the McKinleys were on the island before the Mormons, and had resided among the Indians for many years. In business relations, the Indians had always found that Mr. Mckinley treated them fairly and with respect. Because of this, the Indians not only considered him a fine neighbor but almost a father. They then informed Strang that if he or any Mormon hurt as much as one hair on the heads of any of the McKinleys, the Indians would come over from Garden Island and exterminate them.

A year later, so many new followers of Strang had migrated to the island that Mckinley no longer felt safe, even with Indian protection, so he moved himself and his family to the mainland. With the departure of the McKinleys, Strang was now supreme on Beaver.

Although the report of McKinley's daughter is probably fairly accurate from what she learned from her father, his telling of the events were probably exaggerated. She also shared the irrational hatred that many held for the Mormons. It is difficult to know how many of Strang's actions against the post were altruistic and how many were motivated by the wish to be king of everybody on Beaver Island. None the less, the Mormon leader had done his homework. He knew that the major trading activity between Garden Island natives and McKinley's post on Whiskey Point was done in fish and whiskey. He traced the amounts of whiskey which came from warehouses on Mackinac Island directly to Whiskey Point. Since Strang was a teetotaler he may have felt that selling of firewater by McKinley to the aboriginal people was a terrible moral corruption. It might also have offended him to see how little the Indians were getting for their fish. Strang wanted to control Beaver Island economically as

Part of Garden Island's Native American Cemetery

well as politically, and religiously, which he did during his short reign.

King James later sent a Mormon teacher to Garden Island. It is not surprising that the teacher was ill-received by the native population. A high percentage of the Indians were Catholic, which made them strongly resist Mormon doctrine. Even more upsetting to them was the fact that this new messiah had stopped their ready supply of watered-down whiskey, and Mormon fishermen began dominating the fishing grounds originally used by the Indians.

Indians continued to live on Garden Island, mostly unmolested by white encroachment, and maintained some of their original heritage until well into the twentieth century. The native population, however, began to decline before the turn of the century, not because of expulsion by manipulating whites, but because of the magnet of civilization. Its creature comforts slowly lured the Indians away, particularly members of the younger generation. In the first quarter of this century, there were more than a dozen families still eking out a living on the island, but the number gradually dwindled until the 1940s, when it was reduced to one solitary Indian who still lived there year-around. This Indian farmer-fisherman stayed loyal to his island until his death in 1947, and he lies today in the island's Indian cemetery. With the demise of Pete Monatou, year-round Indian residents on the island had become history.

Aside from Catholic missionaries, the first known white man to live on the island for an extended time was a Scottish trader named James Morey, or Murray. Shipwrecked on nearby Whiskey Island and rescued by Garden Island Indians, he married a native woman and lived with the Indians on the island for about ten years. He was held in high esteem by the native population, because of his knowledge of improved agricultural methods and his skill in dealing with white traders to get better prices for Indian goods. When he received word that his father was dying back in Scotland, he left the island in hopes that he could reach that far-away shore before his father succumbed. Ironically, he fell victim to a fatal plague on shipboard, and died during his return voyage, while his father recovered from his illness. The old Scotsman did learn that he now had a grandson on the island, and he sent the young half-Indian a full uniform, complete with kilt made of the family tartan. Whites visiting or passing close to the island probably wondered if their vision was playing tricks on them to see a young Indian running around the island in kilts. James Moray was the great-grandfather of the Indian lady Kee, who does research on herbs and herbal medicine on the island during the summer months.

Sometime during the nineteenth century, Garden Island had its first year-round white homesteaders. Possibly the first and most successful of these white settlers was John Vincent. Born before 1820 in southern Michigan, he had learned not only farming but many skills that were used in the lumber camps of Michigan. Following the lumber camps northward he eventually came to the Town of Naubinway on the southern coast of the Upper Peninsula, 17 miles due north of Garden Island. There, in 1843, he met and married Josephine Metty. She was the daughter of Louis Metty, who came from the Detroit area and was one of the original settlers of that village. The point of land that forms part of the town harbor is still known as Metty's Point. Taking his bride to Garden Island, John Vincent established a homestead, built a substantial house and raised a family of 12 children. Since so much of Garden Island is swampy and unsuitable for large scale farming operations, Vincent concentrated his commercial efforts in other areas. He planted a large orchard, raised cattle, farmed enough acreage to feed his large family and did some lumbering.

Vincent also was a skilled carpenter. Sitting in the middle of one of the richest fishing grounds of the Great Lakes, nearby Beaver Island had a high demand for fishing boats. Vincent and his son Henry, who was reputed to have been a better carpenter than his father, became builders of fishing boats of exceptional quality. The boats they produced were of such merit they were much in demand, and became the family's major source of income. Because of their reputation as legendary boat builders, the field that once contained their boatyard is still occasionally called "The Boatbuilder's Clearing." Vincent was a strict man who believed in a high degree of efficiency. Each of his grown children were given a certain area of responsibility on this multi-purpose homestead, and was in charge of the activities that took place there. One daughter was in charge of the kitchen, another in charge of all barn activities, and so on. One of his sons, John Jr., married an Indian girl and lived with her in the Indian village on the other side of the island. Many of his children continued to take an active part in this thriving family community of diverse businesses, and remained on the island with the senior John Vincent until his death in 1909 or 1910. He had been the anchor of this family enterprise, and with his passing it began to fall apart. Henry remained at the homestead and continued to build boats for a few more years. In 1915, when John Jr. moved with his Indian wife into the house, he became the last of the Vincents to live there.

The cemetery for the Island's white settlers is found just west of this clearing, and was established by the Vincent family. This burial ground for the island's white homesteaders contains the graves of over 30 people. It might have become lost if it were not for two graves with permanent marble headstone. The markers on all graves except those two were made of materials that have not survived. The two who's graves are marked in marble are those of two Danish settlers, Ecedius and Christina Larsen. Their homestead is the one known today as the Dane's Farm. These headstones misled a state mapmaker to erroneously assume the Vincent, or Boatbuilder's Clearing, was the site of the Larsen homestead and cemetery, and so identified them on a state map.

Besides the Vincent house, there were three other homesteads along the eastern border of the island, and all of them were built and lived in by immigrants from Denmark. At this writing, existing information available to this author about these Scandinavians is sketchy. If anyone has further details about them, or corrections to the material below, I would be delighted to hear from them and make corrections and/or additions to future editions of this book.

The boatbuilder, John Vincent holding horses in back of his house, circa 1905. Area is an empty field today

Pictures courtesy Laurence Vincent

All the Danish immigrants had known each other before coming to the island, and were related either by blood or marriage. Apparently after the first of these families settled on the island, they reported to relatives back home that the island's physical surroundings were not unlike those on their Danish islands, and they encouraged them to come and homestead.

Two brothers by the surname of Jensen built homes fairly close to each other on the eastern shoreline of the island, about a mile southeast of the Vincent place. The one closest to the Vincents, , identified as "The Dane's Farm" on the 1771 state map, was occupied by Matt Jensen, who lived with his wife on the island until their deaths in the 1930s. Matt was a carpenter and fisherman. After the fishing season each year, he would cut timber from which he made both railroad ties and fence posts. He then transferred them to Beaver Island to await shipment elsewhere. He apparently loved the island, and hated to leave it. Each year his wife tried to persuade him to spend the winter on nearby Beaver Island, but he refused. By the 1920s they were probably the only remaining white homesteaders staying on the island year-around. Since no one was living with them the winters must have been lonely affairs.

Matt's wife died during one of those solitary winters in the early 1930s. He wanted her taken to Beaver for internment, instead of in the cemetery found behind the Vincent homestead. Not wishing to share his house with her corpse through the winter, he went to a point on the southern end of the island and built a huge bonfire to attract some Beaver Islander to come to his aid in transporting her remains across the channel. He had to keep the fire burning for three days until someone on Beaver noticed and came across to see what was the matter. After his death, the house was deserted. Matt's skill as a carpenter is emphasized by the fact that the walls of his house and workshop are still standing. The house had beautiful hardwood floors, and visitors reported that these buildings remained in excellent condition

Matt Jensen's Barn and workshop in 1988

as long as the roofs held, which they did well into the 1950s. The ruins of the Matt Jensen complex are the only surviving structures of any size that were built by these white island homesteaders.

Peter Jensen built his homestead just less than a quarter mile south of his brothers. He had several sons, and fished with his brother Matt in a boat they called the Panther. Later he joined the lighthouse service and left the island for good. This clearing is identified on the state map as "Little Pete Nielsons." Little Pete and his sister Lena had moved in with Peter, and continued to live there for a few years after he left the island. When Lena married Matt Jensen, Little Pete moved in with his sister and brother-in-law, and the Peter Jensen home was no longer maintained. It has entirely disappeared, but the clearing with the remains of an old automobile are still visible today. Little Pete stayed on with his brother-in-law as a handyman for a few years before moving to the mainland. Lena stayed on until her death, which caused Matt to build the three-day bonfire.

Another Danish settler had a homestead about a half mile southwest of the original

Pete Jensen place, near Jensen's Point. Ecedius Larsen, better known as Gillis, was a fisherman who probably did some subsistence farming and logging as well. His wife, Christina, was the sister of Pete and Matt Jensen. A son they named Arthur was born on the island in 1898. Gillis apparently felt he could carry on better with his fishing business on Beaver, for he moved his family to that nearby island about 1911 and built a home on the north shore of Beaver Harbor. Apparently Mrs. Larsen was attached to Garden island, for she expressed a wish to be buried there upon her death. She died during the winter of 1913, and her body was carried across the ice for burial in the cemetery behind the Vincent house. Relatives of the Vincents wondered why she wanted to be buried on the island, since her husband and 15 year old son remained on Beaver. She might have been influenced by the fact that her brother Matt and his wife still lived on the island. Gillis taught his son to be a fisherman, a livelihood that both would follow the rest of their lives. When Gillis died in 1923, Art saw to it that his father was laid to rest next to his wife on Garden, and had gray marble headstones placed at their graves. The headstones of the Larsens are the only ones that have survived, and they are easily found today.

Another family whose lives were also woven into the fabric of the Vincents were the Wachtners. William Wachtner, the son of a lighthouse keeper, was born at Omena, Michigan in 1877. Because his father had kept the light on Beaver Island, William was familiar with Garden Island. He became a fisherman, and often plied the waters off Garden island in his sailboat to obtain his catch. In those pre-refrigeration days the young Wachtner salted his fish on Garden Island, then transferred them to Beaver Island for resale. the young fisherman was attracted to John Vincent's daughter Lydia, who managed the barn and cattle operation for her father. The attraction was mutual, for the two young people married and built their first home at Graham's Point on the westernmost tip of the island. It was there in 1902 that the first of their nine children was born. He was named after his father and is still alive at this writing. Graciously sharing his reminiscences with this author, William Jr. was an excellent source of information about the island's white settlers during the first quarter of this century.

The growing Wachtner family moved across the island to Peter Jensen's house, which they shared with Little Pete Nielson and his sister. This placed them in close contact with both the Danish and the Vincent families. Apparently, William Sr. felt that economic opportunities were better for his growing family on the mainland so he departed to nearby Naubinway, where his wife's mother had family connections. But he transferred his family back to the island in 1907, and moved into John Vincent's house. The following year, twin daughters were born in the Vincent home. When John Vincent died, William Wachtner may have aided John's son Henry in the family boatbuilding business at the close of the fishing season. In 1911, William again moved his family back to Naubinway, but returned to the island the following year.

William Wachtner had a brother named John, who was also a fisherman. He joined William on the island in 1912, completing a partially-constructed house that stood near the schoolhouse which someone had abandoned some years before. After he moved in his father began spending the winter months in this new home when the lighthouses were closed. John's new home was a little over a half mile from Matt Jensen's place, and was connected by what is known today as "The Dane's Trail." John and Matt often fished together during the angling season.

The period between 1910 and 1915 was the busiest for the island's schoolhouse.

William Wachtner Jr. remembers that in those days there were fewer than 20 students in attendance. Six of the young students, including William Jr., were from the Wachtner family, six were Jensens, four were Vincents and three Indian children. During their first year at school, the little Wachtner twin sisters who had been born in the Vincent house, were towed to school over the snowcovered ground to school each day in a small sleigh. It was pulled by two large dogs led by William Jr. and his younger brother. School was in session only five months a year, and classes were conducted by a Mrs. Gallagher. William found that when his family returned to the Upper Peninsula, the island children were academically far behind the mainland children at the same grade level.

During the winter of 1914, William and John Wachtner's father died in the Vincent house. The following year, William's wife died in the same house. She was still a young woman, but she bore nine children in 12 years. The horrendous task of providing for such a large brood on an isolated island must have ben an overwhelming task, and her exhausting existence must have weakened her considerably. William Wachtner had seen his father, his father-in-law, his wife and one of his own infant children die in that house in the short period of five years. After his wife's death, he left the island for good and moved back to Naubinway. The end of a lumber boom had reduced the town's population drastically, so he moved his family into a house that had been deserted by the former loggers.

If Garden Island was never again to be the Wachtners' home, they often returned in the summertime to harvest some of the abundant crop of wild berries. Although William Wachtner lived on to the ripe old age of 92, he never remarried. In the same year that the Watchners left the island, John Vincent Jr. moved with his native wife from the Indian village to the traditional Vincent homestead. He remained in the house that his father had built for a few years, but apparently was the last occupant of the Vincent home to live there any length of time. After his departure, the house was no longer maintained, and began to deteriorate. Today the once-substantial house has totally disappeared. The location of the once-proud thriving Vincent homestead and boatyard is now an empty field. Only the marked graves of Gillis and Christina Larsen in the nearby cemetery indicate that this was once the heart of a small but thriving community of white homesteaders.

Since no further year-round homesteads were established on the island after this time, the last quarter of the nineteenth and the first fifteen years of the twentieth centuries were Garden Island's golden age of white settlement. Like the disappearing white homesteaders the Indian population, too, had dropped off considerably. William Wachtner Jr. remembers there were only four Indian families still living on the island in 1915, when his father moved his household back to the Upper Peninsula. During the 1920, the House of David religious colony on High Island (See High Island History), would take Sunday excursions to Garden Island in the summertime. In the large open area next to Indian Harbor they spread a rich picnic assortment of cakes, vegetable dishes and gallons of homemade ice cream. In the field, they held baseball games as well, something they would not have done if there had still been Indian families living there.

Since most of the Indians, as well as the Vincent and Wachtner families, were Catholic the Franciscan Order had maintained a small church on the island during the late nineteenth and early twentieth centuries. William Wachtner remembered that a priest would visit the island a couple times a year for services, baptisms, communions and funerals. By the late 1920s, the island population had diminished to a point where there were almost no parishioners left to be ministered to. The church was closed, and sold to an individual who soon resold the property to another for the price of one steer. Nothing remains of the church today.

Although homesteading on the island for both Indians and whites was largely over before World War I, another economic activity kept some migratory residents on the island off and on for several years. After the demise of the woodburning steamboats, logging on all the islands of the Lake Michigan Archipelago was at a miniscule level, supplying islanders what they needed for home consumption and a few speciality items that could be processed

Site of Northcutt Mill on Northcutt Bay in 1987

profitably. But, as the great lumber boom that took place on the north Michigan mainland used up most of the existing climax forests during the latter part of the nineteenth century, island woodlands attracted the attention of logging interests on the mainland.

This resulted in several small lumber operations on various parts of the island, that would operate a year or two then disappear. Around the center of their operations, a small shantytown would be built for the workers, which would vanish when the operation closed down. Hikers still occasionally encounter small formally-cleared areas, rapidly being reclaimed by nature, that were once the sites of such operations. One such lumber camp became large and consistent enough that it briefly had its own post office. In 1912, a man named Bellinsinger became the only official postmaster in the island's history. He kept the post office and a small general store in his cabin near Garden Island Harbor. Since a small group of woodcutters and mill workers built residences surrounding his cabin, they gave this small hamlet the name of "Success." But, Success wasn't very successful, for the post office was officially registered with the government for only one year. Bellinsinger did stay on the island, and apparently operated his store for a few more years. The partially-collapsed walls of his cabin and the clearing around it are the only visible reminders of this short-lived village.

Most of that settlement's workers were connected with the Northcutt Mill, which was the best-known and probably the largest of the timber operations of that era. It was located on a very attractive sand bay on the southern end of the island, and named after the man responsible for building it. Northcutt was a very tall Texan, who had apparently come east to take part in the Michigan lumber boom. He met and married a lady from the Petoskey area, who was reputed to be over six feet tall herself. In 1912, he built a sawmill along the bay that now bears his name. He brought over his brother-in-law, who acted as engineer. He also took up residence on the island close to the Bellinsinger post office. William Wachtner remembered that many islanders including members of the Vincent and Wachtner families, and some island Indians worked at the mill. The operation was large enough that mainland workers were also brought in. William himself worked at the mill during the busy seasons as a 13-year-old boy, for 50 cents a day.

The operation included a large steam engine to supply power for the mill and a large dock built in Northcutt Bay. They manufactured fish boxes that were in plentiful demand because of the rich fish harvest of whitefish and lake trout that extended throughout the Beaver chain in those days. When two workmen were killed in a mill accident, their fellow workers buried them close to the shore, and fenced in their graves with heavy anchor chains that had been salvaged from shipwrecks. The graves were a prominent landmark for many years, but unfortunately the whereabouts of the graves are lost, for vandals have long since stolen the anchor chains.

Wooden cross on Pete Monitou's grave

Though the mill operated successfully for several years, like the lost graves of the workmen, not a trace of it is left today. With the demise of the Northcutt Mill, the days of turning out finished wooden products such as boats, fence posts, trail ties and fish boxes at this and other island locations were pretty much over. Since that time, there have been several smaller timber operations on various parts of the islands, but the logs were hauled elsewhere to be cut into lumber. Although the virgin forests have long since been harvested, there has been no substantial lumbering on the island for almost 40 years. This has given the island time to recover from the clearcutting scars of the commercial woodcutters, and today most of the island surface is covered with large stands of second and third growth timber.

Except for the workmen in the short-lived lumber camps, no long term settlers who wish to make their living from the soil and the sea came to replace the Vincents and the Danes. The death of Matt and Lena Jensen in the 1930s ended the history of successful white homesteaders on the island. The last long-term homesteader was the Indian named Pete Monatou, a combination of farmer-fisherman-lumberman who raised his family on the island. When his children left, Pete, by then an old man, stayed on. When he died in 1947 at the age of 76, the era of both white and Indian homesteading on the island came to a permanent end. His grave is marked by a simple wooden cross in the Indian cemetery, and the cabin in which he raised his family is now in ruin. The fallen log walls are still visible today on the southern edge of his homestead clearing, found on the southeast corner of the island. Although with time, the clearing and cabin will disappear his name will survive. For, like the Jensens, the bay nearest his home is named after him.

Today people come to Garden Island to fish, to hunt, to sequester themselves on their sailboats in the isolation of the snug harbor or to hike its many trails in solitude. Surrounded by heavy forests and thoughts of its history, Garden Island offers those who visit it a woodland mystique that is extraordinary and rare.

Chapter XIII

GARDEN ISLAND TRAILS

INTRODUCTION

Because of the location of harbors and docks, High Island and the Manitous have standard landing sites that most hikers use as a beginning point. Not so at Garden, for there are at least three prime landing areas to be considered by the prospective hiker. Each offers some protection to boats, and easy access to the more important trails on the island. This has left this writer with a bit of a problem on exactly how to approach the trail description of the eastern-most of these islands. Since hikers will have to decide before their arrival which site they will choose for their debarkation point, the following descriptions gives the merits of the different locations, and may help the hiker in deciding which of the three initial jumpoff places he or she will use. After deciding the section that best suits your plans, you can then turn to the specific trail descriptions of that area for further information. The trail descriptions that start from each area are grouped under that area's heading. By reading them before your arrival, they may also aid you in deciding where you want to land, and where you want to spend the bulk of your exploring time.

Northcutt Bay (Point A) is one of two large bays on the southern end of the island. It lies west of Monatou Bay, and is the better of the two for landing because it is deeper, allowing boats to get closer to shore before running out of bottom. It also is not surrounded by large swamps along much of its shoreline as is Monatou Bay. There is a marvelous sand beach around a good part of the bay. The woodland area along this sand perimeter makes an ideal campsite, possibly the nicest on the island. It is also the closest and most easily reached location from St. James Harbor on Beaver Island making it the shortest trip over open water to reach the island. The Northcutt Trail which begins here, gives easy access to all the trails on the southern part of the island. Although it is about two miles from the beginning of the Center Trail at Indian Harbor, backpackers planning an extended stay on the island might wish to camp here for a couple of days doing the southern trails, then change campsites to Indian Harbor to explore the northern trails. Northcutt Bay's biggest disadvantage may be for people with their own boats who plan to leave them anchored for extended periods of hiking. Although the protection is good, it does not offer the almost total security from rough weather for watercraft that is found at the other two locations. Trail descriptions from this bay begin on page 292.

Garden Island Harbor (Point B). The best place to land is near the southern end of the harbor, behind Little Island, at the landing point for the D.N.R. cabins. Not only are boats offered much protection by the sheltering effect of the lee of Little Island and the sand spit at the southern end of the bay, but there is often a small and somewhat wobbly dock that one can use at the cabin landing area. The water level at the end of the dock is only a little over a foot deep so only shallow draft boats will be able to come up right alongside for unloading. The very rocky and uneven beach, surrounded by a forest of thick density, crowds out any

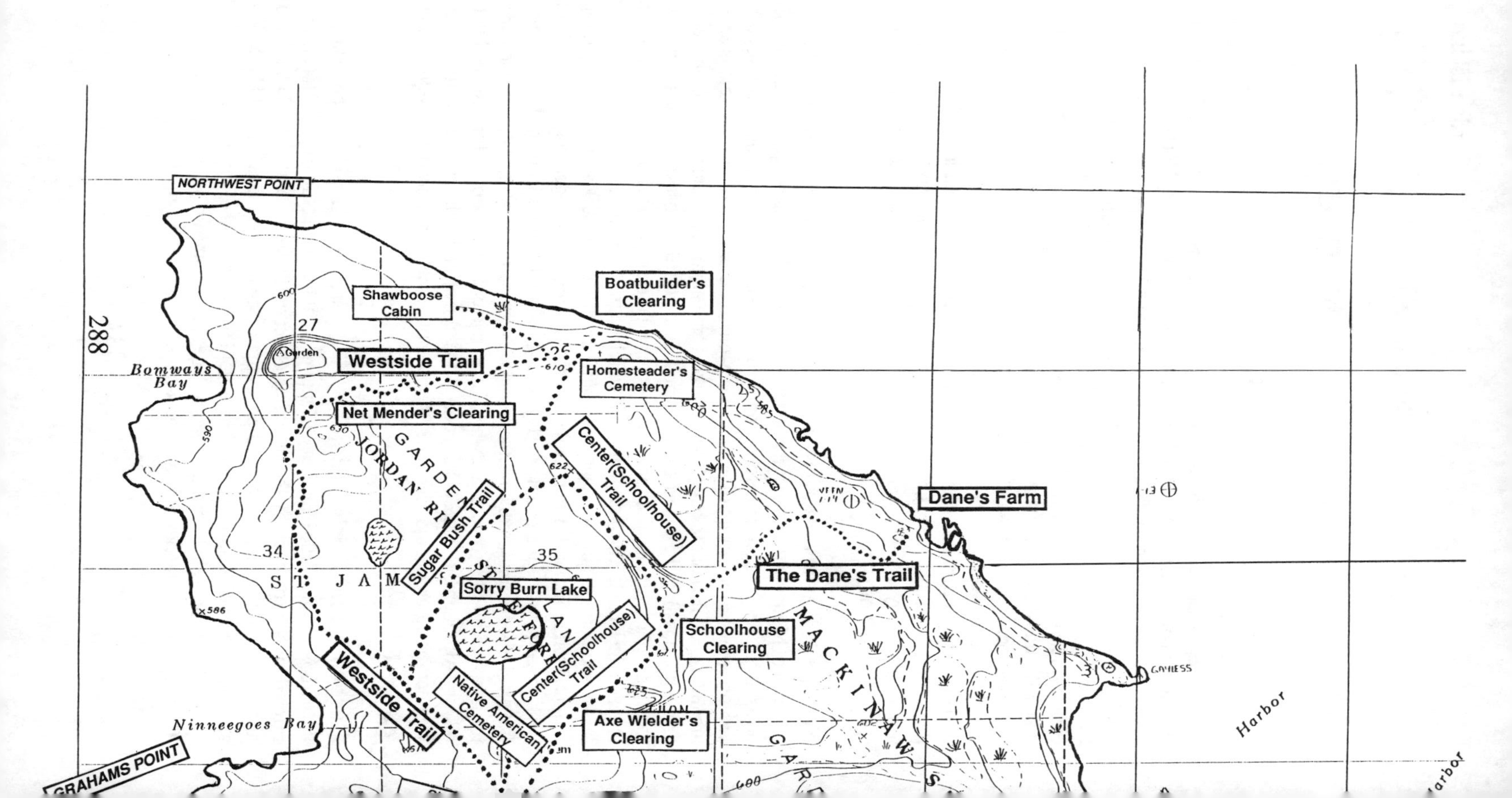
NORTHWEST POINT
Shawboose Cabin
Boatbuilder's Clearing
Westside Trail
Homesteader's Cemetery
Net Mender's Clearing
Center(Schoolhouse) Trail
Dane's Farm
The Dane's Trail
Sugar Bush Trail
Sorry Burn Lake
Schoolhouse Clearing
Center(Schoolhouse) Trail
Westside Trail
Native American Cemetery
Axe Wielder's Clearing
GRAHAMS POINT
Bomways Bay
Ninneegoes Bay
Harbor
GARDEN
JORDAN RIV
ST JAM
MACKINAW
27
34
35

GARDEN ISLAND

GARDEN ISLAND HARBOR

LITTLE ISLAND

D. N. R. Cabins

Harbor Trail

The Triangle

Post Office Trail

Northcutt Trail

Pete Monatou's Trail

Cabin Ruin

STURGEON BAY

MONATOU BAY

NORTHCUTT BAY

A

B

C

D

GARDEN ISLAND

KILOMETERS 1 .5 0 1 2

METERS 1000 0 1000 2000

MILES 1 .5 0 1

FEET 1000 0 1000 2000 3000 4000 5000 6000 7000 8000 9000 10 000

CONTOUR INTERVAL 5 METERS
SUPPLEMENTARY CONTOUR INTERVAL 2.5 METERS
AND 1.5 METERS ALONG SHORELINE

GARDEN ISLAND

Southern end of Garden Harbor

good areas to set up camp near this landing. There is a small open area around the two state D.N.R. buildings, but the close proximity to these structures hardly enhances any kind of wilderness feeling. A more appropriate clearing for camping is found at the junction of the Harbor Trail and the Post Office Trail, about a three-minute walk from the cabins. There is a small trail down to the water at this opening, but its terminus at the shoreline is difficult to find from the harbor, so it is easier to find this clearing by taking the short walk from the area of the D.N.R. Cabin. If you are day-hiking from a boat this is a good vicinity for covering the southern trails, for the distances to Northcutt Bay and The Pete Monatou Trail are within reasonable walking times from the cabin area. Walking to the north shore of the island, by using the Center or Danes Trails, makes for much longer day hikes, but can be done by any hiker in good shape. If the area around the D.N.R. cabins isn't an ideal base camp location, it still is a good starting point for backpacking to other parts of the island. Trail descriptions from this area begin on page 293.

Indian Harbor (Point D). Found at the north end of Garden Island Harbor, most of this narrow inlet is quite shallow, restricting its approach to shallow draft boats. But, the landing site on its north bank is close enough to the mouth of Indian Harbor that deeper offshore anchorage is not far away. This is the closest landing point to the most visited spot on the island, the section of the large Native American Cemetery that contains the Spirit Houses. Adjacent to the harbor is the large open area that once was the site of an Indian village, which offers several choices for good campsites. It is the best general location for day hiking on the north end of the island. Southern day-hikes can also be carried out from this campsite but the distances are somewhat longer and requires walking both directions on the Harbor Trail. Trail descriptions for Indian Harbor begin on page 299.

Hikers, intending to camp the first few days near Indian Harbor exploring the trails of the northern part of the island, might think about later relocating themselves at Northcutt Bay, reserving a day or two for exploring the southern sections of the island.

Suggested Day Loop Hikes.

To better acquaint you with some hiking possibilities from each of the aforementioned landing sites, I have included some possible loop hikes from both the Northcutt Bay and the Indian Harbor areas. This may also help you decide on a choice of landing sites.

FROM NORTHCUTT BAY (Point A). Northcutt, Sturgeon, Monatou Bay Loop. If the waters of Lake Michigan are not at high levels (and you will not make this journey after long periods of extended rain) a pleasant loop hike can be made from either Northcutt Bay or the D.N.R. cabins. Take the Northcutt Trail from the bay and follow it until it T's into the Pete Monatou Trail. Turn right, and follow the Monatou Trail, taking the brief side trail to Sturgeon Bay. Then follow the Monatou Trail into the clearing at the end of the trail. Take the small trail that connects the clearing with Monatou Bay on the right side of the clearing, or walk to the ruins of the Monatou cabin, then walk due south through a narrow section of trees to the shore. Follow the shoreline west around Monatou Bay. Much of the shoreline area is swampy, so you may find that it is too soggy a way to go. If so, you can always retreat and return the way you came. If you do continue around Monatou Bay, it is not necessary to walk to the end of the small peninsula that separates the two bays. When the line of trees along the west side of the bay becomes thin enough, you can cut across the little peninsula to its Northcutt side.

FROM INDIAN HARBOR (Point D). The Boatbuilder's, Blind Net Mender West Side Loop. Take the Center Trail to the Boatbuilder's Clearing. Follow the West Side Trail to the Net Mender's Clearing. Continue on the West Side Trail south to the junction with the Center Trail, but be aware that parts of this trail are quite vague beyond the Net Mender's Clearing, and you can easily lose its thread. Take the Center Trail south, back to Indian Harbor.

The Indian Cemetery, Sugar Bush, Schoolhouse Loop. Follow the Center Trail the short distance north to the junction with the West Side Trail. Follow the West Side Trail, with the short side trip to the Native American Cemetery. Continue on the West Side Trail to the junction with the Sugar Bush Trail. Follow the faint Sugar Bush Trail north until it deadends into the Center Trail. Follow the Center Trail south through the Schoolhouse Clearing back to Indian Harbor.

Dane's Farm, Boat builder Loop. Take the Center Trail to the Schoolhouse Clearing. Follow Dane's Trail to Dane's Farm. Follow shoreline north to the Boatbuilder's Clearing and return on the Center Trail.

TRAIL DESCRIPTIONS
Starting at Northcutt Bay (Point A)

Northcutt Bay has such an easy approach and comparatively level shaded land directly behind the beach, that day-hikers with picnic lunches will occasionally boat over from Beaver Island to spend a pleasant morning and afternoon. As mentioned earlier, there are lovely camping areas, including some rustic benches, found near the shore. Having sand and small pebbles, the beach and a gradually sloping lake bottom make it an ideal place for a swim, when the weather is cooperating. A wooden sign hung up on a tree which is becoming difficult to read with the passage of time states:

This island is your privilege
Keep it clean
Troop 67. Battle Creek Michigan

There is an outhouse of sorts, fashioned of black plastic suspended on two trees, that I found was still in good condition in 1988. This Northcutt beach area, found on the northwest corner of the bay, is close to the primitive john and the trailhead. It offers excellent sites for camping. If strong winds and rain make camping near the beach unpleasant, one may find a far more sheltered area just off the Northcutt Trail a couple of minutes away from the beach. East of this area along the beach is the site of the former Northcutt Lumber Mill. This once-active sawmill was owned and operated by a man of that name who had originally come from Texas (See history section). A few cement slabs seen along the beach are the only visible signs left of the mill.

Northcutt Trail
From Northcutt Bay to the Post Office Trail, Pete Monatou Trail and the Triangle

Distance: To Post Office Trail 0.1 mi., to Pete Monatou Trail 0.4 mi.; to The Triangle 0.8 mi.
Walking Time: To the Triangle 15 to 20 minutes.

GENERAL REMARKS. This is the only easily-followed trail from this bay and it acts as a gateway trail to the rest of the island. At the Triangle it links with the Harbor Trail, which connects you with all the trails on the northern end of the island. By taking the short cut Post Office Trail, you have a quick way to the vicinity of the D.N.R. cabins and the trails on the southwest corner of the island. The old Post Office Trail was used daily by many mill's workers, for they lived by the Post Office in a short-lived hamlet called Success. The Northcutt Trail is an easy, wide and fast woodland path.

TRAIL DESCRIPTION. Look for the only easily seen path that heads north leading away from the bay's north west corner. In less than a hundred yards from the shore, the trail has an easy uphill section about six foot long, taking you above an old shore line. You can look right just beyond the rise and see a small flat open area which makes a good alternate campsite. It is out of sight of the water, but does offer much better wind protection than the

Department of Natural Resources' cabins on Garden Island

beach areas. Less than five minutes beyond this point, you will come on an easily seen trail coming in from the left. This is the Post Office Trail that, in less than a 15 minute walk, will take you to the Harbor Trail and the site of the former village of Success. It is the quickest way to get to the vicinity of the D.N.R. Cabins, and the trails on the southwest corner of the island. If you follow it, you will come to an open area to the right, where, almost buried beneath small trees, are the ruins of an old cabin that once served as a small general store and island post office. A couple minutes beyond this point, the Post Office Trail T's into the very prominent Harbor Trail.

If you do not turn left on the Post Office Trail, but continue straight ahead on the Northcutt Trail, you will find that in about seven to eight minutes it T's into the Pete Monatou Trail. From here, the two trails share the same path to The Triangle. If you wish to go to the Harbor Trail, turn left and in about a quarter of a mile, you will come to the southern spur of The Triangle. At this writing, the right side of the Triangle is a bit grown up, so following the Triangle's southern line is a bit easier. It soon dead-ends into the Harbor Trail.

Starting at the D.N.R. Cabins (point B).

The land approach to the D.N.R. Cabin is behind Little Island close to the southern corner of Garden Island Harbor. There usually is a small unsteady dock there that can be used by boats of very shallow draft. The biggest drawback for extended hiking and camping here is the lack of a good camping area, with the closest open area of any size being about a three minute walk from the landing site. Not counting outhouses and a big shed, there are two separate main buildings. When first viewing this site, I was reminded of an entry someone wrote in the log book kept here which read:

> "This place gives you the feeling of remoteness hard to find
> outside of Canada. The cabin is just
> primitive enough to be comfortable."

The first of the main buildings that comes into view is a log structure, which serves as a combination bunkhouse and storage area for small boats and other equipment used by the D.N.R. The other is a shuttered green tarpaper-covered building with a small porch in front. The shack-like appearance on the outside gives little clue to the rustic secure and snug feeling of its white-walled interior. Equipped with a stove and gas lamps, which work if there is propane in the outside tanks, the kitchen is well-stocked with food, which is to be used in emergency by hikers or boaters who become stranded on the island during times of inclement weather. The unwritten tradition is that you leave whatever food you have left over, and don't use the supplies on the shelves unless it is a true emergency. There is also an oil drum type wood stove, and a good supply of cut wood, which is also there for emergency use by people who have been soaked or nearly frozen by severe weather. Use of the cabin is reserved for D.N.R. personnel, various university scientific groups doing research on the island, and for emergencies. A sign on the front door reads:

> Although maintained for the use of D.N.R. personnel and authorized university groups this building may be used for emergency shelter. Please be responsible. Leave it as clean or cleaner than you found it.
> Michigan Department of Natural Resources.

If no one is occupying the cabin, it is perfectly all right to enter and look around, for the cabin is not kept locked to give easy access to those who need to use the facility in an emergency situation. With this open door policy, the cabin has been seriously vandalized on several occasions. The cabin's usual welcoming condition is due to a group of retired D.N.R. employees who spend up to a week each year doing interior cleanup and necessary repairs to the building. Their only compensation is the satisfaction of keeping this facility useable for those who need it, and the fun of spending a few days on an island they obviously love. Their reports, written in the log during past years show that they often find the interior an unholy mess, and more unfortunately, occasional destruction to parts of the property. It is sad to think that even in this remote semi-wilderness setting, there is a small minority of individuals visiting the island whose Hun-like behavior falls below the intelligence level of Neanderthals and might render this emergency haven unusable for someone who needs it for survival.

Visitors will see that the building is in three distinct sections. The original structure, which is now the kitchen area, was built by Indians as a homestead. Immediately behind the kitchen, one finds the first part of the bunk house, which is an add-on made by a lumber company. The south wing of the dormitory was later added by a group of researchers, doing an in depth study of the coyotes of the island.

South West Island Trails

Distance: Both Trails one way from the D.N.R. Cabin .07 mi. each
Walking Time: Either trail one way 20 minutes or less.

GENERAL REMARKS. These two trails south of the D.N.R. Cabins are quite level, easy to follow, and one can hike both of them in a combined walk in less than an hour. Although they traverse heavy timber growth, the cleared area occupied by the trails is often at least 15 feet wide. They were used as roads by various lumber companies, often to access points where timber could be loaded on boats. One of the trails passes the site of a former lumber camp, then takes you to the beach, close to the southernmost tip of the island. The other leads to a shallow pond, often inhabited by waterfowl. From there you can proceed to a small bay south of Garden Island Harbor, and a peninsula that forms the southwest tip of the harbor.

TRAIL DESCRIPTION. Follow the trail in front of the green D.N.R. cabin south. In about two minutes of walking, the trail makes a left turn. You can look right at this point and see that the trees have been cleared to the waterfront, which probably served as a handy landing site for a timber company. Less than 30 feet beyond this turn, just before the trail heads into the woods, there is another trail coming in from the right. Turn right, and follow that trail. If you wish to follow the trail leading into the forest, you will find that in less than ten minutes it disappears, as do a couple of spurs leading from it. The trail to the right proceeds straight ahead in a southerly direction for a couple more minutes, before making another left turn. Again, as there was at the first left turn, there is a cleared area to the right that goes to Garden Island Harbor. Three to four minutes walking beyond this turning, look for a trail going off to the right. Mark the spot in your mind, for if you are going to do both trails this is the turnoff for the trail that takes you to the small southwest bay south of Garden Harbor, and the harbor peninsula that you will follow on your return trip. If you wish to go only to this area, and not take the trail to the southwest shore, skip the next paragraph.

In a couple more minutes the trail to the southwest shore becomes more closed in, and soon it skirts the right side of an area of thinned out trees that once was the site of a lumber operation. At its southeast corner, the trail goes off diagonally to the right, enclosed in a canopy of heavy forest. The first time I walked this segment, I was alone and the heavily wooded terrain made me feel like I was Little Red Riding Hood on her way to Grandmother's House. When you arrive at the rocky beach, the north end of Beaver Island is dead ahead, a little less that two miles away. Part of High Island, as well as tiny Trout and Whiskey islands, are also visible west of Beaver.

On your return, it should only take you about 10 to 12 minutes to reach the southwest bay junction. After a left turn, this southwest path continues straight ahead for almost five minutes, before turning right. A couple of minutes later, you will see an open area on your left, with a pond at its far end. Turning left there, facing the open area, you can see a break in the trees, which gives you access to a small bay on the southwest corner of the island. If the weather has been dry and you want to walk to the shore and hike to the end of the peninsula on the southern end of Garden Harbor, you can cut directly across the opening to the break in the trees. During wetter times, the direct approach will call for sloshing through a mucky bottom, and it may be easier to follow the tree line that borders the left side of the area to the break. Once the beach is reached, it will take you about ten minutes of shore walking to reach the end of the peninsula, where you have good views of Beaver's northwest corner, the northern end of High Island, and both Trout and Whiskey Islands. Often the reef extending beyond the point will give you the pleasure of watching waves breaking in two directions. When I have walked to this end of land alone, it has always left me with a feeling of eerie isolation and loneliness.

The Harbor Trail

GENERAL REMARKS. Although this curving trail follows the shoreline of Garden Harbor, it is almost never in sight of it. Wide, level and easily followed it functioned as a major road on the island for many years. Not only does it connect the hiker with all the trails on the northern end of the island, but also with all the important southern trails as well. It also acts as a gateway to the southern trails for those starting from the vicinity of Indian Harbor. You will find the description of this trail heading south from **Point D** grouped with the Indian Harbor trails.

Harbor Trail North
from The D.N.R. Cabins (Point B) to the Post Office Trail, the Triangle (Point C) and the Indian Village (Point D)

Distance: To the Post Office Trail .03 mi; to the Triangle 0.5 mi; to Indian Village 1.5 mi. Walking Times: To the Post office Trail 3 to 4 minutes; to the Triangle 10 to 15 minutes; to Indian village 40 to 50 minutes.

TRAIL DESCRIPTION. When you walk away from the dock at Point B to where the first D.N.R Cabin is in sight, the trail turns left away from the buildings. Not only is the trail wide, but the cleared area between the trees is also quite wide, cutting through a dense forest on each side. In about three to four minutes you will come to a clearing on the right. There is a fire ring lined with a circle of field stones in the clearing, where someone has built wooden benches from drift wood. It is the only open site suitable for camping for quite a distance. There is also a narrow path on the left, cut through the trees to the harbor. This clearing was once the site of Success, a small village of lumbermen and fishermen. The only standing evidence of this small hamlet are the ruins of a log cabin, which once functioned as a small general store and the island post office. The trail that begins here and connects with the Northcutt Trail, as well as the clearing, are named after it. The building is not visible from the Harbor Trail, but is not far away. When you approach the southern edge of the clearing, look right where you will find the Post Office Trail going off in that direction, skirting the field's southern end. If you wish to see the remains of the old building, walk a few yards down this trail and you will see it on the left, partly buried in tree growth. If you are looking for a quick way to Northcutt Bay, take the Post Office Trail eastward, and in a half mile it will T into the Northcutt Trail. Turn right there, and in a couple of minutes you'll be on the beach.

If you continue on the Harbor Trail, another quarter mile brings you to the south west corner of the Triangle at Point C. Turn right here for the Pete Monatou Trail and the Northcutt

Hikers on Harbor Trail near D.N.R. cabins

Trail. Another three minutes should bring you to the north corner of the Triangle. A half mile beyond this point, where the trail turns slightly to the right, there is an open area to the left, with a wide path that ends at the harbor. There you have nice views of Little Island and points west.

In less that half a mile, the trail swings left and makes straight for the shore, crossing over a low natural stone ridge running parallel to the rocky beach. Looking dead ahead from the shore you can see a small point on the southern side of Indian Harbor, with the view of the open lake to the left of the point. There is also another small point to the right on the other side of Indian Harbor, which forms a small bay immediately to your right. How you proceed from here depends upon the water level of Lake Michigan. If it is not near the record high level reached in 1987, you have an easy shoreline walk about two thirds the way around the little bay. As you reach the curve around the bay you will see a small swampy area set back from the shore. Approaching it, you will see a small stream known as Sucker Creek emptying into the bay, which drains a huge swamp further inland. Sucker Creek is unusual in the fact that it is one of only two streams on all four islands that flows continuously throughout the warmer seasons of the year, even through periods of drought. It is easily crossed, however, unless Lake Michigan is high enough to push the creek's mouth back into the swamp. In that case see the paragraph after the next one for an alternative route.

If you can cross the creek, proceed along the shore almost to the curve at the end of this little bay. Just before it begins curving round look for a trail to the right which crosses a small grassy area running parallel to the shore. In a few feet, the trail enters the large open area of the old Indian village. After passing a few old fruit trees on your left, which stand almost in the middle of this open area, the trail T's into The Center (Schoolhouse) Trail. This is the site of an Indian village which had its beginnings in the nineteenth century. At the turn of the century, there were about 20 Indian families making their homes here, but by World War One the family units had been reduced to four. A left turn at this junction will soon take you to the shore of Indian Harbor. A right turn will lead you across the island.

If you cannot cross Sucker Creek without getting into the swamp, follow the beach

Cabin ruins of the post office and general store in village of "Success."
Photo taken in 1987

back to the point where the trail originally took you to the shore. Cross over the small rocky barrier that parallels the shore, and walk about 25 feet back up the trail. Look left and in the trees you will see a trail that parallels the shore. Follow it until you reach a small grassy opening. Turn right and follow a not-too-distinct trail which will soon make a big U curve and take you to the banks of Sucker Creek. At this point it has a stone bottom and is easy to cross. Not long after the crossing, you will enter another small grassy area, but the bottom of this one is often mucky, with pools of standing water. Once across it and into the trees on firmer ground, this faint trail T's into an old road. Turn left on the road, and follow it to a small bay. Turn right and follow the bay shore almost to the curve. Look right to find the trail explained in the paragraph above.

Pete Monatou's Trail

Distance: 2.2 mi.
Walking Time: 55 minutes to one hour 10 minutes.

GENERAL REMARKS. Pete Monatou was probably the last person who lived and worked on Garden Island year-round for most of his life. He fished, farmed and did odd jobs to earn a hand-to-mouth living until he died at the age of 74. In 1944 he was laid to rest in the Indian Cemetery. The simple wooden cross that marks the location of his grave is still readable today, and is found in the middle of the most visited part of that cemetery. The trail takes you to the clearing that once was his farm, near the southeast corner of the island on the eastern side of the bay that bears his name. The only visible structure of this once active farming homestead are the walls of his deteriorating log cabin home.

This walk also offers easy access to beautiful but shallow Sturgeon Bay, with good views of Hog Island, and some excellent sand beaches on the south east corner of the island. This trail was almost unusable until 1985, when a Youth Corps group from the lighthouse project on Beaver Island cleared it of underbrush and deadfalls. I first walked it two years later, and found that it already was becoming difficult to find in many areas, showing how fast nature can reclaim these trails if they are not often walked. My companions and I cleared everything except the deadfalls in 1988, so it should be reasonably easy to follow for a few more years.

TRAIL DESCRIPTION. Starting at either the north or southwest corner of the Triangle at **Point C** the trail runs simultaneously with the Northcutt Trail. The path is quite distinct for the first half mile, to the point where the Northcutt Trail branches off to the right. The Northcutt turnoff is easy to find, because many hikers coming from that bay use this way to get to the Harbor Trail. Northcutt Bay is an easy walk of less than a half mile from this junction.

From this point, the Monatou Trail proceeds straight ahead but is less distinct. Beyond this junction, you will have occasional deadfalls to get around, but none should prove difficult. You will also notice that the places where the trail is hard to find tend to be in the open, rather than the heavily wooded areas. After about a half hour of walking, the trail will bring you quite close to Sturgeon Bay, and you can get glimpses of it through the dense tree cover. Just before one large snaggle of deadfalls, where it is necessary to leave the original road and detour around the obstruction on a narrow trail to the left, there is a short narrow trail going through the thick tree cover that will take you to the shore of the southern part of Sturgeon Bay. The walk to this attractive bay of sand beaches, and its view of Hog Island, only takes a couple of minutes.

Once beyond the Sturgeon Bay cutoff, the trail almost unnoticeably begins to swing westward, away from that bay in the direction of Monatou Bay. When you encounter a couple of small open areas, you are really in isolated clearings that once were part of the Monatou farm, but now are closed off by forest growth. The trail begins breaking out into, and following the right side of, the main clearing of the homestead. Despite patches of encroaching forest, there is still a good deal of open land left. By following along the right side of the field, you may find a short trail that has been hacked out through the heavy forest wall between the field and the shore to Monatou Bay. If you follow the large field to its southern end, you will find the remains of Pete Monatou's cabin, just within the tree line. Although there is no trail, it is not hard to walk further south behind the cabin through the trees to this southern shore.

Trails Starting at Indian Harbor (Point D)

The Indian Harbor landing at **Point D** is the used by most boaters who wish to see the Indian Cemetery's spirit houses. It is also the best place to take the various hikes found on the north end of the island. Southern island trails can also be reached from here, by using the connecting Harbor Trail. Although the narrow and shallow Indian Harbor at the north end of the larger Garden Island Harbor is not hard to find, the beginning of the Center Trail is usually not visible from the water. The beginning of this path, which passes through the site of the old Indian village and functions as the link to all the important trails of this area, is partly blocked from view by high shore grass. To find the trailhead, put yourself ashore near the northeast point of Indian Harbor. Then walk along the shore about 50 yards west of that point. You should easily find the place where the trail heads due north from the shore, cutting narrowly through the tall grass lining the beach. The wide open area next to the shore is the former site of an Indian village of many families, during the last half of the nineteenth century. Still a quite active hamlet at the beginning of this century, its Indian residents were mostly gone by the beginning of World War I. Although all traces of these former occupants have vanished, the area they cleared gives campers many choices for good tent sites, and fuel for the imagination of what might have seen here a hundred years earlier. In this clearing, the Center Trail, which leads to all the trails to the north, junctions with the Harbor Trail, forming the connection with all the trails to the south.

Harbor Trail South
from the Indian Village (point D) to the Triangle (Point C), the Post Office Trail and the D.N. R. Cabins (point B)

Distance: to the Triangle 1 mi.; to the Post Office Trail 1.3 mi.; to the D.N.R. Cabins. 1.5 mi.
Walking Times: to the Triangle 20 to 30 minutes; to the Post Office Trail 25 to 40 minutes; to the D.N.R. Cabins 40 to 50 minutes.

GENERAL REMARKS. This easily followed wide trail acts as a corridor between this central section of the island and several important trails grouped at its southern end.

TRAIL DESCRIPTION. This trail begins moving east, away from the Center Trail close to the middle of the Indian village area, and soon approaches the beach of a very small bay. Turn left, and follow the shore. If the water level of Lake Michigan is not extraordinary high, the next part of the walk is an easy one, for as the shore begins curving to the right you will reach the banks of Sucker Creek. Although it is always flowing during the warm months, it is easy to cross. If the lake water is high, forcing a crossing of the creek back in a swamp, the route is far more complicated (See the paragraph below for directions). Once across Sucker Creek, you follow the shore for about another hundred yards until there is a wide break in the shoreline trees to the left. In that break, there is a wide path moving away from the shore. It is here the Harbor Trail leaves the shore line, and it stays out of sight of the harbor for the rest of its easily-followed course.

If the water is high, and you find the mouth of Sucker Creek back in the swamp, just before reaching the swamp look for a path to the left which is hidden from view by tall shore grass. When you find this path, you will see it is on an old road, but you do not follow this road very long. Keep an eye out to the right for a narrow path that takes you into the woods. It will soon take you into a small open bog area where the walking can be quite sloshy. Once across this bog and onto drier land back in the woods, this indistinct trail soon reaches Sucker Creek. After making the easy stream crossing, the trail briefly heads inland before making a large U-turn to the right. Follow it back to the shore where you have two options. On a small open area just short of the shore line, you will be able to see a trail that parallels the shoreline behind the trees. You can follow it until it dead ends into a wide swath cut in the forest, which is the continuation of the Harbor Trail. Or you can proceed straight ahead from this small open area the short distance through the tall grass to the shore. Turn left and follow it until you see the opening on the left, which is the continuation of the Harbor Trail.

Leaving this shoreline, the trail gradually swings to the right and in about a quarter mile you will see a wide opening to the right, which you do not take unless you want another view of Garden Harbor. About a half mile beyond this point, you may see an overgrown trail to the left. This is the northwest corner of the Triangle at Point C, which is the junction for both the Pete Monatou and Northcutt Trails. If you wish to follow one of those trails, it is better to continue on the Harbor Trail about another three minutes to the southwest corner of the Triangle, for unless it has been recently cleared, the northern part is more grown over then the southern part. A left turn there puts you on the Pete Monatou Trail and the Connection to the Northcutt Trail.

You have less than a quarter mile to go before reaching the north end of a large cleared area to the left of the trail. There you will see a fire ring circled with field stones, with a couple of benches someone has fashioned out of driftwood. A small village known as Success was located here. In the early part of this century, it served as a home for men engaged in lumbering and fishing. Its only remaining building is in an advanced state of ruin, and is not visible from this trail. Since it once housed the island post office, the path that connects this trail with the Northcutt Trail bears that name. The Post Office Trail starts at the opposite end of the clearing, and borders its south side. If you want to see the remains of the building, follow this trail for a hundred feet or so and look to the left where you will be able to see it buried in small trees. When continuing along the Harbor trail, you only have about three minutes more walking before you come in sight of the first of the D.N.R. cabins.

The Center (Schoolhouse) Trail
From Indian Harbor (Point D) to the Schoolhouse Clearing and the Boatbuilder's Clearing (Point E)

Distance: to West Side Trail 0.2 mi.; to Schoolhouse clearing 0.8 mi.; to north shore 2 mi.
Walking Time: To Schoolhouse Clearing 20 to 30 minutes, to north shore 45 minutes to one hour.

GENERAL REMARKS. Although this trail crosses the island a little north of its true geographical center, it is the only trail that begins and ends at the beaches of the north and south shore. Those wishing to walk the Harbor Trail, or take the shortest path to the Indian Cemetery will only be on this trail briefly. Hikers wishing to walk the Dane's Trail, visit the Homesteader's Cemetery, the Boatbuilder's Clearing, Shawboose Cabin or the Net Mender's Clearing, possibly doing one of the various loop hikes, will cover a good part of this most frequently used of the island's longer trails. It is also often called the Schoolhouse Trail, because there once was a small schoolhouse found in the clearing that bears its name. Never very large, the school operated less than six months a year to give some basic reading, writing and elementary math instruction to both Indian children and the offspring of the homesteading families who lived on the island year round. Often walked and easily followed, the gentle uphill grades of the Center Trail hardly suggest that it comes close to the island's highest elevation.

TRAIL DESCRIPTION. To find the trailhead see Starting at Indian Harbor above. After two minutes or less of walking across the clearing of the old Indian village, you will junction with the Harbor Trail coming in from the right. This trail links you with all the island's southern paths. Continuing straight ahead, the Center Trail begins to go up a slight rise at the southern end of the clearing, enters a copse of small trees and soon junctions with another easily identified trail on the left. This is the West Side Trail. The first part of this trail is often walked, because a left turn here takes one to the Indian Cemetery turnoff in less than two

Spirit houses near the Center Trail

minutes. If you want to make a quick side trip to this Native American Burying Ground you can walk from this junction to its most interesting section in less than five minutes.

Just beyond this intersection, the Center Trail enters a hardwood forest, and after about five minutes of walking in this pleasant woodland, the trail rises slightly. Keep your eye peeled to the left for you should be able to see three comparatively recent spirit houses just off the trail. This is the eastern end of the Indian Cemetery, which extends from its location near the West Side Trail eastward to this point. There are over 3,000 Native Americans buried in this cemetery, but existing spirit houses are found only here and in one other section near the West Side Trail. Today thousands of graves are unmarked and unidentified. One of the three spirit houses belongs to Sawanigan, whose name is carved in a nearby tree. Another of this immediate group of spirit houses is the resting place of Keewaydin, also known as "The Axe Wielder." But as some readers might mistakenly think, this nickname was not the result of being an eighteenth-century scalp collector. He was a modern Indian whose feats with an axe in splitting logs were legendary. Reputed to have had the only log cabin on the island with absolutely straight walls, his skill improved after a few drinks. A few feet beyond these graves the trail enters a clearing which was once the axe wielder's homesite. Alas, the straight walled cabin of Keewaydin, whose name translates as "The West Wind," is no longer existent for us to admire.

A look at the map shows that the biggest lake on the island, with the interesting name of Sorry Burn is found about a fifth of a mile north west of the Axe Wielder's Clearing. This interesting story of how the lake was named was told to Keewaydinoquay, quite a few years ago. The storyteller was an elderly lady, who spent much of her childhood on the island, and during her teen-age years served as the teacher in the one-room island schoolhouse. When she was a child, her parents built a homesteader's cabin along the shore of the lake, but it was destroyed by a brush fire. Unknown to the white family, a few island Indians had been burning off overgrown fields that they wished to use for growing herbs, but a sudden change in wind direction and increase in wind velocity caused the fire to get out of hand, and the cabin was consumed in flames. Later, much to the family's amazement, a group of Indian women appeared, carrying some undetermined large objects.

Although the days of frontier Indian raids were almost a hundred years in the past, the family still did not know if the burning was deliberate or accidental. They were afraid that the approaching women might be planning to do further mischief. As the Indian women approached, the white homesteaders could see that the bundles carried by the native Americans were large bolts of cloth, which they held out to the white family, showing by gesture that the cloth was being presented as a gift. Neither side spoke the language of the other but the Indian women kept repeating two English words over and over again, "Sorry burn. Sorry burn." It dawned on the white family that the ladies were trying to tell them with these two words that the burning of their home was a regrettable accident, and they were offering the cloth as a goodwill gesture for the loss of their cabin.

The distance to the lake is only about a quarter mile, but there is no path to it. Although it is a pretty little body of water, the approach is difficult, and the surrounding shore is quite swampy, unsuitable for camping or swimming.

In less than ten minutes after crossing the Axe Wielder's Clearing, you will enter the south west corner of a much larger field, much of which has been claimed by juniper bushes. Named the Schoolhouse Clearing, because the ruins of that small building are still found here, it is about halfway between Indian Harbor and the Boatbuilder's Clearing. A visitor might assume that this site was cleared to locate a small hamlet, but such was not the case. This is one of the clearings on the islands that was used for agriculture. It is also the site of an important road junction, for roads coming from the Boatbuilder's Clearing and the Dane's Clearing joined here at this southwest corner of this clearing, on their way to Garden Harbor. Since the Dane's Trail is hard to follow through the juniper bush growth, it is more easily found at the opening's north-west corner (See Dane's Trail description).

The Center Trail follows along the west side of the field, and if you wish to see the few shattered remains of the old schoolhouse, follow the trail to the point where it leaves the clearing at its north west corner. Walk eastward near the northern border of the field, until you see a copse of trees intruding into the clearing. Buried in these trees, a few boards representing partial walls and sections of the shingled roof lie upon the ground, the only evidence left of that simple frontier-like center of rudimentary education.

Once beyond the clearing, the trail follows a usually-wide ridge top whose elevation is only three feet below the highest point of the island. When this path begins an easy descent, you will know that the junction with the West Side Trail, the Homesteader's Cemetery and Boatbuilder's Clearing at Point E is not far away. The first of these reached is the West Side Trail, which will be the first easily identified path that T's into the Center Trail from the left. Even if you do not plan a return walk on this trail, you will use part of it if you wish to go to the Net Mender's Clearing, or the Shawboose Cabin and the Kee Compound (See West Side Trail description).

The Vincent family in front of their island home, circa 1910. John Sr. is seated on right. William Wachtner Jr. is child seated on left
Courtesy Laurence Vincent

It is here that the Center Trail comes closest to the Homesteader's Cemetery. To find this cemetery, continue straight ahead on the Center Trail about 40 feet beyond the West Side Trail junction, and look to the right. Through the trees you should be able to see the large marble gravestones of Ecedius Larsen, who lived from 1872 to 1923, and his wife Christina, 1867 to 1913. There are at least 12 others buried here, mostly members of the Vincent and Wachtner families (See history section). But like thousands of the island's Indian graves, markers identifying the resting places of these white settlers are not easily seen or have disappeared entirely. A few feet beyond the cemetery, the Center Trail drops into a large clearing which was once the site of a homestead originally settled by John Vincent. He and his large family prospered here during the latter part of the nineteenth and the early part of this century. Vincent's major business enterprise was building fishing boats. Some of the best boats used by Beaver Island fishermen were built here. The buildings of this activity, including the homestead, have disappeared but the area today is still known as the Boatbuilder's Clearing (See history section). After going up a slight rise in the clearing, Lake Michigan comes into view, where you can descend through tall grass to a pebble beach. On clear days you can see the Upper Peninsula at Millecoquins Point near the small town of Naubinway Michigan about 17 miles away. Off to the northwest, the Lansing Shoal Light crib is also visible from this point, about six miles away.

The Dane's Trail

Distance: 0.8 mi.
Walking Time: 20 to 25 minutes.

GENERAL REMARKS. With the exception of the Vincents all the north shore settlers were immigrants from Denmark. These Scandinavian settlers busied themselves with fishing, small-scale lumbering and agriculture. The Dane's Trail leads to a complex where crop raising, if not the only activity, was surely carried on. With the exception of the small Shawboose cabin, the best remaining examples of buildings primarily constructed and used as homes on the east side of the island, are two larger log structures found in the Dane's Clearing. Although they have not been maintained and the roofs have fallen in, the four walls of these two buildings are still in place giving some idea of their size. This homesite, built by Matt Jensen, was probably the last to be occupied by year-round white residents over an extended time. Matt and his wife lived here until their deaths in the 1930s. Their buildings remained in very livable condition through the 1950s, with unbroken windows and good hardwood floors still in place, but time and much vandalism over the last 30 years have taken their toll. Nonetheless, they still represent the most interesting and best preserved ruins on the island today. The trail is easy to follow, but several deadfalls call for some skirting over, under and around them, slowing up a normal hiking pace.

TRAIL DESCRIPTION. To find the trailhead, take the Center Trail to the northwest corner of the Schoolhouse Clearing. Then follow the north end of that field around the clump of trees, hiding the remains of the schoolhouse, and continue to the northeast corner of the field. As you approach that corner, the old Dane's Trail road enters the trees. The site is easy to find, because there is a sand mound about a foot high that parallels the old road for about 30 feet on its eastern side, just before going into the forest. There are also two orange blazes painted on two trees on each side of the road as it enters the forest.

The trail continues on the old road making a slow sweeping turn to the right and another to the left, which the hiker may not be aware of. As the road comes alongside the Dane's Clearing, it becomes immersed in a thick maze of small trees. The trail turns left away from the old road and penetrates the thick woods on a narrow path for about 30 feet before breaking out into the sizable Dane's Clearing. Almost immediately in front of you is a large log structure, whose walls are still quite high. This building was not the house, but a working part of the farm, probably a combination barn and workshop. Walk around its right side, and you will see a large doorway with a sizable opening to the left of the door, which resembles a narrow picture window. It apparently was used as an entrance port for large equipment of some kind. This building probably played some part in Matt's winter occupation of making fence posts. With this building on your left, continue walking to the next visible large log structure, which once was the main house of the complex. In 1988 the frame of one window was still in place on the north wall. To the west of the building, a large field still has a few scrawny apple trees left over from a once-active orchard. There are other wooden structures, but none are made of logs, so their deterioration has been faster and all their walls and roofs lie on or close to the ground. A tree barrier stands between this farming complex and the lake, but if you follow the tree line along the eastern edge of the field, there is a break in the trees giving you easy access to the water. Along the shore there are the remains of an old boathouse.

Just before reaching the trees, along the shore line you may see to your right the beginnings of a road heading south, that once connected this homestead with another further south, known as Little Pete Nielson's. Although Little Pete was probably the last of the Danes to live at this homesite, it was built and lived in for many years by the brother of Matt Jensen. Here Peter Jensen fished, farmed, lumbered and raised several sons. When he left the island to join the Lighthouse Service, Little Pete, who had been living with the family, stayed on.

Interior and exterior of the Matt Jensen House in 1988

Little Pete Nielson apparently eked out a bare living at this homestead, in a variety of pursuits, but later moved in with Matt Jensen.

The old road to Little Pete's soon becomes so grown over that for all-practical purposes it is impassable. If you want to visit his homesite, you can follow that road briefly for a short distance until it becomes chocked in a snaggle of small trees. Turn left there and pass through some high grass until you reach the lakeshore. Walk south along the shore, passing a prominent point followed by a smaller one. Then, about 50 yards past this second point, look right for a break in the trees. There is little left in this clearing. In a perfunctory inspection of this location we found the remains of one boiler and the partial body of an old truck, which dates from the era of the Model T. So little is left of this rust heap, that it is beyond the point of any type of restoration.

Overgrown section of West Side Trail

A road once ran from here in a southeast direction to the homestead of Gillis Larsen. Although he and his wife permanently moved to Beaver Island in 1911, they are both buried in the Homesteader's Cemetery on this island, and have the only gravesites marked with modern stones. It would probably be easy to follow the shore down to the site of the Larsens' homestead, but I have never done so.

There also was a road going north, connecting the Dane's farm with the Boatbuilder's Clearing, but like the overgrown path to Little Pete Nielson's and the Larsens', it would take a herculean effort to follow it. The best way to walk from one clearing to the other, I assume, would be to follow the shore. Since I have not walked that shoreline, I cannot tell you if there are any major obstacles along the way.

The West Side Trail

GENERAL REMARKS. In its strategic location along the northwest side of the island, this trail offers several excellent loop hikes and side trip possibilities. Since the West Side Trail begins and terminates near opposite ends of the Center Trail, hikers may find either its north or south junction with that trail by reading the description of the Center Trail. At this writing, the biggest drawback to the West Side Trail is that it has become so overgrown in some areas that for many hikers it will become an illusive and sometimes impossible trail to follow. When I tried to walk this trail northward on my first island visit in 1987, the trail totally disappeared, just beyond its junction with the Sugar Bush Trail. I made repeated attempts to find, it only to become totally lost, and I had to rely on my compass to keep me from wandering hopelessly around in the forest. In 1988, I tried walking it in its opposite southerly direction, and was able to complete the entire trail. There were a few places where the trail disappeared close to where I had lost it the year before, but by scouting ahead, my companions and I were able to find it again beyond the obliterated sections.

Why was I able to complete it one year and not the next? There are probably three reasons which made the second hike successful. First, I think the trail is easier to follow south than north. Second, 1988 was a drought year and the weeds were far lower. Third, I had two companions with me the second year, and three pairs of eyes are far more effective than one. There is a chance that someone might clear this obscure section of the trail before your visit

Tribal Indian Cemetery sign

to the island. You can check its condition by seeing how difficult it is to follow when you arrive. At this writing, it can be followed south from its beginning near the Homesteader's Cemetery without undue difficulty for a far longer distance than in its northern direction. The early part of the West Side Trail heading north to the the Native American Cemetery turnoff is quite easily identifiable. The difficult sections lie beyond, particularly after the junction with the Sugar Bush Trail. By reading the trail descriptions below, you can ,decide what is most suitable for your own hiking agenda, if the overgrown segments have not been cleared.

West Side Trail North Direction from the Center Trail junction near the Indian Village to the Center Trail junction near the Boatbuilder's Clearing

Distance: to Indian Cemetery Junction 0.1 mi.; to Sugar Bush Trail 0.5 mi.; to the Net Mender's Clearing 1.5 mi.; to Center Trail junction near the Boat builder's Clearing 2.3 mi. Walking times: to Indian Cemetery junction 2 to 3 minutes; to the Sugar Bush Trail 12 to 20 minutes; beyond the sugar Bush Trail difficult to estimate.

TRAIL DESCRIPTION. Since the first part of this trail is used for the walk to the Indian Cemetery, its frequency of use makes the left turn from the Center Trail just north of the Indian village easy to identify. The hiker stays on this trail only about two minutes before reaching the short trail that leads to the heart of the burial ground. A sign on the right side of the trail fastened to a tree reads:

Native American Cemetery
Circa 1851 to the Present
Michigan Historic Registry #405
National Historic Site Registry #1978

Franciscan Priest escorting body from Beaver to Garden Island for interrment in the Indian Cemetery, circa 1930

Courtesy Archie La Freniere

Some older spirit houses in the Native American Cemetery

There is also another sign giving the same information in Indian pictographic language.

In less than three minutes, the trail to the right leads you to a collection of spirit houses of many sizes, shapes and various conditions, appropriately found in an area of high

A Recent sprit house with close-up of sign above door

ground in the depth of a hardwood forest. Although there are over 3,000 Indians buried here, only a handful of spirit houses are visible today. When surrounded by these humble wooden structures in this deep forest setting, the visitor may experience feelings of awe and reverence, surrounded by the presence of the omnipotent spirit of the invisible Manitou. The purpose of the spirit house is not unlike the old Egyptian idea of the pyramids, a house where the soul could continue to dwell after the death of the body. The Christian influence is also seen here, for a few graves are marked by modern headstones. A simple wooden cross placed here in 1947 marks the grave of Pete Monatou. He was the last Indian resident who made the island his year-round home. This land was recently purchased from the Roman Catholic Church by an Indian council and is now under its control. Remember, you are visiting their cemetery. Treat it with the respect it deserves.

When returning to the West Side Trail, it is obvious that most people proceed no further north, for the trail immediately becomes narrower and much less distinct. Nonetheless, it is still easy to follow northward for almost another half mile. In less than 10 minutes, the hiker should enter and cross the left side of what once probably was a clearing for some lumbering activity, but is now wildly overgrown, choked with high weeds and small trees. In 1987, these weeds were up to my shoulders, and it took a good deal of pushing to get through, but in the following dry year they only managed to reach my waist. If the weeds obliterate all visible evidence of the path, proceed directly across the opening and pick up the trail when you reach the opposite tree line. In less than five minutes you should arrive at the Sugar Bush junction, which is rather prominent. At this junction it seems as though the West Side Trail just makes a right turn, but that turn is the beginning of the Sugar Bush Trail. The West Side Trail does not turn but almost invisibly proceeds straight ahead. At this writing, it is just beyond this point, for all practical purposes, that the trail disappears to all but gifted Indian trackers. If you decide to do a little boondocking to see if you can make it through to the Blind Net Mender's Clearing, be sure to carry a compass.

West Side Trail South Direction from the Center Trail junction near the Boatbuilder's Clearing to the Center Trail junction near the Indian Village

Distance: To Shawboose Cabin Trail 0.1 mi.; to Shawboose Cabin 0.6 MI.; to the Net Mender's Clearing 0.8 mi.; to Sugar Bush Trail 1.8 mi.; to junction with the Center Trail 2.3 mi.
Walking Times: to Shawboose Cabin Trail 6 to 10 minutes; to Shawboose Cabin 15 minutes; to the Net Mender's Clearing 16 to 20 minutes; to the Sugar Bush Trail and beyond, difficult to estimate.

TRAIL DESCRIPTION. The trail is easily followed to the cutoff of the Shawboose cabin area, which is a little over a half mile from the trailhead. Since the Shawboose Side Trail is more often followed, the West Side Trail becomes a less distinct path, which goes off to the left. This cutoff must be carefully watched for, or the hiker will soon find himself coming to the Kee compound at the Shawboose Cabin. If you want to visit the Shawboose Cabin, follow the more distinctive right path at this junction. It is an easy walk of about a half mile to this old structure. It is also known as the Golden Cabin, for it was later owned and occupied by white occupants of that name. This building and the D.N.R. cabins are the only structures on the island that are maintained and lived in during the summer months. Built in the 1840s by an Indian named Jonas Shawboose, it is occupied from the late spring to early fall by his grandniece, whose Indian name is Keewaydinoquay. In the Ojibwa tongue this translates to "woman of the northwest wind," but most people shorten the long name to Kee. A retired high school science teacher from Leland, Michigan, Kee also taught Native American philosophy at the Milwaukee campus of the University of Wisconsin. Her botanical research includes the collecting and use of herbs and medicines found on the island, as utilized by her Indian ancestors. Aided by visiting assistants, she gathers and catalogues the various plants during the growing season, and publishes articles on her findings and other Indian lore and traditions.

The West Side Trail beyond this junction is not nearly as distinct as it was before the Shawboose cutoff, but is easy enough to follow to the Net Menders Clearing. It should take you less than 20 minutes to reach this little field, once the home site of Blind Ben Keeway, where his small barn stands, with its four walls and rafters still in position. Despite his loss of sight, Blind Ben was an Indian net mender by trade. His expertise at repairing nets was phenomenal, and in the days when commercial fishing was a major industry in the area, both white and Indian fisherman from Beaver Island and the Upper Peninsula sought Blind

Blind Ben Keway's Barn in 1988

Ben's services in repairing their nets.

Finding the continuing West Side Trail from the south west corner of the clearing is not difficult. It is quite wide and easy to follow for at least another half mile, which brings one near the Sugar Bush Trail junction. This area of a half mile or less has two or three places where the trail disappears. It often is difficult to find the trail on the other side of these segments. Anyone camping near Indian Harbor who can find their way through this maze of trees and underbrush to a recognizable trail at the sugar Bush junction, will save themselves a very long reverse walk back the way they came. Don't try it, though, unless you have a compass and are comfortable not knowing exactly where you are or when and how soon you shall be able to return to recognizable locations.

The Sugar Bush Trail

Distance: 1 mi.
Walking Time: 20 to 30 minutes.

GENERAL REMARKS. This short trail is a pleasant walk through a large hardwood forest of mostly maple trees. It begins on the West Side Trail less than a half mile north of the Indian Cemetery turnoff, and connects with the Center Trail about halfway between the Schoolhouse Clearing and the Boatbuilder's Clearing. As its name implies, this maple forest was a center for the island Indians who gathered maple sap and then boiled it down to produce their supply of natural sugar.

TRAIL DESCRIPTION. Since this narrow path does not lead to any better-known point of island interest, it is seldom walked, and if it was found in lower damper areas, it would long since have become impossible to follow. But set in a deep hardwood forest on higher elevation for most of its distance, the trees' leafy canopy keeps the underbrush at a minimum, saving it as a hiking possibility for the observant trail walker. This trail is seldom prominent and in places quite faint, but with attentive observation, a sharp-eyed hiker should be able to follow its tracings with little difficulty. it does call for concentration on route-finding, but the reward is a beautiful walk through a charming high ground forest.

PART V
HIGH ISLAND

Chapter XIV
Introduction And General Remarks

Not quite 50 years ago, an old Indian chief whose name was Paul Kenawabiske, was forced to abandon his home on High Island because it was no longer possible for him to make a living there. When he settled on nearby Beaver Island, he told his old friend Archie La Freniere that High Island was the most beautiful and of all the Lake Michigan islands. He

Only habitable buildings on the island, The D.N.R. Cabins

also told Archie, owner of the Shamrock, Beaver Island's only saloon, that High Island was the most desirable place that the old chief had ever lived. Many who have spent enough time on the island to have an intimate feeling for its surroundings would understand why the old Indian had such a passionate affection for his former home.

High Island is the smallest of the four major islands in this book, and is fifth in size of the islands in the entire archipelago. From its southwest to its northeast corner it is just under four miles in length, and at its widest point about two miles across. Its land mass of 5.8 square miles makes it two square miles smaller and one mile shorter than Garden Island. Although it lies south of both Beaver and Garden, it is about the same distance from Michigan's Upper Peninsula, because Scott Point along the U. P.'s shore projects south into Lake Michigan due north of High Island. The island is entirely owned by the State of Michigan, and like Garden Island, is part of the Beaver Island State Wildlife Research Area.

The only habitable buildings on the island today are two cottages that were built in comparatively recent times as summer homes. Today, they are maintained by the Michigan Department of Natural Resources, and are occasionally used by work parties and survey crews of that department, various university research groups and for emergency shelter. Several years ago, the D.N.R. planted grouse on the island, hoping that the birds would thrive, and it would become a prime location for grouse hunting in season. An in-depth study of the grouse population was carried on for a few summers by a graduate student who lived on the island during the warmer months. The population of these birds varied wildly from year to year, for reasons which were not quite clear. Today the island count of this game bird is small, and hunters have not been attracted in any numbers. Since there are no deer or small game animals in appreciable number, there has been little interest in making the trip from Beaver to hunt. The one very pretty island lake has no outlet, and its stagnant waters are void of fish. The island does have a large population of non-poisonous snakes. Not as many as Garden, but nonetheless they are there in appreciable numbers. Those souls who visit the island are usually attracted for three main reasons: its natural beauty, for many consider it to be the prettiest of the Beaver group, its isolation, or its birds.

Modern Voyageur canoers on north High Island Beach. Beaver Island in background

Island Restrictions

With two exceptions, the entire island is open for recreational camping, day hiking or backpacking. The two locations where restrictions apply have been wisely chosen to protect major nesting grounds of island birds. The first is the long slightly hooked sand spit that extends out from the northeast end of the island for about a half mile. It is a major rookery for thousands of water birds, which include two varieties of gulls and two breeds of terns. This area always is closed to hikers, but this is no real disappointment to visitors, for the entire spit can be viewed easily from high ground near its beginning. The other area lies across the island on its western shore, along Great Sand Bay. This beautiful stretch of curving sand beach is closed only during the nesting season of the endangered Piping Plover, lasting from May through early August (See Introduction to Hiking the High Island Trails).

Like the paths of Garden, the trails on the island are not maintained. Most of them are remnants of human occupation of the past. Many that were quite visible just a few years ago have all but disappeared. Others, because of the footfalls of present-day visitors, are quite easy to follow, and several others lie vaguely between the two extremes. Some of these paths, whose outlines are almost invisible during the spring and summer months, become quite discernible in the fall. The trail descriptions will give you a good idea of the conditions of the trails in the late 1980s.

It is easy to picture High Island as a satellite to the nearby and considerably larger Beaver Island, as is Garden Island, but it is more remote and harder to get to, lying exactly four miles due west of the bigger island. Like both North and South Manitou it faces a 60-mile stretch of open water between them and the Wisconsin shore, broken here only by the diminutive Gull Island. Because of this western exposure, High and the Manitous have prominent sand bluffs, running along most of their western shores. The greatest altitude on High Island is almost 250 feet above Lake Michigan, and since this high point is on open ground, it offers one of the most spectacular panoramic views found on any of the islands. From this high point which gives this island its name, open water can be seen in almost every direction. Its western shore differs from the Manitous because it has a wide sandy plain between the western beach and the high dunes, whereas the Manitou bluffs rise up almost immediately behind the shore. The bluffs of High Island act as buffers to Beaver Island, protecting much of the larger island's western shore from the prevailing west winds. From Mt. Pisgah, the highest point on Beaver, one gets a nice panoramic view of its smaller sister island to the west.

High Island style shower

Despite the short four miles of water that separate the two islands, High is in many ways the most remote of the four major islands of this book, and the least visited. Although one could launch a small boat from Beaver's western shore, the usual debarkation point is St. James harbor on the opposite side of Beaver. This makes a trip of over 11 miles of open water from one island to the other. Sometimes the four miles of water between the two islands is like a polished surface, and one could make the crossing in a john boat or small open canoe. But one might have to wait many weeks for the weather to produce that mirror-like illusion. I once tried to make that crossing in a 12-foot runabout on a relatively calm day. A half mile out from Beaver's windward shore, unexpected swells almost breached the gunwales of my small craft. I turned back, realizing that to continue westward would be the height of fear and folly. Unless you are an experienced Great Lakes sailor, with a boat that can handle heavy weather, you should hire one of the experienced commercial boat operators on Beaver Island to take you across. High Island harbor has an easy deep water access on its eastern side. Unless there are heavy eastern winds, it is a safe anchorage for boats properly secured. Winds from the southeast are particularly dangerous, and if they reach a high velocity they could easily drive a boat ashore. Since this is not the prevailing wind direction boats are usually safe enough, but skippers should keep a sharp weather eye when ashore. This harbor is often used by cruising sailors, who come in under sail during the morning or early afternoon, drop the hook and dinghy to the shore. After taking short exploratory hikes on the island, they return to eat their evening meal aboard, then bunk in for the night, and with the fresh breeze of early morning, sail into open water and disappear.

Romance of the Past

Like Garden, High Island was in the recent past a fragmentary outpost of an aboriginal people who preferred to live on the periphery of the white man's world, unable to surrender to it totally. The island never had any long-lasting secular hamlet of any size. Religious enthusiasm did bring loyal believers here to form a town-sized colony that flourished for a brief period.

Because of its remoteness, the island can conjure up thoughts of romantic isolation. Although hardly tropical in its environment, the island nonetheless can produce a most Robinson Crusoe-like feeling in any solitary hiker. High Island offered me an experience unique in my life. On my first four-day visit to the island I was its sole inhabitant for two of those days. Walking the shores and backcountry paths, I was aware of the romance of its historical past. As I wandered through the ruins of the once active colony of an odd sect of gentle believers who called themselves Israelites, I could almost feel their ghostly presence seeking salvation and a life-span of a thousand years. I also found a few remains of Indian cabins, whose occupants once shared the island in peace with the Israelites. Then too, with the island being reclaimed by nature, the hand of man is being visibly erased from great sections of its surface, leaving one's mind more in harmony with this recovering wilderness.

Personal Feelings

One day, when I was the island's sole occupant, I was thoroughly enjoying a long hike along Great Sand Bay. On the distant western horizon my eyes caught a column of black smoke revealing the presence of a distant ship. With all except the top of its smoke stack and superstructure hidden from view by the curvature of the earth, the mostly-hidden ship was the only visible reminder of the industrial society to which I belong. The symbol was far away and I felt happily detached from that world. The feeling of being the sole occupant of a beautiful beach stretching for almost seven miles, backed by mountainous tree-covered dunes, was overwhelmingly stimulating. As I walked along that beach, enjoying the sunshine on that warm August day, this detachment from everything man-made produced a feeling of pure serenity deep within me. I was well aware it was only a brief moment of euphoria. Though the distant smoke was the only visible reminder of civilization, I was quite aware that I belonged to that world. The momentary ecstasy would fade to depression and loneliness if I stayed on the island for an expended period of time, especially when weather became grim. If the exhilaration could not be maintained and extend for long periods, at least for that moment the isolation was glorious. With not a single human to tread upon my oneness with the natural world, I seemed not a stranger to it, but absorbed and embedded into its grain, rhythm and structure.

I wondered then how long one would have to stay isolated on an island, void of

Looking across Great Sand Bay from its southern end

timepiece or radio, before the natural cycle of the sun would comfortably replace the measured beat of civilization. How long would it be before one adapted to the rhythm of the natural world, and felt comfortable without the rigid and regimented time signatures of hours and minutes? What would it be like not to talk to, or even see, another human being for a week. Colin Fletcher claims that isolation in a wilderness setting for that amount of time brings about a new identification with the world that can be obtained in no other way. But it will only work if the week is not interrupted by a single human intrusion. One could accomplish that here in the fall. I often wondered that if I tried it, would I last the week.

The reader may wonder why I have spent so much time discussing personal thoughts of sequestering myself in seclusion on a distant isle. I find it an antidote to the ceaseless and relentless human activity that lies not far away. In many cases, thousands of vacationers seeking summer recreation, are compressed in the peninsula known as Michigan's little finger. Here they encounter what they came to leave behind. In Charleviox and other neighboring cities, the summer momentum often produces traffic jams bordering on gridlock, with sidewalks, restaurants and shops crowded enough to remind one of the Christmas rush at home. Everything seems to be hurry, hurry. Those who take the 27-mile ferry ride to Beaver Island feel an immediate slowdown from the frenetic rush of summer commercialism. People to be sure, but in smaller doses, miles of little-used gravel roads, long stretches of nearly-deserted beach and not a single traffic light in the island's only town. Beaver Island lies halfway between a maximum and minimum of human activity. One step further west from Beaver, one finds the exact opposite of the mainland's frenetic pace. For on High Island one finds not a single stop sign, nor one solitary boutique selling souvenirs or imported sweaters. No autos, no roads, no offroad vehicles, and possibly no people. It is the ultimate contrast from the mainland just 23 miles away. Most vacationers, especially those who covet air conditioning and showers in an effort to carry the city with them wherever they travel, would be immensely unhappy to spend more than an hour or two on High island. But there are the others, for whom I write.

A bit of warning should be added to these dreams of splendid isolation. If you are in poor health, this would be a good island to avoid. I feel that If you are not well, you should not go to High Island, especially alone, unless that is where you wish to die.

Chapter XV

A Short History of High Island

Although there have been no recent archaeological investigations on either High or Garden Islands to determine possible habitation by Archaic Indian cultures, it can be assumed that by the time of the late Archaic or the Woodland period Indians probably landed on sporadic brief seasonal visits (See chapter entitled A Brief Early History of the Lake Michigan Archipelago). As the white man usurped more and more territory on Michigan's Lower Peninsula during the early decades of the nineteenth century, some Indians, looking for enclaves where they might survive with part of their heritage still intact, sought out the uninhabited islands of the Lake Michigan archipelago. Prominent among these were Beaver, Garden, High and South Fox. A treaty of 1836, between the Ottawas and the U. S., allowed the Indians living on the islands to stay there unmolested for a period of five years. The Indian negotiators had misread the government's terms for they thought that the islands were given to them in perpetuity instead of the short five year period.

Because of its size, excellent harbor and strategic location alongside the major north-south shipping lane, Beaver Island was soon dominated by white traders. Although some Indians remained there up until the establishment of the island's Mormon kingdom, many had transferred to either Garden or High Island. To protect these island Indians from further encroachment, the federal government worked out a new treaty In 1855. It stipulated that the lands of Garden and High Island could not be sold, and the Indians living there could not be forcibly removed from them. It did not give ownership of the land to the Indians, or guarantee that the islands would be held permanently for exclusive Indian use. Although these terms were later amended to allow white ownership of island land, the arrangement did allow these native islanders some breathing space. There was at least partial Indian occupation of the island for many years, lasting until 1940.

The stamina of these isolated Island Inhabitants is suggested by one story of almost unbelievable extreme human endurance. This feat was reported to have been carried out by and Indian named Dan Cornstalk, who called High Island his home. He was hired to carry the winter mail across the ice to the mainland from Beaver Island, a trip which involved not just a walk to the closest mainland point such as Cross Village, but walking all the way to Mackinaw City almost 40 miles away. This never would be an easy glide across miles of smooth ice, but meant climbing and skirting around high ridges of ice made by the buckling of the frozen surfaces from the tremendous pressure of the shifting ice crust. There were also detours around open water for, even in the coldest of winters, there are always unfrozen stretches. According to the story, when he arrived at Mackinaw city only half of his daylight hours were used up. He picked up the waiting island mail and return to Beaver the same day. Arriving at St. James before dark he would then walk across Beaver and as darkness descended, cross four more miles of open ice back to his home on High Island. The round trip from High Island to St. James alone is about 20 miles. That in itself is a hike that would test the endurance of a very healthy hiker. Walking a 100 miles mostly over the rough lake ice in a single day would require physical and mental powers that seem beyond human ability. It is reported that this remarkable achievement was carried out by Dan Cornstalk on several occasions. Roundtripping it across the frozen wastes to Mackinaw and back places it in the realm of the super human which possibly only Dan Cornstalk and the mythological gods of ancient Greece could accomplish.

Since Garden and High Islands are only nine miles apart and in sight of one another, the Indians maintained tribal and family ties between them well into the twentieth century. William Wachtner Jr, who was born on Garden Island in 1902 and left it in 1913, remembers witnessing smoke signals used by the Indians in transmitting news of weddings, funerals and other tribal matters between the two islands. He told this author that shortly after seeing the signals, canoes from one island would soon depart for the other, usually to attend a funeral.

Franciscan missionaries from Harbor Springs had proselytized among the Indians on both Garden and High Islands, so a high percentage had been baptized into the Catholic faith. The Indian population of High Island in the nineteenth century numbered close to a hundred. These numbers were high enough that the Franciscans built a church there in the 1890s, named The Assumption of Our Lady. A priest was sent over from the mainland two to three times a year. The church was active well into the twentieth century, but with the steady decline of the Indian population, it was finally sold in 1942 for $100. The statue of the Virgin, the church bell, pews, altar and other accoutrements were moved to the Catholic church on Beaver Island.

The Religious Communities

Few Caucasians tried living on High Island, but for one brief period in the twentieth century, it did have a sizeable year-round white population. This was not because a group of of secular whites settled on High Island, for it never had a successful colony of independent homesteaders as did Garden. There were, however, two distinct periods in High Island history of attempted white homesteading, both operated communally by iconoclastic religious splinter groups. The latter of the two would bring the largest number of white inhabitants that the island would ever know.

The first and least successful of these attempts was made in 1850, by followers of James Strang, who had proclaimed himself as the Mormon King of Beaver Island. Trying to turn High Island into a satellite of the mother island kingdom, Strang's followers did little to cement relations between themselves and the resident Indian population and were therefore ill-received by the mostly-Catholic Indians. Following the catastrophic demise of King James' Beaver Island kingdom the only white residents of High Island were seasonal itinerant white fishermen who made no real attempts at year-round homesteading.

In the early twentieth century, when the mainland had been mostly timbered out, lumber interests managed to gain control of much of the island. They established a logging camp, but went bankrupt before they had cut much of the island's timber. This set the scene for High Island's most unusual human experience. It had its beginnings with another man who, like James Strang, was a religious spellbinder. The two men both sported red beards, and were referred to as King. The second of these self-proclaimed divines was named Benjamin Purnell.

Unlike James Strang, King Ben had little education, and never proclaimed himself to be a secular king as Strang had, for his title as monarch came not from his followers, but from the press. Nonetheless he proclaimed himself as a divine messenger of the Almighty. Born in 1861 in the Appalachian hills of Kentucky, Ben Purnell, without much formal education, became a spellbinding itinerant fire and brimstone type of preacher. At a prayer

House of David lumberyard with village in background

Logs ready for shipment along shore of High Island Bay, circa 1920

Courtesy Don Cole

The Rising Sun landing members of the House of David at their High Island dock Courtesy Leelanau County Historical Society

High Island Bay today. It was along this shoreline that the Israelites Dock and stacked logs seen in the other pictures was located

meeting held in Detroit in 1895, he claimed to have had a vision, in which he was told that he had been chosen as the last of the seven messengers of God. The first of the messengers was a humble English household servant named Joanna Southcott, who had received her heavenly message in 1792. Purnell claimed, as the last of the seven messengers, to have been sent to earth to unravel life's mysteries, and to gather together the elect. They would become a select group, which would eventually number 144,000 of the faithful, to await the millennium. When this cataclysmic event happened, all except the elect would perish, leaving them the entire globe for a thousand years of life in an earthly paradise. Gathering together a devoted group of followers they settled in Benton Harbor, Michigan, to await the glorious day. They named this religious colony the Israelite House of David. Referring to themselves as Israelites, the organization became widely known as the House of David. Most of the followers were not Jews, but believed that they were still members of the ancient tribes of Israel, and that Benton Harbor had become the new Jerusalem.

Ben laid down laws that all believers were supposed to follow. The faithful could neither use tobacco nor drink alcoholic beverages. As vegetarians, they allowed no consumption of meat, including fish and chicken. Cutting of hair was also forbidden. The locks of longtime House of David members of both sexes often hung to their waists. Since shaving was also forbidden men endowed with heavy facial hair had substantial beards of prolonged lengths. Marriage was allowed, but King Ben had published an edict known as "The Virgin Law," which stated that marriages could not be consummated until the beginning of the millennium.

What set this fringe communal sect apart from many other non traditional religious groups of the early twentieth century was its financial success. Like many other similar

Village of the Israelites, circa 1920

Courtesy Don Cole

communal groups, members of the sect were required to give all their worldly possessions to it. Apparently, Ben had a real eye for business, and gathered around him capable managers to run the various enterprises in which his organization became involved.

Purnell's House of David was, in some essential ways, similar to the Shakers and Ben might have been influenced by the two Shaker colonies that once flourished in his home state of Kentucky. Both First Messenger Joanna Southcott and the founder of the Shaker movement, Ann Lee, were born in England of the humble servile class in the eighteenth century. Both religious organizations lived as communal groups, practiced celibacy and attracted a high percentage of highly skilled artisans and shrewd businessmen from diverse countries.

The practical business side of the House of David's activities included a canning factory, an extensive cold-storage plant, several fruit farms, hotels and a first-class professional baseball team which traveled widely throughout the country. They owned the public transportation system of Benton Harbor, and one of the outstanding amusement complexes of the early twentieth century. Called Eden Springs Park, it was the Disneyworld of its day, attracting over 250,000 visitors a year.

When the island lumber company went bankrupt, their holdings became available for purchase. Purnell and his managers saw this as a golden opportunity for an outpost to supply raw materials to the home organization. Ben was aware that the island's forests still held extensive timber that could be used in the construction of new buildings at Benton Harbor, and for profitable sale on the commercial market. The island also offered plenty of land for vegetable gardens and orchards, which could supply the mother colony with many staples of their vegetarian diet. Its isolation would remove the Israelites further from the worldly temptations of the non believers. In 1912, Purnell bought the land, and the colony was established. With the industriousness of the Believers, extensive lumbering and gardening operations were soon to bear fruit.

After a short time, a large sawmill and a portable shingle mill were in operation. A blacksmith shop, an Ice house, bakery, underground storage cellars and various buildings to house the faithful were soon erected. One such building, constructed with eight sides, was incorrectly called "King Ben's Castle" by outsiders. Its real purpose was to house the unmarried female members of the group, and it was known to the followers as "The House of Virgins." It was guarded at night to keep the men out and the women in. Contemporary photographs show that, although they might have been substantially built, the structures were randomly constructed, with no formal plan or any distinguishing architectural style to set them off from any other type of shantytown. The Israelites were friendly, and got along well with both their Indian neighbors and the Irish on Beaver Island. There are a few oldtimers on Beaver Island today who remember the Israelites, and speak of them warmly, agreeing that they were desirable neighbors. During their most active periods the Israelite population on the island numbered between 120 and 150.

Raymon Nelson, who was brought to the island as a boy by his Israelite parents, and lived there for seven happy years, remembered there were over 100 Indians also living on the island during the 1920s. He thought that the island Indians were divided into about twelve main families. Raymon remembers that although the Indian population was outwardly friendly, they kept mainly to themselves. With a year-round island population well above 200, High Island had become large enough to warrant a public school. One began operation, and included Indian children as well as offspring of the Israelites who had been born before their parents joined the House of David. Some of the lady teachers were House of David members, others came from Beaver Island, and one was an Indian.

Unlike Garden Island there is no observable cemetery visible on High Island, for either the white or the Indian population. The Indians preferred to inter their departed in the large traditional tribal cemetery on Garden Island. House of David members looked upon the death of one of their numbers as an omen of weakening faith or a sign of lapsing into sinful ways, for the Israelites felt that God would keep the true believers healthy until the great millennium. It was rumored that members who passed from this life on the island were sneaked out and buried surreptitiously on other islands. One wonders what unknown graves may exist on nearby Whiskey and Gull Islands.

A large dock was built to accommodate boats big enough to handle the large amounts of logs that were shipped from the island. During the navigational months, movements of goods and people between the island and Benton Harbor was carried out by a steamship purchased by the Israelites, named the Rising Sun. When a vicious storm in 1918 drove her aground, and wrecked her off Sleeping Bear Point, the ship was replaced with a less pretentious sailboat, named the Rosabelle. This schooner plied the waters safely between the two ports until the fall of 1921. During October of that year, she had taken on a cargo of 600 bushels of potatoes and timber at High Island to be delivered to Benton Harbor. She never arrived at her home port, and was found several days later floating upside down in the open lake. None of the 28 people aboard survived, and their bodies were never found. Although the House of David community was still prosperous, apparently Purnell felt that the loss of two ships in three years was unnecessarily expensive and no large boat was ever bought to

The Rising Sun built in 1888
Courtesy Leelanau County Historical Society

The Rising Sun wrecked off Sleeping Bear Point
Courtesy S .B.D. National Lakeshore

replace them. It was less costly to ship goods across the four miles of open water to Beaver Islands to await further shipment. Goods were also easily moved during the freeze over, when sleds pulled by horses or moved by sail could move across the ice to Beaver Island. During the early years of the colony, the logging operations were extensive, but with time the island forests were depleted and the Israelites increased their farming acreage until there were close to 200 acres under cultivation.

A publication written some years ago claims that Purnell used the island as a sort of Siberia, a place to send troublemakers as punishment and isolation from the larger group at Benton Harbor. There is no solid historical evidence to support this allegation, and much to suggest that this idea was the product of the author's imagination and personal prejudice. Living survivors of the House of David who spent several years of their childhood on the island have stated that they never heard such an opinion expressed by their elders. Archie LaFreniere, who still lives on Beaver Island and knew many island Israelites personally over

The Roseabelle lost with all hands in 1921

several years, told this author that not only were the Israelites a friendly warmhearted group, but they never mentioned anything which would suggest that they lived on High Island as a sort of punishment.

There was, however, trouble brewing in Paradise. It did not come from the colony but from the mother polis. The serpent in this modern Eden took the shape of sexual mischief. Apparently, Ben wasn't waiting for the millennium for his moment of sexual fulfillment. As early as 1906, the first of several charges of sexually molesting his female followers were charged against him. In 1924, he disappeared for three years to avoid prosecution for sexual misconduct, but he was finally discovered hiding out in his Benton Harbor community. Brought to trial in 1927, he was accused of public immorality. Thirteen young women testified at that trial that he had persuaded them to have sexual intercourse with him. Under oath, they individually told the court that Ben had explained to them it was necessary to sexually submit to him as part of a purification ceremony he called "blood cleansing." The decision of the court was that Benjamin and his wife must leave the Benton Harbor community, and the House of David was to be disbanded. Ben was then to be tried for rape, but he died before the trial began.

Although the original decision was overturned by appeal two years later, the damage had been done. Ben's followers kept his dead body warm with hot water bottles for several days, waiting for him to miraculously ascend to heaven, but when his corpse began to decompose, they were forced to place their fallen saint in the earth. As death found Ben to be as human as the rest of us, many of his followers became disillusioned. Without the religious fervor that his magnetic personality created, the binding spirt of the movement was gone. A power struggle then ensued between King Ben's wife, Mary, and a local judge named

Ruins of what was probably an Indian home

Dewhirst to determine which would be the new leader of the Israelites. The judge, who was also a believer, took over most of the group's extensive holdings, including the property on High Island. The island community, which had very much favored Mary's leadership, soon fell apart, and gradually the colony disbanded. During the 1950s, their holdings were sold to a resident of Beaver Island who wished to use the island as a cattle ranch.

After the Israelites

By 1940, only six Indian fishermen families still inhabited the island. On Armistice Day of that year, a furious storm wrecked their boats and nets. Since the fishing grounds were no longer as bountiful as they once had been, it would have called for too large a financial investment to start anew. The Indians who left their homesteads and crossed over to Beaver Island became the last of High Island's year round inhabitants. In less than 15 years, High Island had seen its population high of close to 300 dwindle to none at all.

When one of the Indians, known as Little Joe, moved to Beaver he left four horses on the island. Each summer, he took salt blocks over to High, but did little else to maintain them. Having the entire island to roam in they soon became quite wild and thrived in their new freedom, even through the severe winters. Occasionally mainland visitors wanted to be taken to the island to observe the feral horses, and In 1950 one such couple who had decided to bivouac on the island got more than they bargained for. When they went looking for the horses the equines found their camp. Returning to basecamp, the island explorers found the steeds had discovered a rain coat that suited their palates and had eaten most of it. The camp marauders then topped off their feast with a box of brillo pads, and managed to break most of the eggs the campers had brought along. Before the arrival of these visitors, it had been reported that one of the horses had not been sighted for some time. The campers found that the unfortunate horse had fallen into an old cellar and, unable to free himself, had starved to death. The remaining three horses lived free and without mishap on the island for a total of 13 years.

Horse leaving Beaver Island Ferry before swiming ashore in High Island Bay

Courtesy Archie La Freniere

The stories about the High Island feral horses gave a horse trader named Jess Underwood an idea. It seemed to him an ideal place to raise wild horses that could be used for rodeos. With that in mind, he hired the Beaver Island Ferry to deliver a group of horses to High Island. They were pushed off the ferry into the offshore waters of the island and forced to swim ashore. The whole operation had a carnival air about it, for the upper deck of the ferry was loaded with onlookers, who had taken the ride to watch the horses swim ashore. This action soon brought a wave of adverse publicity, especially from animal welfare groups, who felt that leaving the horses unattended on the island during the severe winters was inhumanly cruel, and would cause the horses much suffering. Although no one from the House of David had lived there for many years, they still owned a large part of the island. Disliking the wave of bad publicity, the Israelites made Mr. Underwood herd the horses back across the ice to Beaver Island that winter.

Warren Thompson, who then lived on Beaver Island, reasoned that even if people were sentimental about the horses' winter survival they most probably would not get that upset about a bovine population spending the winters on High Island. The island contained plenty of natural forage for grazing, so cattle would be almost self-sufficient. There were no predators on the island that would threaten cattle, no fences were needed, rustling was a remote possibility, and the island was easily accessible by small plane. With this in mind Mr. Townsend bought the House of David land from the financially troubled Israelites and placed a herd of cattle there. He maintained a small airstrip built across one of the former fields of the Israelites, which was just a short flight from the Beaver Island airports. After several years, when the state was planning to turn the uninhabited islands of the Beaver Group to a wildlife research area, he sold his holdings on High Island to the state.

One of the first ideas the State Division Of Natural Resources had for the island was to develop and promote it as a good area for hunters of small game birds especially grouse. Many birds were brought over, and a graduate student named Douglas Whitcomb spent three summers on the island researching the activities of the grouse for the D.N.R. The population of this game bird fluctuated widely, and never reached proportions large enough to interest many hunters.

If the grouse experiment was not entirely successful, another part of the island's bird population has attracted much interest and scholarly attention in the last few years. High Island is thought to have as many as 10,000 sea birds nesting during the summer. The greatest concentration is in a rookery found on a sand spit on the northeast corner of the island. This sand spit, which juts out about a half mile and curves slightly, like a giant fishhook, has up to 2,000 nests. Both Herring and Ring-Billed Gulls, as well as the Common and Caspean Tern, share the spit, but do so in a well-established pecking order. The powerful and larger gulls use the more desired seaward part of the spit, while the terns must use the part more open to predators, closer to its root on the main island. The Herring Gulls are the first of the spit's residents to arrive in the spring, often beginning their nestbuilding on ground still covered with snow. This natural aviary has attracted the attention of researchers from the Department of Fisheries and Wildlife of the University of Minnesota, and these trained professionals have conducted onsight observations over the summer months on the island for many years. The researchers have found that snakes and fox are the birds' greatest natural enemies. They have also found that the endangered Piping Plover is again nesting on the western shore of the island's Great Sand Bay. Two breeding pairs successfully raised chicks there in 1987. Other birdlovers have also built nesting boxes for Bluebirds on several locations throughout the island, in hopes of increasing their numbers.

Today's visitors will find that, except for the two cottages maintained by the D.N.R., the hand of man is rapidly disappearing from the island. All that remains of the once-thriving colony of Israelites are a few standing walls and others now on the ground rotting back into the earth. Some sturdy log walls of Indian cabins are still in place, but without their roofs they too are slowly deteriorating. New forests of the once nearly denuded island are rapidly growing up, squeezing out old roads, invading and reclaiming the large vegetable fields of the Believers. The only visible clue that the island once had a landing strip is a high telephone-type pole, still with the metal ring of a windsock attached to it, standing on the edge of the former landing field. New trees that have taken root on the former runway, have become natural guardians to make sure that conventional fixed-wing aircraft will never land there again. Each year, the island recovers more and more from the brief invasion of civilization. As it slowly returns to a refreshing outpost of wilderness, the long, deep watery moat known as Lake Michigan acts as guardian shield and protects it from the increasing and restless populations of the mainland.

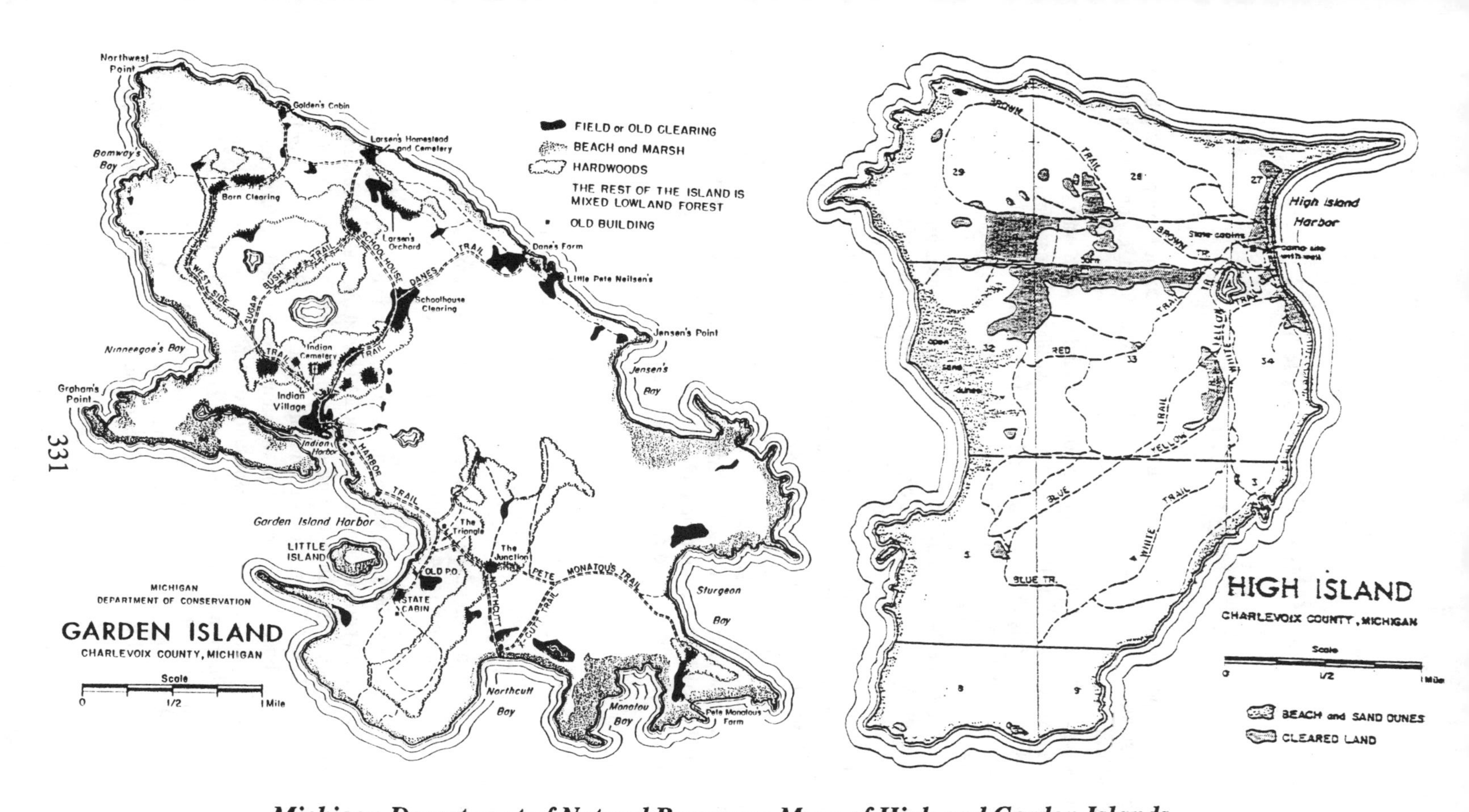

Michigan Department of Natural Resources Maps of High and Garden Islands
Many of the trails on these older maps are difficult or impossible to follow today.

Chapter XVI

HIGH ISLAND TRAILS

INTRODUCTION

One major consideration that should be taken into account when planning hiking trips on the smallest of this four-island book, is whether Great Sand Bay on the west side of the island is open or closed. This will often seriously affect the plans of hikers who wish to pursue longer and more detailed exploration of the island on beach walks and loop hikes. Since the west side's Great Sand Bay is such a lovely area, hiking and camping there has many scenic rewards. But at this writing the bay and its adjacent table land is closed from May 1 to August 15, to protect an established nesting area for the endangered Piping Plover. There were two nesting pairs in 1987.

Except for the long sand spit at the northeast corner of the island the shore lines on the north end, the entire east shore and the southwest shore, and most of the island's interior are always open for hikers. Because of the island's diminutive size, even long loop hikes can be accomplished in a single day. Hikers can establish a base camp on the east side, possibly on one of the open areas on the ledge near the old House of David village, and dayhike from there. By far the most popular walk on the island is the Top O'the World Trail, hereafter called the T.O.T.W. Trail. This hike can be turned into a partial loop hike by using the Alternative Woodland Trail either going or returning. Another walk that begins along the T.O.T.W. Trail is the loop trail around Lake Maria. If Great Sand Bay is not closed to hikers, longer loop hikes to be considered are around either the north or south end of the island, using the T.O.W.T. Trail as the outward or return leg of that loop.

TOP O' THE WORLD (T.O.T.W.) TRAIL

Distance: to top of dune: 1.5 miles; to west shore on Great sand bay 2 miles.
Walking time: to dune top 35 to 45 minutes; to west shore 50 minutes to one hour.

GENERAL REMARKS. This trail's unusual name comes from the magnificent panorama one gets from its highest point on a dune top, some 240 feet above Lake Michigan's shores. On reaching the highest elevation in the Beaver Group, the hiker is rewarded with an almost 360 degree view of Lake Michigan and surrounding islands. Mt. Pisgah on Beaver Island is almost as high, but much of the view from the summit is blocked by surrounding trees, allowing a good view only to the west. The sensation of standing on the highest land elevation within eye range, with so much water in view in almost every direction, gives one the feeling that one indeed stands on the top of the world. If you gain this easily-reached summit on a clear day, you will be able to see more islands than from any other high point in the entire Lake Michigan Archipelago. Even the distant Upper Peninsula is just barely visible on the northern

Eastern section of T.O.T.W. Trail. Although not maintained, trail is easy to follow

horizon, poking its head up above the curvature of the earth. The brief but very steep climb up through loose sand to the dune's summit is the only difficult part of this trail. There is also one very mucky section alongside the site of an old beaver dam, but this area can be avoided by using the Woodland Alternative Trail. Since the T.O.T.W. Trail is mostly in semi open fields, the Woodland Alternative Trail makes a nice contrast that can be used in either direction as one leg of a loop hike. **For the T.O.T.W. Trail East see page 341**

Top o'the World (T.O.T.W) Trail West from High Island Bay to Great Sand Bay

TRAIL DESCRIPTION. The trailhead for this most popular hike is found in a harbor-like area on the north east corner of the island known as High Island Bay. Because of the large sand spit to the north, the harbor is not only protected from the prevailing westerlies, but from northern breezes as well. Beaver Island, some four miles to the east, gives some protection in that direction but the bay is open to the rare southeast wind. Most people will land on the shore of this lovely bay which happens to be the best and closest place to disembark from Beaver Island, and the best anchorage. The trail is the only really well-developed path that leads directly away from the bay. It is found a little bit south of the bay's mid point. Ornithologists residing in one of the island's state's cabins during the early summer often erect poles right at the trailhead, to protect their inflatable boat. Since these poles are visible much of the year, the trail is usually quite easy to find.

Heading due west, the trail is a track of loose sand, through the surrounding light groundcover. In about three minutes walking, the trail curves slightly to the right and the two

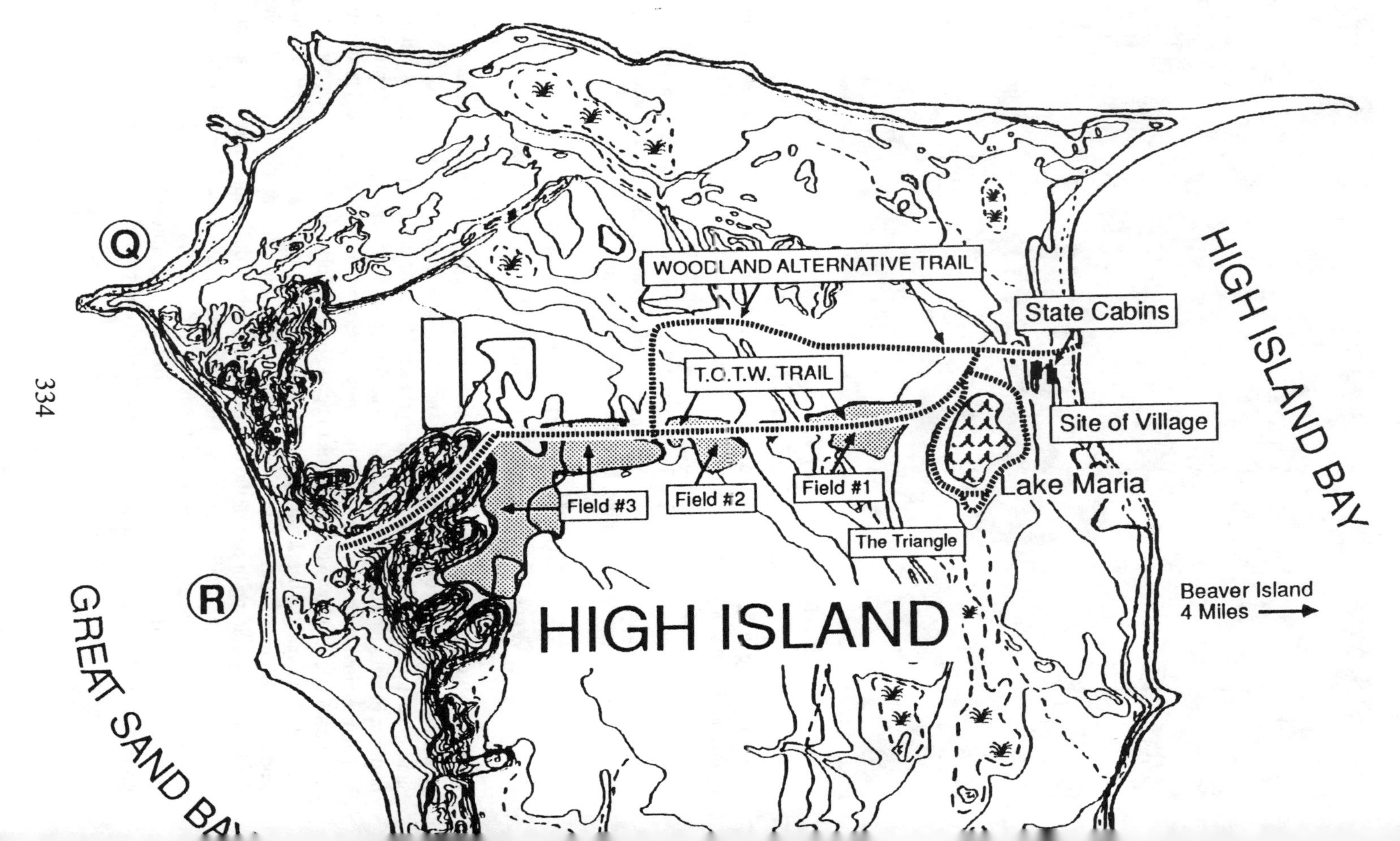
HIGH ISLAND BAY
WOODLAND ALTERNATIVE TRAIL
State Cabins
T.C.T.W. TRAIL
Site of Village
Lake Maria
Field #1
Field #2
Field #3
The Triangle
Q
R
HIGH ISLAND
Beaver Island
4 Miles
GREAT SAND BA

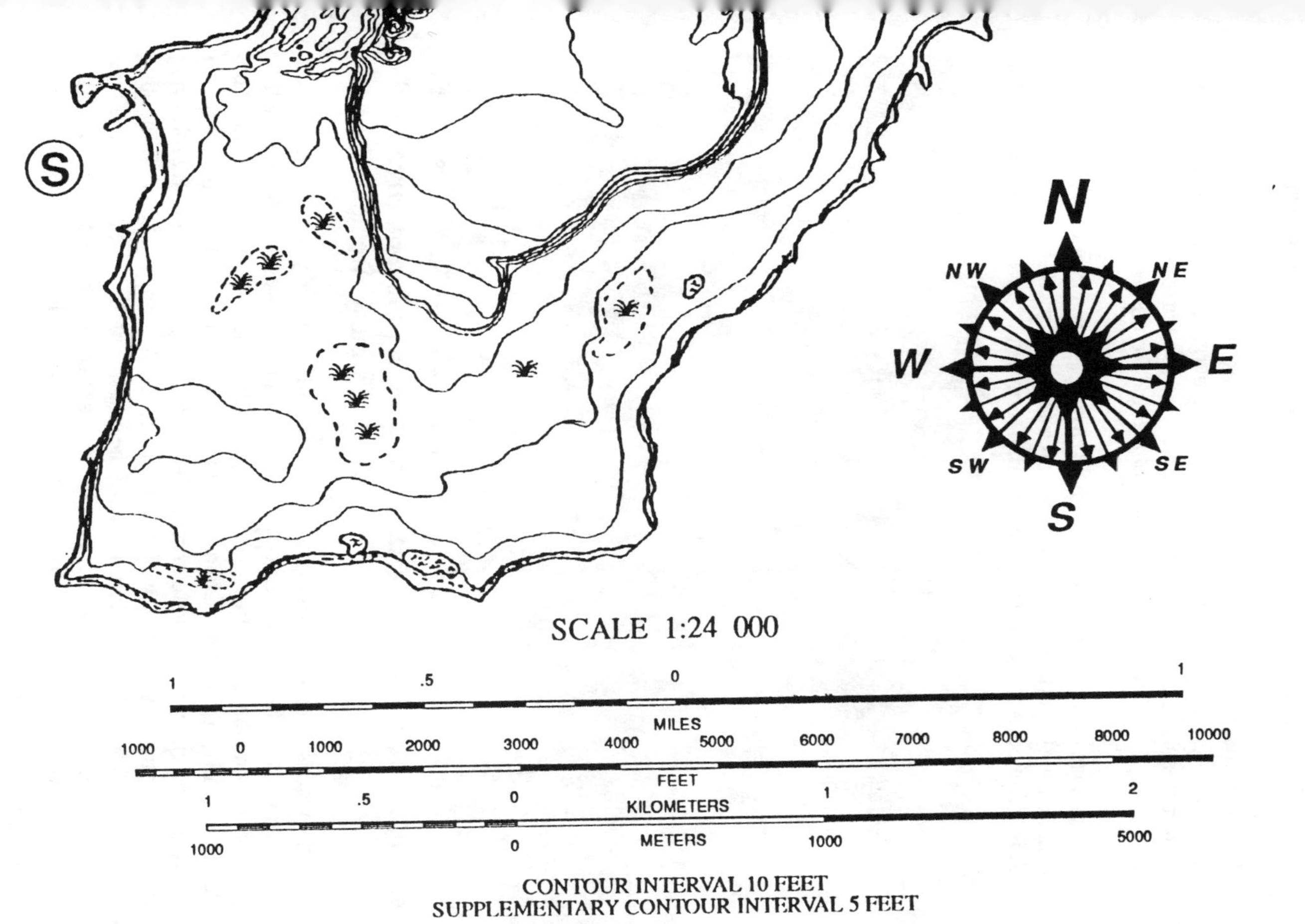

CONTOUR INTERVAL 10 FEET
SUPPLEMENTARY CONTOUR INTERVAL 5 FEET

HIGH ISLAND

white state cabins come into view. The trail curves to the right, crossing in front of the right cabin named Alpha. During the summer months this cabin is often occupied by university groups doing research, especially bird studies, or by members of the Department of Natural Resources (see picture on pg. 314). Both cabins have signs on them that read:

> Although maintained for the use of D.N.R. personnel and authorized university groups this building may be used for emergency shelter. Please be responsible. Leave it as clean or cleaner than you found it.
>
> Michigan Department of Natural Resources.

The cabin to the left, named Omega, is still structurally sound but in 1988 we found the interior had strong odors from some sort of research activity carried on within its confines.

A few feet beyond the Alpha cabin, the trail turns left in a westerly direction, and

House of David farmers harvesting crops on High Island, circa 1920

Courtesy Archie La Freniere

heads into the woods. About 25 feet into the trees, the trail has an easy rise which lasts less than 50 feet, and is the only elevation rise on this entire trail until the west side dune is reached. About 30 feet beyond the rise, there is a pronounced fork in the trail. The right fork is the Woodland Alternative Trail which rejoins the T.O.T.W. Trail in 1.2 miles, and can be used as an alternative on either the outward or return leg of the hike (See pg. 344). By following the left fork, in less that two minutes walking time the T.O.T.W. Trail junctions with another trail that comes in from behind on the left. This is the east side of the Lake Maria Loop Trail (See pg. 346). In less than two more minutes, you will see another trail coming in from the left and an open field in front of you. The left trail is the west side of the Lake Maria loop and the opening in front of you is Field #I.

The trail enters the northeast corner of Field #I, and parallels its northern side. Once the site of intense cultivation by the House of David community, the field was actively farmed until 1927. This field is far less grown over than others used by that organization, because it was cleared anew in the 1950s, when it was used as an airplane landing strip by the new owner of the island, who was using it for cattle raising. When you are about halfway across the field you can look left and see a tall wooden post, which still has the metal ring of the windsock in place. When you leave the northwest end of Field #I, after passing through some scrubby trees, you will be walking along a corridor about 20 feet wide bordered by trees, on what was once an old road linking Fields #I and #2.

When the trail meanders right as it enters a copse of small aspen you will cross a drainage area that runs from the northwest to the southeast. Although there is no running stream, it still makes for a bit of sloshy walking during normal to wet summers. Beavers used this natural drainage and built a long low dam across it. This created a shallow lake in which they built a lodge. The pond and lodge were active in 1987, but during the drought year of 1988 the pond dried up and the beaver left for wetter climes. The trail takes you up to a point where the beaver dam is easily visible. The beaver may return in wetter years and continue to maintain the dam. If they do, you will get a good view of both the lodge and the pond by walking to the dam. The trail however, continues not at the dam, but goes off to the left about 15 to 20 feet back from the beaver construction. Wandering through the small aspens, the trail soon comes to a narrow trough, which is often full of water. If it is not dry and you wish to keep your feet from getting soaked, the beaver have accommodated you, for dead ahead you can see the continuation of the beaver dam. Climb up on the dam and turn left. In about ten feet along this very narrow walk you will come to a place just beyond the trough where you can jump down from the dam and proceed.

Just beyond this drainage area, the trail enters Field #2. Since it has not been maintained since 1927, it is far more grown up than the previous field, and it will not be many more years before it will not look like an open area. More and larger clumps of tree growth are making the area a patchwork of quasi-forests and field. There is a collapsed old House of David barn near the northwest side of the open field, but it now lies buried in the encroaching northern tree line. Since the walls and roof are down, this huge pile of decaying lumber is difficult to find and seldom visible from the trail.

Near the west end of Field #2, you will encounter a fence line that briefly parallels the trail to the right. The first post has a Blue Bird box nailed to it. A few feet further you will approach a small open area to the right. On the left, there is a narrow round wooden fence post, which has several wooden braces supporting it. If you look right here, you can see a fence line alongside a narrow copse of small trees. The wire part of the fence has been pushed down, making the fence line easily crossed. This is the junction with the west end of the **Woodland Alternative Trail,** which you may wish to follow on your return. Keep proceeding west from here, and in less than a half minute you will cross another fence line, where the old fence wire is also low enough that it is easily stepped over. You are now less than a half minute from the northeast corner of Field #3. It is far larger than any field on the island, but as you enter it you will see that like Field #2, it is rapidly being reclaimed by trees. Paralleling the north side of the field, the trail takes you through an old orchard. Despite the age of the trees, they are still producing apples which, if not a gourmet's delight, are quite edible.

After a three to four minutes walk through the old orchard, look for two upright iron wheels, which are part of an old piece of farm machinery, on the right side of the trail. On

Beaver pond along T.O.T.W. Trail in 1987

Lodge in same beaver pond as above, 1988

my second trip to the island, one of my hiking companions had been raised on a farm in Kentucky, recognized it immediately as an old McCormick mower. He had ridden one as a boy on his uncle's farm. About two minutes beyond the mower, the trail returns to the forest, but stays there less than a minute before returning to an open field. During that brief time in the woods, you will pass a sizable pile of field stones on the right. They were probably deposited over 70 years ago by the House of David farmers, after removing them from the nearby fields. The open space lying beyond this small patch of woods is much smaller than

Field #3, and I assumed this field was the one shown on the topo map lying north of the big field. But after examining the map, I realized that field was much larger than the one I was standing in. One of my companions suggested that this might be a part of Field #3, which had become isolated from the rest of the field by heavy tree growth to the south. To test this idea, we hiked north, to see if we could find that northern field, and find it we did, making an interesting discovery on the way. Not far into the woods, we happened upon the ruins of a log cabin which still had three of its walls standing.

Eating apples from old House of David Orchard near Field #3 alongside T.O.T.W . Trail

The T.O.T.W. Trail crosses this small isolated corner of Field #3, heading directly toward the tree line to the west. There is a Bluebird box on a tree close to where the trail returns to the forest. If you would like to see the old cabin, turn to the right when you are about 30 yards from the western tree line, and cross the remaining part of the field northward. Once you are in the forest You should see the cabin almost directly in front of you.

When you follow the T.O.T.W. Trail into the woods, you are almost to the most demanding part of this hike, for before you lies the dune line. The trail, which climbs the heavily forested leeward side of the dune, is very steep and in loose sand. You slide back almost as much as you gain upward with each step. Small trees and bushes that line the trail often are handy for pulling yourself up the slope, and this difficult uphill segment is usually behind you in a little over five minutes. When the trail turns left and breaks out of the trees, the worst is behind you and you are almost at the top.

If you reach the summit of this high dune on a clear day, you will easily see what inspired some imaginative hiker to give this trail its name. Some seven miles due west, almost

Looking west from high point on T.O.T.W. Trail

lost in the incredible blue of Lake Michigan, is Gull Island. Looking east across the open fields which you have just crossed, you can see the sand spit at the north east end of High Island Bay, pointing to the west shore of Beaver Island. The western end of Garden Island is visible just northwest of Beaver. On Beaver Island, the easily-seen large blowout leads to the top of Mt. Pisgah, that island's highest elevation. The southern view is partly blocked by trees but parts of North and South Fox Islands can be seen, and appear from this location as though they are melded into a single land mass. A few years ago a bird researcher who spent most of the summer on the island climbed to the trail's summit on the evening of the Fourth of July. Blessed with a crystal clear, smog free night when the sky was brilliantly illuminated by hundreds of constellations and the Milky Way, rocket displays from nearby Beaver Island and several more distant mainland sites gave her an unforgettable visual experience, combining both man-made and celestial fireworks.

Standing 240 feet above Lake Michigan, you can look down at a small part of the beach of Great Sand Bay. When the area is open to hikers, and you don't mind the climb back up, and have the time to do so before dark, a walk along the shores of this two-mile sandy enclave is well worth the time. The rugged tableland between the perched dunes and the shore is a nesting ground for the Piping Plover. Since there are less than 20 known nesting pairs in the entire Great Lakes region, the bird is on the endangered species list, and this westside bay is closed between May 1 and August 15. If you have come during the unrestricted time, you can walk to the shore from this high point in 15 minutes or less.

You begin the descent to the beach down a moderately steep grade through the open sand of a small blow-out, before hitting a tree line. The grade of the trail moderates somewhat as you enter the grove of conifers. About a minute later, you return to open sand, and the trail again steepens until it reaches a second tree line. When entering the trees, you will see a short moderately-steep uphill section, before it breaks out again into the open dunes. As you drop

Dunes alongside Great Sand Bay with Gull Island on the horizon. One hiker is standing near dead sentinental tree.

down, you will notice a ridge rising above and paralleling the trail on the right. Eventually you reach the edge of a declining section of that ridge, which at that point is a narrow spine. From there, you can drop down over its opposite side across another open sand depression, and cover the uneven table land to the shore. But before you drop off the ridge, notice two things. Look back uphill from where you came and memorize the scene. This will aid you in finding the trail on your return. Also notice that at the foot of that sand depression there stands a trunk of a long dead, and branchless tree, looking like a lone sentinel. This weathered trunk can also help you in locating the trail if you intend using it as a return route to High Island Bay.

Once on the shores of Great Sand Bay, you are on one of the loveliest stretches of unspoiled sand beach in the entire state of Michigan, and usually you share it only with your immediate companions. (If you intend to follow the shore doing a southern loop walk see page 354.)

TOP O' THE WORLD (T.O.T.W.) TRAIL
East from Great Sand Bay to High Island Bay

GENERAL REMARKS. If you are using this trail as a return from Great Sand Bay after a north or south shore walk, remember that the area from the bay to the top of the dune may only be crossed during the non restricted months. If you have not hiked this trail previously in the other direction, you might want to scan the description of the trail's westerly direction (Pg. 333) for I have

Looking east toward Beaver Island from high point on T.O.T.W. Trail

left out some details in this eastbound description to cut down on redundancy.

TRAIL DESCRIPTION. If you have entered Great Sand Bay by walking around the north end of the island, your first unrestricted view of the bay will occur at **Point Q.** From there, it should take you about 20 minutes to reach a lesser, somewhat rocky but minor protrusion at **Point R.** When approaching it, look east above the tableland for a spinelike ridge that is clear of trees. When you turn east and cross the tableland and approach a small open area of sand directly below the ridge, look for an upright limbless dead tree about 15 foot high, that stands like a lonely sentinel at the edge of the open sand. Climb the open sand up to the western edge of the spiny ridge just beyond the dead tree, and drop over its edge. There the trail becomes visible, and parallels the narrow ridge below it in a westward direction up the dune. The trail enters a narrow band of trees, but soon breaks out into the open again. Then it crosses a second tree line. Once through this second band of trees, you can see the top of the trail, and the steepest part of the climb begins. Most hikers find this 240-foot elevation gain from the bay takes 15 to 20 minutes. If you are favored with a clear day, your effort will be rewarded with a grand view.

When you begin descending the eastern side of the dune, you soon enter the forest. As you cross into the trees, you will have very steep going in loose sand. Take it slowly, and be careful not to get a foot tangled in tree roots on the way down. The descent is over in less than five minutes, and you have the last serious elevation change on this trail behind you. A short walk on level ground soon takes you out of the trees, and into the northwest corner of Field #3. Because of heavy tree growth on your right, this section of the field has been cut off from its larger southern part. After crossing this isolated section, the trail returns you briefly into the woods and curves slightly to the right. As you walk through this small copse, you will

Old McCormic mower near Field #3 once used by the House of David Colony

pass a large pile of field stones on your left, before returning to the north east part of Field #3.

As you cross the northern section of the field, the trail will take you through an old apple orchard. You may be able to locate an old McCormick mower half-hidden in the high grass to the left. Not long after you leave the field, you will cross an old fence line, with part of the wire still attached to the lower parts of the fence. Almost immediately you come into a small open area that has a thin wooden fence post on the right, diagonally supported by a few extending wooden braces. At this point, you can see another trail coming in from the left. The T.O.T.W. Trail goes straight ahead here, but the left path is the beginning of the Woodland Alternative Trail. You can see from this point that the Woodland Alternative Trail goes through a break in a tree line and crosses another fence about 30 feet away. Either path will take you back to High Island Bay. (for the Woodland Alternative Trail see Pg. 345).

If you opt to stay on the T.O.T.W. Trail, another two minutes will bring you into Field #2. It has grown up so much that it is hard to tell that about 60 years ago it was an active agricultural area.

As you leave the field, you enter a swampy area that has a once active beaver pond to the left. You will come to a shallow trough of water where you turn left and walk a few feet before turning right and crossing it. If the season has been wet, you can avoid splashing through this trough by continuing a short distance more to the beaver dam. Climb up the narrow dam, turn right and edge along its narrow top for a few feet before dropping down again on the other side of the trough. Once past the beaver dam you will walk through an area that is part scrub and small trees for about five minutes, before entering Field #1. This field

Child from House of David Colony with island grown vegetables, circa 1920

Courtesy Beaver Island Historical Society

is far more open than the others, for it was cleared a few years ago when it was used as a landing strip for a cattle ranching operation. As you walk along the northern border of the field, look to the right, and you will be able to see a high wooden post about the size of a telephone pole which still has one ring of a former wind sock attached. As you return to the woods at the east end of the field, you will come to a fork in the trail. The right fork is the western end of the Lake Maria Loop Trail. Continuing on the left fork you will come to a second fork in the trail. The right fork is the east end of the Lake Maria Trail, and if you have not seen this small lake, you need only to follow the right fork side trail for less than five minutes before you come to another small trail to the right, that takes you down to its shore.

From this junction on the T.O.T.W. Trail, you have only about three minutes of walking before the left fork descends about 30 feet and breaks out of the trees, close to the D.N.R. cabins. Just before going down that easy grade, you may notice another trail coming in from the left. This is the other end of the Woodland Alternative Trail. The trail turns right, passing in front of the Alpha Cabin, before turning left towards the bay. Past a small copse of trees, another couple of minutes walk puts you on the shore of High Island Bay.

WOODLAND ALTERNATIVE TRAIL

Distance: 1.2 mi.
Walking Time: 30 to 35 minutes.

GENERAL REMARKS. Originally, this trail was used by the House of David community as a road to a large field they kept under cultivation, and to give access to the timber on the northern part of the island. It makes a pleasant alternative path for about two thirds of the distance to or from the Top O' the World Dune. You can use it to convert the T.O.T.W. into

Isrsaelites harvesting timber during winter months

a partial loop hike on either the outward or return leg. Although it will add about 10 minutes walking time to your hike, it is entirely in the forest, offering more protection from the sun and a cooler walk than the more open T.O.T.W. Trail. It also avoids the swampy area around the beaver pond, which can save you some sloshing around during soggy summers or after periods of extended and excessive rainfall.

TRAIL DESCRIPTION east to west. (For west to east see below.) To find the trailhead see the westerly direction of the T.O.T.W. Trail. You will find this trail branches off to the left just a couple minutes away from the Alpha Cabin. Once you have taken the right fork away from the T.O.T.W. Trail you will find this delightful woodland path goes almost in a straight line. After about 15 minutes of walking, the trail forks. Follow the left fork. This split in the trail is not always obvious, so if you come to a point where you can see a field through the trees paralleling the trail on your left, you have missed the correct fork in the trail. You may also notice there is an old rail fence running between the field and the trail. Retreat until you locate the correct fork. Once you are on this left fork, you will find the trail curving left and within a minute, you can look right and see the field through the trees. Again, the trail goes in a straight line, paralleling the whole south end of the field, which stays visible through the trees. This straight segment will take another five minutes of walking before the trail makes a decided left curve and begins heading south. In just a few feet you will see a line of old fence posts on your right. With the posts paralleling you in a straight-line walk, you have about a 10 minute walk before breaking out into a small open area. At the south end of this open space, the trail crosses an old fence line, which still has wire that has been pushed down for an easy crossing. A few feet beyond this fence line, the trail Ts into the T.O.T.W. Trail (For continuing westward on the T.O.T.W Trail see pg. 337).

WOODLAND ALTERNATIVE TRAIL
From West to East

TRAIL DESCRIPTION. As this trail leaves the junction with the T.O.T.W. Trail between Field #I and Field #2, it heads due north, and in a few feet, crosses an old fence line, then takes you through a small open area. In less than a minute, the trail returns to the forest, and you have a straight line walk paralleling some old fence posts on the left. In a little over a quarter of a mile, where you can see a heavy fence post on the left that may once have been the location of a gate, the trail jogs slightly to the right. About a minute beyond, the trail turns right and begins another straight line walk to the east, paralleling the southern end of a field that is visible through the trees on the left. In about five minutes the trail begins to curve right to the southeast. Another trail comes in from behind in this vicinity, and junctions from the left, but it is not easily seen. This is the last and the longest lap on this trail, and it will be 15 minutes or more before you rejoin the T.O.T.W. Trail. There is one fork about halfway along this section, with the more prominent left fork being the correct choice. When you hit the T.O.T.W. Trail, a left turn will bring you to the Alpha Cabin in a little over a minute.

LAKE MARIA LOOP TRAIL

Distance: 1 mi.
Walking Time: 25 to 30 minutes.

GENERAL REMARKS. Lake Maria is a good example of the type of small lake often found on this island chain. These lakes are unusual, because they have no stream or any type of surface water flowing out of them. Geologists theorize that this type of lake was formed when the retreating glacier left behind huge ice balls, which eventually melted and created such lakes. All four of this book's islands have examples of this type of lake, and if you have a desire to see one, Lake Maria is a good choice, because it is easy to get to and perhaps the prettiest (see photo on pg. 40). If you don't have time to do the entire loop, but would like to see the lake, the best lakeside viewing point is less than a five minute walk from the T.O.T.W. Trail.

If you are camped near the old village or near the Alpha Cabin, the close proximity of these areas to the lake makes it available for a relaxing bath. The waters of Lake Michigan are usually on the cool side, and the bottom along the shoreline of High Island Bay is rocky. The shallow areas of Lake Maria reach pleasantly warm temperatures on sunny days, and the easiest accessible shoreline has a nice sand beach. There is one major drawback to what seem to be an idyllic location for a wilderness bath. Once in the water, you find the lake bottom is covered with a mustard-colored soup-like silt, which will not support you. You have to swim out to deeper water to have a good bath, and you must keep swimming, for the bottom simply will not hold you up. I once let my body sink into this goo to see how far down I would go before reaching a solid bottom. When I had sunk almost to my waist and was still going down, I aborted the experiment.

TRAIL DESCRIPTION. Follow the T.O.T.W. Trail west to the junction with this trail. After making the left turn from the T.O.T.W. Trail, in about a minute and a half you will come to another prominent fork. You can see that the right fork takes you down to the shoreline, which is now visible, and is the easiest and best place to get an overall view of Lake Maria. If you wish to continue around the lake, you take the left fork which heads in the general direction of the old village and out of sight of the lake. In less than three minutes, the trail swings right and parallels the back side of the former village which is to the left. As it makes this swing, you may see a trail on the left which connects this loop walk with the village trail. None of the village ruins are seen from this trail. A little further on there is another visible trail that diagonally crosses the loop trail, but to continue the loop walk do not turn.

The trail then curves right in a southwesterly direction. About 15 minutes from the trailhead you reach another fork. This a junction of old roads which forms a triangle.

The easily identified left fork, which goes roughly straight ahead, will soon junction with the south east point of the triangle and continue for about another five minutes before petering out. Follow the less visible right fork at this triangle junction, and In less than a minute the right fork Ts into another trail. This is the south west point of the triangle. By turning right at this junction, the lake will soon be seen through the trees below you on the right. As you curve around the south end of the lake, you will see a couple of smaller trails that cross this one heading directly to the lake shore. They are beaver slicks. Rounding the end of the lake and heading northward, the trail again takes you out of sight of the water. You will pass a couple of open areas on the right, which lead to a nice west shore lake view. But walking over to the view has one major drawback. Most of the field you have to cross to get there is a huge patch of poison ivy. Only a short walk beyond this point, the trail junctions with the T.O.T.W. Trail almost at the east end of Field #1. A right turn takes you back to the Alpha Cabin, and a left in the direction of the western dunes.

THE VILLAGE TRAIL

GENERAL REMARKS. Photographs taken over 60 years ago help one conjure up a picture of the old House of David Village where one expects a half demolished ghost town, similar to movie versions of the old west. Ghost town it is, but what is left of this religious colony is a far cry from the hamlet that once domiciled over 100 souls. Most of the buildings have disappeared completely, and of the few that remain, not a single one still supports a roof. But visitors whose imagination can fill in the emptiness between piles of broken, rotting boards and parts of iron bedsteads not slept in for over half a century, may feel empathy with the fervent, gentle but somewhat strange religious artisans. These simple island dwellers had little contact with the rest of the civilized world, and were often cut off completely from it for months each winter. They endured and survived here for over a decade, working to supply the mother church at Benton Harbor with food and lumber (See history section). Some hikers may experience a feeling of warmth toward the souls who once lived and worked in this once-thriving commune. These religious socialists were searching for a more serene existence than they had found in the secular world.

The overgrown condition of the trail leading to the village makes it obvious that few present-day island visitors visit this former village. Indeed, there is little to see. Most visitors are not romantics. They carry with them across the water their hurried mainland existence, with a general indifference and ignorance of history. They find no time or little reason to speculate about the ruins of this dead hamlet or the people that once inhabited it.

TRAIL DESCRIPTION. If you follow the T.O.T.W. Trail west from the shore of High Island Bay toward the state cabins, in about a half minute from the beach, you will notice a break in the trees on your left. This is the beginning of a long open section, lying south of the trail, perched on a ledge paralleling and overlooking High Island Bay. Since the village site also lies to the south, you can go that direction, but there is a better way. Continue on the T.O.T.W. Trail a couple more minutes until you come to the second break in the trees on the lefthand side. Turn left there, and head south across this smaller field, which unfortunately has some poison ivy. Before you reach the tree line, you should be able to pick up a faint trail

House of David Village, Circa 1920

Courtesy Archie La Freniere

Standing wall of structure in House of David Village in 1987. It is possibly part of the building on left in photo above

that was once part of a village road leading you into the trees. The trail here is quite overgrown, but despite its choked condition, you should be able to follow it. You may see another overgrown trail going off to the right. It leads to the island's interior and soon T's into the Lake Maria Loop Trail.

Don't turn, but continue south, and in less than a minute beyond this junction and

(Left) *Log house in village complex as it looked circa 1950s. It possibly last served as an Indian home*

(Below) Same log structure in 1988

about three minutes from the T.O.T.W. Trail you will see on the right a flattened small building, with its downed roof still covered with wooden shingles. As you continue south you will soon see the highest standing wall that still survives in the village. It is set back into the trees on the right. You see the interior wall of a moderately large building where lathing and inside plastering is still very much in evidence.

Continuing south, you will soon pass the uninteresting remains of another small building, with one wall still partly standing. It had a cellar and most of the remains have fallen into it. Another 50 feet beyond this ruin, the trail begins a straight, wide and easily-located path, following a long corridor through a small copse. When a field opens on the right, turn into it and after a few feet turn left again and you will soon come to the remains of a rather large log cabin with three of its walls still standing. Although used by the celibate religious community, this cabin was probably built by Indians before their arrival. Since Indians were on the island until 1940, the Native Americans might have lived in and maintained it long after the departure of the long bearded Israelites. At this point, you can look west and see still another smaller log structure. If you walk toward the lake through the open area from the larger cabin, you can see another ruin entangled in the trees. It is found on the righthand side just before you reach the ledge at the beach. There are still parts of old iron beds that can be seen in what were once the confines of the building.

More open areas, which probably were part of the village, are found south of this point, but nothing of much significance is left, and there is no easily-followed trail. If you do wander through this collection of small and often connecting open fields, you may find a mound in the shape of a horseshoe, surrounding the ruins of another building. Since the ground level inside the mound is slightly lower than the immediate area, it probably indicates that the building once had a large cellar, and has fallen into it. When I saw it, I wondered if it might be the site of the Roman Catholic chapel maintained for Indian use that was located south of the village.

SHORELINE PERIMETER WALK
including North and South Loop hikes

Distance: North Loop 6.6 mi.; South Loop 8.6 Mi.; Perimeter 11.2 mi.
Walking Time: North Loop 3 to 4 hours; South Loop 4 to 5 hours;
Perimeter 7 to 9 hours.

GENERAL REMARKS. High Island has wonderful shoreline hiking and is the easiest of the four islands to circumnavigate. If you are an addicted beachwalker like this writer, you will find the island gives you some of the best opportunities to do so. Not only are there two magnificent large bays, made up almost entirely of sand beach, there is only one half mile stretch at normal water levels of 576 feet where you would have to either walk through shallow water to get around windfalls or retreat to a ledge for a forest walk. When the lake level reaches a high point of 578 feet, however, as it did in 1987, much of this circumference walk becomes exhaustively difficult. If you are visiting the island when Great Sand Bay is not closed, there are three different ways one can use the beaches for long loop hikes. The first and shortest is the North Loop hike. Beginning on High Island Bay, following the shore northward, then west along the north shore and south again on the western side of the island, this loop covers the first half of Great Sand Bay. The return leg of the journey is accomplished by following the T.O.T.W. Trail eastward over the top of the dune, and back across the interior of the island to the east shore.

The advantage of this hike is that it has the most area of sand beach hiking and the least rock hopping. Its disadvantage is that it has a stretch where one must venture out into the shallow water or retreat into the woods to avoid climbing over many windfalls. The South Loop follows the T.O.T.W. Trail westward across the island from the harbor area to Great Sand Bay. From there, you would follow the shore line southward to the island's southwest tip, then proceed northward back to the starting point on High Island Bay. The biggest disadvantage to this loop is that it has more rock hopping and pebble beach walking than the North Loop, and is two miles longer. Either hike however is easily done in a single day, with time left over, so you could make these trips without lugging all your camping gear. Either walk could also be done in reverse as well.

Since both hikes call for crossing the tableland where the Piping Plovers nest, these loop hikes would be impossible during the nesting period, when the area along Great Sand Bay is closed. There is one way, however, which is technically against the rules during the restricted months, but would not endanger the nesting area. If one hikes the entire perimeter of the island without using the T.O.T.W Trail, staying close to the water's edge on the two-mile beach walk around Great Sand Bay, no damage could be done to the nest sites. The plovers do not nest on the open sand but in the rough tableland immediately behind the beach. Walkers staying close to the shore and staying out of the scrub brush areas directly behind the beach would cause the nesting birds no harm. This would give hikers the opportunity of walking the two mile stretch of unspoiled sand beach along Great Sand Bay during the months when it is closed. In this writer's estimation, this is one of the loveliest wilderness beaches in Michigan. The opportunity of walking along its pristine shore, unhampered by any man-made structure, with the added charm of the perched dunes and blowouts rising over 200 feet above you to the east, can make you feel at one with nature, especially if you happen to walk it alone.

Young robust hikers can manage encircling the entire island in a single day but for most of us breaking it into a backpack overnight is a more sensible plan. If you do it as an overnight during the restricted season, remember not to set up camp in the vicinity of Great Sand Bay. When following a shoreline, no one really needs a trail description to keep from getting lost, but the following comments will help you keep tabs on yourself along the way. Those interested in following only the north loop should start with the trail description below. If the south loop is on your agenda start with the T.O.T.W. Trail's westward description, and pick up the island loop hike notes at Great Sand Bay.

SHORELINE PERIMETER WALK NORTH END

TRAIL DESCRIPTION. If you want to keep your boots dry, it is a good idea to carry a set of sneakers along. The easiest way to cover the half mile stretch of fallen trees is by walking around them in the shallow water. It is also a good idea to carry both a long-sleeved shirt and long pants, for the sand flies can be murderous.

After 15 to 20 minutes of walking north along the shoreline of High Island Bay, you will be close to the fence that divides the long sand spit from the rest of the island. The spit is closed during the nesting season, for it is one of the prime nesting sites for up to 2,000 nesting pairs of sea gulls and terns. The fence was placed there not only to keep out humans, but predatory animals as well. A bird researcher told me the greatest danger to the eggs and young chicks comes not from the two-or four-legged mammals, but from snakes who slide through the fence as though it wasn't there. Fox and careless humans also take their toll. On my visit in 1987, the fence was still in fairly good condition, but a year later winter ice had wiped out the shoreline sections completely. Its presence was nothing more than a reminder that it was a no-man's-land boundary line which respectful humans will not cross.

The half-mile narrow stretch of sand, shaped like a big scythe, is a nesting site used by two different types of gulls and two types of terns. The fence also functions as a handy structure on which to hang signs to warn uninformed human trespassers of the ecological damage they could cause by venturing out on the spit during the nesting season. Because of weathering, the signs were almost unreadable in 1987. Some birds nesting here travel as far as South America during the winter months, and one of the gull species returns early enough to begin nest building in the snow. There are active nests here through the second week of August, so you should never venture out on the spit. Even if you stick to the shoreline the

Bird sanctuary on spit, north end of High Island Bay. Beaver Island in the background

panic your presence would create among the fleeing birds might easily cause eggs to be broken by the frightened birds and young fledglings to be trampled to death.

As you walk north, crossing the narrow neck of land between the bay and the north shore of the island, climb the hill west of the fence up to the scrub line. This raises you high enough above the spit for a good panoramic overlook of that half mile long sandy bird sanctuary. As I paused there during the height of the nesting season one early July, the terns apparently felt that my presence was a real menace to their nests. Although I was a good 50 yards away from the fence, I stood there both thrilled and mesmerized as one after another of the birds flew directly at me in a straight line, missing the top of my head by what seemed like inches. Coming head on, their streamlined little bodies looked like tiny English Spitfire fighter planes on a strafing attack, and if their wings had suddenly started to spark flaming tracer bullets, I wouldn't have been too surprised. Although it was a thrilling experience, I did not linger, for I wanted to relieve the anxiety of those worried little terns.

As you drop down to the north shore, you will see that another long sandy beach walk continues west, almost in a straight line with about a mile of it visible from here. You will also have a good view of Trout Island, a little over two miles to the northwest. The owner of that island built an airstrip, which runs almost from one end of it to the other. Whiskey Island is the other small island visible to the north east, about five miles away.

On one August walk along this shore, I was suddenly inundated with nasty biting sand flies. In less that 30 seconds, over 50 of them landed on my exposed legs and began biting away. I had learned earlier that repellent has little effect on these pests, so I hastily changed my shorts for the long pants I carried in my daypack.

A pleasanter memory of this beach happened a year earlier, when I saw a large voyageur canoe pulled up on the beach. It was a modern version of the type the French fur trappers used over 200 years ago in their great lakes navigation. It belonged to a church group which had paddled it from Garden Island some nine miles away. They were making camp on the beach for the night before continuing their motorless trip around the island.

Although the curvature of the earth hides its land surfaces from view, the tree tops of Michigan's Upper Peninsula sometimes can be seen from this shore on very clear days. They shimmer almost like a mirage on the lake's surface, some 15 miles away. It will not be long before you reach an area where northern slopes of the island come up almost to the shoreline. Although this embankment is not high, many trees that once grew at its edge have tumbled across the narrow beach and out into the water. Here you make your choice of shallow wading around the fallen trees or climbing the ledge and working your way through the heavy overgrown forest. I once got caught in a vicious squall at this section and the speed of the wind and pelting rain made the difficult walk through the heavy underbrush of the forest a grudging, difficult necessity. This section of obstructed beach lasts for only a half mile, and if you opt to make the passage via the lake and have sun to warm the shallow water, it's fun splashing around the windfalls. As you get close to the northwest tip of the island, you will see the inland bank to your left decline into a swampy area, containing a small pond. The beach walk is now a rocky one, and you will soon be at the stone laden northwest point. A reef just below the water's surface often makes double wave lines coming diagonally toward each other. Your walking time to this corner from High Island Bay will probably be under an hour and a half. Trout Island to the north is just under two miles away. If you look in a southerly direction from this point, you will have your first view of Gull Island. This diminutive island, which is slightly over a mile long, is part of the Michigan Island National Wildlife Refuge.

As you begin your walk south along the west shore line towards Point Q at the north end of Great Sand Bay, a low land protrusion divides the shoreline into two small bays of rocky and pebble beach. When you arrive at **Point Q** you are on the most westerly protrusion of land on the island, and at the head of Great Sand Bay. The bay itself is over two miles long, and in looking south, nearly all of it is visible. Almost equally divided into two mini-bays by **Point R** about halfway between the northern and the southern end of the bay, the walk along its shores is entirely of sand except in the immediate vicinity of **Points Q** and **S.** If you are going to walk this lovely beach during the months when it is closed, make sure you stay close to the shore and do not venture into the tableland behind the beach or attempt to take the T.O.T.W. Trail back to High Island Bay. You are committed to proceeding either around the southern shore of the island or returning the way you came.

As you head south, you will see the dunes and blowouts rising above you to the east. If you are walking through the area when it is open and you are going to take the T.O.T.W. Trail to complete the north loop, you walk almost to **Point R** before beginning the climb up the dune (See T.O.T.W. Trail east on pg 341).

SHORELINE PERIMETER WALK
South End

From **Point R** there is still about a mile of sand beach walking before you reach the end of Great Sand bay. The largest blowout on the island is soon visible, rising over 200 feet above on your left. If you wish to climb to its top, you will have excellent views to the west and south. Gull Island, which is slightly over a mile in length, lies almost due west. This elevation also gives you a particularly nice panorama of the southern part of High island, as well as North and South Fox Islands beyond. From this vantage point, there is an illusionary view of these two islands, for they appear as though they are separated only by a narrow channel, when the actual distance between the two is about five miles. Looking north, the high bald of the T.O.T.W. Trail is also easily seen.

Shortly before you reach **Point S**, the sand of the beach gives way to rock, and you have either stones or pebbles as walking surfaces all the way to High Island Bay, a distance of about four and a half miles. It is unnecessary to walk out to the end of the rocky peninsula at **Point S**, for if you look left you will see easy places where you can cut through the narrow tree line and across to the other side of that thin land spit. This is about the halfway mark between **Point R**, and the southwest tip of the island, and it will consume around a half hour of rock hopping and walking pebble beaches to reach this southern proximity. From there, you are about the closest you get to both Gull Island seven miles due west, and the two Fox Islands almost due south. Beaver Island comes prominently into view to the east and will be readily visible for the rest of the walk. The distance between the southwest and southeast corners of the island is just about a mile.

After you have walked about half the distance of this southern coast, you will pass the first of two small ponds visible from the shore. Another five minutes will bring you alongside the second pond which is over twice as large as the first. A half mile beyond this second pond, the shoreline swings to the left, beginning the northern part of the hike. You have a little over two miles of varying small bays and points before coming to High Island Bay. After about 15 minutes of walking along the eastern shore, one point of interest which you will pass is a break in the sandy bank. Through this bank a stream flows into the lake during times of heavy rain. Although usually dry, this small estuary is distinctive, because it is the only such outlet on the entire island. Once you reach the curve of High Island Bay, with its long sandy spit reaching eastward, you might want to climb the small ledge to the plain where the House of David village once stood, and find your way north through small stands of trees and fields back to the T.O.T.W. Trail.

OTHER HIKING POSSIBILITIES TO CONSIDER

GENERAL REMARKS. An old D.N.R. map and the new edition of the U.S.G.S. topographic map show many old trails that are much easier to follow on paper than in reality. Over sixty years have passed since most of these paths and roads were actively used for various farming and timbering operations, and several of them no longer exist at all. Since there are no large browsing animals such as deer, underbrush is often thick, and normal plant growth has nearly choked most of the paths out of existence. Within that natural tangle are windfalls and deadfalls by the thousands, making both boondocking and following these old paths exhaustive work. To aid the more adventurous, I include here what I found in trying to follow some of them.

TRAIL HEADING SOUTH FROM THE TRIANGLE ON THE LAKE MARIA LOOP TRAIL

The trail shown on both maps shows an old road heading south from the triangle on the Lake Maria Loop eventually reaching the eastern shore of Lake Michigan, about a quarter of a mile south of High Island Bay. This would be a nice short loop walk following a pleasant section of beach and forest, with views of Lake Maria, if the trail could still be followed to the beach. I discovered that the trail immediately south of the triangle is quite distinct and easy to follow in the early stages, though there are many deadfalls across it. I had high hopes that this recognizable trail would reach the Lake Michigan shore. After making two different attempts, I found that in about five minutes of walking the trail simply disappears. One side trail to the left, located fairly close to the end of the passable section, also soon ended in a wilderness tangle.

TRAIL STARTING ON THE EASTERN END OF FIELD # 1

This trail follows the eastern border of Field #1 in a south west direction. Once past the canopy of small trees at the southeast corner of Field #1, the woodland section is quite distinct. In about five minutes of walking, the deadfalls became so thick it became snail's pace work getting over or around them. Although one can easily see the swath cut through the trees when looking skyward, the physical exertion needed to proceed was not worth the small chance of any appreciable scenic reward.

TRAIL FROM FIRST FORK ON THE WOODLAND ALTERNATIVE TRAIL

When following the Woodland Alternative Trail north from the D.N.R. cabins this is the path that proceeds straight ahead when the Alternative Trail forks left, to follow the southern end of an old field. This segment follows the eastern edge of that field, and an old log fence is still visible on the left. For the first three to four minutes, the trail is comparatively easy to trace, but it gets increasingly difficult to follow in the next couple of minutes, and finally gives out altogether, far short of the northern shore.

TRAIL AT THE SOUTHERN END OF FIELD #3

Of the four trail segments mentioned here, it is the hardest to find, but might be the easiest to follow. Beginning near the south east end of Field #3, it meanders south, coming quite close to the western dune ridge. Rapidly being reclaimed by encroaching trees, Field #3 has been segmented into many separate parcels. This has made the original large farming tract more of a patchwork than a single entity. The old road follows the southeastern border of the field, although it is now hard to tell exactly where that boundary is. The topo map only

Author's first trip to High Island was aboard this historic restored lighthouse keeper's boat

shows the trail beginning south of the field, when actually it comes up to it, running along the southeast border. Because it comes very close to the opposite side of two blowouts, various strenuous loop hikes might be used with this trail forming the eastern link, but where exactly one would need to climb the very steep tree covered dune to come out on top of the high open sand is a guessing game for the adventurous. As it headed south, the trail looked easy to follow but since we found the trail late in the day and had left our compass back at camp, we could not follow it too long without the real possibility of loosing ourselves in the darkness of the boondocks. My companions and I were day hiking, and were not equipped to spend the night, so retreated to the T.O.T.W. Trail while we still had enough light to find our way. This leaves me with a new corner of the island to investigate on a future trip, and it may be one for you as well.

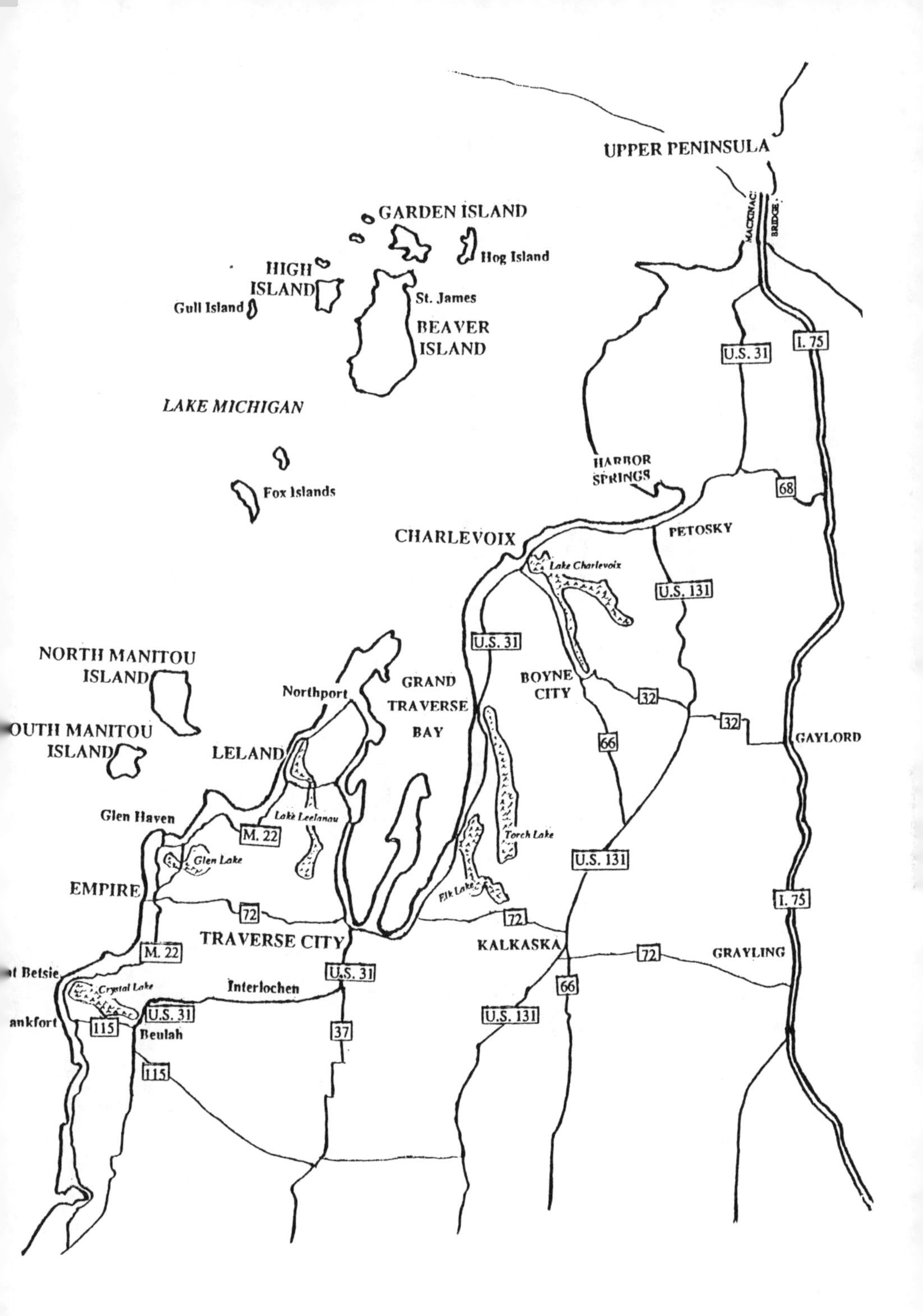
UPPER PENINSULA
MACKINAC
BRIDGE
GARDEN ISLAND
Hog Island
HIGH
ISLAND
Gull Island
St. James
BEAVER
ISLAND
LAKE MICHIGAN
U.S. 31
I. 75
Fox Islands
HARBOR
SPRINGS
68
CHARLEVOIX
PETOSKY
Lake Charlevoix
U.S. 131
U.S. 31
NORTH MANITOU
ISLAND
Northport
GRAND
TRAVERSE
BAY
BOYNE
CITY
32
32
OUTH MANITOU
ISLAND
LELAND
66
GAYLORD
Glen Haven
Lake Leelanau
M. 22
Torch Lake
Glen Lake
U.S. 131
EMPIRE
Elk Lake
I. 75
72
72
TRAVERSE CITY
KALKASKA
72
GRAYLING
M. 22
t Betsie
Crystal Lake
Interlochen
U.S. 31
66
ankfort
115
U.S. 31
Beulah
U.S. 131
37
115

AREA MAP

NOTES

NOTES

NOTES

NOTES

NOTES